The X Window System®

Programming
and Applications
with Xt
OSF/Motif® Edition

Douglas A. Young

Hewlett-Packard Laboratories
Palo Alto, California

Prentice Hall, Englewood Cliffs, New Jersey 07632

Library of Congress Cataloging-in-Publication Data

Douglas A. Young. — OSF/Motif ed.

   The X window system : programming and applications with Xt /

      p.   cm.

   Includes bibliographical references.

   ISBN 0-13-497074-8

   1. X Window System (Computer system) I. Title.

QA76.76.W56Y67 1990

005.4'3—dc20   89-29224
                                                  CIP

Cover design: *Photo Plus Art*
Manufacturing buyer: *Ray Sintel*

Back cover line art:
courtesy of John Humphrys

 © 1990 by Prentice-Hall, Inc.
A Division of Simon & Schuster
Englewood Cliffs, New Jersey 07632

Printed in the United States of America

10 9 8 7 6 5 4

ISBN   0-13-497074-8

Prentice-Hall International (UK) Limited, *London*
Prentice-Hall of Australia Pty. Limited, *Sydney*
Prentice-Hall Canada Inc., *Toronto*
Prentice-Hall Hispanoamericana, S.A., *Mexico*
Prentice-Hall of India Private Limited, *New Delhi*
Prentice-Hall of Japan, Inc., *Tokyo*
Simon & Schuster Asia Pte. Ltd., *Singapore*
Editora Prentice-Hall do Brasil, Ltda., *Rio de Janeiro*

To Teri and D.C.

CONTENTS

PREFACE

Window-based user interfaces have become a common feature of most computer systems, and users are beginning to expect all applications to have polished user-friendly interfaces. Unfortunately, a user interface that is easy to use is seldom easy to build. Some experts estimate that as much as 90 percent of the total effort required to develop a typical window and mouse-based application goes into the user interface. This makes moving software between different window systems a significant task. The X Window System provides a standard window environment that allows application programmers to spend more time improving their programs and less time porting to new user interface platforms.

This book views the X Window System as a complete platform for building user interfaces, consisting of three major components: Xlib, the Xt Intrinsics, and a widget set. A number of widget sets are currently available. An earlier version of this book used Hewlett-Packard's Xhp widget set for purposes of examples, primarily because it was available in the public domain. This edition now uses the OSF/Motif widget set for all example programs. While the general principles described in this book are relatively independent of any particular widget set, I hope that the use of a widely available widget set for the examples will make the book more useful to X programmers.

In the brief history of X, programmers have first focused primarily on the server and Xlib levels, and then on designing and writing toolkits and window managers. So far, little effort has been spent writing real, commercial applications that tap the potential of the X Window System. I believe that time has now come, and I hope this book helps in some small way to make this happen.

This book is intended for the programmer who wants to understand how to write applications using the X Window System. The facilities provided by X, the Xt Intrinsics, and the OSF/Motif widget set are introduced through examples that illustrate how these features can be used in real programs. The Xlib and Xt Intrinsics reference manuals thoroughly explain how individual functions work, but they don't show how to put these pieces together. This book demonstrates typical ways to combine the facilities provided by Xlib, Xt and Motif to form working applications.

There are several audiences this book *does not* address. The first is the reader who is completely unfamiliar with using X and needs to know how to install the system, how to run various X-based applications, and so on. This book is for programmers, and assumes at least a minimal exposure to X as a user. This book is also not intended as a detailed reference manual for advanced X programmers. Instead, it explains and demonstrates the concepts involved in programming with X in enough detail to allow the reader to understand how to write X-based applications without explaining every aspect of every widget or function call. This book also does not emphasize the particular user interface style promoted by Motif. It uses the Motif widget set as the basis for exploring the features of X and the X Toolkit, without any particular focus on the Motif behavior and appearance guidelines.

The information in this book is based on the 1.0 release of the Motif widget set and the corresponding Motif version of the Xt Intrinsics. Motif is currently based on the X11R3 version of the X Window System. Like most large software systems, both X and Motif are evolving systems, and some details will necessarily change with time. All examples are written in the C programming language, and the book assumes at least a basic knowledge of that language. Window systems are inherently graphical in nature, and it might useful for the reader to have some familiarity with basic raster graphics, although no knowledge of graphics algorithms is needed.

ACKNOWLEDGMENTS

Many people contributed to this book, either directly by reviewing all or part of it, or indirectly through discussions regarding the topics in this book. At the risk of forgetting someone, Arlene Azzerello, Martin Cagan, Dan Garfinkel, Audrey Ishizaki, Phil Gust, Warren Harris, Oliver Jones, David Lewis, Niels Mayer, Bob Miller and Pam Raby all helped to improve this book with their suggestions. Steve Friedl and Rick Kelly deserve special mention for their thorough and thoughtful reviews of early drafts. Many people on the xpert mailing list also contributed by asking interesting questions and often providing answers, and also by suggesting ways to improve the first version of the book. Last, but certainly not least, my greatest thanks must go to my wife Teresa, who tirelessly edited nearly every draft of this book and cheerfully put up with my long nights at the keyboard. I could not have finished this book without her. I would like to thank my management at Hewlett Packard Laboratories for their encouragement and also everyone at Prentice Hall, particularly Karen Gettman, Mike McDermott, and John Wait, for their early support of this effort. Of course, all errors in the examples or the information in this book are my responsibility alone.

Douglas Young

1

AN INTRODUCTION TO
THE X WINDOW SYSTEM

The X Window System is an industry-standard software system that allows programmers to develop portable graphical user interfaces. One of the most important features of X is its unique device-independent architecture. X allows programs to display windows containing text and graphics on any hardware that supports the X protocol without modifying, recompiling, or relinking the application. This device independence, along with X's position as an industry standard, allows X-based applications to function in a heterogeneous environment consisting of mainframes, workstations, and personal computers.

X was developed at Massachusetts Institute of Technology (MIT), with support from the Digital Equipment Corporation (DEC). The name, X, as well as some initial design ideas were derived from an earlier window system named W, developed at Stanford University. X was designed at MIT's Laboratory for Computer Science for Project Athena to fulfill that project's need for a distributed, hardware-independent user interface platform. Early versions of X were used primarily within MIT and DEC, but with the release of version 10, many manufacturers expressed interest in X as a commercial product. The early versions of X were designed and implemented primarily by Robert Scheifler and Ron Newman from MIT and Jim Gettys from DEC, although many additional people contributed to X, Version 11. Version 11 of the X Window System is supported by a consortium of hardware and software vendors who have made a commitment to X as a standard base for user interfaces across each of their product lines. The X Consortium supports and controls the standard specification of the X Window System. X is available on most UNIX systems, Digital's VAX/VMS operating

1

system, and also many personal computers. Many companies have also begun to produce hardware specifically designed to support the X protocol.

One important difference between X and many other window systems is that X does not define any particular user interface style. X provides *mechanisms* to support many interface styles rather than enforcing any one *policy*. Many window systems — the one used by Apple's MacIntosh, or Microsoft Windows, for example — support a particular style of user interface. In contrast, X provides a flexible set of primitive window operations, but carefully avoids dictating the look or feel of any particular application's user interface. Instead, X provides a device-independent layer that serves as a base for a variety of interface styles. Therefore, the basic X Window System does not provide user interface components such as button boxes, menus, or dialog boxes often found in other window systems. Most applications depend on higher level libraries built on top of the basic X protocol to provide these components.

1.1 THE CLIENT-SERVER MODEL

The architecture of the X Window System is based on a *client-server* model. A single process, known as the *server,* is responsible for all input and output devices. The server creates and manipulates windows on the screen, produces text and graphics, and handles input devices such as a keyboard and mouse. The server provides a portable layer between all applications and the display hardware. The X server typically runs on a workstation or personal computer with a graphics display, although some vendors offer dedicated X terminals that implement all or part of the X server in hardware or firmware.

An application that uses the facilities provided by the X server is known as a *client.* A client communicates with the X server via a network connection using an asynchronous byte-stream protocol. X supports many network protocols, including TCP/IP, DECnet, and Chaos. Multiple clients can connect to a single server concurrently, and an individual client can also connect to multiple servers.

The X architecture hides most of the details of the device-dependent implementation of the server and the hardware it controls from clients. Any client can communicate with any server, provided both the client and the server obey the X protocol.

In addition to providing device independence, the distributed architecture of X allows the server and clients to run on separate machines located anywhere on a network.[1] This feature has many potential applications. For example, imagine an interactive teaching program executing on a school's main computer that can display information on inexpensive personal

---

1. The server and client(s) often run on separate machines within a local area network. However, X can also handle not-so-local configurations transparently. I once had an interesting opportunity to use this feature to read my electronic mail during a trip to Europe. The X-based mail program (the client) ran on my workstation in Palo Alto, California, while the X server ran on a workstation in Bristol, England! Although the response of the system suffered slightly from the satellite transmission time, X worked perfectly. The mail program was completely unaware that I was interacting with it from a location several thousand miles away.

computers located at each student's desk. In this scenario, the teaching program is a client that communicates with multiple servers, one for each student's display. Each student interacts with the program concurrently through a window on his or her local machine. The same program is also connected to another display located at the teacher's desk, allowing the teacher to check the progress of any individual student or the class as a whole. While one window on each of the students' machines provides an interface to the remote teaching program, other windows on a student's machine can provide interfaces to other clients. For example, each student can use a window to interact with an electronic mail system running on a central mail server. Still another window can provide an interface to an editor running locally on the student's machine.

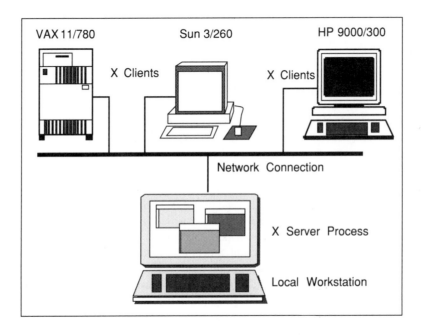

Figure 1.1 The client-server model.

1.2 DISPLAYS AND SCREENS

The terms *display* and *screen* are often used interchangeably to refer to a cathode ray tube (CRT) used by the computer to display text and/or graphics. However, X uses the term *display* to mean a single X server process, while a *screen* is a single hardware output device. A single X display can support many screens. X uses the terms *display* and *server* interchangeably. There is normally only one server per central processing unit (CPU).

Before a client can communicate with the X server it must open a connection to the server. Once a client establishes this connection, it can use any of the screens controlled by the server. X provides a security mechanism that allows a server to deny clients executing on other hosts the right to connect to a display. This mechanism works on a per-host basis.

1.3 RESOURCES

The X server controls all *resources* used by the window system. Resources include windows, bitmaps, fonts, colors, and other data structures used by an application. The X server maintains these resources privately within the server, to enable clients to use and share these data structures transparently. Client programs access each resource through a *resource identifier*, usually referred to simply as an ID. A resource ID is a unique identifier assigned by the X server.

The X server usually creates and destroys resources at the request of a client. Also, the server usually destroys most resources automatically when the client that requested them disconnects from the server. X allows clients to specify the *shutdown mode* of a resource. The shutdown mode controls the lifetime of a resource. The default mode destroys all resources allocated for a client when that client breaks its connection with the server.

1.4 REQUESTS

When a client application needs to use a service provided by the X server, the client issues a *request* to the server. Clients typically request the server to create, destroy, or reconfigure windows, or to display text or graphics in a window. Clients can also request information about the current state of windows or other resources.

The X server normally runs asynchronously with respect to its clients and all clients run asynchronously with respect to each other. Although the server processes requests from each particular application in the order in which they arrive, requests are not necessarily processed immediately. Requests from clients are placed in a queue until the server is able to process them, and clients do not wait for the server to respond to requests. Applications can request the server to handle requests synchronously, but this usually results in poorer performance, because each request to the server suffers a round-trip over the network connection.

1.5 BASIC WINDOW CONCEPTS

The most fundamental resource in X is the *window*. A window simply represents a rectangular section of the screen. Unlike windows in some other window systems, an X window has no title bar, scroll bar or other decorations. An X window appears as a rectangle with a background color or pattern. Each window also has a border. Applications can combine two or more windows to create scroll bars, title bars, and other higher-level user interface components.

The X server creates windows in response to requests from clients. The server stores and maintains the data structure representing a window, while clients refer to the window using the window's ID. Clients can issue requests to the server to alter the window's size, position, color, or other characteristics, and can also request the server to place text in a window or perform graphical operations on a window. Although the server creates each window at the request of a specific client, any client can request the server to manipulate the window, provided it has access to the window's ID. For example, X window managers use this feature to control the position of all windows on the screen.

1.5.1 The Window Hierarchy

X organizes windows as a hierarchy, referred to as the *window tree*. The top window in this window tree is known as the *root window*. The X server automatically creates a root window for each screen it controls. The root window occupies an entire physical screen, and cannot be moved or resized. Every window except the root window has a *parent* window (also known as an *ancestor*) and can also have *children* (also known as *descendents* or *subwindows*). Windows that share the same parent are known as *siblings*.

Fig. 1.2 and Fig. 1.3 illustrate this hierarchical model and show the relationship between several windows. Fig. 1.2 illustrates how a set of windows might appear on the screen, while Fig. 1.3 shows the window tree formed by these windows. Windows A and B are children of the root window, while Windows C and E are children of Window A. Window G is a child of Window E. Similarly, windows D and F are children of Window B and Window H is a child of Window F.

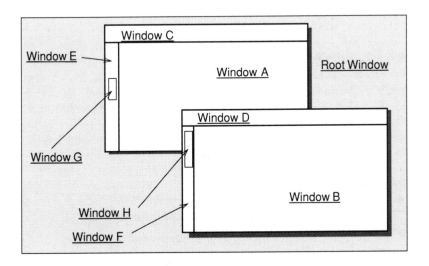

Figure 1.2 A typical window hierarchy.

X places few restrictions on the size or location of a window, but only that portion of a window that lies within the bounds of its parent is visible; the server *clips* the remaining portions to the boundaries of the parent window.

X allows siblings to overlap in a way that resembles a collection of papers on a desk. The *stacking order* determines which windows or portions of windows appear to be on top (and therefore are visible). If two windows occupy overlapping regions on the screen, the window that is higher in the stacking order completely or partially *obscures* the lower window. For example, in Fig. 1.2, Window B is higher in the stacking order than Window A. Clients can request the X server to alter a window's position in the stacking order (for example, raising a window above all other windows). A window's stacking order can only be altered relative to its siblings. Therefore, from a user's viewpoint, a window's descendants raise and lower with the window.

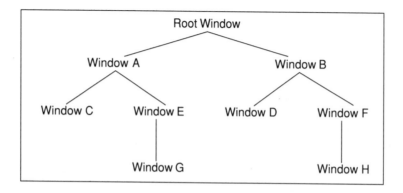

Figure 1.3 Window tree for Fig. 1.2.

1.5.2 The X Coordinate System

Each X window, including the root window, has its own integer coordinate system. The coordinate of the upper left corner of each window is *(0, 0)*. The *x* coordinate increases toward the right and the *y* coordinate increases toward the bottom. Applications always specify the coordinate of a point on the screen relative to some window. A window's position (the upper left corner of the window) is always specified relative to the coordinate system of its parent window. For example, in Fig. 1.4, Window A is positioned at coordinate *(50, 100)* relative to the coordinate system of the root window. However, the coordinate of this point is *(0, 0)* relative to Window A. Each window's coordinate system moves with the window, permitting applications to place text, graphics, or sub-windows in a window without regard to the window's location.

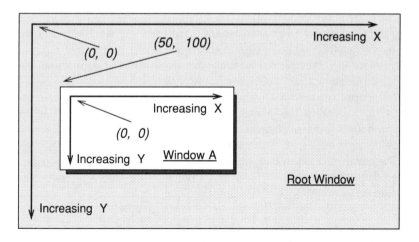

Figure 1.4 The X coordinate system.

1.5.3 Mapping and Window Visibility

Although each X window is associated with a rectangular region on the screen, windows are not necessarily visible to the user all the time. When the server creates a window, it allocates and initializes the data structures that represent the window within the server, but does not invoke the hardware-dependent routines that display the window on the screen. Clients can request the server to display a window by issuing a *map* request. Although a window is considered to be *mapped* if a client has issued a map request for that window, it still might not be visible for any of the following reasons:

- The window is completely *obscured* by another window on the screen. The window becomes visible only if it or the obscuring window is moved such that the window is no longer obscured, the obscuring window is removed from the screen, or the stacking order of the two windows changes so that the obscuring window is lower in the stacking order than the other window.

- An ancestor of the window is not mapped. Before a window can appear on the screen, every ancestor of the window must be mapped. A window that is mapped, but has an ancestor that is not mapped, is said to be *unviewable*. The window automatically becomes *viewable* when all ancestors are mapped.

- The window is completely clipped by an ancestor. If a window is located completely outside the visible boundaries of any ancestor, it is not visible on the screen. The window becomes visible if the ancestor or ancestors are resized to include the region occupied by the window, or if the window is moved to lie within the visible boundaries of all ancestors.

1.5.4 Maintaining Window Contents

In an overlapping window system, each window's contents must be preserved when that window is covered by another window, so that the contents can be restored later. Many systems maintain and restore the contents of a window in such a way that applications are unaware of the process. Such windows are sometimes known as *retained-raster* windows, because the window system generally saves the contents of the window as a *bitmap*, or *raster*.

In X, the responsibility for maintaining the contents of a window lies with the client that uses the window. Some implementations of X support retained rasters, or *backing store* as this technique is known in X, but applications must not depend on this feature because there is no guarantee that all server implementations can provide this service for all windows. Saving complete raster images for every window on the screen places a huge demand on the memory resources of the server's computer system as the number of windows increases. It is usually more efficient for the X server to notify a client when a window is *exposed*, and rely on the client to redisplay the contents of the window. Every X client must be prepared to recreate the contents of its windows at any time. This places some additional burden on the application programmer, although this is seldom a problem because most applications maintain internal representations of the contents of their windows anyway. The backing store feature is best used to support computationally-intensive applications that have difficulty recreating their output quickly. For servers that do not support backing store, such applications must usually resort to saving the current contents of its windows as an off-screen image.

Many X servers also support *save-unders*. A save-under is a technique of saving the image on the screen, *under* a particular window, so that the image can be restored when the window is moved to a new location or removed from the screen. This is done by taking a snapshot of an area of the screen just before this area is covered by a window. For save-unders to work, the state of the screen and all windows on the screen must be held constant between the time the snapshot is taken and the time the image is restored. Save-unders are used primarily when creating popup menus and other small transitory windows to achieve a smooth visual effect.

1.6 EVENTS

The X server communicates with clients by sending *events* to the client applications. The server generates events as a direct or indirect result of a user action (for example, pressing a key on the keyboard, moving the mouse, or pressing a mouse button). The server also generates events to notify the client of changes in the state of its windows. For example, the server sends a client an **Expose** event when a window's contents needs to be restored. X supports thirty-three types of events, and provides a mechanism that allows clients to define additional event types.

The server sends events to a client by placing the event on a first-in, first-out (FIFO) queue that can be read by the client. Each event consists of a packet that reports the type of event, the window in which the event occurred, and other data specific to the particular type of event.

Most X applications are completely *event-driven* and are designed to wait until an event occurs, respond to the event, and then wait for the next event. The event-driven approach provides a natural model for interactive applications. Chapter 5 discusses events and the event-driven model in detail.

1.7 INPUT DEVICES

X supports a variety of input devices. Depending on the implementation, a server can support tablets, track balls, scanners, and other data input and pointing devices. However, the most common input devices are the keyboard, used for textual input, and the mouse, which serves as both a pointing device and a selection device.

1.7.1 The Mouse

A mouse is a device that allows the user to point to locations on the screen and also to issue commands by pressing buttons. The user points to a screen location by controlling the position of an image on the screen known as a *sprite*.

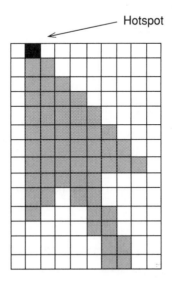

Figure 1.5 A typical mouse cursor.

The sprite is sometimes referred to as the *mouse cursor* although X usually uses the term *pointer*. The user controls the location of the sprite by moving the mouse on the user's desk.[2] The server maintains the sprite and tracks the location of the mouse. Clients can ask the server to report events when the sprite enters or leaves a window, changes position, or when the user presses or releases a mouse button. Clients can also query the server to determine the current position of the sprite, and can change the size and appearance of the sprite as well. This feature is often used to indicate the current task or state of the application. For example, the mouse cursor might assume the shape of a diagonal arrow (see Fig. 1.5) when the user points to a location on the screen, change to a vertical arrow when the user uses a scroll bar, and change to an hourglass when the application is busy.

Every mouse cursor has a *hotspot*. A hotspot is the point within the mouse cursor that defines the precise location of the sprite on the screen. The sprite is said to be *contained* by a window if the mouse cursor's hotspot is inside the visible region of the window, or one of its sub-windows. The sprite is *in* the smallest window that contains the hotspot.

1.7.2   The Keyboard

The server generates an event each time a key changes state. The information in the event structure includes a code identifying the key that was pressed or released. The client can translate this code into an ASCII character code if desired. The key code is independent of any particular keyboard arrangement to allow applications to handle a variety of keyboards made by different manufacturers.

1.8   WINDOW MANAGEMENT

A *window manager* allows the user to control the size and location of windows on the screen. In many window systems, the window manager is inseparable from the rest of the window system. In X, a window manager is an ordinary client application. However, X provides some features intended to allow window managers to control the size and placement of windows. For example, window managers can request that the X server *redirect* requests dealing with the structure of a window to the window manager rather than acting on the requests directly. If an application issues a map request for a window and a window manager has requested that such events be redirected, the X server sends a **MapRequest** event to the window manager. The window manager then has the opportunity to take some action before

---

2. Because of the close relationship between the motion of the mouse and the motion of the sprite on the screen, users often talk of the position of the mouse when they really mean the position of the sprite. For example, someone might say "the mouse is in the window." Of course the mouse is really on the desk; the sprite or mouse cursor is in the window. This tendency to interchange "sprite" and "'mouse" appeared in the names of some library routines in older versions of X, such as XWarpMouse(), that moved, or "warped" the position of the sprite (not the mouse!) to a new location. X11 consistently uses "pointer" in names of functions and macros that refer to the sprite. Thus the X10 function XWarpMouse() is known as XWarpPointer() in X11.

mapping the window, or can even refuse to map the window. Some window managers use this feature to place or resize windows according to a set of layout rules. For example, a *tiling* window manager might first rearrange or resize other windows already on the screen to ensure that no windows overlap. Many window managers use this feature to add a frame or title bar to the window before mapping it.

Window management is a complex subject that affects not only how users interact with a system, but also how applications interact with each other and with the X server. The *Inter-Client Communications Conventions Manual* (ICCCM) defines the protocol all window managers and applications should follow to interact properly with each other. In practice, these guidelines are of the most concern to those few programmers who design window managers[3] and user interface toolkits, or those programmers who choose to program directly with the Xlib C library.

1.9   THE APPLICATION PROGRAMMER'S INTERFACE TO X

Although the X server protocol is defined at the level of network packets and byte-streams, programmers generally base applications on libraries that provide an interface to the base window system. The most widely used low-level interface to X is the standard C language library known as Xlib.[4] Xlib defines an extensive set of functions that provide complete access and control over the display, windows, and input devices. Similar libraries also exist for LISP and ADA.

Although programmers can (and do) use Xlib to build applications, this relatively low-level library can be tedious and difficult to use correctly. Just handling the window manager conventions can require hundreds of lines of code. Many programmers prefer to use one of the higher-level toolkits designed to be used with X. In addition to the X Toolkit discussed in this book, there is InterViews (built at Stanford University), Andrew (from Carnegie Mellon), Xray (developed at Hewlett Packard), and CLUE (developed at Texas Instruments), to name just a few. Most of these toolkits are based on Xlib, but are generally easier to use and hide many implementation details from the programmer.

---

3. Developing new window managers has been a popular activity among X programmers. Many programmers gained their initial understanding of X by writing new window managers. Consequently, X users have had the benefit of the many window managers that are available in the public domain. One early X window manager was simply named "wm". This window manager was intended only for early X11 developers, not for public use. The source to wm was kept primarily in a file named "test.c"! In spite of the implications of this file name, wm served early developers well, and provided a model for some other window managers. Other popular X window managers include "uwm" (Ultrix Window Manager), "awm" (Ardent Window Manager), "twm" (Tom's Window Manager), and a tiled window manager, "rtl" (which takes it name from the Siemens Research Technology Laboratory).

4. The X Consortium recognizes two types of "standards," exclusive and non-exclusive. Xlib is an example of an exclusive standard. The Consortium will not recognize or adopt any other C-language interface to the underlying X protocol as a standard. Non-exclusive standards such as the Xt Intrinsics are considered part of the X Window System, but the Consortium may recognize other similar interfaces as well.

This book discusses a standard toolkit known as the X Toolkit. The X Toolkit consists of two parts: a layer known as the Xt Intrinsics, and a set of user interface components known as widgets. The Xt Intrinsics supports many different widget sets. The examples in this book use the Open Software Foundation (OSF)'s Motif widget set. However, from an application programmer's viewpoint, most widget sets provide similar capabilities. A programmer who is familiar with one widget set should be able to quickly learn to use any other widget set. Both the Xt Intrinsics and the Motif widget set are written in C and are built on top of Xlib. The Motif widget set implements user interface components, including scroll bars, menus, and buttons, while the Xt Intrinsics provides a framework that allows the programmer to combine these components to produce a complete user interface. Fig. 1.6 shows the architecture of an application based on a widget set and the Xt Intrinsics.

The Xt Intrinsics and the Motif widget set are smoothly integrated with Xlib, so applications that use the facilities of the higher level library can also use the functions provided by Xlib when needed. This book shows how the application programmer can use Xlib, the Xt Intrinsics, and a widget set such as the Motif widget set as a complete system for constructing user interfaces.

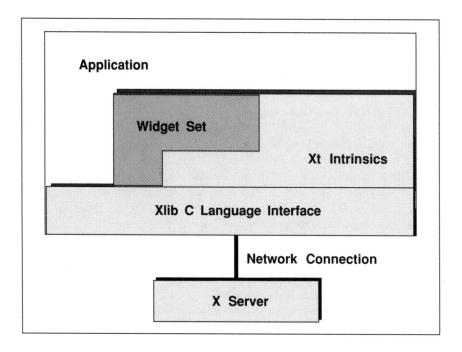

Figure 1.6 Programmer's view of the complete X Window System.

1.10 SUMMARY

This chapter presented the overall architecture of the X Window System and introduced some basic terminology. X provides a powerful platform that allows programmers to develop sophisticated user interfaces that are portable to any system that supports the X protocol. X is based on a network-transparent client-server model. The X server creates and manipulates windows in response to requests from clients, and sends events to notify clients of user input or changes in a window's state.

X does not support any particular interface style, and strives to be policy-free. Applications are free to use the X primitives to define their own type of user interface, although it is easier for an application to fit into an existing environment if the application follows a few guidelines. The easiest way for a programmer to follow these basic guidelines is to use a higher level toolkit, such as the Xt Intrinsics.

Many window systems refer to the entire system as a "window manager." In X, a window manager is a client, no different from any other client, that allows the user to move and manipulate windows. Users can choose from a variety of window managers, and therefore the programmer should not design an X application in such a way that it depends on a particular window manager. For the most part, X applications should function properly even when there is no window manager at all, although the ICCCM protocol forces applications to rely on the existence of an ICCCM-compliant window manager for some services.

Most programmers find it easiest to base their applications on a toolkit, such as the X Toolkit. The Intrinsics layer of the X Toolkit defines an architecture for combining user interface components known as widgets. Widgets are user interface components that can be combined to create complex user interfaces. The following chapters use Xlib, the Xt Intrinsics, and the Motif widget set to build examples that demonstrate many of the features of X. Chapter 2 introduces the Xt Intrinsics and demonstrates a simple X-based application.

2

PROGRAMMING WITH
THE Xt INTRINSICS

This chapter introduces the application programmer's interface to the X Window System, concentrating on the Xt Intrinsics layer of the X Toolkit. Following X philosophy, the Xt Intrinsics attempts to remain policy-free, and provides only those mechanisms that do not affect the look or feel of an application's user interface. The Xt Intrinsics serves as a framework that allows programmers to create user interfaces by combining an extensible set of user interface components. These components are known as *widgets*, and include *scrollbars*, *title bars*, *menus*, and *dialog boxes*. Widgets consist of an X window along with some procedures that operate on the window. The Intrinsics provides a small core set of widgets, and additional widgets are available from many sources.

Most programmers use a combination of Xlib, the Xt Intrinsics, and a widget set to write X-based applications. We refer to these programmers as *application programmers*. The Xt Intrinsics defines an architectural model for widgets that also allows programmers to extend the toolkit by creating new types of widgets. We refer to a programmer who creates new widgets as a *widget programmer*.

This book describes the Xt Intrinsics and the OSF/Motif widget set.[1] This chapter introduces a few of the basic functions included in the Xt Intrinsics layer and presents a simple application using the Xt Intrinsics and a simple widget.

---

1. The version of the Xt Intrinsics provided as part of the Motif toolkit may differ slightly from the MIT version of the Intrinsics, due to extensions required to support Motif-specific features. However, while the Motif version of the Xt Intrinsics must be used with the Motif widgets, the versions are substantially the same from the viewpoint of the application programmer.

2.1 NAMING CONVENTIONS

Each layer of the application programmer's interface to X follows its own naming conventions. The names of all Xlib functions and user-accessible data structures begin with the capital letter **X**, and use a mixed case convention. When function names are composed of more than one word, the first letter of each word is capitalized. For example:

```
XCreateWindow()
XDrawString()
```

All Xlib macros also follow this mixed case convention, but do not begin with the letter **X**. For example:

```
DisplayWidth()
ButtonPressMask
```

Xlib also follows some conventions intended to make it easier to remember the argument order used by each Xlib function. The first argument to nearly every Xlib function is a pointer to a **Display** structure. If the function requires a resource identifier as an argument, the resource ID immediately follows the display argument. *Drawables* precede all other resources. A *drawable* is any resource that can be the object of a graphics request. In X, this can be either a window or a pixmap. Whenever a function requires both a *source* and a *destination* drawable, the source argument always precedes the destination. When the function parameters include size and location specifications, *x* always precedes *y*, *width* always precedes *height*, and the *x, y* pair always precedes the *width, height* pair. For example, consider the argument order of the following Xlib function:

```
XDrawRectangle(display, drawable, gc, x, y, width, height)
```

As specified by the argument ordering conventions, the first argument to this function is a pointer to a display. The next two arguments are resources. The first of these is a drawable, and must precede the second resource (a graphics context). Finally, the *x, y* location precedes the **width** and **height** of the rectangle.

The Xt Intrinsics uses naming conventions similar to those used by Xlib. All functions and macros use mixed case and begin with the letters **Xt**. Unlike Xlib, the Intrinsics layer does not distinguish between functions and macros. For example:

```
XtCreateWidget()
XtSetArg()
```

The Xt Intrinsics also uses string constants to specify names of resources. Defining strings as constants promotes consistency and also assists the programmer by allowing the compiler to detect spelling errors. These resource strings fall into three categories: resource *name strings*, resource *class strings*, and resource *representation strings*. Chapter 3 discusses the meaning of these terms. By convention, the Xt Intrinsics defines resource name strings by adding the prefix **XtN** to the string. For example:

```
#define XtNwidth    "width"
```

Resource class strings use the prefix **XtC**:

```
#define XtCBackground    "Background"
```

A resource representation string is defined by adding the prefix **XtR** to the string:

```
#define XtRInt    "Int"
```

Different widget sets often follow their own conventions for naming functions, types, and variables. For example, nearly all external symbols and functions in the Motif widget set start with the letters **Xm**:

```
XmNlabelPixmap
XmTextGetString()
```

The Motif widget set also uses the **Xm** prefix when defining symbols for the resource strings used by the Motif widgets. For example:

```
#define XmNlabelString   "labelString"
```

In addition, Motif redefines the resource strings provided by the Xt Intrinsics, using its own naming conventions. For example, Motif defines the symbol:

```
#define XmNwidth   "width"
```

This book uses the Xt Intrinsics version of these symbols whenever they exist, to make it clear which symbols are defined by the Intrinsics and which are specific to Motif.

The class names of Motif widgets use a mixed case convention, and begin with the letters **Xm**. For example:

```
XmRowColumn
XmPushButton
```

By convention, each widget class pointer consists of the name of the widget class followed by the word **WidgetClass**. In the Motif widget set, widget class pointers begin with the letters **xm**. For example:

```
xmRowColumnWidgetClass
xmPushButtonWidgetClass
```

The first time a function is used in this book, the syntax of the function is given as it is used in a program. For example, the first time we discuss the function **XtNextEvent()** it is shown as:

```
XtNextEvent(&event)
```

The complete definition of these functions, including the type declarations of all parameters, can be found in the appendixes at the end of this book.

To differentiate functions and variables defined by the examples presented in this book from those defined by Xlib, the Xt Intrinsics, or the Motif widget set, all functions and variables defined by examples use a combination of lowercase letters and underscores. For example:

```
refresh_screen()
main_window
```

This book builds a small library of useful routines as we present examples of the various features of X and Motif. To distinguish these reusable library functions, all functions and symbols in this library begin with the letters **xs_**. For example:

```
xs_create_quit_button()
xs_concat_words()
```

2.2 THE X TOOLKIT PROGRAMMING MODEL

The X Toolkit provides application programmers with a specific model for writing applications. All X applications are normally designed to be event-driven. However, the X Toolkit builds on this event model to create something we might call a dispatch-driven programming model. Xlib applications usually have a switch statement inside an event loop. The **switch** statement looks at the type of each event and performs some action based on the information in the event. If the application uses multiple windows, the program also has to determine in which window the event occurred and take that into consideration. For applications with many windows, the **switch** statement can become quite long and very complex. The X Toolkit hides this process and *dispatches* all events to the appropriate user interface component. So, instead of writing one large switch statement to handle the logic of the program, programmers who use the X Toolkit write small functions to deal with specific events that occur within each component. This approach allows programs to be written in a much more declarative style (when A happens, do B) that greatly simplifies the logic of most applications. With this model, most applications that use the Xt Intrinsics follow a similar format, and every X Toolkit application performs several basic steps. These are:

1. **Initialize the Intrinsics.** This step establishes a connection to the X server, allocates resources, and initializes the Intrinsics layer.

2. **Create widgets.** Every program creates one or more widgets to construct the program's user interface.

3. **Register callbacks and event handlers.** Callbacks and event handlers are application-defined functions that respond to user actions and events that occur within each widget.

4. **Realize all widgets.** Realizing a widget creates the X window used by the widget.

5. **Enter the event loop.** Most X applications are completely event-driven, and are designed to loop indefinitely responding to events. The event loop retrieves events from the X event queue and dispatches the event to the appropriate event handler or callback function associated with the widget in which the event occurred.

Within this basic framework, the details of individual applications may vary widely, of course. However, most applications differ primarily in how they organize widgets and what callbacks and event handlers they define. Section 2.4 presents a simple example that demonstrates these steps. But first, the following section looks at the Xt Intrinsics functions that implement each of these steps.

2.3 BASIC Xt INTRINSICS FUNCTIONS

Before looking at an example application, this section briefly discusses a few of the fundamental Intrinsics functions that implement each step of the programming model outlined in the previous section. Besides implementing the X Toolkit programming model, these Intrinsics functions provide the primary application programmer's interface (API) to all widgets.

2.3.1 Initialization

All applications must begin by establishing a connection to the X server. Applications that use the X Toolkit must also perform some initialization of the Xt Intrinsics before calling any other Intrinsics function. The simplest way to do this is to call the function:

```
XtInitialize(name, class, options, noptions, &argc, argv)
```

This function establishes a connection between the client and the X server and then initializes the resource database used by the X resource manager. The first two arguments to **XtInitialize()** specify the *name* and the *class* of the application. The **name** argument specifies the name by which the program was invoked, for example "emacs", while the **class** argument indicates the more general category to which the application belongs, for example, "Editor". Although this is the basic intent of application names and classes, this is not precisely the convention that has evolved. By convention, the class name of an application is the same as the name of the application, with the first letter changed to upper-case, unless the name of the application starts with the letter X, in which case the first two letters are changed to upper case. So the class name of a program named "emacs" is "Emacs", but the class name of a program named "xterm" is "XTerm".

The X resource manager uses the name and class of an application to determine what resources the program uses. It also extracts resources from the application's command-line arguments. The Intrinsics recognizes several common command-line arguments by default. These are destructively removed from the program's **argv** array and placed in a resource data base. The value of **argc** is decremented accordingly. Notice that **XtInitialize()** requires the address of **argc**. This allows the function to decrement the actual **argc**, rather than a copy. The third and fourth arguments allow an application to specify how the Intrinsics should interpret application-specific command-line arguments and are discussed in Chapter 3.

After initializing the Intrinsics layer, **XtInitialize()** creates and returns a TopLevelShell widget. This widget serves as a container for all other widgets in the calling application.

XtInitialize() is a convenience function that calls other Intrinsics functions to initialize the Intrinsics layer, open a connection to the display, and create an initial shell widget. This function is adequate for most simple applications and is used for most examples in this book. Section 2.5 discusses the functions that perform each of these steps independently.

2.3.2   Creating Widgets

Rather than dealing directly with windows, applications built using the Xt Intrinsics use *widgets*. A widget is a complex data structure that combines an X window with a set of procedures that perform actions on that window. In addition to the ID of the X window used by the widget, the widget structure contains additional data needed by these procedures. Chapter 12 examines the internal structure of a widget in detail. However, application programmers usually only need to understand a widget's external, public interface to use the widget in a program. This public interface consists primarily of the functions discussed in this chapter, along with the customizable resources supported by the widget.

Widgets form a hierarchy similar to the X window tree, known as a *widget tree*. The root of every widget tree must be a special type of widget known as a *shell* widget. Shell widgets must have exactly one child widget. The shell widget serves as a wrapper around its child, providing an interface between the child widget and the window manager. The window used by a shell widget is created as a child of the root window of the display.[2] **XtInitialize()** creates an initial shell widget. Applications that use multiple, independent windows must create an additional shell widget for each top-level window. The function

XtCreateWidget(name, class, parent, args, nargs)

provides the general mechanism for creating all widgets except shell widgets. The **name** argument is an arbitrary string that identifies the widget. Widget names do not need to be unique, although it is often useful if they are. (See the discussion of the resource manager in Chapter 3). The **class** argument is a widget class pointer that specifies the type of widget to be created. For example,

xmScrollBarWidgetClass

---

2. Most X11 window managers reparent application's top-level windows so that they are no longer a direct child of the root window. However, shell widgets are initially created as children of the root window.

specifies an XmScrollBar widget. Each widget class provides a header file that exports the widget's class pointer. This file must be included in any application that uses the widget class. For example, an application that creates a Motif XmScrollBar widget must include the file ScrollBar.h, which contains the declaration of **xmScrollBarWidgetClass**. This book assumes the header files for the Motif widgets are located in the directory /usr/include/Xm. The **parent** argument to **XtCreateWidget()** must be a widget that already exists. This widget can be a shell widget or any other type of widget that allows children. The arguments **args** and **nargs** specify values for resources used by the widget. If the application does not need to specify any widget resources, **args** can be given as NULL. **XtCreateWidget()** creates and returns a widget, which must be declared as type **Widget** by the program. For example, the following function creates and returns a ScrollBar widget named "scroller" as a child of another widget.

```
Widget create_scroll_bar(parent)
  Widget parent;
{
  Widget scroll_bar;
  scroll_bar = XtCreateWidget("scroller",
                               xmScrollBarWidgetClass,
                               parent, NULL, 0);
  return scroll_bar;
}
```

XtCreateWidget() allocates and initializes many of the data structures associated with the widget, but does not create the window associated with the widget. The function

XtRealizeWidget(widget)

creates a window for the widget. Once **XtRealizeWidget()** is called for a particular widget, the widget is said to be *realized*. If a widget has children, **XtRealizeWidget()** also realizes its children. Applications can use the function

XtIsRealized(widget)

to check if a widget is realized. Notice that it is an error to realize a widget if its parent is unrealized, because the window owned by the parent widget must exist before the child's window can be created. Normally, applications simply call **XtRealizeWidget()** once, giving the top level shell widget as an argument.

The function

XtDestroyWidget(widget)

destroys a widget and its children, and frees the server resources used by the widget. The X server also automatically frees all resources used by an application, including the window used by each widget when the program exits or otherwise breaks its connection to the server.

Most Xt Intrinsics functions require a widget as the first argument. However, Xlib functions cannot deal directly with widgets, and instead require a pointer to a **Display** structure, window IDs, and so on, which are normally hidden from the programmer by the Intrinsics. The Intrinsics defines several functions that are useful when combining Xlib and Xt Intrinsics functions. These functions retrieve the data structures and resource IDs required by Xlib functions from a widget. The function

XtDisplay(widget)

returns a pointer to the Xlib **Display** structure used by the widget, while

XtScreen(widget)

returns a pointer to the Xlib **Screen** structure used by the widget. The function

XtWindow(widget)

retrieves the ID of the window used by the widget. This window ID will be **NULL** if the widget has not yet been realized. The display pointer and screen structure can be retrieved as soon as the widget has been created.

2.3.3   Managing Widgets

Except for shell widgets, all widgets must be *managed* by a parent widget. A widget's parent manages the widget's size and location, determines whether or not the widget is mapped, and also controls input to the widget by controlling the input focus. For example, some widgets arrange their children into rows and columns, while others group their children in scrollable lists, and still others allow the user or the programmer to specify the location of each child widget.

To add a widget to its parent's managed set, the application must use the function:

XtManageChild(widget)

The child widget is managed by the parent widget specified in **XtCreateWidget()**. The Intrinsics also provides a convenient function that creates a widget and then calls **XtManageChild()** automatically:

XtCreateManagedWidget(name, class, parent, args, nargs)

This function is convenient for the programmer, but is not always the best way to create and manage widgets. When a widget is managed, its parent is notified. Often the parent widget must perform some calculation or rearrange its other children to handle the new widget properly. Many times it is more efficient to create a group of widgets first, and then manage them at the same time, by passing an array of widgets to the function:

XtManageChildren(widgetlist, num_widgets)

This reduces the work a parent widget must do, because the widget can compute the layout of all children at once rather than as each individual widget is managed. The reduction in the number of requests made to the server, by eliminating repeated shuffling and resizing of windows, can be dramatic. In general, finding ways to reduce the number of server requests results in a more efficient program.

2.3.4   Event Dispatching

When an application uses Xlib directly, it must look at each event and perform an action based on the type of the event. If the application uses multiple windows, the information in the event structure must also be examined to determine the window in which the event occurred. If an application has many windows, using a **switch** statement to handle events can become complicated.

The Xt Intrinsics provides a much simpler and cleaner way to handle input events. The Xt Intrinsics looks up the widget corresponding to the window in which each event occurs and looks for an *event handler*, a function registered by the application or by the widget itself to respond to a specific X event in a particular widget. If the Intrinsics finds an event handler registered with the widget in which the event occurred,[3] it invokes the function automatically. The procedure of finding the proper widget and invoking the appropriate handler for an event is known as *dispatching* the event. The function

    XtDispatchEvent(&event)

dispatches a single event. Applications can use the function

    XtNextEvent(&event)

to obtain the next event from the X event queue. This function waits until an event is available in the application's event queue. When an event is available, the function returns after copying the event at the head of the queue into an event structure supplied by the application. **XtNextEvent()** also removes the event from the queue. Because most X applications are entirely event driven, the heart of nearly every X application is a loop that gets events from the X event queue and then uses **XtDispatchEvent()** to invoke an event handler for that event. This event loop can be written as:

```
while(TRUE) {
  XEvent event;
  XtNextEvent(&event);
  XtDispatchEvent(&event);
}
```

---

3. Strictly speaking, an event never occurs within a widget. Events can only occur relative to a window. However, since there is normally a one-to-one correspondence between a widget and the window created and controlled by a widget, there should be no confusion if we talk about events as if they occur within a widget.

Since this section of code is almost always identical in every X application, the Intrinsics provides it as a function:

```
XtMainLoop()
```

Notice that there is no way to exit this loop. We must arrange another way for the application to exit.

2.3.5 Setting Widget Resources

Most widgets allow the programmer to affect the way the widget appears or behaves by specifying values for resources used by the widget. Here, the term *resource* simply means any data used by the widget. The function **XtCreateWidget()** allows the programmer to pass an array specifying these resources. Resources are specified using an **Arg** data structure defined as:

```
typedef struct {
    String   name;
    XtArgVal value;
} Arg, *ArgList;
```

The **name** member is a string that indicates the name of a resource to be set to the value stored in the **value** member. If the size of the resource stored in the **value** member is less than or equal to the size of **XtArgVal** (the definition of which is system-dependent), the value is stored directly in the structure. Otherwise the **value** member represents a pointer to the resource.

Resources are often specified using a static array of **Arg** structures. For example, the width and height of a widget can be specified by creating an argument list, such as:

```
static Arg wargs[ ] = {
    { XtNwidth,   300 },
    { XtNheight,  400 },
};
```

Then, passing the **Arg** list as an argument to **XtCreateWidget()**, with a statement like

```
XtCreateWidget("sample", xmPushButtonWidgetClass,
               parent, wargs, XtNumber(wargs));
```

creates a widget 300 pixels wide and 400 pixels high. The macro **XtNumber()** determines the length of a fixed-size array. Using **XtNumber()** allows the programmer to change the size of the **Arg** array easily and eliminates the use of "magic numbers" in the code to indicate the length of the array. In some programs the definition of the **Arg** array might be placed in a separate header file, or even used in multiple places, making it difficult to keep track of a hard-coded number.

It is often more convenient for the programmer to use the macro

```
XtSetArg(arg, name, value)
```

to set a single value in a previously allocated argument list. For example:

```
Arg args[10]; /* Allocate enough space for future arguments */
int n = 0;
XtSetArg(args[n], XtNwidth,  300); n++;
XtSetArg(args[n], XtNheight, 400); n++;
XtCreateWidget("sample", xmPushButtonWidgetClass,
                  parent, args, n);
```

This approach has one primary advantage over the technique shown earlier: it allows the programmer to place the values of the resources used by a widget close to the point in the program where the widget is created. This often produces programs that are easier to understand because it is easier to see which resources have been specified for each widget. On the other hand, using this approach with lengthy lists of options makes a program longer and hides the structure of a program. This book uses this second style, primarily because none of the examples set more than a few resources in the program. Using a consistent style such as the one used here helps to minimize mistakes when using this approach. Because **XtSetArg()** is a macro that references its first argument twice, the variable used as an index to the **Arg** array can not be auto-incremented inside **XtSetArg()**.[4]

Applications can also use the function

```
XtSetValues(widget, arglist, nargs)
```

to alter the resources used by a widget after it is created. For example, the following code segment does not provide an argument list when the widget is created. In this case, **XtCreateWidget()** creates the widget using default values specified by the widget and resources set in the user's resource files (see Chapter 3). After the widget has been created, we can use **XtSetValues()** to alter the widget's width and height.

```
Arg  args[10];
int  n = 0;
widget = XtCreateWidget("sample", xmPushButtonWidgetClass,
                          parent, NULL, 0);
XtSetArg(args[n], XtNwidth,  300); n++;
XtSetArg(args[n], XtNheight, 400); n++;
XtSetValues(widget, args, n);
```

The Intrinsics also allows programmers to retrieve the current value of most widget resources, using the function:

```
XtGetValues(widget, arglist, nargs)
```

---

4. If this bothers you, it is simple to define a new macro that allows the index to be auto-incremented:
   #define SETARG(arg, n, v) { Arg *_tmp = &(arg) ; _tmp->name = (n) ; _tmp->value = (XtArgVal) (v) ;}

The argument **arglist** must be an **Arg** array that specifies pairs of resource names and addresses of variables allocated by the calling function. **XtGetValues()** retrieves the named resources from the specified widget and copies the data into the given address if the size of the resource is less than the size of **XtArgVal**. Otherwise, **XtGetValues()** stores a pointer to the resource in the location specified by the application.

For example, the following code fragment retrieves the width and height of a widget, and also a character string kept in a hypothetical **XtNstring** resource:

```
Arg          args[10];
Dimension    width, height;
char         *str;
int          n = 0;
XtSetArg(args[n], XtNwidth,  &width); n++;
XtSetArg(args[n], XtNheight, &height); n++;
XtSetArg(args[n], XtNstring, &str); n++;
XtGetValues(widget, args, n);
```

When **XtGetValues()** returns, **width** and **height** contain copies of the widget's **XtNwidth** and **XtNheight** resources. Notice that **width** and **height** are declared as type **Dimension**. Declaring variables as the wrong type when retrieving resources is a common error that can result in subtle bugs because the Intrinsics copies the data bitwise into the provided address. The most common error is to request the width, height, or position of a widget as an **int**. The width and height of all widgets should be retrieved as type **Dimension**, while a widget's x, y position must be requested as type **Position**.

Although **width** and **height** contain copies of the widget's resources, the variable **str** contains a pointer to the widget's **XtNstring** resource. This is because the size of **Dimension** is smaller than or equal to the size of **XtArgVal**, but the size of the entire character string is greater than the size of **XtArgVal**. Instead of copying the entire string, **XtGetValues()** copies the *address* of the resource into **str**. If the calling application intends to modify this string, it should allocate space for the string and copy it. In all cases, the calling application is responsible for allocating and deallocating resources retrieved using **XtGetValues()**.

2.4 AN EXAMPLE: memo

We have now discussed enough basic functions to examine a simple application that uses the X Toolkit. This first example, memo, is a simple program that displays any command-line arguments not recognized by the Intrinsics in a window. It is useful for displaying brief notes or memos on the screen. The example illustrates each of the steps in the Xt Intrinsics programming model discussed in Section 2.2, except that this example defines no event handlers or callbacks.

```c
/****************************************************
 * memo.c: Display a message in a window
 ***************************************************/
#include <X11/Intrinsic.h>
#include <X11/StringDefs.h>
#include <Xm/Xm.h>
#include <Xm/Label.h>

extern XmString xs_concat_words();

main(argc, argv)
    int        argc;
    char       *argv[];
{
    Widget     toplevel, msg_widget;
    Arg        wargs[1];
    int        n;
    XmString   message;
    /*
     * Initialize the Intrinsics
     */
    toplevel = XtInitialize(argv[0],"Memo",NULL,0,&argc,argv);
    /*
     * If a message is given on the command line,
     * use it as the XmNlabelString argument for the widget
     */
    n = 0;
    if ((message = xs_concat_words(argc-1, &argv[1])) != NULL){
       XtSetArg(wargs[n], XmNlabelString, message); n++;
    }
    /*
     * Create the XmLabel widget.
     */
    msg_widget = XtCreateManagedWidget("msg",
                                       xmLabelWidgetClass,
                                       toplevel, wargs, n);
    /*
     * Realize the widgets and enter the event loop.
     */
    XtRealizeWidget(toplevel);
    XtMainLoop();
}
```

All X applications must include some standard header files. Every application that uses the Intrinsics must include the file Intrinsic.h. The file StringDefs.h provides some standard string constant definitions, while the file Label.h includes definitions required to use the XmLabel widget. Applications that use the Motif widget set must also include the file Xm.h before any Motif widget header file.

Let's look at each step of this program. The first executable line of the example initializes the Intrinsics, and creates a TopLevelShell widget.

```
toplevel = XtInitialize(argv[0], "Memo", NULL, 0,&argc, argv);
```

The name of the program is specified by **argv[0]**, while the class name of this application is **Memo**. Both **argc** and **argv** are modified by **XtInitialize()**. The function removes any command-line arguments recognized by the toolkit from **argv** and decrements **argc** accordingly.

Next, **memo** calls the application-defined function **xs_concat_words()**. This function concatenates the command-line arguments contained in the array **argv[]** into a single string.[5] The first member of **argv** is not passed, because, by UNIX convention, it contains the name of the program. If the command-line contains a message, the lines

```
n = 0;
if ((message = xs_concat_words(argc - 1, &argv[1])) != NULL){
    XtSetArg(wargs[n], XmNlabelString, message); n++;
}
```

set an entry in an **Arg** array to the string containing the message to be displayed. This array is then used as an argument to **XtCreateManagedWidget()**.

```
msg_widget = XtCreateManagedWidget("msg",
                                    xmLabelWidgetClass,
                                    toplevel, wargs, n);
```

This statement creates an XmLabel widget to display the string retrieved from the command line. The widget class pointer is specified as **xmLabelWidgetClass**, and the widget's name is "**msg**". The widget is a managed child of the **toplevel** shell widget created by **XtInitialize()**.

The next step is to realize the top level shell widget. Realizing a widget also causes the widget's children, in this case the XmLabel widget, to be realized. Finally, the program enters the main event loop. **XtMainLoop()** never returns. At this point, the message window appears on the screen and the program loops endlessly, processing events. The XmLabel widget automatically handles all resize and exposure events generated by the server.

This example also requires an auxiliary function, **xs_concat_words()**, which can be written as:

---

5. Motif uses an abstract data structure known as a compound string, instead of the traditional null terminated array of characters. Compound strings allow more flexibility and language independence.

```
/*********************************************************
 * concat.c: utility function to concatenate
 *           an array of strings into a single
 *           compound string with spaces between words.
 *********************************************************/
#include <X11/Intrinsic.h>
#include <X11/StringDefs.h>
#include <Xm/Xm.h>

XmString xs_concat_words(n, words)
    int    n;
    char *words[];
{
    XmString    xmstr;
    int         i, len = 0;
    /*
     * If there are no words just return an empty string.
     */
    if (n <= 0)
        return (XmStringCreate("", XmSTRING_DEFAULT_CHARSET));
    xmstr = (XmString) NULL;

    for (i = 0; i < n; i++)  {
      XmString tmp;
      if (i > 0){ /* Prepend all but first word with a space */
          tmp   = XmStringCreate(" ", XmSTRING_DEFAULT_CHARSET);
          xmstr = XmStringConcat(xmstr, tmp);
      }
      tmp = XmStringCreate(words[i], XmSTRING_DEFAULT_CHARSET);
      xmstr = XmStringConcat(xmstr, tmp);
    }
    return (xmstr);
}
```

This function converts each null-terminated character string in the **words** argument into a *compound string*, an abstraction used by Motif to represent strings. Each compound
string is then concatenated to form a single compound string, with each word separated by a
space. The type **XmString** represents a compound string. The function

XmStringCreate(string, char_set)

creates a compound string from an array of ASCII characters. The **char_set** argument is a
string that identifies a set of fonts that can be used. For now we can just use a default character set defined by Motif.

If the **words** array is empty, **xs_concat_words()** creates and returns an empty compound string. Otherwise it uses the function

XmStringConcat(string1, string2)

to concatenate each entry in the array and form a single compound string. Chapter 9 explains compound strings along with the functions used to create and manipulate them in more detail.

Fig. 2.1 shows the widget tree formed by the **memo** example. The figure shows each widget's name above its class name (shown in italics). Most, but not all, widget trees directly correspond to the X window tree created by the application. This widget tree is very simple, but later examples will produce much more complex widget trees. This figure shows the root of the window tree as the program name and class, with the top level shell widget implied, but not shown.

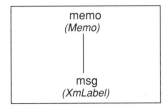

Figure 2.1   The widget tree created by memo.

2.4.1   Building and Using memo

The **memo** example can be compiled and linked with the X libraries with the UNIX shell command:

```
cc -o memo memo.c concat.c -1Xm -1Xt -1X11
```

This compiles the files memo.c and concat.c and links the Xlib, Xt Intrinsics, and Motif widget libraries with the program. The ordering of the libraries is significant. All widget libraries must precede the Intrinsics library, which must precede the Xlib library.

We can now invoke **memo** from a UNIX shell in an X terminal emulator, for example:

```
memo Hello World
```

This produces the message window shown in Fig. 2.2.

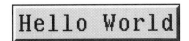

Figure 2.2   memo's message window.

Depending on the window manager you use, **memo** might appear complete with a title bar and other decorations added by the window manager. Fig. 2.3 shows the **memo** window with a title bar and several other gadgets added by the Motif window manager, **mwm**.

Figure 2.3 memo's window with window manager decorations.

One practical application of **memo** is to invoke it from a *makefile*. A makefile is a script used by the UNIX **make** utility, which manages compilation of applications. For example, consider a basic makefile that can be used to build **memo** itself:

```
#############################
# Makefile for memo.c
#############################
memo:memo.o concat.o
     cc -o memo memo.o concat.o -lXm -lXt -lX11
     memo Program Compiled Successfully
```

Now, the shell command

```
make memo
```

builds **memo** and uses **memo** itself to announce the successful compilation.

One obvious problem with **memo** is that there is no way to exit the program. In fact, **memo** provides no way to handle user input of any kind. The rest of this chapter discusses several ways to solve this problem, including event handlers, callbacks, and action procedures.

2.4.2   Creating a Utilities Library

As we demonstrate different parts of X, this book occasionally presents functions and utilities that are useful in more than one program. Some of these functions combine widgets to perform some higher level task, while others have little to do with X, but are useful nevertheless. For example, the function **xs_concat_words()** is a simple, self-contained procedure that we will use again in other examples. It is convenient to place these functions in a library where applications can use them by linking the library with the program. Libraries are useful for grouping collections of small functions into a single module that can be linked with any program needing any of the functions. A library also serves a second purpose in this book, by reducing the number of times a simple function used by multiple examples must be presented. The first time such a reusable function is defined, we will add it to our library. Then, when we discuss examples that use the same function, we can simply refer to the library. We can start a library used by nearly all examples in this book with the function **xs_concat_words()**. We will name this library libXs. (The letters "Xs" stand for "X-sample library".) The library consists of an archive file that stores the relocatable compiled functions, and a header file containing definitions and declarations needed to use the library. At this point the file libXs.h contains only the following lines:

```
/***********************************************
 * libXs.h: Header file for X-sample library
 ***********************************************/
extern XmString xs_concat_words();
```

We will add to this library throughout this book, as we find other useful functions. Refer to Appendix F for the complete libXs.h header file.

We can create a library containing **xs_concat_words()** with the commands:

```
cc -c concat.c
ar ruv libXs.a concat.o
```

These commands compile concat.c into an object file, and then archive the file into the library file libXs.a. It is common practice to place library files in some standard location such as

```
/usr/lib
/usr/local/lib
```

where they can be found by the linker. Assuming this is done, we can build **memo** with the command:

```
cc -o memo memo.c -lXs -lXm -lXt -lX11
```

This command compiles the file memo.c and links the resulting object file with the libXs library as well as the Motif and X libraries.

2.4.3 Event Handlers

An event handler is a procedure invoked by the Intrinsics when a specific type of event occurs within a widget. The widget programmer can define event handlers to handle some, all, or none of the X events. The application programmer can also use the function

```
XtAddEventHandler(widget, eventmask, nonmaskable,
                  handler, client_data)
```

to register additional event handlers for events that occur in a widget. This function registers an application-defined function specified by the argument **handler** as an event handler for the event or events specified in the **eventmask**. The argument **eventmask** must be one of the standard X event masks defined in the file X.h. The event handler can also be registered for more than one event by specifying the inclusive-OR of two or more event masks. The Xt Intrinsics automatically invokes the given handler function when one of the event types specified by **eventmask** occurs within the widget's window. Applications can register multiple event handlers for the same event type and the same widget. When an event occurs, each handler registered for that event type is called. However, the Intrinsics does not define the order in which multiple event handlers are invoked. Applications can use the argument **client_data** to specify some data to be passed as a parameter to the event handler. This argument can be given as **NULL** if the event handler does not require any application-specific data.

Some X events that applications need to handle have no event mask. These events are said to be *nonmaskable* because they are sent to all applications whether an application selects them or not.[6] To register an event handler for a nonmaskable event, the argument **nonmaskable** must be set to **TRUE**. Since nonmaskable events have no event mask, the **mask** argument must be specified as **NoEventMask**. The form of every event handler is:

```
void handler(w, client_data, event)
   Widget   w;
   caddr_t  client_data;
   XEvent   *event;
```

Every event handler is called with three arguments. The first argument is the widget in whose window the event occurred. The second argument is the client data specified by the application when registering the event handler. The event handler usually coerces this argument to the expected data type.[7] In C, this can be done by simply declaring the **client_data** argument to be the expected type in the definition of the event handler. The last argument is a pointer to the event that caused this function to be invoked. Event handlers never return a useful value, and should be declared to be of type **void.**

We can use an event handler to provide a way to exit from the **memo** program. First we must define an event handler that simply exits when it is called. Before calling **exit()**, it is a good idea to close the application's connection to the X server. This isn't absolutely necessary, because the server will notice that the connection has been lost when the client exits. However, it is cleaner to request the server to close the connection and perform cleanup of the application's resources, using the function:

XtCloseDisplay(display)

The **quit()** event handler can be written as:

---

6. The nonmaskable event types are ClientMessage, MappingNotify, SelectionNotify, SelectionClear, and SelectionRequest. Most of these events are used for interclient communication, and are discussed in Chapter 11.

7. The Xt Intrinsics uses the type caddr_t to indicate an untyped pointer. On the author's system, caddr_t is defined as:
      typedef caddr_t char *

```
void quit(w, client_data, event)
  Widget   w;
  caddr_t  client_data;
  XEvent  *event;
{
  XtCloseDisplay(XtDisplay(w));
  exit(0);
}
```

Next, we must register the event handler with the Xt Intrinsics so that it can be called when the appropriate event occurs. For example, let's redesign the **memo** program to exit when the user presses a mouse button in the message window. The new version of **memo** simply adds the line

```
XtAddEventHandler(msg_widget, ButtonPressMask, FALSE,
                  quit, NULL);
```

to register the **quit()** event handler for **ButtonPress** events. Notice that this version of **memo** includes the header file libXs.h (see Section 2.4.2) and must be linked with the libXs library which contains the **xs_concat_words()** function. The new version of **memo** can be written as:

```
/**********************************************
 * memo.c: Adding an event handler
 **********************************************/
#include <X11/Intrinsic.h>
#include <X11/StringDefs.h>
#include <Xm/Xm.h>
#include <Xm/Label.h>
#include "libXs.h"

extern void quit();

main(argc, argv)
   int     argc;
   char   *argv[];
{
  Widget       toplevel, msg_widget;
  Arg          wargs[1];
  int          n;
  XmString     message;

  /*
   * Initialize the Intrinsics
```

```
          */
    toplevel = XtInitialize(argv[0],"Memo",NULL,0,&argc, argv);
    /*
     * If a message is given on the command-line,
     * use it as the XmNlabelString argument for the widget
     */
    n = 0;
    if ((message = xs_concat_words(argc-1, &argv[1])) != NULL){
        XtSetArg(wargs[n], XmNlabelString, message); n++;
    }
    /*
     * Create the XmLabel widget.
     */
    msg_widget = XtCreateManagedWidget("msg",
                                        xmLabelWidgetClass,
                                        toplevel, wargs, n);
    /*
     * Register the event handler to be called when
     * a button is pressed
     */
    XtAddEventHandler(msg_widget, ButtonPressMask, FALSE,
                      quit, NULL);
    /*
     * Realize the widgets and enter the event loop.
     */
    XtRealizeWidget(toplevel);
    XtMainLoop();
}
```

2.4.4   Callback Functions

Some widgets provide hooks that allow applications to define procedures to be called when some widget-specific condition occurs. These hooks are known as *callback lists* and the application's procedures are known as *callback functions*, or simply *callbacks*, because the widget makes a "call back" to the application-defined function. Each widget maintains a callback list for each type of callback it supports. For example, every widget supports a **XtNdestroyCallback** callback list. Each callback on this callback list is invoked before the widget is destroyed. Callbacks are different than event handlers because they are invoked by the widget rather than the Intrinsics, and are not necessarily tied to any particular event. Applications can add a callback to a widget's callback list with the function:

```
    XtAddCallback(widget, callback_name, proc, client_data)
```

The argument, **callback_name**, specifies the callback list to which the callback function **proc** is to be added. The application can use the **client_data** argument to specify some application-defined data to be passed to the callback procedure by the Intrinsics when the callback is invoked.

The form of every callback procedure is:

```
void CallbackProcedure(widget, client_data, call_data)
     Widget   widget;
     caddr_t client_data;
     caddr_t call_data;
```

Like event handlers, callback functions do not return any useful value, and should be declared as type **void**. The first argument to every callback function is the widget for which the callback is registered. The second parameter is the **client_data** specified by the application in the call to **XtAddCallback()**. The last argument contains data provided by the widget. The type and purpose of this data can be determined by checking the documentation for the specific widget. In Motif, this argument is always a pointer to a structure. At a minimum, this structure contains a pointer to the X event that caused the callback and a widget-specific code that indicates the reason the callback was invoked. The structure containing this basic information is defined as:

```
typedef struct {
     int       reason;
     XEvent   *event;
} XmAnyCallbackStruct;
```

Some Motif widgets use structures containing additional information, but these structures always contain **reason** and **event** fields.

The **memo** example in Section 2.4.3 uses an event handler to exit the application when a **ButtonPress** event occurs. Another way to do this is to use a callback procedure. However, the XmLabel widget used in the earlier versions of **memo** supports only the **XmNhelpCallback** callback list. To demonstrate callbacks, we must modify **memo** to use a subclass of the XmLabel widget, the XmPushButton widget class, which supports three additional callback lists:

XmNactivateCallback   **XmNarmCallback**   **XmNdisarmCallback**

When the user presses a mouse button inside an XmPushButton widget, the widget invokes the functions on the **XmNarmCallback** list. If the user releases the mouse button while the sprite is contained within the XmPushButton widget, the functions on the **XmNactivate-Callback** are called, followed by the functions on the **XmNdisarmCallback** list. If the user moves the sprite out of the XmPushButton widget's window before releasing the mouse button, only the functions on the **XmNdisarmCallback** list are invoked.

We only need to change a few lines of code to use an **XmNactivateCallback** function instead of an event handler to exit the program. First, we must change the definition of **quit()** to the form used by a callback function.

```
void quit(w, client_data, call_data)
    Widget      w;
    caddr_t     client_data;
    XmAnyCallbackStruct *call_data;
{
    XtCloseDisplay(XtDisplay(w));
    exit(0);
}
```

Then we must replace the line

```
XtAddEventHandler(msg_widget,ButtonPressMask, FALSE,
                    quit, NULL);
```

from the previous version of **memo** with the line:

```
XtAddCallback(msg_widget, XmNactivateCallback, quit, NULL);
```

We must also include the header file PushB.h, instead of Label.h and create the **msg_widget** as an XmPushButton widget rather than an XmLabel widget by replacing **xmLabelWidgetClass** with **xmPushButtonWidgetClass**. With these changes, the widget calls all functions on its **XmNactivateCallback** list, including **quit()**, when the user presses and releases a mouse button in the message window.

The difference between using the event handler and a callback may seem to be insignificant, since we accomplished the same task using both. However, there is at least one important advantage to using callback functions. With callbacks, the method used to exit the **memo** program is no longer tied directly to a specific X event, but instead is tied to a more abstract *action*, in this case the action of *activating* the button widget. Further, the user can usually use the *translation manager* facility provided by the Xt Intrinsics to customize the action that invokes a callback. The next section discusses the translation manager, and shows yet another way that we can make **memo** respond to user actions.

2.4.5   Using The Translation Manager

The Xt Intrinsics's translation manager provides a mechanism that allows the user to specify a mapping between user actions and functions provided by a widget or an application. For example, the user can use the translation manager to alter the action that causes the **memo** program from the previous section to exit. Adding the line

```
memo*XmPushButton.translations:   <Key>q:   ArmAndActivate()
```

to the user's .Xdefaults file specifies that the action procedure "**ArmAndActivate()**" should be bound to the action "<Key>q". This action procedure is defined by the Motif Xm-PushButton widget. It invokes all callback functions on both the **XmNarmCallback** and **XmNactivateCallback** callback lists.

In its most basic form, a translation table consists of a list of expressions. Each expression has a left side and a right side, separated by a colon. The left side specifies the user action that invokes the procedure given on the right side. The left side can specify modifier keys and also sequences of events. For example, we could specify that the message window of the **memo** program should be armed and activated after a mouse button has been pressed and released, by specifying:

```
*translations:<Btn1Down>,<Btn1Up>: ArmAndActivate()
```

We can specify that a modifier key must also be held down while a mouse button is pressed, for example:

```
*translations: Ctrl<Btn1Down>:     ArmAndActivate()
```

Multiple bindings can be specified in a single translation table. However, the more complex the translation table, the more chance there is for unwanted interaction between the entries. More specific events should always precede less specific events. For example, in the specification

```
# WRONG
*translations:  <Btn1Down>:     Arm() \n\
                Meta<Btn1Down>: Activate()
```

the second button action overrides the first, because specifying no modifier keys is the same as specifying all modifier keys and the translation manager scans the translations for each event and uses the first match it finds. The correct way to specify that <Btn1Down> without the Meta key invokes the **Arm()** procedure is:

```
# CORRECT
*XmLabel*translations:  Meta<Btn1Down>: Activate() \n\
                        <Btn1Down>:     Arm()
```

When multiple translations are given, each specification must be separated by a newline character (' \n'). It is often convenient to use a backslash to break the translations across multiple lines.

These examples show how the translation manager maps between a user event and a corresponding procedure defined by a widget. However, applications can also define new action procedures, using the function:

```
XtAddActions(actions, num_actions)
```

The **actions** argument must be an array of type **ActionsRec**. This structure consists of a string that defines the public name of the action procedure and a pointer to a procedure that performs the action. For example, we can register an action procedure **quit()** for the **memo** program as:

```
static XtActionsRec actionsTable [] ={
                {"bye",    quit},
                };
```

The string, "**bye()**" is the name by which the action is known to the translation manager. The procedure **quit()**, which must be declared before referencing it, takes four arguments and can be written as:

```
static void quit(w, event, params, num_params)
      Widget     w;
      XEvent     *event;
      String     *params;
      Cardinal   *num_params;
{
  XtCloseDisplay(XtDisplay(w));
  exit(0);
}
```

The first argument specifies the widget in which the user action occurred, while **event** is a pointer to the X event that caused the procedure to be invoked. The **params** argument is an array of strings containing any arguments specified in the translation, while **num_params** indicates the length of this array.

If we use **XtAddActions()** to register this action list with the translation manager, the user can define a translation for the **bye()** action in the .Xdefaults file. For example:

```
memo*XmLabel*translations: Ctrl<Key>q:    bye()
```

The **bye()** action is specified using a function-like syntax to allow parameters to be passed to the action procedure. For example, if the translation were defined as

```
memo*XmLabel*translations: <Key>q:     bye(10, Goodbye)
```

the **quit()** procedure's **params** argument would contain two entries when the translation manager calls **quit()**.

Programmers often need to specify translations programmatically. This can be done using the function

```
XtAugmentTranslations(widget, translation_table)
```

or the function

```
XtOverrideTranslations(widget, translation_table)
```

Both of these functions register a translation table with a particular widget. **XtAugmentTranslations()** merges a list of translations with the list of current translations supported by the widget. It does not override existing translations specified by the widget or the user. **XtOverrideTranslations()** also merges the two lists, but replaces existing translations with entries from the new translation list whenever there is a conflict.

A translation table is a structure of type **XtTranslations**. The function

```
XtParseTranslationTable(source)
```

compiles a string containing a translation specification into a **XtTranslations** structure. For example, we can programmatically define translations for **memo** as:

```
static char defaultTranslations[] =  "<Key>q:  bye()";
```

In the body of the program, we must call **XtParseTranslationTable()** to compile this string. For example:

```
trans_table = XtParseTranslationTable(defaultTranslations);
```

Then we must add the translations to the existing translations for the message widget with:

```
XtAugmentTranslations(msg_widget, trans_table);
```

We can now write a new version of **memo** that uses the translation manager to exit. This version uses the XmLabel widget to display the message, although the XmPushButton widget could also be used.

```
/************************************************************
 * memo.c: Defining application actions and translations
 ************************************************************/
#include <X11/Intrinsic.h>
#include <X11/StringDefs.h>
#include <Xm/Xm.h>
#include <Xm/Label.h>
#include "libXs.h"
static void quit();

static XtActionsRec actionsTable [] = {
  {"bye",    quit},
};
static char defaultTranslations[] =  "<Key>Q:  bye()";

main(argc, argv)
    int             argc;
    char            *argv[];
{
```

```
Widget              toplevel, msg_widget;
Arg                 wargs[10];
int                 n;
XmString            message;
XtTranslations  trans_table;
/*
 * Initialize the Intrinsics
 */
toplevel = XtInitialize(argv[0],"Memo",NULL,0,&argc,argv);
/*
 * Register the new actions, and compile translations table
 */
XtAddActions(actionsTable, XtNumber(actionsTable));
trans_table=  XtParseTranslationTable(defaultTranslations);
/*
 * If a message is given on the command-line,
 * use it as the XmNlabelString argument for the widget
 */
n = 0;
if ((message = xs_concat_words(argc-1, &argv[1])) != NULL){
  XtSetArg(wargs[n], XmNlabelString, message); n++;
}
/*
 * Create the XmLabel widget.
 */
msg_widget = XtCreateManagedWidget("msg",
                                   xmLabelWidgetClass,
                                   toplevel, wargs, n);
/*
 * Merge the program-defined translations with
 * existing translations.
 */
XtAugmentTranslations(msg_widget, trans_table);
/*
 * Realize all widgets and enter the event loop.
 */
XtRealizeWidget(toplevel);
XtMainLoop();
}
```

Using the translation manager to map between action procedures and events provides a flexible way for programmers to design customizable applications. It also provides a simple way for the application programmer to extend the behavior of any widget.

2.5   APPLICATION CONTEXTS

Most of the Xt Intrinsics functions described in this chapter are convenience routines. These functions are adequate for most applications and also are compatible with the earlier versions of the Intrinsics. However, most of these functions simply call other routines that require an additional parameter, known as an *application context*. Application contexts allow multiple logical applications to exist in a single address space. Each context corresponds to a logical application that has its own independent event loop and connection to the X server. Application contexts reduce re-entrancy problems in the toolkit, and also allow applications to use multiple displays. Each application context maintains a list of displays opened by the function **XtOpenDisplay()**.

Applications can create a unique application context using the function:

XtCreateApplicationContext()

This function returns a context, whose type is **XtAppContext**. Every application must have at least one application context. Applications that use the convenience functions described in this chapter use a default context automatically created by the Intrinsics.

The programmer can destroy an application context using the function:

XtDestroyApplicationContext(app_context)

This function destroys the context and closes the connection to the X server used by the context.

The function **XtInitialize()** is a convenience function that calls three other Intrinsics functions. These are:

XtToolkitInitialize()

XtOpenDisplay(app_context, display_name, app_name, app_class, options, noptions, &argc, argv)

XtAppCreateShell(app_context, classname, class, display, args, nargs)

XtToolkitInitialize() initializes the Xt Intrinsics. Unlike **XtInitialize()**, it does not open a connection to the server, nor create an initial shell widget. **XtOpenDisplay()** opens a new connection to the X server using the given application context. If a **NULL** context is specified, **XtOpenDisplay()** uses the default application context. **XtAppCreateShell()** creates a top-level shell for the application. Applications that use application contexts should call these functions directly rather than using **XtInitialize()**. Fig. 2.4 shows the functions that require application contexts and the corresponding convenience functions that use the default application context.

<u>Convenience Routine</u>	<u>Context Routine</u>
XtMainLoop()	XtAppMainLoop()
XtNextEvent()	XtAppNextEvent()
XtProcessEvent()	XtAppProcessEvent()
XtPeekEvent()	XtAppPeekEvent()
XtPending()	XtAppPending()
XtAddInput()	XtAppAddInput()
XtAddTimeOut()	XtAppAddTimeOut()
XtAddWorkProc()	XtAppAddWorkProc()
XtCreateApplicationShell()	XtAppCreateShell()
XtInitialize()	XtToolkitInitialize()
XtAddConverter()	XtAppAddConverter()

Figure 2.4 Xt Intrinsics convenience functions.

Let's look at the skeleton of the **memo** example, this time using application contexts:

```
/************************************************************
 * memo.c: Skeleton Using Application Contexts
 ***********************************************************/
/*
 * Includes and global declarations......
 */
main(argc, argv)
    int     argc;
    char    *argv[];
{
  XtAppContext    app;
  Display         *dpy;
  /* Other declarations ..... */
  /*
   * Initialize the Intrinsics
   */
  XtToolkitInitialize();
  /*
   * Create a context.
   */
  app = XtCreateApplicationContext();
  /*
   * Open the display.
   */
  dpy = XtOpenDisplay(app, "", argv[0], "Memo", NULL, 0,
                      &argc, argv);
```

```
    /*
     * Create a toplevel shell.
     */
    toplevel = XtAppCreateShell(app, "Memo",
                                applicationShellWidgetClass,
                                dpy, NULL, 0);
    /*
     * Extract message and create message widget here .....
     */
    XtRealizeWidget(toplevel);
    XtAppMainLoop(app);
}
```

2.6 SUMMARY

This chapter briefly introduced the key concepts of the Xt Intrinsics layer. We learned how to create and display a widget on the screen, explored four implementations of a simple X application, and introduced event handlers, callbacks, and the translation manager. Using the Xt Intrinsics and a widget set has many advantages over using Xlib directly:

- Using a higher level library reduces the amount of code that must be written by the application programmer, and helps make an application easier to understand and modify.

- The customization facilities provided by the Xt Intrinsics allow the end user to modify the behavior of applications in a consistent way.

- Standard widgets that provide essential components needed by many applications are available, eliminating the need for each programmer to re-implement these components for each application.

- A project with unique user interface requirements can create new widgets that can be used alone or mixed with an existing widget set. When many applications need to work together, using a common set of widgets is an excellent way to ensure consistency across all applications.

One major advantage of the Xt Intrinsics is the degree to which it is integrated with Xlib. Using the Intrinsics and a widget set does not prevent the programmer from calling Xlib functions directly. Most applications use a combination of the Xt Intrinsics framework, a set of widgets, and Xlib functions. Whenever an appropriate widget set is available, it is generally better to use these higher level facilities than to program directly with Xlib. However, when writing callbacks and event handlers, the programmer often needs to use Xlib functions as well.

The following chapter introduces the X resource manager, a facility that provides a simple and consistent way for users to customize applications. Chapter 4 introduces the Motif widget set and shows how to combine widgets to create more complex interfaces.

3

THE X RESOURCE MANAGER

Managing resources is an important part of programming with X. It is difficult to write or even use any significant X Toolkit application without understanding the X resource management facilities. This chapter explains what resources are and shows how both the programmer and the user can use the resource manager to customize applications.

3.1 WHAT IS A RESOURCE?

X programmers often use the word *resource* to mean different things, depending on the context in which they use the word. For example, the Xlib documentation refers to windows, graphics contexts, and fonts as resources. These types of resources are maintained by the X server and accessed by clients through a resource ID. Widget programmers generally refer to any internal data required by the widget as a resource. The Xt Intrinsics also allows applications to manage user-customizable data, using the same mechanisms used by widgets. Therefore, we might say that a resource is any user-customizable data. In this broader sense, resources include window IDs, colors, fonts, images, text, names of windows or widgets, positions and sizes of windows, or any customizable parameter that affects the behavior of the application.

By convention, X applications allow the end user to specify most or all resources used by a program. Application programmers should always provide reasonable defaults for all resources required by a program, but should allow the end user to override these defaults whenever possible. It is important to allow the user to customize an application because no matter how well the programmer tries to anticipate the needs of the end user, there is always someone who wishes to alter the behavior of a program.

The X resource manager facility encourages programmers to write customizable applications by providing an easy-to-use mechanism for determining user customizations and specifying defaults. The basic resource manager facilities provided by Xlib allow applications to store and retrieve information from a resource database. The Xt Intrinsics provides a higher level interface, built on the Xlib resource manager, that makes it easy for the application programmer to access the user's options and blend them with the program-defined defaults.

3.2 SPECIFYING RESOURCES

X maintains a database of resources containing user preferences as well as application defaults. The application can determine the proper value of a given resource at run time by querying the database. Traditional databases contain information that is completely and precisely specified. Users of such a database search for information by making imprecise queries. You might, for example, query a bibliographical database for books about the X Window System by requesting information on "windows." This query would return a possibly large list of books about "windows."

The X resource manager uses a slightly different model. In X, the database contains general information about the resources used by applications. For example, a user can specify that "All buttons should be red," or "All terminal-emulator windows should be 24 characters high and 80 characters wide." Applications query the database to determine the value of a specific resource for a specific application: "What color should the mail program's quit button be?" or "How wide should the command window be?"

3.2.1 Names and Classes

The resource manager requires that every application and resource in X have both a name and a class. The class indicates the general category to which each of these entities belongs, while the name identifies the specific entity. For example, a program named "emacs" might belong to the class "Editor". Similarly, the resource "destroyCallback" names a specific callback list. The class name of this resource, "Callback", identifies all callback lists. Both resource names and resource class names are strings. The header file, StringDefs.h, contains a set of commonly used resource names. Programmers can define additional resource names as needed, although they should not create new resource names unnecessarily. Choosing standard resource names and classes whenever possible promotes consistency between applications.

By convention, resource names generally begin with a lowercase letter, while class names begin with a capital letter. Resource names are often identical to the corresponding resource class names, except for the capitalization. For example, the resource name used to specify a foreground color is "foreground" and the resource class name is "Foreground". A widget's class name can be an arbitrary string, but is usually related to its function. The class name of every widget is determined by the widget programmer who designs the widget, while the application programmer determines the widget's name. For example, the class name of the widget used to display a string in the previous chapter is "XmLabel". The **memo** program specified the widget's name as "msg".

As we noted earlier, an application queries the resource database using a complete specification of the desired resource. Resources are completely specified by two strings that together uniquely identify a resource for a particular window or widget. The first string consists of the name of the application, followed by the names of each widget in the application's widget tree between the top widget and the widget using the resource, followed by the name of the resource. Each name in the string is separated by a dot ("."). The second string is similar except that it uses class names instead of resource names. Together, these strings (sometimes referred to resource lists) specify a unique path through the application's widget tree.

Fig. 3.1 and Fig. 3.2 show the widget layout and hierarchy of a hypothetical graphics editor named "draw." According to convention, the programmer has chosen the class name of the application as "Draw". Fig. 3.2 shows the widget tree corresponding to the widget layout in Fig. 3.1, with the class name of each widget in parentheses below the widget's name. We can specify the foreground color of the widget named **button1** in the upper portion of the window with a string containing the resource names

draw.panel.commands.button1.foreground

and a string containing the resource class names

Draw.XmBulletinBoard.XmRowColumn.XmPushButton.Foreground

Notice that the resource name string uniquely identifies **button1**, differentiating it from the other children of the **commands** widget, and also from any other button with the same name but in a different widget hierarchy (such as the **button1** in the **options** widget). The class string, however, can potentially apply to many buttons. In this example, the class string specifies the foreground color of all XmPushButton widgets managed by both the **commands** widget and the **options** widget. This class string also applies to buttons in any other application that contains this exact widget tree.

A resource database consists of a set of associations between resource names or class names and the value of a resource. The user can specify these associations in a resource file, such as the .Xdefaults file in the user's home directory. Each association consists of strings containing resource names or class names, followed by a colon, one or more spaces, and a value. For example, we can specify that the foreground color of **button1** in the **commands** panel should be red by adding the line

draw.panel.commands.button1.foreground: red

to a resource file. We can specify the color of all buttons in this application with the line:

Draw.XmBulletinBoard.XmRowColumn.XmPushButton.Foreground: red

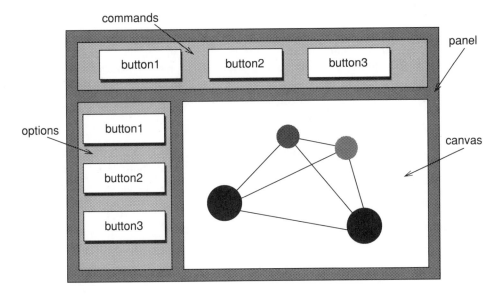

Figure 3.1 An example widget layout.

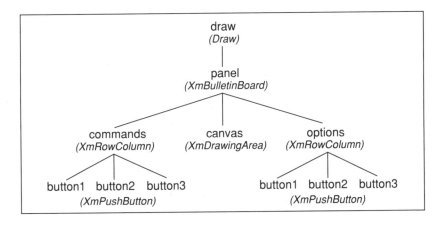

Figure 3.2 Widget tree for Fig. 3.1.

Although this example specifies resources relative to widgets, we can use the same mechanism to specify resources unrelated to any particular widget or window by using the program name and the resource name. For example,

```
draw.bufsize:      100
```

specifies the value of some resource named "bufsize" used by the application.

3.2.2   The Resource Manager's Matching Algorithm

It is often inconvenient to specify the value of every resource using the complete name or class list as in the previous examples. Instead, the resource manager allows us to use an asterisk "*" as a wild card character to represent any number of resource names or class names. For example, continuing to use the widget tree in Fig 3.1 and Fig. 3.2, we can specify the foreground color of a button named **button1** with:

      draw*button1*foreground: red

Notice, however, that there are two buttons in this example named **button1**. This resource specification applies to both buttons, because the asterisk matches both **options** and **commands**. We can be more specific and indicate the foreground color of **button1** in the **commands** widget with

      draw*commands*button1*foreground: red

We can also be more general, and specify all foreground colors used by the application with:

      draw*foreground: red

Or we can specify the foreground color of the **options** widget and all its children with:

      draw*options*foreground: red

Partial resource specifications can also consist of any combination of resource names and class names. For example, we can specify that the foreground color of all widgets belonging to class XmPushButton should be green, regardless of the application, with the line

      *XmPushButton.foreground: green

Although the user can specify resources using incomplete name and class lists, applications must query the database using both the complete name list and the complete class list. At the lowest level, the Xlib function

      XrmGetResource(db, name, class, &type, &value)

is used to query the database. It returns the value and type of the resource that best matches the complete resource name and class name specification. The resource manager uses a matching algorithm to determine if any entry in the resource database matches the requested resource and returns a type and a value for the query. If no match is found, the returned value is **NULL**.

    The matching algorithm uses several precedence rules to arbitrate between multiple matching entries in the resource database. These rules are:

1. Either the resource name or the class name of each item in the query must match the corresponding item in the database entry. For example, a query for the foreground color of **button1**, using the resource name and class name specifications

```
draw.panel.commands.button1.foreground
Draw.XmBulletinBoard.XmRowColumn.XmPushButton.Foreground
```

matches the resource database entry

```
draw.XmBulletinBoard.commands.button1.Foreground: Blue
```

but not

```
draw.XmBulletinBoard.commands.button1.Highlight:   Yes
```

because the class name **Foreground**, specified in the query, does not match the class name, **Highlight**, in the database.

2. Entries in the database prefixed by a dot ("."") are more specific than (and therefore have precedence over) those prefixed by an asterisk ("*"). Therefore, the database entry

```
*commands.Background:      green
```

has precedence over

```
*commands*Background:      red
```

If both these specifications are in the user's resource database, the **commands** widget will have a green background. However, all children of the **commands** widget (here, **button1**, **button2**, and **button3**) will have a red background.

3. Resource names always have precedence over class names. Therefore

```
*button1.Foreground:      red
```

has precedence over

```
*XmPushButton.Foreground:      green
```

because the name **button1** is more specific than the class XmPushButton.

4. Both resource names and class names have precedence over an asterisk. So

```
Draw*XmBulletinBoard*XmPushButton*Foreground: red
```

has precedence over

```
Draw*XmBulletinBoard*foreground: green
```

because the first entry more completely identifies the path through the widget tree.

5. The resource manager compares database entries left to right, and the first items in a resource specification have precedence over successive items. For example, when determining the foreground color of the buttons in Fig. 3.1,

```
draw*XmBulletinBoard*foreground: green
```

has precedence over

```
draw*XmPushButton*foreground: red
```

Specifying resources takes practice and is often a matter of trial and error, particularly as the size of the user's resource files grows and the potential for accidental interactions increases.

3.3 MANAGING APPLICATION RESOURCES

Individual widgets usually manage their own resources and require no action from the application programmer. However, programmers often need to obtain application level resources that have nothing to do with widgets and perhaps little to do with the application's user interface. The resource manager provides the programmer with a consistent mechanism for retrieving all options and resources used by applications. Although Xlib provides the basic resource manager facilities, the Xt Intrinsics provides a higher level interface that is much easier to use. This section discusses and demonstrates how the application programmer uses the resource manager facilities provided by the Xt Intrinsics.

3.3.1   Loading the Resource Database

Every X Toolkit application must begin by initializing the Xt Intrinsics and opening a connection to the X server, often using the convenience function **XtInitialize()**. This procedure also creates a resource database and loads it with the resource specifications in the user's resource files. **XtInitialize()** also extracts options specified on the command line and adds them to the resource database. Because the command-line arguments are added last, they override the corresponding values specified in all resource files. X applications usually do not need to parse command-line arguments directly, but instead use the resource manager interface to obtain command-line arguments.

XtInitialize() loads the resource database from several different places. Fig. 3.3 summarizes the order in which the resource manager loads these files. By default, the Intrinsics first searches for the file

/usr/lib/X11/app-defaults/<class>

where <class> is the class name given to **XtInitialize()**. If this file exists, the resource manager loads it into the resource database. Motif provides the ability to specify an alternate directory for these resource files based on the environment variable **LANG**. If this environment variable is set, it is assumed to specify a directory component in the path:

/usr/lib/X11/<$**LANG**>app-defaults/<class>

This allows language-specific resource files to be provided. Next, if the UNIX environment variable **XAPPLRESDIR** is set, it is expected to specify a directory containing application-specific resource files. The resource manager appends the class of the program to the value of the **XAPPLRESDIR** variable and tries to load the file named by the result. Again, Motif provides a language-independent version of this. The Motif Intrinsics looks first for a file named $**XAPPLRESLANGPATH**<class>. If this environment variable doesn't exist or if the file does not exist, Motif looks for the file **$XAPPLRESDIR**<class>. Next, if the root window has a **RESOURCE_MANAGER** property, the resource manager assumes that this property contains additional options. If this property doesn't exist, the resources in the file named .Xdefaults in the user's home directory are merged into the database. Next, the environment variable **XENVIRONMENT** can contain the name of a resource file. If this environment variable is defined, the resource manager loads the contents of the file. If no such environment variable exists, the resource manager loads the file .Xdefaults-<*host*>, where <*host*> is the name of the machine on which the client is running. We will refer to any of these files used to hold user-defined options as *resource files*. All resource files use the same format as the .Xdefaults file, discussed in Section 3.2.2. Notice that all files and directories are relative to the machine on which the client is running, while the **RESOURCE_MANAGER** property is associated with the root window of the server on which the client is displayed.

---

1. Load /usr/lib/X11/$**LANG**app-defaults/<class>
   where <class> is the class of the application.

2. If step 1 fails, load /usr/lib/X11/app-defaults/<class>
   where <class> is the class of the application.

3. Load $**XAPPLRESLANGPATH**<class>
   where <class> is the class of the application.

4. If step 3 fails, load $**XAPPLRESDIR**<class>
   where <class> is the class of the application.

5. Load data in **RESOURCE_MANAGER** property.

6. If **RESOURCE_MANAGER** property does not exist,
   load $HOME/.Xdefaults

7. Load file specified by $**XENVIRONMENT**.

8. If $**XENVIRONMENT** is not set,
   load $HOME/.Xdefaults-<host>
   where <host> is the machine where the client is running.

9. Load command-line options.

Figure 3.3 Algorithm for loading the resource database.

After processing all resource files, the Intrinsics also merges any recognized options from the application's command line into the resource database. **XtInitialize()** removes all recognized options from **argv** and leaves unrecognized options for the application to process. The Xt Intrinsics supports a standard set of options to ensure that all applications recognize the same command-line arguments. Fig. 3.4 lists these standard command-line options along with the corresponding resource name used to set the option in a resource file. Each application can also define additional options, which are passed in the **option** argument to **XtInitialize()**. Section 3.3.3 discusses the format of these options. Notice that Intrinsics simply recognizes these standard command line options and places the appropriate value in the application's resource database. This has nothing to do with whether or not the application actually uses or responds to these resources. For example, Motif widgets currently use a "fontList" resource to determine the font used for displaying text, and ignores the "font" resource. So, while the Intrinsics recognizes the "-font" command-line option, and will place the corresponding value in the resource database, Motif applications will not be affected.

The "-xrm" command-line flag allows users to specify an arbitrary string to be placed in the resource database. This flag can be used to specify any resource on the command line, using the same syntax as a resource file.

Flag	Resource Name	Type	Example or Effect
+rv	*reverseVideo	None	sets resource to "off"
+synchronous	*synchronous	None	sets resource to "off"
-background	*background	String	-background Black
-bd	*borderColor	String	-bd Black
-bordercolor	*borderColor	String	-bordercolor Black
-bg	*background	String	-bg Red
-borderwidth	*TopLevelShell.borderWidth	Integer	-borderwidth 2
-bw	*TopLevelShell.borderWidth	Integer	-bw 2
-display	*display	String	-display expo:0.1
-fg	*foreground	String	-fg Blue
-foreground	*foreground	String	-foreground Blue
-fn	*font	String	-fn 6x13
-font	*font	String	-font 6x13
-geometry	*TopLevelShell.geometry	String	-geometry =80x24
-iconic	*TopLevelShell.iconic	None	sets resource to "on"
-name	*name	String	-name Console
-reverse	*reverseVideo	None	sets resource to "on"
-rv	*reverseVideo	None	sets resource to "on"
-selectionTimeout	*selectionTimeout	Integer	-selectionTimeout 5
-synchronous	*synchronous	None	sets resource to "on"
-title	.title	String	-title Console
-xrm	N.A.	String	-xrm "*fontList: 6x13"

Figure 3.4 Standard command-line options.

3.3.2   Retrieving Application Resources

Widgets retrieve their resources automatically when they are created. However, applications can also use the resource manager to retrieve the user's application level options and resources, by using an **XtResource** structure to specify the resources to be retrieved from the database. This structure is defined in the header file /usr/include/X11/Xresource.h as:

```
typedef struct _XtResource {
    String    resource_name;  /* Resource name            */
    String    resource_class; /* Resource class           */
    String    resource_type;  /* Desired type             */
    Cardinal  resource_size;  /* Size in bytes            */
    Cardinal  resource_offset;/* Offset from base         */
    String    default_type;   /* Type of specified default */
    caddr_t   default_addr;   /* Address of default resource*/
} XtResource;
```

The **resource_name** member is a string that specifies the name of the resource being retrieved. For example, to retrieve a foreground color, an application uses the string "**foreground**". Whenever possible, the constants defined in the header file Stringdefs.h should be used. This not only encourages consistency between applications, but also allows the compiler to catch spelling errors. For example, StringDefs.h defines the string "foreground" as the constant **XtNforeground**.

The **resource_class** member specifies the class of the resource, and is used by the resource manager's matching algorithm. For a foreground color, the class name is "**Foreground**", or the predefined constant **XtCForeground**. The **resource_type** member is a string that specifies the desired type of the resource. The type can be any valid data type, including any application-defined type. For example, an application might reasonably ask for a color by name (a string) or ask for the pixel value (an integer) that represents the color. The file StringDefs.h also contains definitions of common resource types. By convention, a resource type consists of the name of the type preceded by the letters **XtR**, for example **XtRString** or **XtRPixel**. The **resource_size** member indicates the size, in bytes, of the resource to be retrieved. The **resource_offset** member of the **XtResource** structure indicates a relative address where the resource value should be placed. The Xt Intrinsics provide a utility macro

```
XtOffset(type *, field)
```

which determines the byte offset of a member of a C struct and provides a convenient way to specify relative addresses. The last members of the **XtResource** structure specify a default value for the resource and the type of the default value. The resource manager uses this default if it does not find a match in the user's resource database. This provides a simple way for the application programmer to specify default values for all resources.

Applications can use the function

```
XtGetApplicationResources(widget, base, resources,
                          nresources, args, nargs)
```

to retrieve the resources specified in an array of type **XtResource** from the database. The **widget** argument should specify the top-level shell widget that identifies the name and class of the application. The **base** argument specifies the base address of a data structure where the resource manager is to store the retrieved values. If the offsets specified in the **XtResource** list are absolute addresses, rather than offsets within a structure, the **base** argument can be specified as zero. The next argument, **resources**, is an **XtResource** list, while **nresources** indicates the length of the **resource** list. The last arguments, **args** and **nargs** provide a way for the application to override values in the database. The **args** parameter must be an array of type **Arg** containing resource names and values while **nargs** indicates the number of resources in the array.

Let's look at an example of how an application uses this mechanism. A simple test program, named **rmtest**, retrieves and prints the value of four parameters. The program supplies default values for these resources, but the user can also use the resource manager to customize the parameters. The four parameters are: **foreground** (color), **background** (color), a **delay** parameter, and a **verbose** flag. First we must include the header files Intrinsic.h and StringDefs.h.

```
/***********************************************
 * rmtest.c: simple test of the resource manager
 ***********************************************/
#include <X11/Intrinsic.h>
#include <X11/StringDefs.h>
```

Next, we define a single data structure to store the four parameters:

```
typedef struct {
    Pixel    fg, bg;
    int      delay;
    Boolean  verbose;
} ApplicationData, *ApplicationDataPtr;
```

Then we define an **XtResource** array that specifies how the resource manager should retrieve these resources from the database.

```
static XtResource resources[] = {
{ XtNforeground, XtCForeground, XtRPixel, sizeof (Pixel),
  XtOffset(ApplicationDataPtr, fg), XtRString, "Black"     },
{ XtNbackground, XtCBackground, XtRPixel, sizeof (Pixel),
  XtOffset(ApplicationDataPtr, bg), XtRString, "White"     },
{ "delay", "Delay", XtRInt, sizeof (int),
  XtOffset(ApplicationDataPtr, delay),
```

```
      XtRImmediate, (caddr_t) 2},
    { "verbose", "Verbose", XtRBoolean, sizeof (Boolean),
      XtOffset(ApplicationDataPtr, verbose), XtRString, "FALSE"},
    };
```

The first line of this declaration specifies that the value of a resource with name **XtNforeground** and class **XtCForeground** should be retrieved from the resource database. The function **XtOffset()** determines the offset within the **ApplicationData** structure where the resource manager is to store the retrieved value. This line also specifies that the value should be retrieved as type **XtRPixel**. If the value in the resource database is some type other than **XtRPixel**, the resource manager automatically converts the data to the requested type (See Section 3.3.4). If the resource database does not contain a foreground color specification, the resource manager uses the default value, "Black". Similarly, this resource list specifies that the background color should be retrieved as type **XtPixel**, **delay** as type **XtRInt**, and the flag **verbose** as a **XtRBoolean**.

The specification of the **delay** resource illustrates the use of the **XtRImmediate** type, which allows the default value to be specified directly, rather than as a string to be converted to the expected type.

The body of **rmtest** uses **XtGetApplicationResources()** to retrieve the resources and then prints each value before exiting. Notice that this example specifies the address of the **ApplicationData** structure, **data**, as the base address relative to which the function **XtGetApplicationResources()** is to store the values retrieved from the resource data base.

```
main(argc, argv)
  int     argc;
  char    *argv[];
{
  Widget          toplevel;
  ApplicationData data;

  toplevel = XtInitialize(argv[0], "Rmtest", NULL, 0,
                          &argc, argv);
  /*
   * Retrieve the application resources.
   */
  XtGetApplicationResources(toplevel, &data, resources,
                            XtNumber(resources), NULL, 0);
  /*
   * Print the results.
   */
```

```
    printf("fg = %d, bg = %d, delay = %d, verbose = %d\n",
           data.fg, data.bg, data.delay, data.verbose);
}
```

If none of the resources in the application's resource list are specified in the user's resource files, the resource manager uses the default values in the **XtResource** list. So, with no matching entries in any resource file, running the program gives the following output:

```
% rmtest
fg = 0, bg = 1, delay = 2, verbose = 0
```

Notice that the resource manager converts the foreground and background values from the colors named "Black" and "White" to the pixel values one and zero. These are pixel indexes used by X graphics functions that correspond to the named colors. (Chapter 6 discusses the color model used by X.) Also notice that the resource manager converts the value of **verbose** from the string "FALSE" to the boolean value zero used by convention in C to mean **FALSE**.

Since the class name of this program is "Rmtest", resources can be specified in the class resource file, /usr/lib/X11/app-defaults/Rmtest. Let's create a class resource file containing the following lines:

```
*foreground: Red
*delay:      10
*verbose:    TRUE
```

Now, if we run the program rmtest from a shell, we should see:

```
% rmtest
fg = 9, bg = 1, delay = 10,verbose = 1
```

Again, the pixel values of the foreground and background colors may vary because of X's color model. However, it should be clear that, in this case, the resource manager obtained the values of **foreground**, **delay**, and **verbose** from the class resource file rather than from the application-defined defaults. However, the background color still reflects the default value specified by the application, because the class resource file does not specify a background color.

Class resource files are generally used to define resources that apply to all applications of a particular class. This file is often used by a systems integrator to define resources for all users of the system. For example, a systems integrator might decide for some reason that all applications that belong to the class "Rmtest" should default to verbose mode. This could be done by setting the **verbose** resource to **TRUE** in the class resource file. The class resource file also serves as a good place to document the options that can be set for each application, and is often provided by the programmer or programmers who wrote the application. Comments can be inserted in the file after a "!" character.

End users of an application can selectively override any or all resource specifications in their own .Xdefaults file. Suppose we place the lines

```
*background: Blue
*delay:      20
```

in the file $HOME/.Xdefaults. Now, if we run this program we should see:

```
% rmtest
fg = 9, bg = 13, delay = 20, verbose = 1
```

In this example, the resource manager obtains the values for **foreground** and **verbose** from the class resource file, and retrieves the values of **delay** and **background** from the user's .Xdefaults file.

3.3.3 Retrieving Resources from the Command Line

It is usually more convenient to specify options using resource files than to use the conventional UNIX command-line argument mechanism, because resource files allow defaults to be specified once in a file rather than each time the application is run. Also, resource files allow users to specify general defaults to be used by all applications rather than specifying every option to every program on the command line. In addition, in a window-based environment, applications are less likely to be invoked from a UNIX command shell and more likely to be started from a menu or some type of applications browser. In spite of this, there are many cases where it is convenient or necessary to specify arguments on a command line. One situation were this is necessary is when the user needs to specify options on a per-process basis. For example, a user cannot use a resource file to run one **xterm** (an X terminal emulator program) with a red foreground and another **xterm** with a blue foreground. As one solution to this problem, Xlib and the Xt Intrinsics provide mechanisms for parsing the command-line arguments and placing the contents into the resource database. This allows applications to use the same retrieval mechanism discussed in the previous section to determine the value of command-line arguments.

Applications can use the **options** argument to **XtInitialize()** or **XtOpenDisplay()** to define additional command-line arguments. The **options** argument, which must be an array of type **XrmOptionDescList**, specifies how additional command-line arguments should be parsed and loaded into the resource database. The **XrmOptionDescList** structure is defined as:

```
typedef struct {
    char            *option;     /* argv abbreviation */
    char            *specifier;  /* Resource specifier*/
    XrmOptionKind   argKind;     /* Style of option   */
    caddr_t         value;       /* Default Value     */
} XrmOptionDescRec,  *XrmOptionDescList;
```

The **option** member of this structure is the name by which the resource is recognized on the command line, while the **specifier** is the name by which the resource is known in the resource database. The field **argKind** specifies the format of the command-line arguments and must be one of the values shown in Fig. 3.5.

Argument Style	Meaning
XrmoptionNoArg	Value is specified in **OptionDescRec.value**
XrmoptionIsArg	Value is the option string itself
XrmoptionStickyArg	Value immediately follows the option - no space
XrmoptionSepArg	Value is next argument in **argv**
XrmoptionResArg	A resource and value are in the next argument in argv
XrmoptionSkipArg	Ignore this option and the next argument in **argv**
XrmoptionSkipLine	Ignore this option and the rest of **argv**

Figure 3.5 Command-line parsing options.

Let's see how this works by adding some command-line arguments to the **rmtest** program from the previous section. The command-line options -fg and -bg are predefined by the Xt Intrinsics (see Section 3.3.1) so they are recognized automatically. We can specify command-line arguments corresponding to the other resources with:

```
static XrmOptionDescRec options[] = {
    {"-verbose", "*verbose", XrmoptionNoArg, "TRUE"},
    {"-delay",   "*delay",   XrmoptionSepArg, NULL }
};
```

The **verbose** resource is parsed as type **XrmoptionNoArg**, which means that if this option is present, its value is given by the fourth argument in the **XrmOptionsDescRec**. The Xt Intrinsics will extract the **delay** resource from the command line as type **XrmoptionSepArg**, which means that the value of the resource is given by the next argument in **argv**.

We must add these lines to the file rmtest.c and also change the first line of the program to:

```
toplevel = XtInitialize(argv[0], "Rmtest", options,
                        XtNumber(options), &argc, argv);
```

After making these changes to the **rmtest** program, we can try the new command-line options. Let's assume the contents of the class resource file and .Xdefaults file are the same as at the end of the previous section. We can now override the values in all resource files using command-line arguments. For example:

```
% rmtest -fg green -delay 15
fg = 14, bg = 13, delay = 15, verbose = 1
```

Now the resource manager retrieves the value of **verbose** from the class resource file and the value of **background** from the .Xdefaults file. However, the values of **foreground** and **delay** are specified by the command-line arguments.

Occasionally a programmer needs to override the values in the resource database, possibly because of a calculated condition that makes that option invalid. The resources obtained using **XtGetApplicationResources()** can be overridden by specifying a list of resource names and values as the **args** argument to the function.

3.3.4 Type Conversion

In each of the previous examples, the resource manager automatically converted the requested resources from one data type to another. The resource manager performs these conversions using functions known as *type-converters*. The most common type-converters convert from a string to some other data type, because resource files specify resources as strings. However, type-converters can be used to convert between any two data types, including application-defined types. Fig. 3.6 lists the standard type-converter conversions defined by the Xt Intrinsics, while Fig. 3.7 lists the additional type converters provided by Motif.

From	To	From	To	From	To
String	Boolean	String	Bool	String	short
String	unsigned char	String	Font	String	LongBoolean
String	Fontstruct	String	Cursor	String	int
String	Display	String	Pixel	String	File
XColor	Pixel	int	Boolean	int	Bool
int	Short	int	Pixel	int	Pixmap

Figure 3.6 Type converters defined by the Xt Intrinsics.

From	To	From	To
String	ArrowDirection	String	Orientation
String	Attachment	String	Packing
String	Alignment	String	LabelType
String	IndicatorType	String	EditMode
String	ScrollPolicy	String	VisualPolicy
String	SBDisplayPolicy	String	SBPlacement
String	Char	String	SelectionPolicy
String	ListSizePolicy	String	ProcessingDirection
String	StringDirection	String	SeparatorType
String	ShadowType	String	WhichButton
String	XmFontList	String	XmString
String	XmStringTable	String	DefaultButtonType
String	DialogType	String	DialogStyle
String	ResizePolicy	String	RowColumnType

Figure 3.7 Type converters defined by Motif.

Applications can define additional type conversions by writing a type-converter function and registering it with the resource manager. A type converter is a procedure that has the form:

```
void Converter(args, nargs, fromVal toVal)
        XrmValue    *args;
        Cardinal    *nargs;
        XrmValue    *fromVal;
        XrmValue    *toVal;
```

The arguments **args**, **fromVal** and **toVal** are pointers to structures of type **XrmValue**, which is defined as:

```
typedef struct {
  unsigned int  size;
  caddr_t         *addr;
} XrmValue, *XrmValuePtr;
```

This structure holds a pointer to a value, and the size of the value. The last two parameters of a type converter provide the original data and a way to return the converted value. The type-converter is expected to convert the data in the **fromVal** structure and fill in the **toVal** structure with the result. The **args** parameter is an array of type **XrmValue** containing any additional data required by the converter.

Before the resource manager can use a type converter, the function must be registered with the resource manager. The function

XtAddConverter(from_type, to_type, converter, args, nargs)

registers a type converter with the resource manager. The arguments **from_type** and **to_type** must be strings indicating the data types. Whenever appropriate, the standard names defined in StringDefs.h should be used for consistency. The **converter** argument specifies the address of the type-converter function, while **args** and **nargs** specify any additional arguments that should be passed to the type converter when it is called. The **args** parameter must be an array of type **XtConvertArg**, which is defined as:

```
typedef struct {
    XtAddressMode    address_mode;
    caddr_t          address_id;
    Cardinal         size;
} XtConvertArgRec, *XtConvertArgList;
```

The **address_mode** indicates the type of the data provided and may be one of the constants:

XtAddress	XtBaseOffset	XtWindowObjBaseOffset
XtImmediate	XtResourceString	XtResourceQuark

The **address_id** member specifies the address of the additional data, while the **size** member indicates the size of the resource in bytes. Many converter functions require no additional data and **args** is often given as **NULL**, and **nargs** as zero.

Let's see how this works by writing an example type converter. One useful type converter that the Xt Intrinsics does not provide is a function to convert a string to a floating point number. We can define this type converter as:

```
/*****************************************************
 * str2flt.c: Convert a string to a float.
 *****************************************************/
#include <X11/Intrinsic.h>
#include <X11/StringDefs.h>

void xs_cvt_str_to_float(args, nargs, fromVal, toVal)
     XrmValue    *args;
     Cardinal    *nargs;
     XrmValue    *fromVal, *toVal;
{
  static float result;
  /*
   * Make sure the number of args is correct.
   */
  if (*nargs != 0)
   XtWarning("String to Float conversion needs no arguments");
  /*
   * Convert the string in the fromVal to a floating pt.
   */
  if (sscanf((char *)fromVal->addr, "%f", &result) == 1) {
    /*
     * Make the toVal point to the result.
     */
    toVal->size = sizeof (float);
    toVal->addr = (caddr_t) &result;
  }
  else
  /*
   * If sscanf fails, issue a warning that something is wrong.
   */
   XtStringConversionWarning((char *) fromVal->addr, "Float");
}
```

This type converter first checks how many **args** were given as parameters. Since no additional parameters are needed, the function uses the utility function

XtWarning(message)

to print a warning if the number of arguments is not equal to zero. The type converter uses **sscanf()** to convert the string representation to a floating point value. The **toVal** structure is then filled in with the size of a float and the address of the variable **result**. If **sscanf()** fails, the function

XtStringConversionWarning(from, to);

is used to issue a warning. This function takes two arguments indicating the two data types involved in the conversion.

Notice that the variable **result**, which contains the value returned by the type converter, is declared as static. This is important because otherwise the address of **result** would be invalid after the function returns. Functions that call type converters must copy the returned value immediately, because the type converter reuses the same address each time it is called.

The **xs_cvt_str_to_float()** type-converter is a useful function to add to the libXs library and we will use it again in later chapters. We can test this string-to-float converter by modifying the **rmtest** program from Section 3.3.2. The example now defines the **delay** member of the **ApplicationData** structure as a floating point number, rather than an integer as in the earlier version. We must also change the **XtResource** array to specify that the value of **delay** should be retrieved as type **XtRFloat**. The Intrinsics does not define **XtRFloat**, but we can easily add it to the libXs header file, defined as:

#define XtRFloat   "Float"

The main difference in this version of **rmtest** is that the body of the test application registers the type-converter function before retrieving the application resources.

```
/*********************************************
 * rmtest3.c: floating point version.
 *********************************************/
#include <X11/Intrinsic.h>
#include <X11/StringDefs.h>
#include "libXs.h"

typedef struct {
    Pixel     fg, bg;
    float     delay;
    Boolean   verbose;
} ApplicationData, *ApplicationDataPtr;
```

```
static XtResource resources[] = {
  { XtNforeground, XtCForeground, XtRPixel, sizeof (Pixel),
    XtOffset(ApplicationDataPtr, fg), XtRString, "Black"      },
  { XtNbackground, XtCBackground, XtRPixel, sizeof (Pixel),
    XtOffset(ApplicationDataPtr, bg), XtRString, "White"      },
  { "delay", "Delay", XtRFloat, sizeof (float),
    XtOffset(ApplicationDataPtr, delay), XtRString,"2.5"      },
  { "verbose", "Verbose", XtRBoolean, sizeof (Boolean),
    XtOffset(ApplicationDataPtr,verbose), XtRString, "FALSE"},
};

static XrmOptionDescRec options[] = {
 {"-verbose", "*verbose", XrmoptionNoArg, "TRUE"},
 {"-delay",   "*delay",   XrmoptionSepArg, NULL}
};


main(argc, argv)
    int    argc;
    char *argv[];
 {
  Widget           toplevel;
  ApplicationData data;
  toplevel = XtInitialize(argv[0], "Rmtest", options,
                          XtNumber(options), &argc, argv);
  /*
   * Add the string to float type-converter.
   */
  XtAddConverter(XtRString, XtRFloat, xs_cvt_str_to_float,
                 NULL, 0);
  /*
   * Retrieve the resources.
   */
  XtGetApplicationResources(toplevel, &data, resources,
                            XtNumber(resources), NULL, 0);
  /*
   * Print the result.
   */
  printf("fg = %d, bg = %d, delay = %f, verbose = %d\n",
         data.fg, data.bg, data.delay, data.verbose);
 }
```

We can test this version of **rmtest** using the following class resource file, or by specifying command line arguments.

```
!!!!!!!!!!!!!!!!!!!!!!!!!!!!!!!!!!!!!!!
! Rmtest: resource file for rmtest.c
!!!!!!!!!!!!!!!!!!!!!!!!!!!!!!!!!!!!!!!
*foreground:    Red
*background:    Blue
*verbose:       FALSE
*delay:         23.54
```

Now, if we run this version of **rmtest** from a shell, we should see something like:

```
% rmtest
fg = 9, bg = 1, delay = 23.54, verbose = 0
```

3.4 WIDGET RESOURCE CONVENTIONS

Widgets use the resource manager to retrieve the resources specified by the user when the widget is created. Applications can also set the value of a widget resource by passing an argument list to **XtCreateWidget()** or by using **XtSetValues()** to change the value after the widget is created. Because the resources specified by the programmer are applied *after* the user-specified resources are retrieved from the resource data base, they override the user's chosen options. It is sometimes difficult to determine when a widget resource should be set by an application programmer and when it should be left for the end user. The convention used in this book is as follows:

> *Application programmers should avoid specifying widget resource values in the program except where absolutely necessary to ensure that the application works correctly.*

Application programmers should think carefully whenever they are tempted to hard code resource values into an application. Whenever possible, the programmer should leave decisions regarding widget layout, fonts, labels, colors, and so on, to the end user. Applications that are customizable by the end user tend to be more portable. For example, the label displayed by an XmPushButton widget can be set by the user or the programmer. A programmer could probably justify hard coding the button labels for important functions to prevent the user from using the resource manager to mis-label them. But what if the labels are programmed in English, and the user reads only French? Labels that can be set in a resource data base can be changed easily and without access to source code.

Unfortunately, it is difficult to design a program to be customizable by the end user and still ensure that it works correctly. For example, if command labels can be redefined by the end user, there is nothing to prevent the labels of the buttons from being altered in a misleading way. Imagine a situation where the user has inadvertently switched the labels of the "Delete" and "Save" command buttons of an editor. The results could be disastrous. Documenting software that can be radically customized by the end user is also an enormous problem. Therefore, the approach advocated here is not without flaws.

One way to make programs customizable, while still providing useful defaults, is to provide a class resource file for every program. The programmer can use the class resource file to specify default resources that the user can override in the .Xdefaults file, if desired. The class resource file also provides a useful public place to document the resources and options recognized by an application. The programmer should excercise restraint even when providing a class resource file. For example, specifying colors is asking for trouble.

Even when it is necessary to hard code some resources into a program, using a resource file while developing the application makes it easier for the application programmer to determine the best value for a resource. Rather than recompiling an application every time a resource needs to be changed, the programmer can simply change the appropriate entries in the resource file and run the program again until the proper value is determined. The examples in this book specify few resources in the source code, and many examples are accompanied by a class resource file containing the default resources used by the program.

The important point here is to use common sense when deciding how to control resources. The more customizable an application is, the more easily it can be made to fit the needs of the end user. However, an application that requires the user to do a great deal of setup to even try out the application is unlikely to please a new user.

3.5 SUMMARY

The resource manager provides a simple and powerful mechanism that allows the application programmer to create customizable applications easily. This chapter examined the basic principles of the Xlib resource manager and showed how applications can use the Xt Intrinsics resource facilities to manage application resources. The Intrinsics encourages consistency between all applications by providing a standard set of resource names recognized by all applications. The Intrinsics also assists the programmer by providing an easy-to-use mechanism for handling user-defined resources, command-line options, and programmer-defined defaults.

We have now discussed the general architecture of X, the architecture of the Xt Intrinsics, and the resource manager. The following chapter introduces the widgets provided by the Xt Intrinsics and the Motif widget set, and begins to put these pieces together as we explore more complex applications.

4

PROGRAMMING WITH WIDGETS

Chapter 2 introduced the Xt Intrinsics, a framework that allows programmers to combine user interface components known as widgets to create complete applications. Widgets are simply an X window along with some procedures that manipulate the window. Each widget maintains a data structure that stores additional information used by the widget's procedures. This chapter examines widgets more closely. We will explore the basic widgets provided by the Xt Intrinsics, discuss a few representative widgets from the Motif widget set, and show how we can combine widgets to create a complete user interface for an application.

As this book is being written, the X Consortium has not recognized any widget set as a standard part of the X Window System. However, at least four sets of widgets are freely available as contributed software. These public domain widget sets include: Hewlett Packard's X Widget set, Sony's Xsw widget set, the Athena widget set developed by M.I.T.'s Project Athena, and the Cornell widget set. Several proprietary widget sets are also available. The Open Software Foundation (OSF) and its member companies distribute the Motif widget set and AT&T markets the XT+ toolkit which includes a widget set based on the OPEN LOOK interface style.

The examples in this book use the Motif widget set, designed and widely distributed by the Open Software Foundation. This widget set is available from many of the members of the OSF. The Motif widget set is based on both HP's Common X Interface widget set and Digital Equipment Corporation's XUI widget set. Motif consists of four components: a widget set, a window manager, a style guide, and a user interface description language known as UIL. This book only considers the Motif widget set. The interested reader can refer to the OSF documentation and other sources for more information on the other components of Motif.

Other widget sets provide different appearances or interaction styles, and may offer somewhat different functionality, but from the application programmer's viewpoint should be similar to the widgets used in this book. A programmer who understands the principles of the Xt Intrinsics and is familiar with one widget set should be able to learn to use any other widget set quickly.

While an in-depth look at every available widget provided by Motif is beyond the scope of this book, we can discuss general features of widgets by dividing them into several functional categories. This chapter looks at a few widgets belonging to each category, and provides examples of how they can be used in typical applications.

4.1 WIDGET CLASSES

The Xt Intrinsics defines an object-oriented architecture that organizes widgets into *classes*.[1] In general, a class is a set of things that have similar characteristics. Individual things (objects) are always instances of some class. For example, an object-oriented drawing program might define a class named Rectangle. This class could define various attributes common to all rectangles: color, width, height, position, and so on. To display a particular rectangle on the screen, the program instantiates (creates an instance of) a rectangle. This rectangle has specific values for all its attributes, for example, color: red, width: 10, height: 20, x: 200, y: 325. In the Xt Intrinsics, the function **XtCreateWidget()** creates an instance of the widget class specified by the class argument. In the example in Chapter 2, the message window was an instance of the XmLabel widget class.

Inheritance is another useful object-oriented concept supported by the Xt Intrinsics. In most object-oriented systems, a class can inherit some or all the characteristics of another class, in much the same way that people inherit characteristics from their parents. For example, the drawing program we discussed above could define a class named GraphicalObject that defines the attributes common to all objects that can be displayed on the screen. GraphicalObject might define position and color attributes. Next, we can define subclasses of GraphicalObject, such as Circle and Rectangle. The Circle class inherits the position and color attributes from its superclass, GraphicalObject and adds another attribute, radius. The Rectangle class also inherits the position and color attributes, but adds two more attributes, width and height.

The widget programmer (a programmer who designs new widgets) needs to understand these concepts to create new widget classes. Chapters 12, 13, and 14 discuss how the Xt Intrinsics implements classes and uses the architecture of the Xt Intrinsics to create several new widget classes. However, the application programmer should also understand these concepts because it is possible to characterize the behavior of a widget by knowing its class and

---

1. Object-oriented programming is a programming style that organizes systems according to the objects in the system, rather than the functions the system performs. An object is an abstraction that combines data and the operations that can be performed on that data in a single package.

its superclasses. For example, the Motif set defines an XmLabel widget class that displays text. Because the XmPushButton is a subclass of XmLabel, it is safe to assume that the XmPushButton widget class is similar to the XmLabel widget class. For example, the XmPushButton recognizes many of the same options and uses the same resource names as the XmLabel widget class. However, it adds the features of a button to those inherited from the XmLabel class.

The characteristics that each widget class inherits from its superclass include all resources and all callback lists. For example, all widget classes are subclasses of the Core widget class provided by the Xt Intrinsics. Therefore, because the Core widget class provides a **XtNdestroy** callback list, all widget classes also support the **XtNdestroy** callback list. A widget can also inherit the procedures that define the widget's behavior, including the action list used by the translation manager. Each widget class has a class name used by the resource manager to retrieve resources, and also defines a pointer to a structure known as a widget class. The widget class pointer is used as an argument to **XtCreateWidget()**. For example, the widget class pointer for the Core widget is defined in Core.h as:

```
WidgetClass widgetClass;
```

Therefore,

```
XtCreateWidget("core", widgetClass, parent, NULL, 0);
```

creates an instance of a widget belonging to the Core class.

4.2 INTRINSIC WIDGET CLASSES

The Xt Intrinsics defines several basic widget classes that serve as superclasses for other widgets. These widget classes define the architecture used by all other widgets, and also provide some fundamental characteristics inherited by all other widget classes. The following sections discuss the fundamental widget classes provided by the Intrinsics.

4.2.1   The Core Widget Class

The Core widget class is the most fundamental widget class, and serves as the superclass for all other widget classes. The Core widget's class name is Core and its class pointer is **widgetClass**.[2] The Core widget class provides some basic resources inherited by all widgets.

The Core widget class is an example of a *meta-class*. In the Xt Intrinsics, a meta-class is a class that serves only as a superclass to other widgets. Meta-classes are not designed to

---

2. The remainder of this book simply refers to widgets by their class name, thereby avoiding any more statements like "the Core widget's class name is Core." Appendix B lists the class and class names for the widgets provided by both the Xt Intrinsics and the Motif widget set.

be used directly in applications. In spite of its intended purpose, the Core widget class *can* be instantiated, as illustrated by the following program:

```
/**********************************************************
 * generic.c: Test the Core widget class
 **********************************************************/
#include <X11/Intrinsic.h>

main(argc, argv)
  int    argc;
  char *argv[];
{
  Widget toplevel;
  /*
   * Initialize the Intrinsics.
   */
  toplevel = XtInitialize(argv[0], "Generic", NULL, 0,
                          &argc, argv);
  /*
   * Create a Core widget.
   */
  XtCreateManagedWidget("widget", widgetClass,
                        toplevel, NULL, 0);
  XtRealizeWidget(toplevel);
  XtMainLoop();
}
```

This program simply creates an empty window and displays it on the screen.[3] The application does nothing useful, but does obey all conventions of the X Window System. The program interacts correctly with window managers, and allows the end user to customize all resources supported by the Core widget class. Applications that need a basic window for displaying text or graphics can use the Core widget, although the Motif widget set provides another widget, the XmDrawingArea widget, which is more suitable for this purpose.

4.2.2   The Composite Widget Class

The Composite widget class is a subclass of the Core widget class, and is also a meta-class. All subclasses of the Composite widget class are also known as composite widgets. Composite widgets serve primarily as containers for other widgets. A composite widget *manages* its children, which means that composite widgets are responsible for:

---

3. The Core widget class uses a default size of 0 width by 0 height for its window. Since X does not allow zero width or height windows, this program will generate an error unless a geometry is specified on the command-line or in a resource file.

- Determining the physical layout of all managed children. Each composite widget has a geometry manager that controls the location of each child widget according to its management policy.
- Deallocating the memory used by all children when the composite widget is destroyed. When a composite widget is destroyed, all children are destroyed first.
- Mapping and unmapping its children's windows. By default, a widget's window is mapped when it is managed, and unmapped when it is unmanaged. This behavior can be altered by setting the widget's **XtNMappedWhenManaged** resource to **FALSE**.
- Controlling which child has the keyboard input focus. For example, a multiple field form editor might shift the input focus from one field to the next when the users enters a <RETURN> or a <TAB> key.

4.2.3   The Constraint Widget Class

The Constraint widget class is a subclass of the Composite widget class, and therefore can also manage children. Constraint widgets manage their children based on some additional information associated with each child. This information often takes the form of some constraint on the child's position or size. For example, children can be constrained to some minimum or maximum size, or they can be constrained to a particular location relative to another widget. The Constraint widget class is also a meta-class and is never instantiated directly. Section 4.3.4.3 discusses an example constraint widget.

4.2.4   The Shell Widget Class

The Shell widget class is a subclass of the Composite widget class, but can have only one child. Shell widgets are special purpose widgets that provide an interface between other widgets and the window manager. A Shell widget negotiates the geometry of the application's top level window with the window manager, sets the properties required by the window manager, and generally handles the window manager protocol for the application, as defined by the ICCCM. The following sections briefly discuss several subclasses of the Shell widget class.

4.2.4.1   Top-Level Shells

The TopLevelShell widget class is a subclass of the Shell widget class. **XtInitialize()** creates a TopLevelShell widget that applications usually use as their main top-level window. Applications that use multiple top-level windows can use the functions:

```
XtCreateApplicationShell(name, class, args, nargs)
XtAppCreateShell(context,classname,class,display,args, nargs)
```

to create additional TopLevelShell widgets.

The following program is a modified version of the example from Section 4.2.1 that creates two independent top-level windows. Both windows can be manipulated independently, although both are created by the same client. Notice that applications must realize each top-level shell individually.

```
/**********************************************************
 * twoshells.c: Example of two independent top-level shells
 **********************************************************/
#include <X11/Intrinsic.h>
#include <X11/Shell.h>

main(argc, argv)
    int    argc;
    char *argv[];
{
  Widget toplevel, shell2;
  /*
   * Initialize the Intrinsics, create one TopLevelShell.
   */
  toplevel = XtInitialize(argv[0], "Generic", NULL, 0,
                          &argc, argv);
  /*
   * Create a second TopLevelShell widget.
   */
  shell2= XtCreateApplicationShell("Window2",
                                   topLevelShellWidgetClass,
                                   NULL, 0);
  /*
   * Create a Core widget as a child of each shell.
   */
  XtCreateManagedWidget("Widget", widgetClass,
                        toplevel, NULL, 0);
  XtCreateManagedWidget("Widget2", widgetClass,
                        shell2, NULL, 0);
  /*
   * Realize both shell widgets.
   */
  XtRealizeWidget(toplevel);
  XtRealizeWidget(shell2);
  XtMainLoop();
}
```

4.2.4.2   Transient Shells

Transient shells are similar to TopLevelShells except for the way in which they interact with window managers. Window managers are not supposed to iconify Transient shells separately. If an application's top-level window is iconified, the window manager should also iconify all transient shells created by that application. Applications can create a transient shell by specifying the widget class pointer **transientShellWidgetClass** as an argument to **XtCreateApplicationShell()**.

4.2.4.3   Override Shells

The OverrideShell widget class is also similar to the TopLevelShell, except for the way in which it interacts with window managers. An OverrideShell widget sets the **override_redirect** attribute of its window to TRUE, which instructs the window manager to completely ignore it. OverrideShell widgets completely bypass the window manager and therefore have no added window manager decorations. OverrideShell widgets are often used for popup menus.

4.3   THE MOTIF WIDGET CLASSES

The Motif widget set contains many components, including scroll bars, menus, buttons, and so on that can be combined to create user interfaces. We can divide the widget classes that implement these components into several categories based on the general functionality they offer. For example, some widgets display information while others allow the user to select from a set of choices. Still others allow other widgets to be grouped together in various combinations. The following sections describe a few examples of each of these categories.

The most noticeable characteristic of the Motif widget set is its three-dimensional appearance. Most Motif widgets draw a border around each widget. The top and left sides of this border can be set to one color and the bottom and right sides can be set to another. By setting these areas to the appropriate colors, a three-dimensional shading effect can be achieved, as shown in Fig. 4.1. Notice that by making the top shadow lighter than the background color and the bottom shadow darker, the widget appears to be coming out of the screen. Reversing these colors makes the widget appear to be recessed into the screen. The colors that create this three-dimensional effect can be set by the user or the programmer, although, by default, Motif generates the appropriate top and bottom shadow colors automatically based on the background color.

Another notable feature of the Motif widget set is its resolution independence mechanism. All sizes and dimensions used by Motif can be specified in terms of pixels, multiples of 1/1000 of an inch, multiples of 1/100 of a point, multiples of 1/100 of a millimeter, or multiples of 1/100 of a font size. The default is to interpret size and dimension specifications as units of pixels.

The Motif widget set is also designed to encourage the programmer to follow the Motif style guide which is based on the interaction style of Microsoft's Presentation Manager. However, Motif widgets are customizable in the same way as other widget sets. Therefore, while the Presentation Manager style is encouraged, it is not strictly enforced. In spite of this, programmers who want their applications to fit smoothly with other Motif-based applications would be well-advised to follow the Motif style as closely as possible.

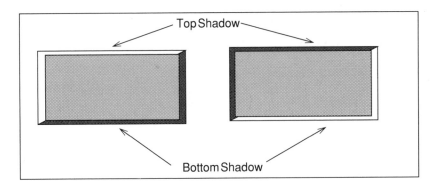

Figure 4.1 Three-dimensional shading in Motif.

4.3.1 Creating Motif Widgets

Every widget in the Motif widget set has its own creation function which creates an unmanaged widget. In most cases, these functions are only provided as a convenience and simply call **XtCreateWidget()** with the appropriate class pointer as an argument. For example, we can create an XmLabel widget with either of the statements:

```
XtCreateWidget(name, parent, xmLabelWidgetClass, NULL, 0);
XmCreateLabel(parent, name, NULL, 0);
```

The arguments to these functions are similar, except that the convenience function does not require the widget's class pointer, and the order of the **parent** and **name** arguments is reversed.

Some Motif creation functions do more than this. For example, the Motif RadioBox widget is simply an XmRowColumn widget with several resources set up in a specific way. The programmer could create a RadioBox widget with either

```
n = 0;
XtSetArg(wargs[n],XmNpacking, XmPACK_COLUMN); n++;
XtSetArg(wargs[n],XmNradioBehavior, TRUE);    n++;
XtSetArg(wargs[n],XmNisHomogeneous, TRUE);    n++;
```

```
XtSetArg(wargs[n],XmNentryClass,
        xmToggleButtonGadgetClass);n++;
XtCreateWidget(name,parent,xmRowColumnWidgetClass,wargs,n);
```

or with the convenience function:

```
XmCreateRadioBox(parent, name, NULL, 0);
```

Still other Motif creation functions create a set of widgets that together implement a user interface component. Since these components are not really widgets, the programmer cannot use **XtCreateWidget()** for these components.

4.3.2   Motif Widget Meta-Classes

The Motif widget set defines several additional meta-classes. The most basic of these is the XmPrimitive widget class, which is a subclass of the Core widget class. The XmPrimitive widget class is never instantiated, and serves only to define some standard resources inherited by its subclasses, including resources to control the three-dimensional appearance. The Xm-Manager widget class is another Motif widget meta-class. It is a subclass of the Constraint widget class, and defines basic resources used by all composite and constraint widgets in the Motif widget set. Both the XmPrimitive and XmManager widget classes provide an **XmN-helpCallback** list which is inherited by all subclasses.

4.3.3   Display Widgets

Motif provides many widgets that display information. These widgets include:

XmArrowButton	XmDrawnButton	XmLabel
XmList	XmPushButton	XmScrollBar
XmSeparator	XmTextEdit	XmToggleButton

The following sections look at several of these widget classes.

4.3.3.1   The Label Widget

One of the simplest display widgets is the XmLabel widget used in Chapter 2. This widget simply displays a string or a pixmap in a window. The XmLabel widget does not support any callbacks, other than the **XmNhelpCallback** supported by all Motif widgets.

4.3.3.2   The PushButton Widget

Several subclasses of XmLabel, such as XmPushButton, XmToggleButton, and XmDrawn-Button, act as buttons and allow the user to select them. When a button is "pushed", its three-dimensional appearance inverts, giving the illusion that the button has been pressed. When the user releases the button, the color returns to normal. These button widgets provide several callbacks in addition to the **XmNhelpCallback** provided by the XmPrimitive widget class. For example, the callback lists provided by the XmPushButton widget class are:

- **XmNarmCallback**: This callback function is called when the button is "'armed". Normally this is when a mouse button is pressed while the sprite is contained in the widget's window. If the resource **XmNinvertOnArm** is TRUE (the default), the button's colors invert, giving the illusion of a button being pressed. When this callback list is invoked, the **reason** member of the call data structure is set to **XmCR_ARM**.

- **XmNactivateCallback**: This callback is invoked when the button is activated. Normally this is when the user releases the mouse button while the sprite is within the widget's window. This callback is not invoked if the user releases the mouse button outside of the widget. The **reason** member of the call data structure is set to **XmCR_ACTIVATE** when this callback list is invoked.

- **XmNdisarmCallback**: This callback is invoked when the widget is no longer armed. By default, this is when the user releases the mouse button. The **reason** member of the call data structure is set to **XmCR_DISARM**.

Let's look at a simple example using the XmPushButton widget to see how these callbacks work in more detail. This program creates a single XmPushButton widget and registers the same callback for each of the callback lists discussed above.

```
/*************************************************
 * pushbutton.c: Test the XmPushButton widget.
 *************************************************/
#include <X11/Intrinsic.h>
#include <X11/StringDefs.h>
#include <Xm/Xm.h>
#include <Xm/PushB.h>

extern void button_callback();

main(argc, argv)
    int    argc;
    char *argv[];
{
  Widget toplevel, button;
  toplevel = XtInitialize(argv[0], "Pushbutton",
                          NULL, 0, &argc, argv);
  /*
   * Create the pushbutton widget.
   */
  button =  XtCreateManagedWidget("button",
                                  xmPushButtonWidgetClass,
```

```
                                        toplevel, NULL, 0);
     /*
      * Add callbacks.
      */
     XtAddCallback(button, XmNactivateCallback,
                   button_callback, NULL);
     XtAddCallback(button, XmNarmCallback,
                   button_callback, NULL);
     XtAddCallback(button, XmNdisarmCallback,
                   button_callback, NULL);
     XtRealizeWidget(toplevel);
     XtMainLoop();
}
```

The callback function is very simple and just prints a message reporting the reason indicated in the call data structure when it is invoked.

```
     void button_callback(w, client_data, call_data)
        Widget                 w;
        caddr_t                client_data;
        XmAnyCallbackStruct  *call_data;
        {
          switch(call_data->reason){
            case XmCR_ACTIVATE:
              printf("Button activated\n");
              break;
            case XmCR_ARM:
              printf("Button armed\n");
              break;
            case XmCR_DISARM:
              printf("Button disarmed\n");
              break;
          }
        }
```

Now we can run the program to see how the button callbacks work. When the user presses a mouse button while the sprite is in the XmPushButton widget, the widget's shadow colors are inverted and the **button_callback()** function is called with the **reason** member of the call data structure set to **XmCR_ARM**. When the user releases the button, **button_callback()** is called with the reason reported as **XmCR_ACTIVATE**, and then called again with the reason given as **XmCR_DISARM**. As the button is disarmed, it also resumes its normal appearance. If the user moves the sprite out of the widget's window before releasing the mouse button, **button_callback()** is called with the reason specified as

XmCR_DISARM. This allows the user to abort a command by moving the sprite out an Xm-PushButton widget before releasing the mouse button, and also allows the application to know that the user has aborted the operation.

The XmPushButton widget provides a convenient way to issue a command. For example, we could have designed the **memo** example in Chapter 2 with a "quit" button rather than having the user click the mouse on the message window. Since many applications need such a button, let's use an XmPushButton widget to write a simple routine for the libXs library that causes an application to exit when the user clicks on the button with the mouse. This function takes a single argument: the parent widget of the button. The function simply adds an XmPushButton widget to its parent widget and registers several callback functions.

Designing a general purpose quit button is not quite as simple as it might at first appear. Applications that use this quit button may need to perform other actions before exiting the application. However, the order in which the functions on a given callback list are invoked is not defined by the Xt Intrinsics. Therefore, it is not sufficient to register an **XmNactivateCallback** function that exits the application, because it is not guaranteed that additional callback functions registered by an application would ever be called. However, we can make use of the three callback lists supported by the XmPushButton widget to solve this problem. The first callback to be called, the **XmNarmCallback**, initializes a flag to **FALSE**. If the button is activated, an **XmNactivateCallback** function sets this flag to **TRUE**. Finally, if this flag is **TRUE** when the button is disarmed, the **XmNdisarmCall-back** function calls **exit()**. Applications that need to perform some cleanup before exiting can add functions to the **XmNactivateCallback** list, because all functions on this callback list will be invoked before the program exits.

```
/***********************************************************
 * quit.c: A utility function that adds a quit button
 ***********************************************************/
#include <X11/Intrinsic.h>
#include <X11/StringDefs.h>
#include <Xm/Xm.h>
#include <Xm/PushB.h>
/*
 * Define three callbacks. Make them static - no need
 * to make them known outside this file.
 */
static void arm_callback(w, flag, call_data)
     Widget       w;
     int          *flag;
     XmAnyCallbackStruct *call_data;
{
 *flag = FALSE;
}
```

```
static void activate_callback(w, flag, call_data)
    Widget      w;
    int         *flag;
    XmAnyCallbackStruct *call_data;
{
  *flag = TRUE;
}
static void disarm_callback(w, flag, call_data)
    Widget      w;
    int         *flag;
    XmAnyCallbackStruct *call_data;
{
  if(*flag){
    XtCloseDisplay(XtDisplay(w));
    exit(0);
  }
}
/*
 * Function to add a quit button as a child of any widget.
 */
Widget xs_create_quit_button(parent)
    Widget  parent;
{
    Widget      w;
    static int really_quit;
    w = XtCreateManagedWidget("quit", xmPushButtonWidgetClass,
                                parent, NULL, 0);
    XtAddCallback(w, XmNarmCallback,
                    arm_callback, &really_quit);
    XtAddCallback(w, XmNdisarmCallback,
                    disarm_callback, &really_quit);
    XtAddCallback(w, XmNactivateCallback,
                    activate_callback, &really_quit);
    return (w);
}
```

To add this function to the libXs library, we also need to add the line

```
extern Widget xs_create_quit_button();
```

to the file libXs.h.

4.3.3.3   The Text Widget

Another useful widget provided by Motif is the XmText widget, which allows the user to edit multiple or single lines of text. In single-line mode, this widget is often used to allow the user to enter a short string, perhaps in response to a question. In multi-line mode, it functions as a complete text editor. A large number of public functions allow the programmer to scroll the text, set the text widget to edit mode or read-only mode, retrieve the text displayed, and so on. The XmText widget class also defines a number of useful callback lists. These include:

- **XmNactivateCallback**: Functions on this callback list are called by the XmText widget's **activate()** action procedure, which is bound by default to the <RETURN> key.

- **XmNfocusCallback**: This callback list is invoked when the XmText widget gets the focus.

- **XmNlosingFocusCallback**: Called when the XmText widget loses the focus.

- **XmNvalueChangedCallback**: This callback list is invoked whenever the text in an XmText widget is modified through the use of **XtSetValues()**, **XmTextSet-String()**, or **XmTextReplace()**;.

- **XmNmotionVerifyCallback**: Called whenever the cursor position changes. This callback uses a **XmTextVerifyCallbackStruct** structure as call data. This structure has the members:

```
int             reason;
XEvent          *event;
Boolean         doit;
XmTextPosition  currInsert, newInsert;
XmTextPosition  startPos, endPos;
XmTextBlock     text;
```

  A function registered as an **XmNmotionVerifyCallback** function can examine the information in this structure to determine if the motion should be permitted. If the motion is allowed, the callback function must set the **doit** member of the **XmTextVerifyCallbackStruct** to **TRUE**. If the **doit** member is set to **FALSE**, the action will not be performed. The **doit** member is initialized to **FALSE** before the callback is invoked.

- **XmNmodifyVerifyCallback**: This callback list is invoked whenever the text in the XmText widget is modified. Like the **XmNmotionVerifyCallback callback list**, functions registered with this callback list can examine the information in the call data structure to determine if the modification should be permitted. If the modification is allowed, the callback function must set the **doit** member of the **XmTextVerifyCallbackStruct** to **TRUE**.

The XmText widget also provides many public functions for manipulating the contents of the widget, as shown in the following partial list:

XmTextGetString()	Retrieves the contents of the XmText widget.
XmTextSetString()	Set the contents of the XmText widget.
XmTextReplace()	Replace the XmText between two positions.
XmTextGetEditable()	Determine if the XmText widget is editable.
XmTextSetEditable()	Set the mode to editable/not editable.
XmTextGetSelection()	Return the text currently selected.
XmTextSetSelection()	Set the text currently selected.
XmTextClearSelection()	Clear the selection.
XmTextSetInsertionPosition()	Go to a position.
XmTextGetInsertionPosition()	Return the current text insert position.
XmTextScroll()	Scroll the widget by lines.

We will demonstrate the XmText widget as well as many of the public functions provided by the XmText widget in the following section and also throughout the rest of this book.

4.3.4   Container Widgets

So far, every example program in this book has created a single widget that occupies the entire top-level window of the application. Because most applications require a more complex interface, the Motif widget set provides many widgets that can be used to combine other widgets. These widgets allow endless combinations of buttons, scroll bars, text panes, and so on, to be grouped together in an application. Widgets that control the layout of multiple children must be subclasses of the Composite widget class. In the Motif widget set, widgets that control the layout of other widgets are also a subclass of the Manager meta-class. The Motif container widgets include:

XmDrawingArea	XmFrame	XmMainWindow
XmRowColumn	XmScale	XmScrolledWindow
XmPanedWindow	XmBulletinBoard	XmForm

The following sections discuss several typical Motif container widget classes.

4.3.4.1   The BulletinBoard Widget

The XmBulletinBoard widget class is a simple example of a container widget. The XmBulletinBoard widget allows children to be placed at absolute (x, y) coordinates within the widget. If no coordinates are provided for children of the XmBulletinBoard widget, the XmBulletinBoard widget places them all at location $(0, 0)$. First, let's look at a simple example that uses a XmBulletinBoard widget to combine several other widgets into a simple form to be filled out by the user.

```
/*****************************************************************
 * formedit.c: Simple example of multiple edit fields managed
 *             by an XmBulletinBoard widget.
 *****************************************************************/
#include <X11/Intrinsic.h>
#include <Xm/Xm.h>
#include <Xm/Text.h>
#include <Xm/PushB.h>
#include <Xm/BulletinB.h>
#include "libXs.h"

void get_text();
char *buttons[] = {"button1", "button2", "button3"};
char *editors[] = {"field1", "field2", "field3"};

main(argc, argv)
   int    argc;
   char *argv[];
{
  Widget toplevel, bb, edit[3], button[3];
  int    i;
  toplevel = XtInitialize(argv[0], "Formedit",
                          NULL, 0 , &argc, argv);
  /*
   * Create the XmBulletinBoard widget that manages
   * the edit fields.
   */
  bb = XtCreateManagedWidget("board",
                             xmBulletinBoardWidgetClass,
                             toplevel, NULL,0);
  /*
   * Create three single line XmEdit widgets
   * and associate a button with each text widget.
   * Assign an XmNactivateCallback callback to each button.
   */
  for(i=0; i < XtNumber(editors); i++)
     edit[i] = XtCreateWidget(editors[i],
                              xmTextWidgetClass,
                              bb, NULL, 0);
  for(i=0; i < XtNumber(buttons); i++){
     button[i] = XtCreateWidget(buttons[i],
                                xmPushButtonWidgetClass,
```

```
                                   bb, NULL, 0);
       XtAddCallback(button[i], XmNactivateCallback,
                     get_text, edit[i]);
   }
   XtManageChildren(edit, XtNumber(editors));
   XtManageChildren(button, XtNumber(buttons));

   XtRealizeWidget(toplevel);
   XtMainLoop();
}
```

This example creates a more interesting widget tree than earlier examples. Fig. 4.2 shows the widget tree formed by the TopLevelShell widget along with the XmBulletin-Board widget and its children. The XmBulletinBoard widget has six children, three XmText widgets and three XmPushButton widgets. The XmText widgets' **XmNeditMode** resource is set to **XmSINGLE_LINE_EDIT** by default, which configures the widget to edit only a single line of text. The user can enter text in the XmText widgets and perform some action on that data by selecting the corresponding XmPushButton widget. In this example, the action is simply to print the current contents of the XmText widget.

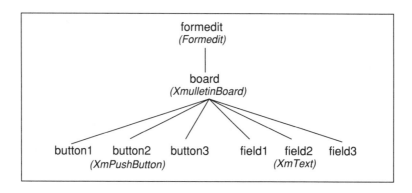

Figure 4.2 The widget tree created by formedit.

The **XmNactivateCallback** procedure, **get_text()**, retrieves the contents of the XmText widget passed to the callback procedure as client data and prints the string. The function **XmTextGetString()**, a public function defined by the XmText widget, returns the entire contents of the XmText buffer as a string. This string is allocated using **XtMalloc()** and should be freed by the application.

```
void get_text(w, textwidget, call_value)
   Widget    w;
   Widget    textwidget;
   XmAnyCallbackStruct *call_value;
{
   char * str = XmTextGetString(textwidget);
   printf("retrieving text: %s\n", str);
   XtFree(str);
}
```

The XmBulletinBoard widget does not control the position of its children. Since this example also does not specify any sizes or locations for the widgets, they will all appear at *(0,0)*, unless we specify the placement in a resource file. The following class resource file defines the widget layout shown in Fig. 4.3.

```
!!!!!!!!!!!!!!!!!!!!!!!!!!!!!!!!!!!!!!!!!!!!!!!!!!!!!!!!!!!!!!!!!
! Formedit: Class resource file for the formedit example
!!!!!!!!!!!!!!!!!!!!!!!!!!!!!!!!!!!!!!!!!!!!!!!!!!!!!!!!!!!!!!!!!
Formedit*button1*labelString:    Name:
Formedit*button2*labelString:    Phone:
Formedit*button3*labelString:    Address:
Formedit*XmText*x:           100
Formedit*field1*y:            10
Formedit*field2*y:            40
Formedit*field3*y:            70
Formedit*XmPushButton*x:      10
Formedit*button1*y:           10
Formedit*button2*y:           40
Formedit*button3*y:           70
```

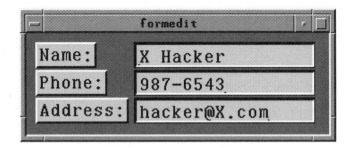

Figure 4.3 An XmBulletinBoard widget.

4.3.4.2   The RowColumn Widget

The XmRowColumn widget is a subclass of the XmManager widget class that organizes its children as rows and columns. This widget can also be used as a RadioBox widget that manages button widgets and allows only one button to be selected at one time, and can also be used as both a pulldown menu bar and a menu pane. The behavior of the XmRowColumn widget can be controlled either by setting appropriate resources or by using one of several convenience functions to create the widget. This section looks at how the XmRowColumn can be used to organize widgets into rows and columns. Later sections look at some of the other uses for the XmRowColumn widget. The XmRowColumn widget provides several resources that determine how it arranges its children:

- **XmNorientation**: This resource determines whether the XmRowColumn widget should lay out its children as row major or column major. This resource may be set to **XmVERTICAL** to select a column major layout, or **XmHORIZONTAL** to specify a row major layout.

- **XmNpacking**: This resource specifies how to pack children of the XmRowColumn widget. It may be one of **XmPACK_TIGHT**, **XmPACK_COLUMN**, or **XmPACK_NONE**. If **XmPACK_TIGHT** is chosen, the XmRowColumn widget packs its children tightly along the major dimension until no more children fit in a given row. At this point a new row is begun. If **XmPACK_COLUMN** is chosen, each child is resized to the size of the largest child, and the children are placed in aligned columns. The number of columns is determined by the **XmNnumColumns** resource. The value **XmPACK_NONE** means that no packing is performed. The widgets are positioned according to their (x, y) positions.

- **XmNnumColumns**: If **XmNpacking** is set to **XmPACK_COLUMN**, this resource determines the maximum number of rows or columns. If the orientation is vertical, this resource indicates the maximum number of columns. Otherwise, it indicates the maximum number of rows.

- **XmNadjustLast**: If this resource is **TRUE**, the XmRowColumn widget resizes the last column of children in each row (if **XmNorientation** is **XmVERTICAL**) to fill any dead space. If **XmNorientation** is **XmHORIZONTAL**, the bottom widget in each column is resized. The default is **TRUE**.

The XmRowColumn widget class supports many other resources, many of which are useful in specific cases, such as when the widget is used as a menu pane. A few of the more generally useful resources include:

- **XmNisHomogeneous**: If this resource is **TRUE**, the XmRowColumn widget can manage only children belonging to the widget class indicated by the **XmNentryClass** resource.

- **XmNisAligned**: This resource specifies whether the text displayed by each child of the XmRowColumn widget should be aligned. This applies only to children that are subclasses of the XmLabel widget class or the XmLabelGadget class.

- **XmNentryAlignment**: If **XmNisAligned** is **TRUE**, this resource specifies the type of alignment used. The possible values are **XmALIGNMENT_CENTER**, **XmALIGN‑MENT_LEFT**, and **XmALIGNMENT_RIGHT**. The default is **XmALIGNMENT_CENTER**.

- **XmNentryBorder**: If this resource is non-zero, it specifies a border thickness which is imposed on all children.

Let's look at a simple example and explore a few of these resources. The following example creates an XmRowColumn widget that manages six XmPushButton widgets.

```
/**************************************************************
 * rctest.c: An example of a row column manager
 **************************************************************/
#include <X11/StringDefs.h>
#include <X11/Intrinsic.h>
#include <Xm/Xm.h>
#include <Xm/RowColumn.h>
#include <Xm/PushB.h>
char * buttons[] = {"button1", "button2", "button3",
                    "button4", "button5", "button6"};
main(argc, argv)
  int    argc;
  char   *argv[];
{
  Widget toplevel, rowcol;
  int    i;
  toplevel = XtInitialize(argv[0], "Rctest", NULL, 0,
                          &argc, argv);
  /*
   * Create an XmRowColumn widget.
   */
  rowcol = XtCreateManagedWidget("rowcol",
                                 xmRowColumnWidgetClass,
                                 toplevel, NULL, 0);
  /*
   * Create six children of the XmRowColumn widget.
   */
  for(i=0;i< XtNumber(buttons); i++)
   XtCreateManagedWidget(buttons[i], xmPushButtonWidgetClass,
                          rowcol, NULL, 0);
  XtRealizeWidget(toplevel);
  XtMainLoop();
}
```

Figure 4.4 shows the **rctest** program.

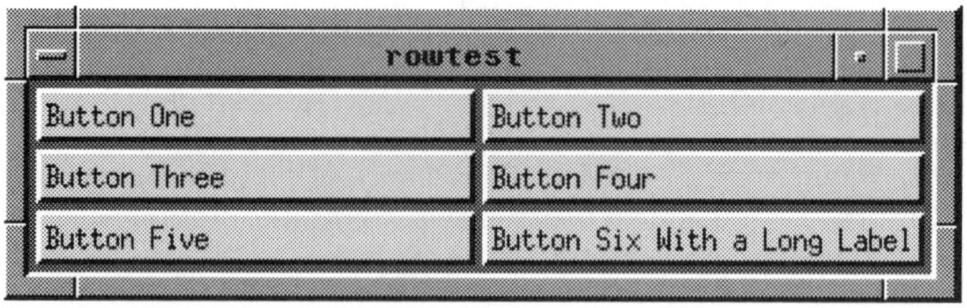

Figure 4.4 An XmRowColumn widget managing three rows.

Now we can try different resource settings and see what affect they have on the arrangement of the XmPushButton widgets. The first set of resources uses the **XmNnumColumns** resource to arrange the buttons into three rows, as shown in Fig. 4.4.

```
!!!!!!!!!!!!!!!!!!!!!!!!!!!!!!!!!!!!!!!!!!!!!!!!!!!!!!!!!
! Rctest: Class Resources for rctest.c
!!!!!!!!!!!!!!!!!!!!!!!!!!!!!!!!!!!!!!!!!!!!!!!!!!!!!!!!!
!
! Specify labels for all buttons.
!
*Rctest*button1.labelString:     Button One
*Rctest*button2.labelString:     Button Two
*Rctest*button3.labelString:     Button Three
*Rctest*button4.labelString:     Button Four
*Rctest*button5.labelString:     Button Five
*Rctest*button6.labelString:     Button Six With a Long Label
!
! Request buttons in 3 rows, by setting orientation to
! horizontal and requesting 3 columns (minor-dimension)
!
*Rctest*orientation:        horizontal
*Rctest*rowcol*numColumns:  3
*Rctest*rowcol*packing:     pack_column
```

We can specify that the XmRowColumn widgets should pack its children as tightly as possible by changing the resource file to include the line:

```
*Rctest*rowcol*packing:     pack_tight
```

This results in the layout shown in Fig. 4.5.

Figure 4.5 A tightly packed XmRowColumn widget.

With the **XmNpacking** resource set to **pack_tight**, the XmRowColumn widget puts as many widgets as possible in each row. When there is no more space on a given row, a new row is started. For example, resizing the **rctest** window results in the layout shown in Fig. 4.6. This layout changes dynamically as the XmRowColumn widget is resized.

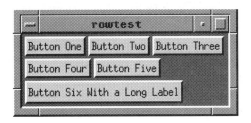

Figure 4.6 A tightly packed XmRowColumn widget.

4.3.4.3   The Form Widget

The XmForm widget class is a subclass of the XmManager widget class that manages its children based on constraints that specify the position of each widget relative to another widget, known as a reference widget. Each widget can have a top, bottom, left, and right reference widget. Each widget can also have an "attachment" specified for each of top, bottom, left, and right. The attachment specifies how the widget's position is related to the reference widget. By carefully specifying the attachments and reference widgets, we can specify how the children of a XmForm widget are positioned, and also how those positions are affected when the XmForm widget is resized.

The XmForm widget attaches additional resources to each managed child that allow the programmer or the user to specify the constraints for each widget. These resources include:

- **XmNtopAttachment**, **XmNbottomAttachment**, **XmNleftAttachment**, **XmN-rightAttachment**: These resources specify how and where a child widget is attached. The possible values are:

  — **XmATTACH_NONE**: Do not attach this side.

- — **XmATTACH_FORM**: Attach the widget to the corresponding side of the XmForm widget.
- — **XmATTACH_WIDGET**: Attach the corresponding side of the child to the reference widget.
- — **XmNATTACH_OPPOSITE_WIDGET**: Attach the child to the opposite side of the reference widget.
- — **XmNATTACH_POSITION**: Attach the corresponding side of the child to the position given by the **XmNtopPosition**, **XmNbottomPosition**, **XmNleftPosition**, or **XmNrightPosition** resources.
- — **XmNATTACH_SELF**: Attach the child to its initial position.
- **XmNtopWidget, XmNbottomWidget, XmNleftWidget, XmNrightWidget**: These resources specify the reference widget for this child, if the corresponding attachment is **XmATTACH_WIDGET** or **XmATTACH_OPPOSITE_WIDGET**.
- **XmNtopPosition, XmNbottomPosition, XmNleftPosition, XmNrightPosition**: These resources specify the attachment position of a widget, if the corresponding attachment resource is set to **XmATTACH_POSITION**. The value is interpreted as a fraction of the corresponding dimension of the XmForm widget. This resource specifies the numerator of the fraction, while the **XmNfractionBase** resource specifies the denominator. By default the value of **XmNfractionBase** is 100.
- **XmNtopOffset, XmNbottomOffset, XmNleftOffset, XmNrightOffset**: These resources specify the offset between the corresponding side of the child and the widget it is attached to.

The XmForm widget retains these relative positions when it is resized, when new children are added or deleted, or when one of its children is resized.

The easiest way to understand how these constraints work is by looking at an example. The following simple program creates an XmForm widget that manages three XmPushButton widgets.

```
/**********************************************************
 * formtest.c: Test the constraints of the XmForm Widget
 **********************************************************/
#include <X11/Intrinsic.h>
#include <Xm/Xm.h>
#include <Xm/Form.h>
#include <Xm/PushB.h>

char * buttons[] = {"button1", "button2", "button3"};

main(argc, argv)
    int    argc;
```

```
      char *argv[];
{
  Widget toplevel, form, wbutton[5];
  int    i, n;
  Arg wargs[10];
  toplevel = XtInitialize(argv[0], "Formtest", NULL, 0,
                          &argc, argv);

  /*
   * Create an XmForm manager widget
   */
  form = XtCreateManagedWidget("form", xmFormWidgetClass,
                               toplevel, NULL,0);
  /*
   * Add three XmPushButton widgets to the Form Widget.
   */
  for(i=0;i< XtNumber(buttons); i++)
    wbutton[i] = XtCreateWidget(buttons[i],
                                xmPushButtonWidgetClass,
                                form, NULL,0);
  XtManageChildren(wbutton, XtNumber(buttons));
  /*
   * Set constraint resources for each button, setting up
   * a shape like this:
   *          button one
   *          button two
   *          button three
   */
  n = 0;
  XtSetArg(wargs[n], XmNtopAttachment,   XmATTACH_FORM); n++;
  XtSetArg(wargs[n], XmNleftAttachment,  XmATTACH_FORM); n++;
  XtSetArg(wargs[n], XmNrightAttachment, XmATTACH_FORM); n++;
  XtSetValues(wbutton[0], wargs, n);
  n = 0;
  XtSetArg(wargs[n], XmNtopAttachment,   XmATTACH_WIDGET);n++;
  XtSetArg(wargs[n], XmNtopWidget,       wbutton[0]);     n++;
  XtSetArg(wargs[n], XmNleftAttachment,  XmATTACH_FORM);  n++;
  XtSetArg(wargs[n], XmNrightAttachment, XmATTACH_FORM);  n++;
  XtSetValues(wbutton[1], wargs, n);
  n = 0;
  XtSetArg(wargs[n], XmNtopAttachment,   XmATTACH_WIDGET);n++;
  XtSetArg(wargs[n], XmNtopWidget,       wbutton[1]);     n++;
```

```
    XtSetArg(wargs[n], XmNleftAttachment,  XmATTACH_FORM);  n++;
    XtSetArg(wargs[n], XmNrightAttachment, XmATTACH_FORM);  n++;
    XtSetArg(wargs[n], XmNbottomAttachment,XmATTACH_FORM);  n++;
    XtSetValues(wbutton[2], wargs, n);

    XtRealizeWidget(toplevel);
    XtMainLoop();
}
```

The constraints[4] specified in this example attach the left and right sides of all three buttons to the parent XmForm widget. The top of **button1** and the bottom of **button3** are also attached to the XmForm widget. The top of **button2** is attached to the bottom of **button1** and the top of **button3** is attached to the bottom of **button2**. Fig. 4.7 shows the initial layout produced by these resources, while Fig. 4.8 shows the layout after resizing the XmForm widget.

Figure 4.7 A Form widget using constraint one.

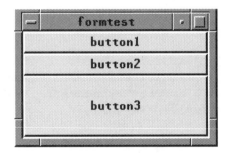

Figure 4.8 Resized version of Fig. 4.7.

---

4. We cannot define these resources in a resource file, because Motif does not provide a way to specify the attachment widget (which is really a pointer) by name. We could write a type-converter (see Chapter 3) to do this, but the order in which widgets are created would still determine which constraints are possible, and therefore a type-converter is not entirely satisfactory.

The number of ways that widgets can be arranged is virtually endless. Although the process of attaching widgets to each other is useful, often we would like to define a layout where relative sizes are maintained as an application's window is resized. Notice that with the previous constraints, only **button3** grew as the XmForm widget was resized. We can specify that all three buttons should maintain some relative size by specifying the attachment as **Xm_ATTACH_POSITION**. Let's change the **formtest** example to do this. Since this type of attachment does not require a reference to a widget, we can set all resources in a resource file. First, remove all the calls to **XtSetArg()** and **XtSetValues()** from the **formtest** program. Then the following resources specify that each button should occupy 30 percent of the height of the XmForm widget and stretch from 1 to 99 percent of the width.

```
!!!!!!!!!!!!!!!!!!!!!!!!!!!!!!!!!!!!!!!!!!!!!
! Formtest: class resource file for formedit
!!!!!!!!!!!!!!!!!!!!!!!!!!!!!!!!!!!!!!!!!!!!!
!
! Make all children resizable and specify
! all attachments as attach_position
!
Formtest*resizable:              TRUE
Formtest*topAttachment:          attach_position
Formtest*bottomAttachment:       attach_position
Formtest*leftAttachment:         attach_position
Formtest*rightAttachment:        attach_position
!
! Set up the buttons to stretch across the entire form
! and each occupy 30 % of the height.
!
Formtest*button1.leftPosition:     1
Formtest*button1.rightPosition:    99
Formtest*button1.topPosition:      1
Formtest*button1.bottomPosition:   31

Formtest*button2.leftPosition:     1
Formtest*button2.rightPosition:    99
Formtest*button2.topPosition:      35
Formtest*button2.bottomPosition:   65

Formtest*button3.leftPosition:     1
Formtest*button3.rightPosition:    99
Formtest*button3.topPosition:      69
Formtest*button3.bottomPosition:   99
```

These relative   positions and sizes are maintained as the XmForm widget is resized, as shown in Fig. 4.9 and Fig. 4.10.

Figure 4.9 Attaching a position in a Form widget.

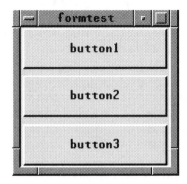

Figure 4.10   Resized version of Fig. 4.9

4.3.4.4   The List Widget

The XmList widget is a useful widget that displays a list of text items and allows the user to select entries on the list. The items displayed by the XmList widget must be specified as an array of compound strings. The XmList widget supports several selection policies and selection callback lists. The selection policies supported by the XmList widget are:

*   **XmSINGLE_SELECT**. When this policy is specified, the **XmNsingleSelectionCall-back** list is invoked when the user presses a mouse button over an item. If an item is already selected, and the user selects a second item, the first item is no longer selected.

*   **XmMULTIPLE_SELECT**. When this policy is specified, the **XmNmultipleSelection-Callback** list is invoked when the user selects one or more items from the list. Items are selected by pressing a mouse button while the sprite is over an item. In this mode, selecting additional items does not unselect previous items.

- **XmEXTENDED_SELECT**. When this policy is specified, the **XmNextendedSelection-Callback** list is invoked when the user selects one or more items from the list. In this mode, the user selects an initial item by pressing the mouse button while the sprite is over the desired item. Then additional items can be selected by dragging the sprite over the desired items. Once all desired items have been selected, the user can end the selection by releasing the mouse button, which invokes the callback.

- **XmBROWSE_SELECT**. When this policy is specified, the **XmNbrowseSelectionCall-back** list is invoked when the user releases a mouse button while an item is selected. The user selects an initial item by pressing the mouse button while the sprite is over an item. Then, while holding the mouse button down, the user can move the selection by dragging the sprite over other items. Only a single item can be selected at any one time.

The selection policy can be chosen by the programmer or the user by setting the **XmNse-lectionPolicy** resource. The default policy is **XmBROWSE_SELECT**. Regardless of the chosen selection policy, the list widget passes the appropriate callback functions a pointer to an **XmListCallbackStruct** as call data. This structure contains the following information:

```
int        reason;
XEvent     *event;
XmString   item;
int        item_length;
int        item_position;
XmString   *selected_items;
int        selected_item_count;
int        selection_type;
```

The **reason** member is set to one of the constants:

```
XmCR_SINGLE_SELECT              XmCR_BROWSE_SELECT
XmCR_MULTIPLE_SELECT            XmCR_EXTENDED_SELECT
```

The rest of this structure contains information about the selected item or items.

Let's see how the list widget works by writing a simple program, **chooseone**, that places its command-line arguments in a list. The example uses the **XmBROWSE_SELECT** selection policy. When the user selects one of the items in the list, the program prints the selection and exits. This program might be useful in a UNIX shell script as a way to allow the user to select from several alternatives. For example, this program could be used as:

```
cat `chooseone *.c`
```

resulting in a window similar to that shown in Fig. 4.11

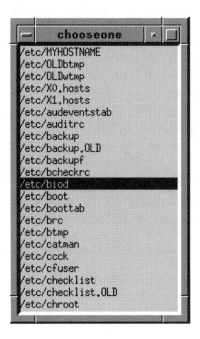

Figure 4.11   An XmList widget.

The main body of the program is written as:

```
/**************************************************************
 * chooseone.c: Test a list widget
 **************************************************************/
#include <X11/StringDefs.h>
#include <X11/Intrinsic.h>
#include <X11/Shell.h>
#include <Xm/Xm.h>
#include <Xm/List.h>

static void browse_callback();

main(argc, argv)
     int    argc;
     char *argv[];

{
   Widget    toplevel, list;
   Arg       wargs[10];
```

```
int        n, i;
XmString *xmstr;
/*
 * Initialize the Intrinsics and check for zero arguments
 */
toplevel = XtInitialize (argv[0], "Chooseone", NULL, 0,
                         &argc, argv);
if(argc <= 1){
   XtCloseDisplay(XtDisplay(toplevel));
   exit(-1);
}
/*
 * Convert all command line arguments to an array of
 * type XmString, ignoring argv[0].
 */
xmstr = (XmString *) XtMalloc(sizeof(XmString) * argc - 1);
for(i = 1; i < argc; i++)
   xmstr[i - 1] = XmStringCreate(argv[i],
                                 XmSTRING_DEFAULT_CHARSET);
/*
 * Create the list widget and register a browse callback.
 */
n = 0;
XtSetArg(wargs[n], XmNitems, xmstr); n++;
XtSetArg(wargs[n], XmNitemCount, argc - 1); n++;
list = XtCreateManagedWidget("list",
                             xmListWidgetClass,
                             toplevel, wargs, n);
XtAddCallback(list, XmNbrowseSelectionCallback,
              browse_callback, NULL);

XtRealizeWidget (toplevel);
XtMainLoop();
}
```

The callback function **browse_callback()** is invoked when the user releases a mouse button over an entry in the list. It simply extracts a character string from the call data, using the function **XmStringGetLtoR()** to convert the compound string contained in the call data structure to a character string, prints the selected item, and exits.

```
static void browse_callback(w, client_data, call_data)
   Widget    w;
   caddr_t    *client_data;
```

```
      XmListCallbackStruct *call_data;
{
   char *text;
   XmStringGetLtoR (call_data->item, XmSTRING_DEFAULT_CHARSET,
                    &text);
   printf("%s\n", text);
   XtCloseDisplay(XtDisplay(w));
   exit(0);
}
```

The XmList widget is particularly useful when combined with an XmScrolledWindow widget to create scrollable lists. Motif provides a convenience function, **XmCreate-ScrolledList()** for exactly this purpose.

4.3.4.5 Menu Widgets

The Motif widget set provides a versatile set of widgets that allow applications to create popup and pulldown menus. A menu consists of a popup Shell widget which manages an Xm-RowColumn widget containing buttons, labels, and occasionally other types of widgets. The buttons are the selectable entries in the menu. Actions can be associated with each menu entry by registering a callback function with each button in the menu. By combining different types of widgets, the programmer can create many different types of menus: pulldowns, popups, cascading pulldowns, cascading popups, and so on.

In this section we will build several different menu types, but first let's look briefly at each of the components of a menu:

- The XmRowColumn widget class is used as both a pulldown menu bar and a popup menu pane. Motif provides convenience functions to create both a popup shell widget (XmMenuShell) and the XmRowColumn widget with the proper resources already set. These are:

  XmCreatePopupMenu (parent, name, args, nargs)
  XmCreatePulldownMenu (parent, name, args, nargs)

- The XmPushButton widget is commonly used as a menu entry. It is used exactly as it has been used in previous examples. Callback functions registered for the **XmNactivateCallback**, **XmNarmCallback**, and **XmNdisarmCallback** lists are called when the menu button is activated, armed, and disarmed.

- The XmCascadeButton widget class is used to popup a submenu. It is managed by an Xm-RowColumn widget and looks much like an XmPushButton widget. However, the Xm-CascadeButton widget can have a pulldown menu associated with it, which appears when the XmCascadeButton is armed.

- The XmLabel widget class is often used to display non-selectable text, a menu title or subtitle, for example.

- The XmSeparator widget displays a line. This widget can be used to delineate different sections of the menu, for example to set the title off from the menu selections.

Creating Popup Menus

Creating a popup menu requires only three basic steps.

1. Create the popup menu pane using **XmCreatePopupMenu()**.
2. Create the items in the menu. These can be XmLabel widgets, XmPushButton widgets, XmSeparator widgets, or XmCascadeButton widgets.
3. Register callbacks for each XmPushButton widget.

To create a menu with a cascading pane, a separate pulldown menu must be created, using the function **XmCreatePulldownMenu()**. This pulldown menu must be created as a child of the menu pane, and must be associated with an XmCascadeButton widget by setting the Xm-CascadeButton widget's **XmNsubMenuId** resource.

Popup menus are displayed by calling **XtManageChild()** in a callback or event handler which is called by the action required to post the menu. This is typically done by pressing a mouse button. For example, we can write an event handler to display a popup menu when a mouse button is pressed as follows:

```
void post_menu_handler (w, menu, event)
   Widget  w;
   Widget  menu;
   XEvent *event;
{
  Arg wargs[10];
  int button;
  /*
   * Make sure the button that caused this event was the one
   * the menupane uses for menu item selection.
   */
  XtSetArg(wargs[0], XmNwhichButton, &button);
  XtGetValues(menu, wargs, 1);
  if (event->xbutton.button == button){
   /*
    * Position the menu over the sprite and post the menu.
    */
   XmMenuPosition(menu, event);
   XtManageChild(menu);
  }
}
```

The XmRowColumn has an **XmNwhichButton** resource that determines which mouse button is to be used for posting menus, selecting menu entries, and so on. Before posting the menu we must retrieve this value and check to be sure the button press that caused the event is the same as the one used to select menu entries. The **if** statement in this event handler ensures that the menu will only be displayed when the correct mouse button is pressed. The function **XmMenuPosition()** computes the position of the menu based on the position of the sprite as reported in the event. Finally, **XtManageChild()** causes the menu to be displayed. When the XmRowColumn widget is configured as a menu, it automatically calls **XtPopup()** to pop up the parent of the menu pane when the menu is managed. Notice that applications must not manage a menu pane when it is created. Managing the menu pane is reserved for displaying the menu.

Let's build an example menu. The following program creates a single menu pane that can be popped up by pressing a mouse button in XmBulletinBoard widget. The menu consists of a title, followed by an XmSeparator widget and three menu entries. The second entry in the menu has a cascading menu pane associated with it. For this example, a single callback function is registered for all entries in the menu. The function simply prints the item the user selects from the menu. Normally, each XmPushButton widget in a menu would have its own callback function to perform the desired action. Fig. 4.12 shows the widget tree created by this example.

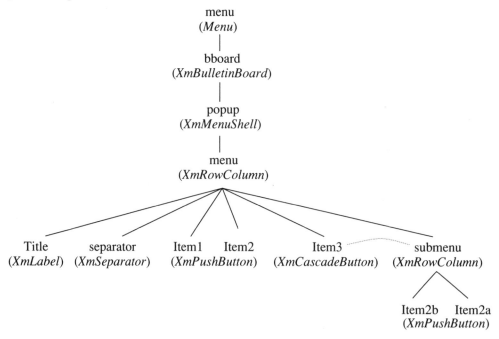

Figure 4.12 An example menu tree.

```
/***************************************************
 * menu.c: First pop up menu example
 ***************************************************/
#include <X11/Intrinsic.h>
#include <X11/Shell.h>
#include <Xm/Xm.h>
#include <Xm/Label.h>
#include <Xm/RowColumn.h>
#include <Xm/PushB.h>
#include <Xm/Separator.h>
#include <Xm/BulletinB.h>
#include <Xm/CascadeB.h>

extern void post_menu_handler ();

void do_it(w, client_data, call_data)
    Widget   w;
    char     *client_data;
    caddr_t  call_data;
{
  printf("%s selected\n", client_data);
}

main(argc, argv)
    int    argc;
    char *argv[];
{
  Widget toplevel, button, bboard, menu, button1,
         button2, button3, submenu, button2a, button2b;
  Arg wargs[10];
  /*
   * Initialize the Intrinsics and create a BulletinBoard
   * widget to be the primary widget in the program.
   */
  toplevel = XtInitialize (argv[0], "MenuTest", NULL, 0,
                           &argc, argv);
  bboard = XtCreateManagedWidget("bboard",
                                 xmBulletinBoardWidgetClass,
                                 toplevel, NULL, 0);
  /*
   * Step 1. Create a popup menu. Add an event handler
   * To the BulletinBoard widget to pop up the menu when
```

```
 * a mouse button is pressed.
 */
menu = XmCreatePopupMenu(bboard, "menu", NULL, 0);
XtAddEventHandler(bboard, ButtonPressMask, FALSE,
                    post_menu_handler, menu);
/*
 * Step 2. Add buttons, labels, and separators to the pane.
 * Step 3. Register callbacks to define the action
 *         associated with each menu entry.
 */
XtCreateManagedWidget("Title", xmLabelWidgetClass, menu,
                          NULL, 0);
XtCreateManagedWidget("separator", xmSeparatorWidgetClass,
                          menu, NULL, 0);
button1 = XtCreateManagedWidget("Item1",
                                    xmPushButtonWidgetClass,
                                    menu, NULL, 0);
XtAddCallback (button1, XmNactivateCallback,
                do_it, "Item1");
/*
 * Add an XmCascadeButton widget to support a submenu.
 */
button2 = XtCreateManagedWidget("Item2",
                                    xmCascadeButtonWidgetClass,
                                    menu, NULL, 0);
button3 = XtCreateManagedWidget("Item3",
                                    xmPushButtonWidgetClass,
                                    menu, NULL, 0);
XtAddCallback (button3, XmNactivateCallback,
                do_it, "Item3");
/*
 * To Create a cascading menu pane:
 *         Create a pulldown menu pane and attach it to the
 *         XmCascadeButton widget.
 */
submenu = XmCreatePulldownMenu(menu, "submenu", NULL, 0);
XtSetArg(wargs[0], XmNsubMenuId, submenu);
XtSetValues(button2, wargs, 1);
/*
 * Add buttons the submenu.
 */
button2a = XtCreateManagedWidget("Item2a",
```

```
                                   xmPushButtonWidgetClass,
                                   submenu, NULL, 0);
    XtAddCallback (button2a, XmNactivateCallback,
                   do_it, "Item2a");
    button2b = XtCreateManagedWidget("Item2b",
                                   xmPushButtonWidgetClass,
                                   submenu, NULL, 0);
    XtAddCallback (button2b, XmNactivateCallback,
                   do_it, "Item2b");

    XtRealizeWidget (toplevel);
    XtMainLoop();
}
```

Fig. 4.13 shows the menu created by this example.

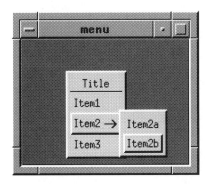

Figure 4.13 A cascading popup menu.

Some applications have many large menus, and creating each menu as in the previous example can be tedious, although the approach allows maximum flexibility in configuring menus and setting the resources of each individual pane and menu button. However, it is often easier to wrap the steps of the menu creation in some higher level functions. Let's try to make this process of creating a menu a little clearer and easier by defining a higher level interface to the menu widgets that we can add to the libXs library. We can separate the menu creation into three steps. First, the contents of the menu must be described in an array. Then, the application must create a popup menu pane to hold the various entries in the menu. Finally, the function **xs_create_menu_buttons()** uses the menu description to create the menu entries, assign the callbacks, and also create any submenus by calling itself recursively.

First, let's look at a structure that defines the menu information needed for each entry in the menu. The following definition needs to be placed in the library header file, libXs.h.

```
typedef struct _menu_struct{
    char*      name;                    /* name of the button      */
    void       (*func)();               /* Callback to be invoked */
    caddr_t    data;                    /* Data for the callback   */
    struct _menu_struct *sub_menu;/* data for submenu          */
    int        n_sub_items;             /* items in sub_menu       */
    char       *sub_menu_title;         /* Title of submenu        */
} xs_menu_struct;
```

This structure records the name of a menu entry, a callback function to be invoked if that entry is selected, and any additional data to be passed to that callback. In addition, if the entry has a submenu attached to it, the structure contains a pointer to an array of type **xs_menu_struct**, the length of the array, and also the title of the submenu. Thus, an array of type **xs_menu_struct** defines a tree of menus and submenus.

Before we look at the function that creates menu entries from this structure, let's look at how this can be used in an application. The following example reimplements the previous cascading menu example, using the libXs menu wrapper.

```
/************************************************************
 * menu2.c: pop up menu example using libXs menu functions
 ************************************************************/
#include <X11/StringDefs.h>
#include <X11/Intrinsic.h>
#include <Xm/Xm.h>
#include <Xm/RowColumn.h>
#include <Xm/BulletinB.h>
#include "libXs.h"

extern void post_menu_handler ();
extern void do_it();

/*
 * Describe the list of menu items for a submenu pane.
 */
static xs_menu_struct sub_menu_a[] = {
  {"Item 2 A" , do_it, "Item 2 A"},
  {"Item 2 B" , do_it, "Item 2 B"}
};
/*
 * Describe the main menu pane.
 */
static xs_menu_struct MenuData[] = {
  { "Item 1" , do_it, "Item One",
```

```
            NULL, 0, NULL },
        { "Item 2" , NULL, "Item Two",
            sub_menu_a, XtNumber(sub_menu_a), "SubMenuA" },
        { "Item 3" , do_it, "Item Three",
            NULL, 0 , NULL }
    };

main(argc, argv)
        int    argc;
        char *argv[];
{
    Widget toplevel, bboard, popup_menu;
    /*
     * Initialize the Intrinsics and create a top level widget.
     */
    toplevel = XtInitialize (argv[0], "MenuTest", NULL, 0,
                                &argc, argv);
    bboard = XtCreateManagedWidget("bboard",
                                    xmBulletinBoardWidgetClass,
                                    toplevel, NULL, 0);
    /*
     * Step 1. Create a popup menu pane and define an event
     *          handler to pop it up.
     */
    popup_menu = XmCreatePopupMenu(bboard, "menu", NULL, 0);
    XtAddEventHandler(bboard, ButtonPressMask, FALSE,
                        post_menu_handler, popup_menu);
    /*
     * Step 2. Create the menu entries from the description.
     */
    xs_create_menu_buttons("Menu", popup_menu,
                            MenuData, XtNumber(MenuData));
    XtRealizeWidget (toplevel);
    XtMainLoop();
}
```

This example is shorter than the previous example and it is also easier to add new entries to a menu. Rather than having to read the code and trying to decipher the menu structure, the menu structure is clearly defined by the **xs_menu_struct** arrays. Adding a new entry requires only defining a callback function and adding an entry to the array that describes the menu.

Now let's look at the **xs_create_menu_buttons()** function. This function loops through the array of menu entries creating an appropriate widget for each entry. If a title is given, the function creates an XmLabel widget as a title, separated from the rest of the menu by an XmSeparator widget. For each item in the menu description, if the name of an entry is given as **NULL**, the function creates an XmSeparator widget. If the entry has a name and a callback function, the function creates an XmPushButton widget and assigns the callback. If the entry has a name, but no callback function, and the **submenu** member is **NULL**, an XmLabel widget is created. Finally, if a submenu is specified, **xs_create_menu_buttons()** creates an XmCascadeButton widget and a pulldown menu pane, and attaches the pulldown menu to the menu entry, after adding the entries in the submenu to the pulldown menu pane by calling **xs_create_menu_buttons()** recursively.

```
/**********************************************************
 * menus.c: Simple menu package
 **********************************************************/
#include <X11/StringDefs.h>
#include <X11/Intrinsic.h>
#include <Xm/Xm.h>
#include <Xm/Separator.h>
#include <Xm/PushB.h>
#include <Xm/CascadeB.h>
#include <Xm/RowColumn.h>
#include <Xm/Label.h>
#include "libXs.h"

xs_create_menu_buttons(title, menu, menulist, nitems)
   char            *title;
   Widget          menu;
   xs_menu_struct  *menulist;
   int             nitems;
{
  Arg        wargs[1];
  int        i;
  WidgetList buttons;
  int        separators = 0;
  /*
   * Allocate a widget list to hold all
   * button widgets.
   */
  buttons = (WidgetList) XtMalloc(nitems * sizeof(Widget));
  /*
   * If a title is given, create Label and Separator widgets.
   */
  if(title){
    XtCreateManagedWidget(title, xmLabelWidgetClass, menu,
```

```
                              NULL, 0);
    XtCreateManagedWidget("separator", xmSeparatorWidgetClass,
                          menu, NULL, 0);
}
/*
 * Create an entry for each item in the menu.
 */
for(i=0;i<nitems;i++){
 /*
  * A NULL name represents a separator.
  */
 if(menulist[i].name == NULL){
   XtCreateManagedWidget("separator",
                           xmSeparatorWidgetClass,
                           menu, NULL, 0);
   separators++; /* Count how many entries aren't buttons */
 }
 /*
  * If there is a name and a callback, create a selectable
  * menu entry and register the callback function.
  */
 else if(menulist[i].func){
   buttons[i-separators] = XtCreateWidget(menulist[i].name,
                                   xmPushButtonWidgetClass,
                                   menu, NULL, 0);
   XtAddCallback(buttons[i-separators], XmNactivateCallback,
                 menulist[i].func, menulist[i].data);
 }
 /*
  * If there is a name, but no callback function, the entry
  * must be a label, unless there is a submenu.
  */
 else if(!menulist[i].sub_menu)
   buttons[i-separators] = XtCreateWidget(menulist[i].name,
                                   xmLabelWidgetClass,
                                   menu, NULL, 0);
 /*
  * If we got here, the entry must be a submenu.
  * Create a pulldown menu pane and an XmCascadeButton
  * widget. Attach the menu pane and make a recursive call
  * to create the entries in the submenu.
  */
```

```
  else{
   Widget sub_menu;
   sub_menu =XmCreatePulldownMenu(menu,
                                menulist[i].sub_menu_title,
                                NULL, 0);
    XtSetArg(wargs[0], XmNsubMenuId, sub_menu);
    buttons[i-separators] =
          XtCreateWidget(menulist[i].name,
                        xmCascadeButtonWidgetClass,
                        menu, wargs, 1);
    xs_create_menu_buttons(menulist[i].sub_menu_title,
                        sub_menu, menulist[i].sub_menu,
                        menulist[i].n_sub_items);
   }
 }
 /*
  * Manage all button widgets. Menu panes are not managed.
  */
  XtManageChildren(buttons, nitems - separators);
 }
```

Pulldown Menus

In addition to popup menus, Motif provides pulldown menus. Pulldown menus are created similarly to the popup menus described in the previous section. The steps for creating a pull-down menu are:

1. Use the **XmCreateMenuBar()** convenience function to create an XmRowColumn widget configured as a menu bar.

2. Manage the menu bar.

3. Use the **XmCreatePulldownMenu()** convenience function to create pulldown menu panes as children of the menu bar widget.

4. For each pulldown pane, create an XmCascadeButton widget as a child of the menu bar widget.

5. Attach the menu panes to the XmCascadeButton widgets, by specifying the menu pane as the XmCascadeButton widget's **XmNsubMenuId** resource.

6. Create the menu entries as desired.

While this seems complex, these are just the same steps required for adding a cascading pane to a popup menu pane. In fact, we can actually use the same libXs menu functions described in the previous section to create pulldown menus easily. To do this, the program needs to create a menu bar, and then simply specifies this menu bar widget as the **parent** argument to

xs_create_menu(). Each item in the topmost **xs_menu_struct** of the menu tree should have only a name and a submenu. The following example illustrates this.

```
/*************************************************************
 * menu3.c: pulldown menu example
 *************************************************************/
#include <X11/StringDefs.h>
#include <X11/Intrinsic.h>
#include <Xm/Xm.h>
#include <Xm/RowColumn.h>
#include <Xm/BulletinB.h>
#include "libXs.h"

extern void do_it();

/*
 * Create the list of menu items for a sub menu pane.
 */
static xs_menu_struct sub_menu_a[] = {
  {"Item 2 A", do_it, "Item 2 A"},
  {"Item 2 B", do_it, "Item 2 B"}
};

/*
 * Describe pulldown pane one.
 */
static xs_menu_struct MenuData[] = {
  {"Item 1", do_it, "Item One",  NULL, 0, NULL},
  {"Item 2", NULL,    "Item Two",  sub_menu_a,
      XtNumber(sub_menu_a), "SubMenuA"},
  {"Item 3", do_it, "Item Three", NULL, 0 , NULL}
};

/*
 * Describe pulldown pane two.
 */
static xs_menu_struct Menu2Data[] = {
  {"Item 2-1", do_it, "Iten 2-One",   NULL, 0, NULL},
  {"Item 2-2", do_it, "Item 2-Two",   NULL, 0, NULL},
  {"Item 2-3", do_it, "Item 2-Three", NULL, 0 ,NULL}
};
```

```
/*
 * Describe the menu bar, giving only the names to appear in
 * the menu bar and pointers to each pulldown pane.
 */
static xs_menu_struct PulldownData[] = {
  {"Menu One" , NULL,  NULL,
    MenuData, XtNumber(MenuData), NULL},
  {"Menu Two" , NULL,  NULL,
    Menu2Data, XtNumber(Menu2Data), NULL},
};

main(argc, argv)
    int   argc;
    char *argv[];
{
  Widget toplevel, bb, menubar;
  /*
   * Initialize the Intrinsics and create a top level widget.
   */
  toplevel = XtInitialize (argv[0], "MenuTest", NULL, 0,
                             &argc, argv);
  bb = XtCreateManagedWidget("bulletin",
                                 xmBulletinBoardWidgetClass,
                                 toplevel, NULL, 0);
  /*
   * Steps 1 and 2. Create and manage a menubar.
   */
  menubar = XmCreateMenuBar(bb, "menubar", NULL, 0);
  XtManageChild(menubar);
  /*
   * Step 3. Create the menu from the description.
   */
  xs_create_menu_buttons(NULL, menubar, PulldownData,
                           XtNumber(PulldownData));
  XtRealizeWidget (toplevel);
  XtMainLoop();
}
```

Fig. 4.14 shows the pulldown menu created by this example.

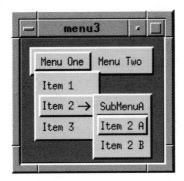

Figure 4.14 A Pulldown menu.

4.3.4.6   Managing Keyboard Focus

One important responsibility of all Motif manager widgets is handling the input focus for its children. Motif supports to different keyboard focus models:

- **pointer**. In this model the widget containing the sprite always receives keyboard events.
- **explicit**. When using this model, the user must click on a widget to specify that the widget is to receive keyboard events. Once the focus is explicitly set, the focus widget continues to receive keyboard input, even if user moves the sprite out of the focus window. The widget can lose the focus if the window manager takes the focus completely away from the application.

The focus model used by an application is determined by the **XmNkeyboardFocusPolicy** resource, which can be set to either **XmPOINTER** or **XmEXPLICIT**. Only display widgets (subclasses of XmPrimitive) and gadgets can have the keyboard focus. Container widgets control which children receive the focus. The process of moving the focus from one widget to another is referred to as "traversal". An **XmNtravesalOn** resource supported by all primitive Motif widgets determines whether or not the widget accepts the focus from a manager widget. The default value of this resource is **FALSE**, which indicates that the widget denies focus. When a Motif widget has the keyboard focus, it has a highlighted border, as determined by the **XmNhighlightColor** and **XmNhighlightThickness** resources.

Depending on the setting of the **XmNkeyboardFocusPolicy** resource, Motif allows the user to change the focus widget in several ways. If the pointer focus model is used, the focus changes as the sprite moves between primitive widgets. If the explicit model is used, the user can set the focus using the mouse, by clicking mouse button one in the widget to get the focus, or by using the <TAB> and arrow keys to move the focus from widget to widget. The manner in which these keys allow the user to traverse a set of widgets depends on the order in which widgets are created and by the way in which the widgets are organized into *tab* *groups*. A tab group specifies a set of widgets within which the user can use arrow keys to traverse the widgets. The user can move between different tab groups using the <TAB> key. A tab group must consist of a single container widget, and can be defined by the function:

XmAddTabGroup (manager_widget)

Tab groups can also be removed with the function:

XmRemoveTabGroup (manager_widget)

Let's see how this works with a simple example. This example creates two XmRow-Column widgets, each of which is placed in a tab group. Each XmRowColumn manages three XmPushButton widgets.

```
/***********************************************************
 * traverse.c: An example of Motif's traversal mechanisms
 ***********************************************************/
#include <X11/StringDefs.h>
#include <X11/Intrinsic.h>
#include <X11/Intrinsic.h>
#include <Xm/Xm.h>
#include <Xm/RowColumn.h>
#include <Xm/PushB.h>
char * buttons_one[] = {"button1", "button2", "button3"};
char * buttons_two[] = {"button4", "button5", "button6"};
main(argc, argv)
    int     argc;
    char    *argv[];
{
    Widget toplevel, rowcol, box1, box2;
    int    i;
    toplevel = XtInitialize(argv[0], "Traverse", NULL, 0,
                            &argc, argv);
    rowcol = XtCreateManagedWidget("rowcol",
                                   xmRowColumnWidgetClass,
                                   toplevel, NULL, 0);
    box1 = XtCreateManagedWidget("box1",
                                 xmRowColumnWidgetClass,
                                 rowcol, NULL, 0);
    box2 = XtCreateManagedWidget("box2",
                                 xmRowColumnWidgetClass,
                                 rowcol, NULL, 0);
    /*
     * Make each child XmRowColumn widget a tab group.
     */
```

```
    XmAddTabGroup(box1);
    XmAddTabGroup(box2);
    /*
     * Create three children of each XmRowColumn widget.
     */
  for(i=0;i< XtNumber(buttons_one); i++)
    XtCreateManagedWidget(buttons_one[i],
                            xmPushButtonWidgetClass,
                            box1, NULL, 0);
    for(i=0;i< XtNumber(buttons_two); i++)
    XtCreateManagedWidget(buttons_one[i],
                            xmPushButtonWidgetClass,
                            box2, NULL, 0);
    XtRealizeWidget(toplevel);
    XtMainLoop();
}
```

Now we can experiment with the Motif's keyboard traversal. To see this, set the **XmN-traversalOn** resource to **TRUE**, give a non-zero value for **XmNhighlightThickness**, and choose a color for the **XmNhighlightColor** resource. For example, you could put the following resource in a resource file:

```
*traversalOn:        TRUE
*highlightColor:     Red
*highlightThickness: 5
```

To see the pointer focus model, also add the resources:

```
*keyboardFocusPolicy: pointer
*highlightOnEnter:    TRUE
```

Now, as you move the sprite across each of the XmPushButton widgets in this example, the button will be highlighted while the sprite remains in the widget. To experiment with the explicit focus model, change the focus policy resource to:

```
*keyboardFocusPolicy: explicit
```

In this mode, this example allows the user to move sequentially from **button1** to **button2** to **button3**, and back again to **button1** using the arrow keys. The <TAB> key moves the focus to the second tab group. Once there, the user can use the arrow keys to move between **button4**, **button5**, and **button6**.

4.4   POPUP DIALOGS

Often we want to display a temporary window to request the user to enter some information or to display a message. The Xt Intrinsics supports several types of popups that allow the programmer to do this. The popup menu widgets discussed in the previous section are one example of a popup widget. However, sometimes the application programmer needs to popup an arbitrary window. In such cases, we can create a popup shell, created using the function:

```
XtCreatePopupShell(name, class, parent, args, nargs)
```

The arguments to this function are the same as the arguments to **XtCreateWidget()**.

A popup shell and its children can be displayed using the function:

```
XtPopup(shell, grab_mode)
```

The **shell** argument must be a popup shell. Applications do not need to realize popup shells, because **XtPopup()** does it automatically. Sometimes popup shells pop up other shells, creating a cascade of popup shells. The cascading menu in the previous section is one example. The **grab_mode** argument allows the programmer to specify how events are dispatched within a cascade of popups. If **XtNgrabNone** is specified, events are processed normally. If the **grab_mode** is **XtNGrabNonExclusive**, device events are sent to any widget in the popup cascade. If the grab mode is **XtNGrabExclusive**, all device events are sent only to the last popup in the cascade.

A popup widget can be popped down using the function:

```
XtPopDown(popup_shell)
```

Because these functions are often used inside callback functions, the Xt Intrinsics provides several callback functions as a convenience. The functions are **XtCallbackNone()**, **XtCallbackNonexclusive()**, and **XtCallbackExclusive()**. Each of these calls **XtPopup()** with the corresponding grab mode. These callbacks also disable the sensitivity of the widget from which the popup was invoked.

Popup shells that are popped up from within one of these callback functions should be popped down using the callback function **XtCallbackPopupdown()**. This callback function expects to be passed a pointer to a structure of type **XtPopdownIDRec** as client data. This structure must contain the shell widget to be popped down, and optionally the widget that initiated the popup. The **XtPopdownIDRec** is defined as:

```
typedef struct {
    Widget shell_widget;
    Widget enable_widget;
} XtPopdownIDRec, *XtPopdownID
```

4.4.1   Motif Dialog Widgets

The Motif widget set builds on the popup facilities of the Xt Intrinsics to create a versatile set of dialog widgets. Motif uses a subclass of the shell widget, the XmDialogShell widget class, as the basis of most popups. However, the programmer seldom needs to deal with this widget class directly because of the convenience functions provided to create different types of dialogs and popups. Most Motif widgets know when they are children of the XmDialogShell widget class and automatically cause their parent shell to popup and pop down when they are managed and unmanaged. This relieves the programmer from handling the details described in the previous section directly.

The following are the Motif widget classes designed to be used as dialog widgets. These widgets can also be used outside of a popup dialog, as we have already demonstrated in previous sections.

- XmBulletinBoard: This widget is the base for many dialogs. It does not impose any ordering or geometry constraints on its children.

- XmCommand: The XmCommand widget is a subclass of the XmSelectionBox widget class. It provides a command input region and also a command history region along with a history mechanism.

- XmFileSelectionBox: This widget class is a subclass of the XmSelectionBox widget class. It is useful for selecting from a list of files.

- XmForm: The XmForm widget was described in Section 4.3.4.3. It uses constraints attached to each managed child to determine the position of each child.

- XmMessageBox: The XmMessageBox widget class is a subclass of XmBulletinBoard used to display a message to the user. The XmMessageBox widget provides a message area, a symbol area, and three buttons, which are labeled "OK", "Cancel", and "Help" by default.

- XmSelectionBox: This is a subclass of XmBulletinBoard which allows the user to select from a list of choices. The choices are displayed in a scrollable list. This widget class also provides "OK", "Cancel", and "Help" buttons.

By setting appropriate resources, many types of dialogs can be created from these basic widget classes. Motif provides a large set of convenience routines to make dialogs easier to create and use. These convenience functions create the following types of dialogs:

BulletinBoardDialog	ErrorDialog	FileSelectionDialog	FormDialog
InformationDialog	MessageDialog	PromptDialog	QuestionDialog
SelectionDialog	WarningDialog	WorkingDialog	

The corresponding convenience functions can be generated by adding "XmCreate" before these names. These types of dialogs are not really new widget classes, but are combinations of an XmDialogShell widget and one of the manager widgets described above. The widget returned by these convenience functions is the manager widget, not the XmDialogShell widget created as the parent of the manager widget.

Now that we've described the basic dialog functions provided by Motif, let's look at how a few of these can be used in an application. First, we will reimplement the example from Section 4.3.4.1 as a popup dialog. The main part of the program simply creates a push-button that pops up the dialog when the user presses a mouse button.

```
/****************************************************
 * dialog.c: Test a popup Dialog widget
 ***************************************************/
#include <X11/StringDefs.h>
#include <X11/Intrinsic.h>
#include <X11/Shell.h>
#include <Xm/Xm.h>
#include <Xm/PushB.h>
#include <Xm/BulletinB.h>
#include <Xm/Text.h>
#include "libXs.h"
void    show_dialog();
void    done_callback();
Widget create_dialog();
void    get_text();

main(argc, argv)
    int    argc;
    char *argv[];
{
  Widget toplevel, button, dialog;
  /*
   * Initialize the Intrinsics and create a PushButton widget.
   */
  toplevel = XtInitialize (argv[0], "Dialog", NULL, 0,
                           &argc, argv);
  button = XtCreateManagedWidget("button",
                                 xmPushButtonWidgetClass,
                                 toplevel, NULL, 0);
  /*
   * Create a popup dialog and a register a callback
   * function to popup it up when the button is activated.
   */
  dialog = create_dialog(button);
  XtAddCallback(button, XmNactivateCallback,
                show_dialog, dialog);
  XtRealizeWidget (toplevel);
  XtMainLoop();
}
```

To popup the dialog, the callback function **show_dialog()** simply manages the dialog widget.

```
static void show_dialog(w, dialog, call_data)
   Widget      w;
   Widget      dialog;
   XmAnyCallbackStruct *call_data;
{
  XtManageChild(dialog);
}
```

The function **create_dialog()** is very similar to the XmBulletinBoard widget example in Section 4.3.4.1, except that this time the XmPushButton and XmText widgets are created as children of a BulletinBoardDialog component. By default, the BulletinBoardDialog widget is set to auto-manage mode, which means that if any button is activated, the dialog will be unmanaged. In this example, we want to allow the user to activate buttons for help and so on without unmanaging the form, so the widget's **XmNautoManage** resource is set to **FALSE**.

```
char *buttons[] = {"button1", "button2", "button3"};
char *editors[] = {"field1", "field2", "field3"};

Widget create_dialog(parent, name)
    Widget parent;
{
  Widget bb, edit[3], button[3], done_button;
  Arg    wargs[10];
  int    i,  n = 0;
  XtSetArg(wargs[n], XmNautoUnmanage, FALSE); n++;
  bb = XmCreateBulletinBoardDialog(parent, "board", wargs, n);
  /*
   * Create three single line XmEdit widgets
   * and associate a button with each text widget.
   * Assign an XmNactivateCallback callback to each button.
   */
  for(i=0; i < XtNumber(editors); i++)
     edit[i] = XtCreateWidget(editors[i],
                               xmTextWidgetClass,
                               bb, NULL, 0);
  for(i=0; i < XtNumber(buttons); i++){
     button[i] = XtCreateWidget(buttons[i],
                                 xmPushButtonWidgetClass,
                                 bb, NULL, 0);
     XtAddCallback(button[i], XmNactivateCallback,
```

```
                    get_text, edit[i]);
}
/*
 * Add a button to let the user pop down the widget.
 */
done_button= XtCreateManagedWidget("done",
                                    xmPushButtonWidgetClass,
                                    bb, NULL, 0);
XtAddCallback(done_button, XmNactivateCallback,
              done_callback, bb);
XtManageChildren(edit, XtNumber(editors));
XtManageChildren(button, XtNumber(buttons));
return bb;
}
```

The dialog widget also manages a button named "done", which has an **XmNactivateCall-back** function registered. This function pops the dialog widget down by unmanaging the dialog widget.

```
static void done_callback(w, dialog, call_data)
   Widget      w;
   Widget      dialog;
   XmAnyCallbackStruct *call_data;
{
   XtUnmanageChild(dialog);


}
```

It is important to notice the model used in this example to pop up the dialog box. The dialog box is popped up in response to an action and stays up until it is popped down. Often programmers want to call a function which pops up a dialog box and blocks until the user responds. Then the function returns some value. This is not the model used here. This example continues to use the event-driven model supported by the Xt Intrinsics. Creating a function that blocks is a more difficult task. The application would have to enter a second dispatch loop and return from the loop after the user is finished with the dialog.

The previous example used the simplest form of a dialog, the BulletinBoardDialog widget. Let's expand the previous example as we look at one of the higher level dialog components, the XmMessageDialog widget. This widget automatically provides a message area and three buttons, an "OK" button, a "cancel" button, and a "help" button.

One facility commonly needed by applications is some kind of help mechanism. The following example uses the XmMessageDialog widget to implement a help mechanism in which the user can ask for progressively more detailed help information. In this example, the programmer specifies the help information by providing an array of strings. The first level of help information is terminated by an empty string. If there is an additional, presumably more detailed, level of help available, this follows the empty string. Two empty strings in a row signals the end of the help text. For example, here's a possible help message which provides three levels of help for the previous dialog example:

```
char *help_str[] = {
  "Fill in the text fields and press the buttons to ",
  "the right when done",
  "",
  "The first text field should contain a persons name",
  "The second field should contain an address",
  "The third should contain a phone number",
  "Edit any field and then press the button to the right",
  "to indicate that the information is completed",
  "",
  "Sorry, more detailed help is unavailable.",
  "",""};
```

To display this message, we must first add a help button to the dialog widget in the previous example. The new version of **create_dialog()** is defined as:

```
Widget create_dialog(parent, name)
    Widget parent;
{
  Widget bb, edit[3], button[3], done_button, help_button;
  Arg    wargs[10];
  int    i,  n = 0;
  XtSetArg(wargs[n], XmNautoUnmanage, FALSE); n++;
  bb = XmCreateBulletinBoardDialog(parent, "board", wargs, n);
  /*
   * Create three single line XmEdit widgets
   * and associate a button with each text widget.
   * Assign an XmNactivateCallback callback to each button.
   */
  for(i=0; i < XtNumber(editors); i++)
     edit[i] = XtCreateWidget(editors[i],
                             xmTextWidgetClass,
                             bb, NULL, 0);
  for(i=0; i < XtNumber(buttons); i++){
     button[i] = XtCreateWidget(buttons[i],
                             xmPushButtonWidgetClass,
                             bb, NULL, 0);
     XtAddCallback(button[i], XmNactivateCallback,
                   get_text, edit[i]);
  }
```

```
    /*
     * Add a button to let the user pop down the widget.
     */
    done_button = XtCreateManagedWidget("done",
                                        xmPushButtonWidgetClass,
                                        bb, NULL, 0);
    XtAddCallback(done_button, XmNactivateCallback,
                  done_callback, bb);
    /*
     * Add a button to let the user ask for help.
     */
    help_button = XtCreateManagedWidget("help",
                                        xmPushButtonWidgetClass,
                                        bb, NULL, 0);
    XtAddCallback(help_button, XmNactivateCallback,
                  xs_help_callback, help_str);
    XtManageChildren(edit, XtNumber(editors));
    XtManageChildren(button, XtNumber(buttons));
    return bb;
}
```

The callback function **xs_help_callback()** takes the array of strings containing the help message as client data and creates and displays a sequence of dialogs. The user can end the help session using the XmMessageDialog widget's "OK" button. When the user selects "OK", the dialog is unmapped. The "help" button is used to request more detailed help. If no additional help is available, this button is not shown. The "cancel" button is not used, and is unmanaged when the dialog is created.

The **xs_help_callback()** callback function creates an XmMessageDialog widget, adds an **ok_callback()** function, which is used to unmanage the dialog widget, and removes the "cancel" button by specifically unmanaging it. Each of the component widgets that make up the message dialog are available to the programmer, through the function:

XmMessageBoxGetChild (dialog, child)

The child parameter specifies which child widget is returned. For the XmMessageBox widget, this parameter may be one of the constants:

XmDIALOG_CANCEL_BUTTON   XmDIALOG_SYMBOL_LABEL
XmDIALOG_MESSAGE_LABEL   XmDIALOG_OK_BUTTON
XmDIALOG_HELP_BUTTON   XmDIALOG_SEPARATOR

After retrieving the XmLabel widget used by the message box, the callback function specifies that the XmLabel widget should display text left-justified.

By default, the XmMessageDialog widget is set to auto-manage mode, which means that if any button is activated, the dialog will be unmanaged. We want to control this ourselves, so the widget's **XmNautoManage** resource is set to **FALSE**.

The callback function counts the number of lines before the empty line in the help message and converts this array of strings to a compound string which is used as the message to be displayed by the message dialog. The function **xs_str_array_to_xmstr()** converts a character string to a compound string with separator components between each line. We will delay the description of this function until Chapter 9. If this is the last level of help, the "help" widget is unmanaged. Otherwise it is managed and the **xs_help_callback()** function is added to the **XmNactivateCallback** list for the help button. The client data for this callback is the remainder of the help string array.

```
#include <X11/StringDefs.h>
#include <X11/Intrinsic.h>
#include <Xm/Xm.h>
#include <Xm/MessageB.h>
#include "libXs.h"
static void xs_ok_callback();
void xs_help_callback(w, str, call_data)
     Widget    w;
     char      *str[];
     caddr_t   call_data;
{
  int        i, n;
  Widget     dialog;
  Widget     label;
  XmString   xmstr;
  Arg        wargs[5];
  /*
   * Create the message dialog to display the help.
   */
  n = 0;
  XtSetArg(wargs[n], XmNautoUnmanage, FALSE); n++;
  dialog = XmCreateMessageDialog(w, "Help", wargs, n);
  /*
   * We won't be using the cancel widget. Unmanage it.
   */
  XtUnmanageChild(XmMessageBoxGetChild (dialog,
              XmDIALOG_CANCEL_BUTTON));
  /*
   * Retrieve the label widget and make the
   * text left justified
   */
```

```
   label = XmMessageBoxGetChild (dialog,
                                 XmDIALOG_MESSAGE_LABEL);
   n = 0;
   XtSetArg(wargs[n],XmNalignment,XmALIGNMENT_BEGINNING);n++;
   XtSetValues(label, wargs, n);
   /*
    * Add an OK callback to pop down the dialog.
    */
   XtAddCallback(dialog, XmNokCallback,
                 xs_ok_callback, NULL);
   /*
    * Count the text up to the first NULL string.
    */
   for(i=0; str[i][0] != '\0'; i++)
     ;
   /*
    * Convert the string array to an XmString array and
    * set it as the label text.
    */
   xmstr  = xs_str_array_to_xmstr(str, i);
   n = 0;
   XtSetArg(wargs[n],  XmNmessageString, xmstr);n++;
   XtSetValues(dialog, wargs, n);
   /*
    * If the next entry in the help string array is also NULL,
    * then this is the last message. Unmanage the help button.
    */
   if(str[++i][0] == '\0')
     XtUnmanageChild(XmMessageBoxGetChild (dialog,
                     XmDIALOG_HELP_BUTTON));
   /*
    * Otherwise add a help callback function with the
    * address of the next entry in the help string
    * as client_data.
    */
   else{
     XtAddCallback(dialog, XmNhelpCallback,
                   xs_help_callback, &str[i]);
   }
   /*
    * Display the dialog.
    */
   XtManageChild(dialog);
}
```

The **xs_ok_callback()** function unmanages the dialog widget to pop the dialog down and end the help session.

```
static void xs_ok_callback(w, client_data, call_data)
    Widget              w;
    caddr_t             client_data;
    XmAnyCallbackStruct *call_data;
{
    XtUnmanageChild(w);

}
```

Fig. 4.16 shows a series of dialogs created by the help callback.

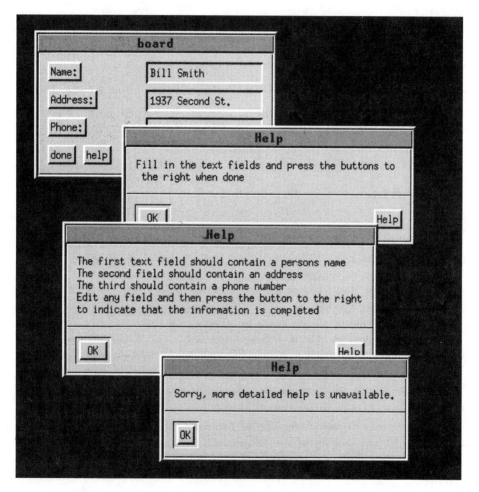

Figure 4.15 The XmMessageDialog displaying help messages.

4.5 GADGETS

In addition to widgets, Motif provides a user interface component known as a gadget. Gadgets are identical to widgets, except that they have no window of their own. A gadget must display text or graphics in the window provided by its parent, and must also rely on its parent for input. Because reducing the number of windows in an application reduces the number of server requests, using gadgets can make an application much more efficient. From the application programmer's viewpoint, gadgets can be used exactly the same as other display widgets, except for the following restrictions. Gadgets cannot support event handlers, translations, or popup children. Gadgets can support callback functions and have the same appearance as the corresponding widgets. Motif provides both widget and gadget versions of several interface components. The Motif gadget classes are:

XmArrowButtonGadget   **XmLabelGadget**   **XmPushButtonGadget**
XmSeparatorGadget   **XmToggleButtonGadget** **XmCascadeButtonGadget**

Gadgets can be created exactly the same as widgets, using **XtCreateWidget()**, by specifying a gadget class pointer as the class argument. For example:

XtCreateWidget("memo", xmLabelGadgetClass, toplevel, NULL, 0)

Gadgets can provide a significant performance improvement and are useful whenever the restrictions noted above are not a problem. One likely place for using gadgets heavily is in menus.

4.6 SUMMARY

This chapter demonstrated how applications can combine various widgets to create a complete user interface. Widgets provide basic user interface components such as scroll bars, buttons, and menus. Applications can use composite and constraint widgets to group simple widgets together to form complex user interfaces.

The widgets in the Motif widget set are powerful enough to meet most of the user interface needs of typical applications. These widgets allow the programmer to display and edit text and graphics, pop up dialog boxes and menus, and display a variety of selection devices, such as push buttons, toggle buttons, and lists. For those applications that need functionality not addressed by existing widgets, the application programmer has two choices:

- Use a primitive widget class, such as the Core widget class or XmDrawingArea widget class, as a window in which to display output. Such applications must use Xlib text and graphics functions to draw the contents of the window.

- Write a new widget to provide the needed function. This is quite feasible, although it requires a good understanding of the widget architecture. Chapters 12, 13, and 14 show how to write new widgets.

The following chapter discusses the events generated by the X server and shows examples of how applications can handle events.

5

HANDLING EVENTS

The X server communicates with clients by sending events. The architecture of the Xt Intrinsics allows individual widgets to handle most common events automatically. For example, most widgets handle the **Expose** events sent by the server when the contents of a widget's window needs refreshed, and also handle configuration events generated by the server when a window is resized. In addition, most widgets use the translation manager to handle keyboard and mouse input. In spite of this, most programmers still find occasions when they must handle events directly, even when using the X Toolkit. Having a good understanding of the events generated by the X server also helps the programmer understand and use the Xt Intrinsics and widgets more effectively.

Chapter 2 provided a brief introduction to events and event handlers. This chapter examines events in more detail and provides examples that use features of the Intrinsics to handle events. The chapter first examines the events and event structures provided by X and Xlib and then looks at the event-handling mechanisms built on top of Xlib by the Xt Intrinsics. We also examine some applications that depend on input from sources other than X events. Events used for interclient communication are discussed in Chapter 11.

5.1 WHAT IS AN EVENT?

An *event* is a notification, sent by the X server to a client, that some condition has changed. The X server generates events as a result of some user input, or as a side effect of a request to the X server. The server sends each event to all interested clients, who determine what kind of event has occurred by looking at the *type* of the event. Applications do not receive events automatically. They must specifically request the X server to send the types of events in which they are interested. Events always occur relative to a window, known as the *source window* of the event. If no client has requested the event for the source window, the server propagates the event up the X window hierarchy until it finds a window for which some client has requested the event, or it finds a window that prohibits the event propagation. The server only propagates *device events* generated as a result of a key, mouse button, or sprite motion. If the server reaches the root of the window tree without finding a client interested in the event, the event is discarded. The window to which the server finally reports the event is known as the *event window*.

The X server places all events in an event queue. Clients usually remove events from the event queue using the Xt Intrinsics function, **XtNextEvent()**. This function fills in an **XEvent** structure allocated by the client. Each event type is defined as a C struct. The **XEvent** structure is a C union of all event types. Appendix D lists the event types as well as the union member corresponding to each event type.

All events contain a core set of basic information, contained in the first five members of every event structure. This information specifies

- the **type** of the event,
- the **display** where the event occurred,
- the event **window**,
- the **serial** number of the last request processed by server, and
- a **send_event** flag that indicates if this event was generated by the server or if the event was sent by another client. The flag is **TRUE** if the event was sent by another client, and **FALSE** if it was sent by the server.

The structure **XAnyEvent** is defined to allow access to those members that are common to all event types. Clients can access this basic information in any event using the **xany** member of the **XEvent** union, for example:

    event.xany.window

The type of every event can also be accessed directly using:

    event.type

Each event contains additional information, specific to the type of the event, that must be accessed using the member of the union corresponding to that event type. For example, the width of a window can be extracted from an **XConfigureNotify** event with

    event.xconfigure.width

5.2 EVENT MASKS

An X application must request the event types it wishes the server to report for each window by passing an *event mask* to the Xlib function **XSelectInput()**, or by registering an event handler for the event using the Xt Intrinsics function **XtAddEventHandler()**. For example, the statement

```
XSelectInput(display, window,
        ButtonPressMask | ButtonReleaseMask);
```

requests the server to generate events when a mouse button is pressed or released in the given window. Fig. 5.1 shows the X event masks defined in X.h. Notice that the names of these masks are not the same as the names of the event types listed in Appendix D.

There is not always a direct correlation between the masks clients use to request events and the types of events reported by the server. For example, a client that selects events with **ExposureMask** may be sent the events **Expose**, **GraphicsExpose**, and **NoExpose**. On the other hand, clients requesting events using **PointerMotionMask** or **ButtonMotionMask** receive a **MotionNotify** event when either type of event occurs. The correspondence between event masks, event types, and event structures is shown in Appendix D.

EventMask	KeyPressMask
KeyReleaseMask	ButtonPressMask
ButtonReleaseMask	EnterWindowMask
LeaveWindowMask	PointerMotionMask
PointerMotionHintMask	Button1MotionMask
Button2MotionMask	Button3MotionMask
Button4MotionMask	Button5MotionMask
ButtonMotionMask	KeymapStateMask
ExposureMask	VisibilityChangeMask
StructureNotifyMask	ResizeRedirectMask
SubstructureNotifyMask	SubstructureRedirectMask
FocusChangeMask	PropertyChangeMask
ColormapChangeMask	OwnerGrabButtonMask

Figure 5.1 Event masks used to select X events.

5.3 EVENT TYPES

We can group the events supported by X into several general categories. The following sections discuss each event category and examine the information contained in these events.

5.3.1 Keyboard Events

The server generates a **KeyPress** event whenever a key is pressed and generates a **KeyRelease** event when the key is released. All keys, including modifier keys, (the <SHIFT> key, for example) generate events. A client can request **KeyPress** events by specifying **KeyPressMask** as the event mask when calling **XSelectInput()** or when defining an event handler. Clients request **KeyRelease** events using **KeyReleaseMask**. The server reports both **KeyRelease** and **KeyPress** events using an **XKeyEvent** structure. In addition to the members common to all X events, the **XKeyEvent** structure contains some additional information:

```
Window        root;
Window        subwindow;
Time          time;
int           x, y;
int           x_root, y_root;
unsigned int  state;
unsigned int  keycode;
Bool          same_screen;
```

The **root** member reports the ID of the root window of the screen where the event occurred. If the source window is a descendent of the event window, the **subwindow** member indicates the ID of the immediate child of the event window that lies between the event window and the source window. For example, assume that a window named BaseWindow has a child named ScrollBar, and that ScrollBar has a child named Slider, as shown in Fig. 5.2 and Fig. 5.3. Also assume that only window BaseWindow has selected **KeyPress** events. If a **KeyPress** event occurs in Slider, the event propagates to BaseWindow. The source window is **Slider**. The event received by BaseWindow indicates BaseWindow as the event window. The **subwindow** member of the event contains the ID of the ScrollBar window.

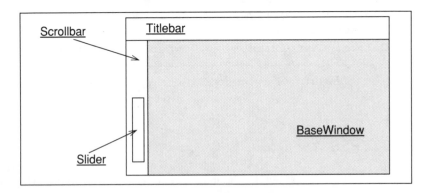

Figure 5.2 Event propagation.

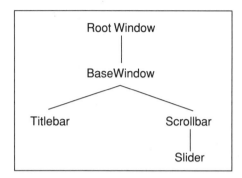

Figure 5.3 Window tree for Fig. 5.2.

The **time** member of an **XKeyPress**edEvent structure indicates the time in milliseconds since the server reset. This information is useful in preventing race conditions that can arise because the X server and its clients run asynchronously with respect to each other.

The **XKeyEvent** structure also contains the coordinates of the sprite relative to both the event window and the root window, as long as the event window is on the same screen as the root window. If this is not the case, the event reports the coordinates of the sprite as *(0, 0)*, relative to the root window.

The **XKeyEvent** structure contains a keycode that uniquely identifies the key that caused the event. Applications can use the Xlib function **XLookupString()** to map this keycode to the character it represents. The Intrinsics also includes several functions for manipulating keycodes.

The **state** member of the event contains a mask indicating which, if any, modifier keys were depressed when this key was pressed. X supports many modifier keys including **<SHIFT>**, **<SHIFTLOCK>**, **<CONTROL>**, as well as up to five additional system-dependent modifier keys.

5.3.2   Pointer Events

The server generates **ButtonPress**, **ButtonRelease**, and **MotionNotify** events when the user presses or releases a mouse button or moves the sprite. The source window for pointer events is always the smallest window containing the sprite, unless some client has *grabbed* the pointer. When the pointer is grabbed, the server reports all pointer events to the window that initiated the grab. The server reports **ButtonPress** and **ButtonRelease** events using an **XButtonEvent** structure. This event structure is similar to the **KeyPress** event structure, but instead of a key code, the **XButtonEvent** structure contains a **button** member which indicates what mouse button was pressed or released. X supports up to five mouse buttons, defined in the file X.h as **Button1**, **Button2**, **Button3**, **Button4**, and

Button5. The mouse buttons can also be combined with a modifier key, such as the **<SHIFT>** or **<META>** key. The state of all modifier keys when the event occurred is indicated by the **state** member.

The server reports pointer motion events using an **XMotionEvent** structure. Clients can request the server to generate motion events whenever the user moves the sprite, or only when the user moves the sprite while holding down a particular button or combination of buttons. However, the server reports all motion events as type **MotionNotify**, using the **XMotionEvent** structure. Clients can determine the state of the mouse buttons (which buttons are up and which are down) by looking at the **state** member of the event.

By default, the server reports motion events continuously as the pointer moves. Clients can also request the server to *compress* motion events and generate events only when the pointer starts or stops moving. Most applications do not need continuous motion events and should request the server to compress pointer motion into *hints*, by requesting motion events with **PointerMotionHintMask**. The **is_hint** member of the **XMotionEvent** structure indicates whether an event indicates continuous motion or a hint. Other members of the event structure report the *(x, y)* position of the sprite relative to both the event window and the root window. The members of the **XMotionEvent** event structure include:

```
Window          root;
Window          subwindow;
Time            time;
int             x, y;
int             x_root, y_root;
unsigned int    state;
char            is_hint;
Bool            same_screen;
```

5.3.3   Crossing Events

The server generates crossing events whenever the sprite crosses the boundary of a window. The server sends an **EnterNotify** event to the window the sprite enters and a **LeaveNotify** event to the window the sprite leaves. The server also generates crossing events when the sprite enters a window because of a change in the window hierarchy. For example, if a window containing the sprite is lowered to the bottom of the window stack so that the sprite is now in another window, the first window receives a **LeaveNotify** event and the second window receives a **EnterNotify** event. Clients must request **EnterNotify** events using the mask **EnterWindowMask** and **LeaveNotify** events using the mask **LeaveWindowMask**. Both crossing events use the **XCrossingEvent** structure, which includes the members:

```
Window          root;
Window          subwindow;
Time            time;
int             x, y;
int             x_root, y_root;
int             mode;
int             detail;
Bool            same_screen;
Bool            focus;
unsigned int    state;
```

The **XCrossingEvent** structure always contains the final *(x, y)* coordinate of the sprite relative to both the event window and the root window. The **state** member of the event structure indicates the state of the mouse buttons immediately preceding the event.

Applications often need to determine the hierarchical relationship of the windows involved in a crossing event. For example, suppose we wish to write a program that highlights the border of its top-level window whenever the window contains the sprite. Highlighting the window border whenever the client receives an **EnterNotify** event, and unhighlighting the border whenever the client receives an **LeaveNotify** event, works correctly unless the window has subwindows. When the sprite enters a subwindow, the top-level window receives a **LeaveNotify** event, even though the sprite is still within the bounds of the window. In addition, if the application has not requested **EnterNotify** events for the subwindow, the server propagates the event to the top-level window, causing further complications. To do this correctly, we must inspect the **detail** member of the event structure. The server sets this member to one of the constants **NotifyAncestor**, **NotifyVirtual**, **NotifyInferior**, **NotifyNonlinear**, or **NotifyNonlinearVirtual**, signifying the different types of window crossings that can occur.

Fig. 5.4 through Fig. 5.7 show the root window, and two children, Window A and Window B. Window A and Window B have subwindows Window C and Window D respectively. The vector in each figure represents a sprite movement starting in one window and ending in the window containing the arrow head. The text at the beginning and end of each line indicates the type of event generated in that window, with the value of the **detail** member of the event structure shown in parenthesis. Fig. 5.4 illustrates the sprite moving from the root window into a child, Window B. The root window receives a **LeaveNotify** event with the **detail** member of the event set to **NotifyInferior**, while Window B receives an **EnterNotify** event, with the **detail** member set to **NotifyAncestor**.

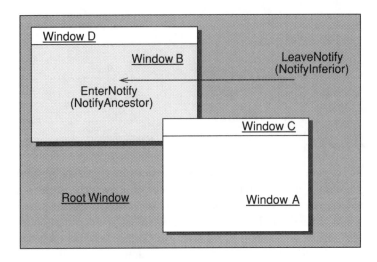

Figure 5.4 Crossing events.

Fig. 5.5 illustrates the opposite situation, where the sprite moves from a window into the window's parent.

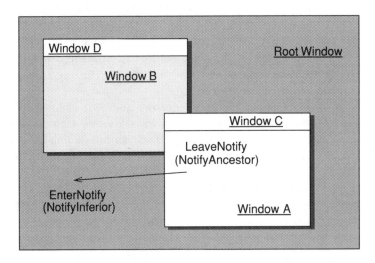

Figure 5.5 Crossing events.

Fig. 5.6 illustrates movement of the sprite between two siblings. In this case, the server sets the **detail** member of each event to **NotifyNonlinear**.

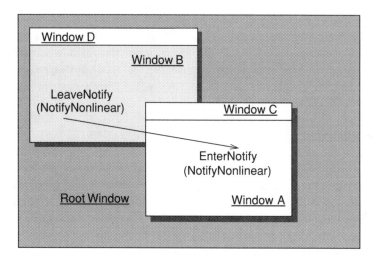

Figure 5.6 Crossing events.

Fig. 5.7 shows the most complex situation, in which the sprite moves between two windows that are more than one level apart in the window hierarchy. In this case, Window C receives a **LeaveNotify** event and Window B receives an **EnterNotify** event. The **detail** member in both events is **NotifyNonlinear**. However, Window A also receives a **LeaveNotify** event, with the **detail** member set to **NotifyNonlinearVirtual**.

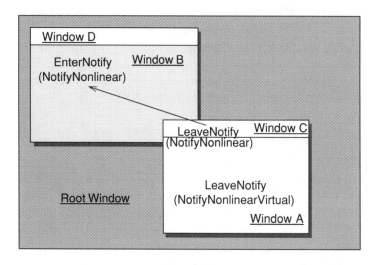

Figure 5.7 Crossing events.

The server also generates crossing events when an application grabs or ungrabs the pointer. When an application grabs the pointer, the server sends the window containing the sprite a **LeaveNotify** event with the **mode** member set to the constant **NotifyGrab**. When the grabbing application ungrabs the pointer, the server sends the window containing the sprite an **EnterNotify** event with the **mode** member set to **NotifyUngrab**. If the crossing event is not a result of a grab, the server sets the **mode** member of the event to **NotifyNormal**.

5.3.4   Focus Events

The window to which the X server sends keyboard events is known as the focus window. The server generates **FocusIn** and **FocusOut** events whenever the focus window changes, usually as a result of a window manager explicitly changing the focus window. Applications wishing to receive these events must select them using **FocusChangeMask**. Focus events are similar to **EnterNotify** and **LeaveNotify** events but are even more complex, because the sprite is not necessarily in any of the windows involved in the change of focus. Most applications that use the Xt Intrinsics do not need to handle focus events directly, because focus is handled by manager widgets.

5.3.5   Exposure Events

The server generates exposure events when a window or a portion of a window becomes visible. Clients must request exposure events using the **ExposureMask** event mask. There are three types of exposure events. The most common type, **Expose**, is generated when the contents of a region of a window are lost for any reason. The server sends a **GraphicsExpose** event when a client attempts to use **XCopyArea()** to copy an obscured region of a window. **NoExpose** events can also be generated when copying areas between drawables. The server generates this event when an application requests **GraphicsExpose** events but no regions are exposed by as a result of a call to **XCopyArea()**. The server reports **Expose** events using an **XExposeEvent** structure, which includes the members:

```
int     x, y;
int     width, height;
int     count;
```

The **XExposeEvent** structure contains the x and y coordinates relative to the upper left corner of the window and the width and height of the rectangular region of the window that has been exposed. The event also contains a **count** member which indicates how many **Expose** events are still pending. If **count** is zero, there are no more **Expose** events pending for this window. However, if the **count** member is non-zero, then *at least* this many events are still pending. Multiple **Expose** events occur primarily when an exposed region consists of more than one rectangular region. Applications that are not capable of redrawing arbitrary regions of windows can ignore **Expose** events with a non-zero **count** member, and redraw the entire contents of the window when the server generates an event whose **count** member is zero. The Xt Intrinsics allows widgets to request that multiple exposure events be *compressed* into a single **Expose** event. The Intrinsics automatically accumulates all **Expose** events until an event with **count** set to zero is received. The Intrinsics then replaces the coordinates in this last **Expose** event with the bounding box of the areas in all previous **Expose** events and invokes the widget's **Expose** event handler with the single **Expose** event.

5.3.6 Structure Control

The server reports structure control events to clients that ask for requests to be *redirected*. Window managers generally use event redirection to exercise control over application's windows. For example, if a window manager requests events using the mask **ResizeRedirectMask**, the X server ignores all requests from other applications to resize windows and instead sends a **ResizeRequest** event to the window manager. The window manager then has the opportunity to act on the request according to its screen management policy. Requests that circulate a window's position in the stacking order, configure the window in any way, or map the window can also be redirected. If a window manager requests events using **SubstructureRedirectMask**, the X server generates **CirculateRequest**, **ConfigureRequest**, and **MapRequest** events instead of acting directly on these requests. Only one application can request the server to redirect events at any one time.

5.3.7 State Notification

Some applications need to be informed when its windows are reconfigured in any way. Clients can use the **StructureNotifyMask** event mask to request events when a window's configuration changes, or **SubstructureNotifyMask** to request notification of changes to a window's subwindows.

Clients that request **StructureNotify** events can receive many different types of events, depending on what changes occur. When a window's position in the stacking order changes because of a call to the Xlib functions **XCirculateSubwindows()**, **XCirculateSubwindowsUp()**, or **XCirculateSubwindowsDown()**, the server generates a **CirculateNotify** event, which uses an **XCirculateEvent** structure. This structure includes the members:

```
Window  event;
Window  window;
int     place;
```

The **event** member of this structure indicates the event window. The **window** member is set to the ID of the window that was restacked. This window is not necessarily the same as the event window. The server also sets the **place** member of this event to the constant **PlaceOnBottom**, indicating the window is below all siblings, or the constant **PlaceOn-Top**, indicating that the window is above all siblings.

The server generates **ConfigureNotify** events whenever a window's size, position, or border width changes. The server reports this event using an **XConfigureEvent** structure. **ConfigureNotify** events are also generated when a window's position in the stacking order changes because of a call to the Xlib functions **XLowerWindow()**, **XRaiseWindow()**, **XRestackWindow()**, or **XRestackWindows()**. The members in the **XConfigureEvent** structure include:

```
Window   event;
Window   window;
int      x, y;
int      width, height;
int      border_width;
Window   above;
Bool     override_redirect;
```

The **event** member of the **XConfigureEvent** structure indicates the event window while the **window** member indicates the window that has changed. The **above** member contains the ID of the sibling window just below the window whose position in the stacking order has changed. If the window is on the bottom of the stacking order, the **above** member of the **XConfigureNotify** event is set to **None**.

The server generates **CreateNotify** and **DestroyNotify** events whenever a window is created or destroyed, respectively. Clients that wish to receive these events must request events for the window's parent using **SubstructureNotifyMask**. The event structure of the **CreateNotify** event contains the IDs of both the new window and the parent of the new window, and also the size and location of the window. The **DestroyNotify** event contains only the event window and the ID of the destroyed window.

Other types of structure notification events include **GravityNotify**, **MapNotify**, **MappingNotify**, **ReparentNotify**, **UnmapNotify**, and **VisibilityNotify**. The application programmer seldom needs to deal with these events directly, because the Intrinsics normally handles them automatically.

5.3.8   Colormap Notification

Applications that need to know when a new color map is installed can request **ColormapNotify** events using the mask **ColormapChangeMask**. Color maps determine the colors available to an application, and are discussed in Chapter 6. The server reports **Col-ormapNotify** events using an **XColormapEvent** structure that contains the ID of the colormap, a boolean value that indicates whether the colormap is new, and a **state** member set to one of the constants **ColormapInstalled** or **ColormapUninstalled**. The members of the **XColormapEvent** structure include:

```
Colormap colormap;
Bool     new;
int      state;
```

5.3.9   Communication Events

X also supports events that allow direct communication between applications, and events that provide a mechanism for exchanging and sharing data between applications. **ClientMessage** events can be used by applications to define additional event types that can be sent between applications using the Xlib function:

> **XSendEvent(display, window, propagate, mask, event)**

Applications cannot specifically request **ClientMessage** events. The server always sends **ClientMessage** events to the destination window. Chapter 11 discusses **ClientMessage** events and shows some examples of direct interclient communication.

The server generates **PropertyNotify** events when the value of a window *property* is modified. Applications interested in receiving **PropertyNotify** events must select the event using **PropertyChangeMask** as an argument to **XSelectInput()** or **XtAddEventHandler()**. Properties and **PropertyNotify** events are discussed in Chapter 11.

SelectionClear, **SelectionNotify**, and **SelectionRequest** events are used by the X selection mechanism for exchanging data between applications. Like **ClientMessage** events, selection events cannot be specifically selected by an application. Selections are also discussed in Chapter 11.

5.4   HANDLING EVENTS WITH THE Xt INTRINSICS

The Xt Intrinsics hides many of the details of handing events from the programmer and allows widgets to handle many of the common X events automatically. As a result, many applications built using the X Toolkit do not need to deal directly with events at all. However, the Xt Intrinsics does provide facilities that allow applications to receive and handle events if needed. Applications can request a specific type of event by defining a handler for that event. The **memo** example in Chapter 2 introduced the use of event handlers. That chapter also discussed the advantages of using callbacks and the translation manager instead of handling the events directly. There are situations, however, where applications need to handle events directly. The following sections explore some ways to use events and event handlers.

5.4.1   Using Event Handlers

This section presents two examples that use event handlers to handle **MotionNotify** events, **ButtonPress** events, and crossing events. These examples illustrate accessing and using the information in the event structures. Later examples demonstrate dynamically installing and removing event handlers.

The first example creates a module that tracks and reports the position of the sprite in an arbitrary widget. We will refer to this module as a *mouse tracker*. For purposes of demonstration, the mouse tracker displays the current position of the sprite in an XmLabel widget, but you can probably imagine more practical uses for tracking the position of the sprite. Let's first examine the body of a simple driver program to test the mouse tracker, named **mousetracks**.

```
/************************************************************
 * mousetracks.c: Driver to test the mouse tracker module
 ************************************************************/
#include <X11/StringDefs.h>
#include <X11/Intrinsic.h>
#include <Xm/Xm.h>
#include <Xm/PanedW.h>
#include <Xm/RowColumn.h>
#include <Xm/DrawingA.h>
#include <Xm/Label.h>
#include "libXs.h"

main(argc, argv)
    int         argc;
    char        *argv[];
{
    Widget          toplevel, panel, command, target;
    /*
     * Initialize the Intrinsics.
     */
    toplevel = XtInitialize(argv[0], "Mousetracks", NULL, 0,
                            &argc, argv);
    /*
     * Create a vertical paned widget, to hold
     * all the other widgets.
     */
    panel = XtCreateManagedWidget("panel",
                                  xmPanedWindowWidgetClass,
                                  toplevel, NULL, 0);
    /*
```

```
 *  Create a command widget to hold both a quit button
 *  and the mouse tracker display.
 */
command = XtCreateManagedWidget("command",
                                xmRowColumnWidgetClass,
                                panel, NULL, 0);
/*
 *  Add a quit button.
 */
xs_create_quit_button(command);
/*
 *  Create the widget in which we track the
 *  motion of the sprite.
 */
target = XtCreateManagedWidget("target",
                               xmDrawingAreaWidgetClass,
                               panel, NULL, 0);
/*
 *  Create the mouse tracker.
 */
create_mouse_tracker(command, target);
XtRealizeWidget(toplevel);
XtMainLoop();
}
```

This test driver initializes the Intrinsics and then creates an XmPanedWindow widget that manages two children, an XmRowColumn widget and an XmDrawingArea widget. The XmPanedWindow widget creates a pane for each widget it manages. The user can adjust the vertical size and position of each pane by using the mouse to move a small control (really a separate widget) known as a *Sash*. The XmDrawingArea widget provides an empty window, used in this example as the window in which the sprite motion is tracked. The XmRowColumn widget manages a quit button (created by the libXs function defined in Chapter 4) and also an XmLabel widget created by the mouse tracker. Fig. 5.8 shows the widget tree formed by the widgets in this example.

The function **create_mouse_tracker()** creates the mouse tracker module, and takes two arguments. The first indicates a parent widget that manages the XmLabel widget created by the mouse tracker. The second specifies the widget in which the sprite position is to be tracked. The mouse tracker only reports the sprite position when the sprite is in this target widget.

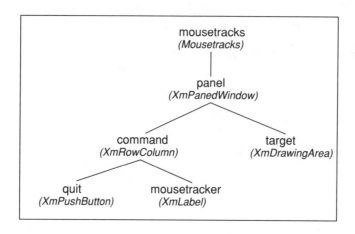

Figure 5.8 The mousetracks widget tree.

The function **create_mouse_tracker()** is defined as:

```
create_mouse_tracker(parent, target)
    Widget    parent, target;
{
    extern void   clear_tracker();
    extern void   track_mouse_position();
    Widget        tracker;
    /*
     * Create the tracker widget and register event
     * handlers for the target widget.
     */
    tracker = XtCreateManagedWidget("mousetracker",
                            xmLabelWidgetClass,
                            parent, NULL, 0);
    XtAddEventHandler(target, PointerMotionMask, FALSE,
                    track_mouse_position, tracker);
    XtAddEventHandler(target, LeaveWindowMask, FALSE,
                    clear_tracker, tracker);
}
```

This function creates an XmLabel widget, **tracker**, as a child of the given parent widget and then registers two event handlers for the **target** widget. The first handles **PointerMotion** events while the other handles **LeaveNotify** events. The **tracker** widget is specified as client data for both event handlers.

The Intrinsics invokes the event handler **track_mouse_motion()** whenever the user moves the sprite within the **target** window. This function extracts the current sprite location from the event structure and displays it in the **tracker** widget. This event handler is defined as:

```
void track_mouse_position(w, tracker, event)
    Widget          w;
    Widget          tracker;
    XEvent          *event;
{
   /*
    * Extract the position of the sprite from the event
    * and display it in the tracker widget.
    */
    xs_wprintf(tracker, "X: %04d, Y: %04d",
               event->xmotion.x, event->xmotion.y);
}
```

The function **xs_wprintf()** is a simple routine that displays text in a widget using the same syntax as **printf()**. Let's wait to describe this function until we have finished describing the tracker module.

It is usually a bad idea to display status information when it is no longer valid, such as when the sprite is no longer in the target window. The **clear_tracker()** event handler clears the contents of the **tracker** widget when the sprite leaves the **target** widget's window.

```
void clear_tracker(w, tracker, event)
    Widget      w;
    Widget      tracker;
    XEvent      *event;
{
  /*
   * Display an empty string in the tracker widget.
   */
   xs_wprintf(tracker, "");
}
```

The mouse tracker could be added to nearly any application without interfering with the normal operation of the program. The Intrinsics allows applications to define multiple event handlers for each event, so the event handlers added by **create_mouse_tracker()** are invoked in addition to any other handlers registered with the target widget for the same events.

This example uses event handlers in a very straightforward way, but we can create more complex variations of this example. For example, let's modify the mouse tracker to report the position of the sprite only while a mouse button is pressed. To do this, we first need to redefine the **create_mouse_tracker()** function.

```
create_mouse_tracker(parent, target)
     Widget    parent, target;
{
  extern void  clear_tracker();
  extern void  track_mouse_position();
  extern void  show_mouse_position();

  Widget         tracker;
  /*
   * Create the tracker widget.
   */
  tracker = XtCreateManagedWidget("mousetracker",
                              xmLabelWidgetClass,
                              parent, NULL, 0);
  /*
   * Set up event handlers on target widget.
   */
  XtAddEventHandler(target, ButtonPressMask, FALSE,
                    show_mouse_position, tracker);
  XtAddEventHandler(target, ButtonMotionMask, FALSE,
                    track_mouse_position, tracker);
  XtAddEventHandler(target,
                    ButtonReleaseMask | LeaveWindowMask,
                    FALSE, clear_tracker, tracker);
}
```

This variation registers three event handlers for the **target** widget. The function **track_mouse_position()** (defined exactly as before) is registered for **MotionNotify** events using the **ButtonMotionMask** instead of the **PointerMotionMask** event mask. This function is only invoked if the user moves the sprite while holding down a mouse button. This version of the mouse tracker registers a new event handler for **ButtonPress** events. This function, **show_mouse_position()**, is defined as:

```
void show_mouse_position(w, tracker, event)
    Widget         w;
    Widget         tracker;
    XEvent         *event;
{
    /*
     * Extract the position of the sprite from the event
```

```
 * and display it in the tracker widget.
 */
xs_wprintf(tracker, "X: %04d, Y: %04d",
          event->xbutton.x, event->xbutton.y);
}
```

This function is nearly the same as **track_mouse_position()**, except that it extracts the position of the sprite from the **XButtonPressedEvent** structure, using the **xbutton** member of the **XEvent** union rather than **xmotion**. We could use the same function to handle both of these events, because the definition of the **XButtonEvent** and **XMotionEvent** event structures are identical, except for the names. The expressions

event->xbutton.x

and

event->xmotion.x

both access the same member in the event structure. However it is not good programming practice to rely on such implementation-dependent details.

In this version of **create_mouse_tracker()**, the function **clear_tracker()** (also defined exactly as in the earlier version) is registered as an event handler for both **LeaveNotify** and **ButtonRelease** events by passing the inclusive-OR of both event masks to **XtAddEventHandler()**. When a single function handles multiple types of events, the event handler can check the type member of the event to determine the event type. In this example, **clear_tracker()** performs the same action in either case.

The function **xs_wprintf()** is a useful function that uses **XtSetValues()** to change the string displayed in any subclass of the XmLabel widget class. The function has a form similar to the C library function **fprintf()**, except that it displays its output in a widget. We will use this function again, so we will place it in the libXs library. The function uses the utility macros found in the UNIX header file /usr/include/varargs.h in combination with **vsprintf()** to handle a variable number of arguments.

```
/**********************************************************
 * xs_wprintf: fprintf-like function for XmLabel widgets
 **********************************************************/
#include <varargs.h>
#include <stdio.h>
#include <X11/Intrinsic.h>
#include <X11/StringDefs.h>
#include <Xm/Xm.h>
#include <Xm/Label.h>

void xs_wprintf(va_alist)
```

```
        va_dcl
{
  Widget    w;
  char      *format;
  va_list   args;
  char      str[1000]; /* Potential overflow situation. */
  Arg       wargs[10];
  XmString  xmstr;
  /*
   * Init the variable length args list.
   */
  va_start(args);
  /*
   * Extract the destination widget.
   * Make sure it is a subclass of XmLabel.
   */
  w = va_arg(args, Widget);
  if(!XtIsSubclass(w, xmLabelWidgetClass))
     XtError("xs_wprintf() requires a Label Widget");
  /*
   * Extract the format to be used.
   */
  format = va_arg(args, char *);
  /*
   * Use vsprintf to format the string to be displayed in the
   * XmLabel widget, then convert it to a compound string
   */
  vsprintf(str, format, args);
  xmstr =  XmStringLtoRCreate(str, XmSTRING_DEFAULT_CHARSET);

  XtSetArg(wargs[0], XmNlabelString, xmstr);
  XtSetValues(w, wargs, 1);

  va_end(args);
}
```

5.5 MANAGING THE EVENT QUEUE

Most applications use the function **XtMainLoop()** or **XtAppMainLoop()** to remove events from the event queue and dispatch them to the appropriate widgets. However, occasionally an application needs to have more control over this process. Xlib provides many functions for examining and manipulating the event queue. These are seldom needed by applications that use the Intrinsics and widgets, although they can be used if needed. The Xt Intrinsics layer provides its own versions of the most common functions for examining the event queue,

XtPending()

and

XtPeekEvent(&event)

XtPending() returns a mask of type **XtInputMask** that indicates the type of input available or zero if the event queue is empty. The possible return values include **XtIMX-Event**, **XtIMTimer**, **XtIMAlternateInput**, and **XtIMAll**. **XtPeekEvent()** copies the event at the top of the event queue into the application-supplied event structure, but does not remove the event from the event queue. **XtPending()** is useful when an application needs to do other tasks whenever there are no events in the event queue. For example, we could write an application's main event loop as:

```
if(XtPending()){
   XtNextEvent(&event);
   XtDispatchEvent (&event)
}
else{   /* Do something else for a while */
   }
```

Notice that this can result in many wasted CPU cycles because the application continuously polls for events. To prevent this, the loop should block for some length of time after the task is completed. This can be done using the UNIX function **select()** to watch for input from the X file descriptor, which can be retrieved from the display using the **ConnectionNumber()** macro:

```
while(TRUE){
   if(XtPending()){  /* If an event is pending, get it and */
      XEvent event;  /* process it normally.              */
      XtNextEvent(&event);
      XtDispatchEvent (&event);
   }
   else{              /* Otherwise do a "background" task */
      struct timeval timeout;
      int readfds = 0;  /* Initialize arguments to select() */
      int maxfds = 1 + ConnectionNumber(XtDisplay(toplevel));
      timeout.tv_sec = 1; /* Set timeout for 1 second. */
      timeout.tv_usec = 0;
      /*
```

```
       * Do something else for a while - insert code here.
       */
      readfds = 1 << ConnectionNumber(XtDisplay(toplevel));
      /*
       * Block for tv.sec or until input is pending from X
       */
      if (select(maxfds, &readfds, NULL, NULL, &timeout) == -1){
        if (EINTR != errno)
            exit(1);
      }
    }
  }
}
```

This approach assumes that the time required to perform the task when no events are available is short, so that the loop returns to process events in a reasonable time period. Sections 5.6 and 5.7 describe slightly different approaches for doing this.

5.6 HANDLING TIMEOUTS

Although many useful X applications only process events from the user, some applications need to perform other tasks as well. The next few sections explore facilities provided by the Xt Intrinsics that extend Xlib's notion of events to allow applications to use the event dispatching mechanism to perform these tasks. One such feature allows applications to register a callback procedure to be invoked by the Intrinsics when a specified interval has elapsed. Applications can use the function

XtAddTimeOut(interval, proc, data)

to register a timeout callback and specify the time delay before it is invoked. **XtAddTimeOut()** returns an ID of type **XtIntervalId** that uniquely identifies this timeout event. The first argument specifies the time interval, in milliseconds, until the Intrinsics invokes the callback function **proc**. The **data** parameter specifies some client data to be passed to the timeout callback function when it is called. The form of a timeout callback is:

```
void proc(data, id)
    caddr_t        data;
    XtIntervalId   *id;
```

where **data** is the client data specified in the call to **XtAddTimeOut()** and **id** is a pointer to the **XtIntervalId** identifier of the timeout event. When a timeout event occurs, the Intrinsics invokes the corresponding callback and then automatically removes the callback. Therefore, timeout events are only invoked once. Clients can use the function

XtRemoveTimeOut(id)

to remove a timeout callback before the timeout occurs. The argument, **id**, must be the **XtIntervalId** of the timer event to be removed.

5.6.1   Using Timeouts as Alarms

Timeout events can be viewed as alarms that can be set to go off some time in the future. This section uses such an alarm to improve the original version of the mouse tracker example from Section 5.4.1. One problem with tracking and reporting all **MotionNotify** events is that both the X server and clients generally have trouble keeping up with the large number of events that can be generated. Moving the sprite across the mouse tracker's target window can slow the entire system because of the overhead involved in generating continuous motion events. This might be acceptable to someone actually using something like the mouse tracker, but what if the user accidently moves the sprite through the mouse tracker's target window on the way to another application's window? It can be frustrating to have the sprite slow down while it passes through the target area, when we are not really interested in the sprite position in the window.

We can solve this problem by using **XtAddTimeOut()** to set an alarm whenever the sprite enters the target window. We can then redesign the mouse tracker so that the position of the sprite is not reported (and no events are generated) until the alarm goes off. By setting the alarm interval appropriately, we can keep the mouse tracker from being activated when the sprite passes quickly through the target window.

In addition to demonstrating the use of timeout events, this version of the mouse tracker also demonstrates several other techniques for using event handlers. The previous examples defined and installed event handlers when the program began. This example dynamically adds and removes event handlers and callbacks within other event handlers. This example also exploits the ability to pass client-defined data to event handlers and callbacks to allow all event handlers access to some common data without resorting to global variables.

In this example, all data used by the mouse tracker and its event handlers is kept in a single data structure, defined as:

```
typedef struct {
    Widget          tracker;
    Widget          target;
    XtIntervalId    id;
    int             delay;
} track_data, *track_data_ptr;
```

The **tracker** member of this structure contains the mouse tracker's XmLabel widget, while the **target** member indicates the widget in which mouse motion events are being monitored. The **id** member of this data structure contains the **XtIntervalId** identifier for the timeout event, and **delay** specifies the time, in milliseconds, that the sprite must remain in the target window before the sprite position is reported. In this example, this delay is set to one second. The function **create_mouse_tracker()** allocates and initializes this structure and then registers a single event handler for the target widget.

```
#define DELAY 1000
create_mouse_tracker(parent, target)
     Widget              parent, target;
{
  extern void       enter_window_handler();
  static track_data data;

  data.delay = DELAY;
  /*
   * Store the target and tracker widgets in the data.
   */
  data.target  = target;
  data.tracker = XtCreateManagedWidget("mousetracker",
                                       xmLabelWidgetClass,
                                       parent, NULL, 0);
  /*
   * Start with a single event handler.
   */
  XtAddEventHandler(data.target, EnterWindowMask, FALSE,
                    enter_window_handler, &data);
}
```

The Intrinsics invokes **enter_window_handler()** when an **EnterNotify** event occurs. The client data for this event handler is a pointer to the **track_data** structure declared in the **create_mouse_tracker()** routine. This event handler does two things. First, it registers a new event handler, **disable_alarm()**. The Intrinsics calls this event handler when the sprite leaves the target window. Second, it adds a timeout callback, **start_tracking()**, to be invoked after the time specified by the **delay** member of the client data structure. Notice that the same client data is also given as the client data argument for the timeout callback.

```
static void enter_window_handler(w, data, event)
    Widget          w;
    track_data      *data;
    XEvent          *event;
{
  extern void  start_tracking();
  extern void  disable_alarm();
  /*
   * When the sprite enters the window, install
```

```
 * a timeout callback, and start the count-down.
 */
XtAddEventHandler(data->target, LeaveWindowMask, FALSE,
                  disable_alarm, data);
data->id = XtAddTimeOut(data->delay, start_tracking, data);
}
```

So, what happens when the sprite quickly passes through the target window? First, the Intrinsics invokes the function **enter_window_handler()**. This function sets an alarm that causes the function **start_tracking()** to be invoked after the specified delay. However, if the sprite leaves the target window before the timeout event occurs, the event handler **disable_alarm()** is called. This event handler is defined as:

```
static void disable_alarm(w, data, event)
    Widget          w;
    track_data      *data;
    XEvent          *event;
{
    /*
     * Remove the timeout callback and then remove
     * ourself as an event handler.
     */
    XtRemoveTimeOut(data->id);
    XtRemoveEventHandler(data->target, LeaveWindowMask, FALSE,
                         disable_alarm, data);
}
```

This function uses **XtRemoveTimeOut()** to remove the timeout callback before it is invoked and also uses **XtRemoveEventHandler()** to remove itself as an event handler. At this point, the mouse tracker is in the same state as before the sprite entered the window, and the only event handler registered is the **enter_window_handler()** function. Notice that in this scenario, no **MotionNotify** events are generated because the mouse tracker never requests motion events.

Now suppose the sprite is still within the target window when the timeout event occurs. In this case, the Intrinsics invokes the timeout callback **start_tracking()**. This callback does three things. First, it removes the **disable_alarm()** event handler, which is no longer needed because the Intrinsics removes timeout callbacks automatically when the timeout occurs. Next, it registers the function **track_mouse_position()** as an event handler for **MotionNotify** events, and last, it registers **leave_window_handler()** as an event handler for **LeaveNotify** events. This sets up the event handlers in the same way as the original example in Section 5.4.1.

```
static void start_tracking(data, id)
    track_data      *data;
    XtIntervalId    id;
{
    extern void  disable_alarm();
    extern void  leave_window_handler();
    extern void  track_mouse_position();
    /*
     * If this function was called, the alarm must have
     * gone off, so remove the disable_alarm event handler.
     */
    XtRemoveEventHandler(data->target, LeaveWindowMask,
                         FALSE, disable_alarm, data);
    /*
     * Now add event handlers to track the sprite motion
     * and clear the tracker when we leave the target window.
     */
    XtAddEventHandler(data->target, PointerMotionMask,
                      FALSE, track_mouse_position, data);
    XtAddEventHandler(data->target, LeaveWindowMask,
                      FALSE, leave_window_handler, data);
}
```

The function **track_mouse_position()** is similar to the previous version in Section 5.4.1, but extracts the tracker widget from the **track_data** structure passed as client data.

```
static void track_mouse_position(w, data, event)
    Widget          w;
    track_data      *data;
    XEvent          *event;
{
  /*
   * Extract the position of the sprite from the event
   * and display it in the tracker widget.
   */
  xs_wprintf(data->tracker, "X: %04d, Y: %04d",
             event->xmotion.x, event->xmotion.y);
}
```

As long as the sprite remains in the target widget, the tracker widget displays the current position of the sprite. When the sprite leaves the target widget, the Intrinsics invokes the event handler **leave_window_handler()**. This function resets the mouse tracker to its initial state by removing the **track_mouse_position()** event handler, clearing the mouse tracker's display widget, and finally removing itself as an event handler.

```
static void leave_window_handler(w, data, event)
   Widget            w;
   track_data        *data;
   XEvent            *event;
{
 extern void  track_mouse_position();
 /*
  * Clear the tracker widget display.
  */
 xs_wprintf(data->tracker, "");
 /*
  * Remove the dynamically installed event handlers.
  */
 XtRemoveEventHandler(data->target, PointerMotionMask, FALSE,
                       track_mouse_position, data);
 XtRemoveEventHandler(data->target, LeaveWindowMask, FALSE,
                       leave_window_handler, data);
}
```

5.6.2   Cyclic Timeouts

Applications often need to perform some action repeatedly at designated intervals. Although the Xt Intrinsics automatically removes timeout callbacks when the timeout event occurs, applications can arrange for timeout callbacks to be invoked at regular intervals by designing the callback to re-install itself each time it is called. An obvious application of this technique is a clock. We can write a digital clock easily using an XmLabel widget and a single timeout callback. The body of the clock program is:

```
/*****************************************************
 * xclock.c : A simple digital clock
 *****************************************************/
#include <X11/Intrinsic.h>
#include <X11/StringDefs.h>
#include <Xm/Xm.h>
#include <Xm/Label.h>
#include <time.h>

void update_time();

main(argc, argv)
```

```
    int             argc;
    char            *argv[];
{
    Widget          toplevel, clock;
    /*
     * Create the widgets.
     */
    toplevel = XtInitialize(argv[0], "Clock", NULL, 0,
                            &argc, argv);
    clock = XtCreateManagedWidget("face",
                                  xmLabelWidgetClass,
                                  toplevel, NULL, 0);
    /*
     * Get the initial time.
     */
    update_time(clock, NULL);
    XtRealizeWidget(toplevel);
    XtMainLoop();
}
```

Before entering the main loop, the program calls the function **update_time()** to display the initial time in the widget. This function uses the UNIX system call **time()** to determine the current time in seconds since 00:00:00 GMT (Greenwich Mean Time), Jan 1, 1970. After rounding the time to the nearest minute, the function calls the UNIX library routine **ctime()** to convert this value to a string representing the current time and date. After displaying the string in the XmLabel wid**get**, the function registers itself as a timeout callback. Each time the callback is invoked, it re-registers itself. The delay until the next timeout event is calculated to occur on the next full minute, to keep the clock reasonably accurate in spite of any variations in the timeouts. The **update_time()** function is defined as:

```
void update_time(w, id)
    Widget          w;
    XtIntervalId    id;
{
    long   tloc, rounded_tloc, next_minute;
    /*
     * Ask Unix for the time.
     */
    time(&tloc);
    /*
     * Convert the time to a string and display it,
     * after rounding it down to the last minute.
     */
```

```
    rounded_tloc = tloc / 60 * 60;
    xs_wprintf(w, "%s", ctime(&rounded_tloc));
    /*
     * Adjust the time to reflect the time till
     * the next round minute.
     */
    next_minute = (60 - tloc % 60) * 1000;
    /*
     * The Intrinsics removes timeouts when they occur,
     * so put ourselves back.
     */
    XtAddTimeOut(next_minute, update_time, w);
}
```

Fig. 5.9 shows the digital clock created by this example.

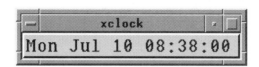

Figure 5.9 xclock: A digital clock.

5.7 USING WORKPROCS

The Xt Intrinsics includes a type of callback function known as a WorkProc that provides a limited form of background processing. This facility works in much the same way as the example using **select()** in Section 5.5. However, WorkProcs allow the programmer to register a callback and hides the details of the event processing from the programmer. A Work-Proc is a callback that is invoked by the Intrinsics whenever there are no events pending. A WorkProc takes only a single argument, which is client-defined data. The procedure is expected to return **TRUE** if the callback should be removed after it is called, and **FALSE** otherwise. Applications can register a WorkProc using the function:

```
XtAddWorkProc(proc, client_data)
```

This function returns an ID that identifies the WorkProc. The **client_data** argument specifies some application-defined data to be passed to the WorkProc. WorkProcs can be removed by calling the function

```
XtRemoveWorkProc(id)
```

where **id** is the identifier returned by **XtAddWorkProc()**. We can use WorkProcs to write a "stopwatch" variation on the clock program from the previous section that updates the time continuously. This example shows how WorkProcs allow a mixture of background processing and event handling. In addition to an XmLabel widget in which time is continuously displayed, this example creates three XmPushButton widgets. One starts the stopwatch, another stops the stopwatch, while the third is a quit button. The main body of the program creates the XmPushButton and XmLabel widgets and registers several callback functions for the XmPushButton widgets.

```
/****************************************************
 * stopwatch.c: A digital stopwatch using workprocs.
 ****************************************************/
#include <X11/Intrinsic.h>
#include <X11/StringDefs.h>
#include <Xm/Xm.h>
#include <Xm/Label.h>
#include <Xm/RowColumn.h>
#include <Xm/PushB.h>
#include <time.h>
#include "libXs.h"

Boolean update_time();
void    start_timing();
void    stop_timing();

long          start_time;
XtWorkProcId work_proc_id = NULL;

main(argc, argv)
   int      argc;
   char     *argv[];
{
  Widget   toplevel, panel, commands, start, stop, timer;

  toplevel = XtInitialize(argv[0], "Stopwatch", NULL, 0,
                           &argc, argv);
  /*
   * Create a XmRowColumn widget to hold everything.
   */
  panel = XtCreateManagedWidget("panel",
                                xmRowColumnWidgetClass,
                                toplevel, NULL, 0);
  /*
```

```
   * An XmLabel widget shows the current time.
   */
  timer = XtCreateManagedWidget("timer",
                                  xmLabelWidgetClass,
                                  panel, NULL, 0);
  /*
   * Add start, stop, and quit buttons and register callbacks.
   * Pass the timer widget to all callbacks.
   */
  commands = XtCreateManagedWidget("commands",
                                     xmRowColumnWidgetClass,
                                     panel, NULL, 0);
  start = XtCreateManagedWidget("start",
                                  xmPushButtonWidgetClass,
                                  commands, NULL, 0);
  XtAddCallback(start,XmNactivateCallback,start_timing,timer);
  stop = XtCreateManagedWidget("stop",
                                 xmPushButtonWidgetClass,
                                 commands, NULL, 0);
  XtAddCallback(stop, XmNactivateCallback,stop_timing,timer);
  xs_create_quit_button(commands);

  XtRealizeWidget(toplevel);
  XtMainLoop();
}
```

The **start_timing()** callback function determines the initial time and registers a WorkProc with the Intrinsics to update the stopwatch display. It uses **time()** to get the current time. Next, in case the user presses the start button multiple times, the function removes any previous WorkProc before registering the function **update_time()** as a WorkProc.

```
  void start_timing(w, timer, call_data)
     Widget                 w, timer;
     XmAnyCallbackStruct    *call_data;
  {
    /*
     * Get the initial time, and save it in a global.
     */
    time(&start_time);
    /*
     * If a WorkProc has already been added, remove it.
     */
```

```
   if(work_proc_id)
     XtRemoveWorkProc(work_proc_id);
   /*
    * Register update_time() as a WorkProc.
    */
   work_proc_id = XtAddWorkProc(update_time, timer);
 }
```

The **stop_timing()** callback function simply removes the WorkProc, if one exists.

```
   void stop_timing(w, timer, call_data)
      Widget                    w, timer;
      XmAnyCallbackStruct   *call_data;
 {
   if(work_proc_id)
     XtRemoveWorkProc(work_proc_id);
   work_proc_id = NULL;
 }
```

The stopwatch display is updated by the WorkProc, **update_time()**, which is called whenever no events are pending. The client data for this function specifies the XmLabel widget in which the time is displayed. The function **update_time()** subtracts the initial time from the current time to obtain the elapsed time in seconds since the user pressed the start button, and then converts the time to minutes and seconds before displaying the elapsed time. Because WorkProcs are called whenever there are no events pending, **update_time()** can be called more often than necessary. Therefore, this function remembers the elapsed time each time the display is updated, and if at least one second has not elapsed, it simply returns.

```
   Boolean update_time(w)
        Widget    w;
 {
   static long elapsed_time, last_time = -1;
   int minutes, seconds, current_time;
   /*
    * Retrieve the current time and calculate the elapsed time.
    */
   time(&current_time);
   elapsed_time = current_time - start_time;
   /*
    * WorkProcs are irregularly called; don't update the
    * display if it's been less than a second since the last
    * time it was updated.
    */
   if(last_time == elapsed_time)
```

```
    return FALSE;
  /*
   * If one or more seconds has elapsed, remember this time,
   * and convert the elapsed time to minutes and seconds.
   */
  last_time = elapsed_time;
  minutes = elapsed_time / 60;
  seconds = elapsed_time % 60;
  /*
   * Display the time as minutes and seconds.
   */
  xs_wprintf(w, "%02d : %02d", minutes, seconds);
  /*
   * Return FALSE so this WorkProc keeps getting called.
   */
  return FALSE;
}
```

The layout for the stopwatch program shown in Fig. 5.10 can be specified using the following resources.

```
Stopwatch*panel*numColumns:           1
Stopwatch*panel*commands*numColumns:  3
Stopwatch*adjustLast:                 FALSE
Stopwatch*packing:                    pack_column
```

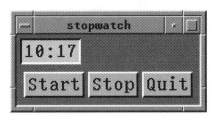

Figure 5.10 The stopwatch program.

5.8 HANDLING OTHER INPUT SOURCES

Many X applications require input from sources other than the X event queue. The Xt Intrinsics provides a simple way to handle additional input sources, such as a UNIX file. Applications can define input callbacks to be invoked when input is available from a specified file descriptor. The function

XtAddInput(source, condition, proc, client_data)

registers an input callback with the Intrinsics. The **source** argument must be a UNIX file number, while **condition** indicates under what circumstances the input callback should be invoked. The **condition** must be one of the constants:

XtInputNoneMask	**XtInputReadMask**
XtInputWriteMask	**XtInputExceptMask**

When the given condition occurs, the Intrinsics invokes the callback function specified by **proc**. The **client_data** parameter allows the application to provide some data to be passed to the callback function when it is called. **XtAddInput()** returns an identifier of type **XtInputId** that uniquely identifies this callback.

Input callback functions have the form:

```
void io_callback(client_data, file_num, id)
    caddr_t     client_data;
    int         *file_num;
    XtInputId   *id;
```

When the Intrinsics invokes an input callback, it passes the **client_data** provided by the application along with a pointer to the file number of the source responsible for the callback. It also provides a pointer to the **XtInputId** associated with this callback.

Input callbacks that are no longer needed can be removed using the function:

XtRemoveInput(id)

The argument, **id**, must be the **XtInputId** identifier for the input callback to be removed.

5.8.1   Using Input Callbacks

This section looks at an example that uses an input callback to read from a UNIX *pipe*. Pipes provide a way to connect the output of one UNIX program to the input of another. This example uses pipes to add a mouse-driven interface to a standard UNIX utility without modifying the code of the original application in any way. The example builds a simple interface for the UNIX calculator program **bc** that allows the user to input commands using the mouse and displays the results in a window. The resulting "desktop calculator," named **xbc**, communicates with **bc** using UNIX pipes. To keep this example simple, **xbc** provides only a few basic arithmetic functions, although it could easily be extended to take advantage of more advanced features of **bc**. Fig. 5.11 shows the window-based interface to **bc**.

Figure 5.11 xbc: A mouse-driven calculator.

The body of the calculator program creates the widgets used as a keypad and the calculator display panel.

```c
/*****************************************************
 * xbc.c: An X interface to bc
 *****************************************************/
#include <stdio.h>
#include <ctype.h>
#include <X11/StringDefs.h>
#include <X11/Intrinsic.h>
#include <Xm/Xm.h>
#include <Xm/PushB.h>
#include <Xm/PanedW.h>
#include <Xm/RowColumn.h>
#include <Xm/Text.h>
#include "libXs.h"

Widget      display;
Widget      create_button();
void        quit_bc();
void        get_from_bc();
void        send_to_bc();
```

```
main(argc, argv)
  int       argc;
  char      *argv[];
{
  Widget    toplevel, panel, keyboard, qbutton;
  Arg       wargs[10];
  int       n;
  toplevel = XtInitialize(argv[0], "Xbc", NULL, 0,
                          &argc, argv);
  /*
   * Create a vertical paned widget as a base for the
   * rest of the calculator.
   */
  panel = XtCreateManagedWidget("panel",
                                xmPanedWindowWidgetClass,
                                toplevel, NULL, 0);
  /*
   * Create the calculator display.
   */
    display = XtCreateManagedWidget("display",
                                    xmTextWidgetClass,
                                    panel, NULL, 0);
  /*
   * Make the keyboard, which manages 5 rows of buttons
   */
  n = 0;
  XtSetArg(wargs[n], XmNorientation, XmHORIZONTAL); n++;
  XtSetArg(wargs[n], XmNnumColumns, 5); n++;
  XtSetArg(wargs[n], XmNadjustLast, FALSE); n++;
  XtSetArg(wargs[n], XmNpacking, XmPACK_COLUMN); n++;
  keyboard = XtCreateManagedWidget("keyboard",
                                   xmRowColumnWidgetClass,
                                   panel, wargs, n);
  /*
   * Create the keyboard buttons. This order makes it
   * look like a typical desktop calculator.
   */
  create_button("1", keyboard);
  create_button("2", keyboard);
  create_button("3", keyboard);
  create_button("+", keyboard);
```

```
    create_button("4", keyboard);
    create_button("5", keyboard);
    create_button("6", keyboard);
    create_button("-", keyboard);
    create_button("7", keyboard);
    create_button("8", keyboard);
    create_button("9", keyboard);
    create_button("*", keyboard);
    create_button("0", keyboard);
    create_button(".", keyboard);
    create_button("=", keyboard);
    create_button("/", keyboard);
    /*
     *  Create a quit button and add a callback that
     *  tells bc to exit.
     */
    qbutton = xs_create_quit_button(keyboard);
    XtAddCallback(qbutton, XmNactivateCallback, quit_bc, NULL);
    /*
     * Add callback get_from_bc() --  invoked when input
     * is available from stdin.
     */
    XtAddInput(fileno(stdin), XtInputReadMask,
            get_from_bc, display);
    /*
     * Exec the program "bc" and set up pipes
     * between it and us.
     */
    xs_talkto("bc");

    XtRealizeWidget(toplevel);
    XtMainLoop();
}
```

Fig. 5.12 shows the widget tree created by **xbc**. The calculator consists of a display area (an XmText widget) and a keyboard area (an XmRowColumn widget). Both of these widgets are managed by an XmPanedWindow widget. The XmRowColumn widget manages five rows of buttons used for input to the calculator.

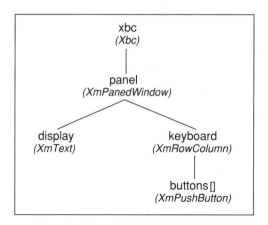

Figure 5.12 The xbc widget tree.[1]

The function **create_button()** takes two arguments, a label for the calculator key and the parent widget of the button. The function creates a single XmPushButton widget and adds the callback **send_to_bc()** to the **XmNactivateCallback** list. The name of the widget is also given as client data, to be used as a string that is sent to **bc** when the user selects the button. This function is defined as:

```
Widget create_button(name, parent)
  char     *name;
  Widget   parent;
{
  extern void send_to_bc();
  Widget       button;
  /*
   * Create a single button and attach an activate callback.
   */
  button = XtCreateManagedWidget(name,
                                 xmPushButtonWidgetClass,
                                 parent, NULL, 0);
  XtAddCallback(button, XmNactivateCallback, send_to_bc,name);
  return (button);
}
```

1.The brackets after the button widget in this figure signifies many button widgets.

The main program also creates a quit button, using the libXs function defined in Chapter 4, and registers an **XmNactivateCallback** function. This callback prints the string "**quit**" when the user activates the button, causing the **bc** process to exit before **xbc**.

```
void quit_bc(w, client_data, call_data)
    Widget    w;
    caddr_t   client_data, call_data;
{
    /*
     * Tell bc to quit.
     */
    fprintf(stdout, "quit\n");
}
```

The line

XtAddInput(fileno(stdin),XtInputReadMask,get_from_bc,display);

in the main program registers an input callback. Whenever input is pending from **stdin**, the Intrinsics calls the function **get_from_bc()** with the **display** widget as client data. We will look at this function shortly, but first we must discuss how **xbc** communicates with **bc**.

Before entering **XtMainLoop()**, **xbc** calls the function **xs_talkto()**. This function starts up the program **bc** and establishes a two-way connection between **bc** and **xbc**, by creating two pipes that connect the **stdin** and **stdout** of the parent process (**xbc**) to the **stdout** and **stdin** respectively the child process (**bc**). This function can be used to establish similar pipes between any two programs.   Initially, **xs_talkto()** creates two pipes and *forks* a new process. The **fork()** function is a UNIX system call that creates a duplicate of the calling process, and returns the *process id* of the newly created process to the parent. Both processes have access to the pipes created earlier. The calling process closes its **stdin** and **stdout** file descriptors and replaces them, using **dup()**, with one end of each pipe. Similarly, the forked process closes its input and output files and replaces them by the other end of the same pipes. Finally the forked process is overlaid by cmd by calling **execlp()**. Notice that this function is a bit over-simplified in that it performs no error checking.

```
#include <stdio.h>
void xs_talkto(cmd)
    char   *cmd;
{
  int   to_child[2], /* pipe descriptors from parent->child */
        to_parent[2];/* pipe descriptors from child->parent */
  int   pid;
  pipe(to_child);
  pipe(to_parent);
```

```
    if (pid = fork(), pid == 0){      /* in the child    */
       close(0);                      /* redirect stdin */
       dup(to_child[0]);
       close(1);                      /* redirect stdout*/
       dup(to_parent[1]);
       close(to_child[0]);            /* close pipes     */
       close(to_child[1]);
       close(to_parent[0]);
       close(to_parent[1]);
       execlp(cmd, cmd, NULL);        /* exec the new cmd */
    }
    else if (pid > 0){                /* in the parent   */
       close(0);                      /* redirect stdin */
       dup(to_parent[0]);
       close(1);                      /* redirect stdout  */
       dup(to_child[1]);
       setbuf(stdout, NULL);          /* no buffered output */
       close(to_child[0]);            /* close pipes */
       close(to_child[1]);
       close(to_parent[0]);
       close(to_parent[1]);
    }
    else {                            /* error!        */
       fprintf(stderr,"Couldn't fork process %s\n", cmd);
       exit(1);
    }
}
```

The UNIX standard I/O (stdio) package normally buffers its output. The function **setbuf()** turns off buffering so that all output from the parent process is sent to the child process immediately. Unfortunately, we can only unbuffer the output in the parent process. To avoid problems, both processes should used unbuffered output, but we do not have access to the child process.

After calling **xs_talkto()**, when **xbc** reads from **stdin**, it is really reading from the pipe connected to the output of **bc**. When **xbc** writes to **stdout** it is actually writing to a pipe connected to the input of **bc**. Notice that **bc** does not have to be modified in any way. As far as **bc** is concerned, it is reading from **stdin** and writing to **stdout**.

This approach can be used to create window-based interfaces to many UNIX applications. However, it is not always as simple as we might wish, partially because of inconsistencies in the output of UNIX commands. In spite of UNIX conventions that encourage small applications that can be piped together in various combinations, the output of UNIX applications is often inconsistent. For example, many applications add headers at the top of each page. Others format their output differently depending on the options specified on the command line.

The same utility may also behave differently on different vendor's machines. Therefore, one of the difficulties in using existing UNIX applications this way is sending the correct input to the application and parsing the results.

The pipe mechanism itself can also cause other problems. Handling all the exceptions and error conditions that can occur when using two-way pipes can be difficult. For example, this version of **talkto()** neglects the problems that can arise when either process exits unexpectedly, and also does not attempt to do any signal handling. Problems can also occur if the maximum buffer size of a pipe is exceeded. This is usually not a problem for **xbc** because only a few digits cross the pipes at any time.

The callback function **send_to_bc()**, invoked each time an **xbc** button is activated, sends a command to **bc**. As a first pass, we could define this function as:

```
/* INCOMPLETE VERSION */
void send_to_bc(w, buffer, call_data)
   Widget      w;
   char        *buffer;
   caddr_t     call_data;
{
   fprintf(stdout, "%s", buffer);   /* Not Good Enough! */
   xs_insert_string(display, buffer);
}
```

This simplified function prints the characters given as client data to **stdout**, (now attached to the input of **bc**), and calls **xs_insert_string()**, a yet-to-be-defined function that appends a string to the current contents of the **display** widget. Although this function shows the general idea, we must write a slightly more complex function to make **xbc** act like a real calculator and also send correct input to **bc**. The complete **send_to_bc()** function is:

```
void send_to_bc(w, buffer, call_data)
   Widget     w;
   char       *buffer;
   XmAnyCallbackStruct *call_data;
{
   static int  start_new_entry = TRUE;
   /*
    * If this is the beginning of a new operand,
    * clear the display.
    */
   if(start_new_entry){
     reset_display();
     start_new_entry = FALSE;
   }
```

```
switch (buffer[0]) {
/*
 * If the user entered and '=', send bc a newline, clear
 * the display, and get ready for a new operand.
 */
case '=':
  fprintf(stdout, "%s", XmTextGetString(display));
  fprintf(stdout, "\n");
  reset_display();
  start_new_entry = TRUE;
  break;
/*
 * If this is an operator, get the previous operand
 * from the display buffer, and send it to bc before
 * sending the operand.
 */
case '-':
case '+':
case '/':
case '*':
case '^':
  fprintf(stdout, "%s", XmTextGetString(display));
  fprintf(stdout, "%s", buffer);
  reset_display();
  break;
/*
 * Anything else must be a digit, so append it to the
 * display buffer.
 */
default:
  xs_insert_string(display, buffer);
}
fflush(stdout);
}
```

This function creates an interface between the input **bc** expects and the behavior we expect from a desktop calculator. A flag, **start_new_entry**, indicates when one calculation sequence has been completed and another one is beginning. If this flag is **TRUE**, the calculator display is cleared and reset using the function **reset_display()**.

Normally, a calculator displays the results of a calculation when the user presses the "=" key. However, **bc** evaluates an expression when a newline character is entered. The first case ('=') in the **switch** statement uses the function **XmTextGetString()** to retrieve the contents of the XmText widget, sends it to **bc** by printing it to **stdout**, and then prints a newline character to get **bc** to evaluate the expression. It also sets the flag **start_new_entry** to **TRUE** to signal the end of a calculation sequence, and calls **reset_display()** to clear the **display** widget.

Calculators display numbers as they are entered, but do not usually display math operators. Therefore, all operators are sent to **bc**, but not displayed. When an operator is selected, **send_to_bc()** prints the current contents of the **display** widget, followed by the operator. It then clears the **display** widget to prepare for the next operand.

The default case handles all digits and calls **xs_insert_string()** to insert the digit at the current position in the **display** widget. The digit is not sent to **bc** until the user presses an operator or the "=" button or any operand.

The function **xs_insert_string()** simply gets the current insert position of the XmText widget and uses the function

> **XmTextReplace(widget, to, from, new_text)**

to replace a zero length string at this position with the text to be appended.

```
/*************************************************************
 * xs_insert_string(): insert a string in an XmText widget
 *************************************************************/
#include <X11/StringDefs.h>
#include <X11/Intrinsic.h>
#include <Xm/Xm.h>
#include <Xm/Text.h>
void xs_insert_string(text_widget, buf)
    Widget    text_widget;
    char      *buf;
{
  int pos = XmTextGetInsertionPosition(text_widget);
  XmTextReplace(text_widget, pos, pos, buf);
}
```

The input callback **get_from_bc()** handles output from **bc**. This function reads from **stdin**, and, after adding a **NULL** to the end of the buffer, calls **xs_insert_string()** to display the string.

```
void get_from_bc(w, fid, id)
  Widget       w;
  int          *fid;
  XtInputId    *id;
{
  char         buf[BUFSIZ];
  int          nbytes, i;
```

```
    /*
     * Get all pending input and append it to the display
     * widget. Discard lines that begin with a newline.
     */
    nbytes = read(*fid, buf, BUFSIZ);
    if (nbytes && buf[0] != '\n') {
    /*
     * Null terminate the string at the first newline,
     * or at the end of the bytes read.
     */
    for(i=0;i<nbytes;i++)
      if(buf[i] == '\n')
          buf[i] = '\0';
      buf[nbytes] = '\0';
      xs_insert_string(display, buf);
    }
}
```

The only complication here is that this function must handle the newline characters that **bc** prints after each result, by ignoring the data if the first character is a newline character and by stripping off any other newlines that appear in the buffer.

The last function, **reset_display()**, simply clears the **display** widget and sets the current insert position to zero.

```
reset_display()
{
  /*
   * Clear the text buffer and go to position 1.
   */
  XmTextSetString(display, "");
  XmTextSetInsertionPosition(display, 0);
}
```

5.9 SUMMARY

This chapter examined many of the events supported by the X Window System and discussed the event-handling mechanisms provided by the Xt Intrinsics. Xlib reports events whenever any aspect of a window's environment changes. The Intrinsics provide a higher level interface to the X event mechanism and also adds the ability to handle input from sources other than the X server using a similar event handling mechanism. Timeout events and WorkProcs provide a simple way to perform tasks not directly related to user input.

This chapter did not discuss some of the most powerful and interesting events provided by X, communication events, which are discussed in Chapter 11.

6

USING COLOR

Previous chapters demonstrated some simple applications using the Xt Intrinsics and the Motif widget set. In these programs, the widgets completely controlled how they displayed the information specified by an application. The next few chapters discuss Xlib facilities that allow applications to display text and graphics directly in windows. Discussing these facilities gives us a better understanding of X and allows us to write applications that cannot be built from existing widgets alone. Before discussing the Xlib text and graphics functions, we need to understand the color model used by X. This chapter discusses how X uses color, and presents a simple color editor as an example.

6.1 THE X COLOR MODEL

X uses a flexible color model that provides a common interface to many different types of display hardware. The color model allows a properly designed application to run equally well on a variety of monochrome and color screens.

It is particularly difficult to design a color model for a window system that supports multiple processes, because most color screens support a limited number of colors. For example, a typical color screen with four bit planes of display memory supports only 16 colors at one time. Often, these 16 colors can be chosen from a large palette of available colors. One common configuration provides a palette of nearly 16 million different colors; however, on a screen with four bit planes, only 16 of these colors can be displayed at any given time.

This might not be a serious problem for systems where one graphics application controls the entire screen. However, in a multiprocess window-based system, many applications are present on the screen at once, and therefore each application competes for the limited number of colors available.

One way to solve this problem is to support only a fixed set of colors used by all applications. Some low-cost personal computers use this approach by providing a small set of basic colors: red, green, blue, magenta, yellow, and so on. All applications must choose from one of these preset colors. Using a fixed palette of colors is not acceptable for X, because portability between many architectures was a basic design goal.

Instead, X uses a unique approach that allows each application to use as many colors as it needs, but also encourages applications to share colors. The approach used by X is based on an allocation scheme, in which an application requests the server to allocate only those colors it needs. If two applications request the same color, the server gives each application a pointer to the same color cell.

6.1.1   Colormaps

The X color model uses a *colormap*. A colormap, sometimes called a color lookup table, is an array of colors. Applications refer to colors using an index into the colormap. The colormap provides a level of indirection between the color index used by an application and the color displayed on the screen. Most displays provide a hardware colormap. To draw a point on the screen, applications place a value in the appropriate location of the display's *frame buffer*. A frame buffer is a large contiguous area of memory. The frame buffer must contain at least one bit for each screen location (pixel) on the screen. The amount of memory corresponding to one bit per pixel is known as a *bit plane*. The number of colors that a screen can display at one time is determined by the number of bit planes in the frame buffer, according to the relation *colors* = 2^{planes}. For example, a frame buffer with three bit planes can support 8 different colors. The value in each pixel of the frame buffer is used as an index into the colormap. The value stored in that location of the colormap is then used to determine the color and intensity of the color shown on the screen for that pixel. Fig. 6.1 shows how a typical hardware display uses the colormap to convert a value in the frame buffer to a color on the screen. This figure illustrates a display with a 3 plane frame buffer. The hardware scans each cell, or pixel, in the frame buffer, and uses the combined value of all planes as an index to the colormap. The value stored in this location in the colormap is then converted to an intensity on the screen. Fig. 6.1 shows a 4 bit colormap for a monochrome display. A display with a single 4 bit colormap and a single color gun can display 16 levels of a single color. Typically, a colormap supports more color intensities by adding more bits to the lookup table. Also, color displays typically divide the colormap into different fields to control each of the red, green, and blue color components.

Each X window has a virtual colormap associated with it. Before the colors in this colormap are reflected on the screen, the colormap must be *installed* into the hardware colormap. Some hardware displays allow multiple colormaps to be installed at once, but many support only one colormap at a time. By convention, X window managers install the colormap of the current focus window, allowing the application using this window to be displayed using correct colors. However, when this approach is used, other applications on the screen are unlikely to be displayed in their true colors, because the colors stored in the hardware color map change, but the indexes used by applications do not.

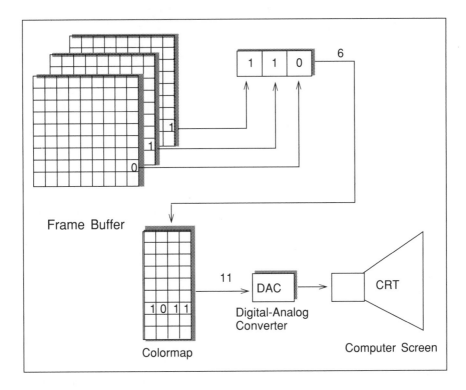

Figure 6.1 A Typical Colormap Architecture.

Applications can often share the same colormap. By default, windows inherit the colormap of their parent, and most applications can use the default colormap of the root window. Applications can use the macro

DefaultColormap(display, screen)

to access the default colormap of any screen. This default colormap is installed by the X server when the server is started. The server normally allocates two colors, black and white, from the default colormap. All other color cells can be allocated by clients. (See Section 6.1.3). Applications can also create their own colormaps. A programmer might consider creating a new colormap when an application needs many colors, requires colors to be placed in particular locations in the colormap, or needs to alter the contents of the colormap dynamically. Applications can use the function

XCreateColormap(display, window, visual, alloc)

to create a colormap. The function returns a unique ID for the new colormap. **XCreateColormap()** uses the **window** argument only to determine the screen where the colormap is used, so this window does not need to be the window associated with the color-map, but only a window on the same screen as that on which the colormap will be used. This function also requires the programmer to specify the *visual type* of the screen. Every screen supports one or more visual types. A visual type is represented by a structure, **XVisual**, de-fined in the header file Xlib.h. This structure contains information about the screen, includ-ing how many colormap entries it supports, whether it supports monochrome, color, gray scale only, and so on. It is possible for a screen to support more than one visual type, al-though it is currently more common for hardware to support only one. The previous discus-sion of colormaps applies most directly to a screen whose visual type is **PseudoColor**. The visual types recognized by X are:

- **PseudoColor**. On a **PseudoColor** screen, pixel values index a colormap to produce independent, dynamically changeable red, green, and blue values. Most of the discussion in this chapter assumes a PseudoColor visual type.

- **StaticColor**. This type is similar to **PseudoColor**, except that the colormap con-tains predefined (fixed) values.

- **GrayScale**. This type is similar to **PseudoColor**, except that only a single color (usually gray) is available.

- **StaticGray**. Screens with a **StaticGray** visual type have a fixed, predetermined monochrome colormap.

- **DirectColor**. Screens that support **DirectColor** decompose the pixel values into separate red, green, and blue fields. Each component is then used as an index into a sepa-rate color lookup table.

- **TrueColor**. This visual type is similar to **DirectColor** except that the colormap contains pre-defined, fixed values.

The default visual structure for a particular screen can be obtained using the Xlib macro:

DefaultVisual(display, screen)

Some hardware supports multiple visual types, in which case the default visual type may not be the correct one to use. You can also get a valid visual type using the Xlib function:

XMatchVisualInfo(display, screen, depth, class, &info)

This function returns a status of **TRUE** if it was able to find a visual type to match the speci-fied screen and depth. It fills in the **info** argument, which is an **XVisualInfo** struct. This structure contains a variety of information about the visual type. In particular, the **visual** member contains a valid visual type. For example, if we wish to determine if we can use a PseudoColor visual type on a certain screen, we could write a code segment like:

```
Status        result;
Display       *dpy   = XtDisplay(widget);
int           screen = DefaultScreen(dpy);
XVisualInfo   info;
Visual        *my_visual;
result = XMatchVisualInfo(dpy, screen,
                          DefaultDepth(dpy, screen),
                          PseudoColor, &info))
if(result)
   my_visual = info.visual;
```

Colormaps contain no colors when first created. Before an application can store colors in a colormap, it must *allocate* color cells. The last argument to **XCreateColormap()** specifies how many entries in the colormap should be allocated initially. This argument must be one of the constants **AllocNone** or **AllocAll**. The value **AllocNone** must be used for screens with a static visual type.

The function

XInstallColormap(display, cmap)

installs a colormap as the current colormap used by the display. When a colormap is installed, the screen instantly reflects the colors in the new colormap, and the server sends a **ColormapNotify** event to all windows associated with the newly installed colormap. By convention, this function should not be used by applications. X window managers use this function to install the colormap associated with an application's top-level window when the application gets the input focus. By default, a window inherits its parent's colormap. It is common for applications to inherit the colormap of the root window. Applications that need to use a different colormap can use the function

XSetWindowColormap(display, window, cmap)

to associate a colormap with a window. Applications that wish to use their own colormap should use this function to set the colormap of their top-level window and rely on the window manager to install it for them.

Applications can use the function

XFreeColormap(display, id)

to free a colormap when it is no longer needed. The **id** argument must specify a resource ID of a colormap.

6.1.2 Standard Colormaps

X supports the concept of *standard colormaps*. Colormaps may be stored in a property (see Chapter 11) in the X server, where they can be retrieved by any application that wishes to use them. Xlib defines the property names for several standard colormaps, including

RGB_DEFAULT_MAP, **RGB_BEST_MAP**, and **RGB_GRAY_MAP**. Notice that only the *names* of these colormaps are defined. The colormaps, as well as the exact organization of the color-maps, are not precisely defined. These colormaps exist only if some application (most often a window manager) defines them and stores them in the server.

A standard colormap can be stored in the server using the Xlib function:

XSetStandardColormap(display, window, cmap, property)

Once a standard colormap has been stored in the server, applications can use the Xlib function

XGetStandardColormap(display, window, &cmap, property)

to retrieve a standard colormap from the server.

6.1.3 Allocating Colors

Once an application has access to a colormap, it can allocate colors in that colormap. The Xlib functions that allocate colors make use of an **XColor** structure. This structure includes the members:

```
unsigned long  pixel;
unsigned short red, green, blue;
char           flags;
```

Colors are specified by the intensity of each of their red, green, and blue (RGB) compo-nents. The values of these components can range from 0 to 65535, where 0 corresponds to the lowest intensity of a color component, and 65535 corresponds to the highest intensity. The X server scales these values to the range of color intensities supported by the hardware. For example, we can initialize an **XColor** structure representing bright white with:

```
XColor color;
color.red   = 65535;
color.green = 65535;
color.blue  = 65535;
```

We can initialize a color structure to represent bright red with:

```
XColor color;
color.red   = 65535;
color.green = 0;
color.blue  = 0;
```

Color cells of a colormap can be *read-only* or *read-write*. The color components in a read-only cell can not be altered, and therefore can be shared between all applications that use the same colormap. Attempts to change the value of a read-only cell generate an error. A read-write cell cannot be shared between applications, because the application that allocated the cell can change it at any time.

The Xlib function

XAllocColor(display, cmap, &color)

allocates a read-only entry in a colormap. This function requires an **XColor** structure containing the RGB components of the color to be allocated. If some other application has already allocated the same color as a read-only cell, the same cell is reused and the **pixel** member of the **XColor** structure is set to the value of the existing colormap cell. Otherwise, **XAllocColor()** attempts to store the given color components in the next available cell of the colormap **cmap**. If successful, the function fills in the **pixel** member of the **XColor** structure to the newly allocated color cell and returns a status of **TRUE**.

To see how this function is used, let's write a function named **get_pixel()** that allocates a color cell from the default colormap and loads it with a color. The function takes a widget and the red, green, and blue components of the desired color as input. It returns a pixel index that refers to the specified color.

```
get_pixel(w, red, green, blue)
   Widget  w;
   int     red, green, blue;
{
   Display *dpy =  XtDisplay(w);
   int      scr =  DefaultScreen(dpy);
   Colormap cmap = DefaultColormap(dpy, scr);
   XColor   color;
   /*
    * Fill in the color structure.
    */
   color.red   = red;
   color.green = green;
   color.blue  = blue;
   /*
    * Try to allocate the color.
    */
   if(XAllocColor(dpy, cmap, &color))
      return (color.pixel);
   else {
      printf("Warning: Couldn't allocate requested color\n");
      return (BlackPixel(dpy, scr));
   }
}
```

Whenever color allocation fails, applications should always be prepared to use one of the default values, usually black or white, available in all visual types. Applications can use the macros

```
BlackPixel(display, screen)
WhitePixel(display, screen)
```

to access the default pixels representing black and white on a particular screen.

Because new colors are allocated in the next available cell of the colormap, applications must not assume that the index representing a particular color in a shared colormap is the same each time the application runs. The exact index used to refer to a particular color depends on the order in which all applications request the colors.

Applications sometimes need to know the color components stored in any pixel index of a colormap. The function

```
XQueryColor(display, cmap, &color)
```

fills in the RGB components of the **color** structure corresponding to the **pixel** member of that structure. The function

```
XQueryColors(display, cmap, colors, ncolors)
```

fills in the RGB components of an array of colors.

Sometimes applications need to set up the colormap in a specific way, controlling the colors in each cell. Such applications should first allocate the number of color cells needed, using the function:

```
XAllocColorCells(display, cmap, contig, planes,
                 nplanes, cells, ncells)
```

This function allocates *ncells* * $2^{nplanes}$ read-write color cells. Applications that do not need to control the bit planes of the screen can specify **nplanes** as zero.[1]

The function **XAllocColorCells()** allocates read-write color cells. If the application requires the color cells to be contiguous, it must set the **contig** argument to **TRUE**. Otherwise the planes and cells are allocated from wherever they are available. **XAllocColorCells()** fails and returns a status of **FALSE** if it cannot allocate the exact number of planes and cells. If the function is able to allocate the requested number of colors, it returns the allocated color cells in **cells**, which must be an array of unsigned integers created by the application. If the application requests one or more planes, the **planes** argument, which must also be an array of unsigned integers, returns the allocated planes.

Once color cells are allocated, applications can use the function

```
XStoreColor(display, cmap, &color)
```

to alter the values stored in each cell of the colormap. The **color** argument must be an **XColor** structure containing both the **pixel** value and the **red, green** and **blue** values

---

1. A common mistake is to attempt to allocate all planes and all color cells. This generates more colors than the screen supports. For example, on a screen with 4 bit-planes (and therefore 16 colors), a request such as

    XAllocColorCells(display, cmap, TRUE, planes, 4, cells, 16);

    attempts to allocate $16 * 2^4$, or 256 colors.

to store in that cell. Let's see how this works by defining a function, **load_rgb()**, that loads the colors red, green, and blue into three consecutive color cells of the default colormap. The pixel indexes are assigned to the parameters **red**, **green**, and **blue**.

```
load_rgb(w, red, green, blue)
    Widget  w;
    int     *red, *green, *blue;
{
    Display *dpy  = XtDisplay(w);
    int      scr  = DefaultScreen(dpy);
    Colormap cmap = DefaultColormap(dpy, scr);
    XColor   color;
    unsigned int  cells[3];
   /*
    *  Try to allocate three consecutive color cells.
    */
    if(XAllocColorCells(dpy, cmap, TRUE,
                        NULL, 0, cells, 3)){
      /*
       *  If successful, store Red in the first allocated cell,
       *   green in the second and blue in the third.
       */
      color.red = 65535;
      color.green = color.blue = 0;
      *red = color.pixel = cells[0];
      XStoreColor(dpy, cmap, &color);

      color.green = 65535;
      color.red =  color.blue = 0;
      *green = color.pixel = cells[1];
      XStoreColor(dpy, cmap, &color);

      color.blue = 65535;
      color.red = color.green = 0;
      *blue = color.pixel = cells[2];
      XStoreColor(dpy, cmap, &color);
    }
    else{
      printf("Warning:Couldn't allocate color cells\n");
      *blue = *red = *green = BlackPixel(dpy, scr);
    }
}
```

The function

XStoreColors(display, colormap, colors, ncolors)

stores values in multiple color cells with a single request. The **colors** argument must be an array of **XColor** structures and **ncolors** indicates the number of colors in the array.

Xlib also provides functions that allow applications to refer to colors by their symbolic names. Color names are stored in a database along with their RGB components. The location and format of this database is operating-system-dependent. On UNIX systems, the color database files are usually found in the directory /usr/lib/X11/. The file rgb.txt contains a human-readable version of the database.

The color database distributed with X defines many common colors, and users can add additional colors. The function

XLookupColor(display, cmap, name, &color, &exact)

returns the color components corresponding to a named color in the color database. If the color exists in the database, **XLookupColor()** fills in the **red**, **green**, and **blue** members of the **XColor** structures **color** and **exact**. The **color** argument contains the closest color supported by the hardware, while **exact** indicates the precise value of color components specified in the color database. The **cmap** argument must specify a colormap ID. **XLookupColor()** uses this colormap only to determine the visual type of the screen on which the color is used. This function does not allocate or store the color in the colormap.

Applications can also allocate colors by name, using the function:

XAllocNamedColor(display, cmap, name, &color, &exact)

This function is similar to **XAllocColor()**, except that the color is specified by name. Let's use **XAllocNamedColor()** to write a function called **get_pixel_by_name()**. This function is similar to the **get_pixel()** function described earlier, but it returns a pixel index for a named color.

```
get_pixel_by_name(w, colorname)
  Widget w;
  char  *colorname;
{
  Display *dpy  = XtDisplay(w);
  int      scr  = DefaultScreen(dpy);
  Colormap cmap = DefaultColormap(dpy, scr);
  XColor   color, ignore;
  /*
   * Allocate the named color.
   */
  if(XAllocNamedColor(dpy, cmap, colorname, &color, &ignore))
    return (color.pixel);
```

```
    else{
      printf("Warning: Couldn't allocate color %s\n",colorname);
      return (BlackPixel(dpy, scr));
    }
  }
```

6.2 EXAMPLE: A COLORMAP EDITOR

This section demonstrates how these Xlib color functions can be used in a program named **coloredit** that allows the user to edit a colormap interactively. The color editor allocates color cells in a colormap and allows the user to alter the red, green, and blue components stored in each cell. This program allows the user to change the colors used by other applications by installing a new colormap which duplicates the default colormap of the screen. Changes made to the colormap are only effective while the color editor has the input focus (and therefore has its colormap installed).

Fig. 6.2 shows the window layout of the **coloredit** program. The rows of widgets near the top of the editor display the colors available for editing. The user chooses a color cell to be edited by selecting one of these colors using the mouse. The selected color can then be edited using the three sliders located below the color pane. Each slider allows the user to set the intensity of one component of the current color. When the user selects a color, each of the three sliders moves to the position corresponding to the red, green, and blue values of the selected color. An XmLabel widget also displays the numeric values of the red, green, and blue components of the current color.

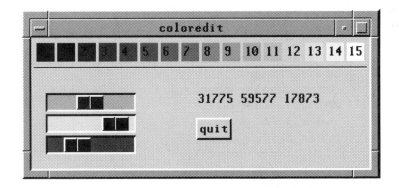

Figure 6.2 The coloredit program.

6.2.1   The Header File: coloredit.h

The file coloredit.h includes the Xt Intrinsics and Motif header files for the widgets used by **coloredit**, declares several callbacks, and defines the resources and global parameters used in the example.

```
/******************************************************
 * coloredit.h: Header file for coloredit
 ******************************************************/

#include <X11/StringDefs.h>
#include <X11/Intrinsic.h>
#include <Xm/Xm.h>
#include <Xm/BulletinB.h>
#include <Xm/Separator.h>
#include <Xm/Scale.h>
#include <Xm/RowColumn.h>
#include <Xm/Label.h>
#include <Xm/PushB.h>
#include "libXs.h"

#define MAXCOLORS    256

Display     *dpy;
Colormap     my_colormap;
XColor       current_color;
int          ncolors;

Widget       red_slider,
             blue_slider,
             green_slider,
             color_display_panel;
void         slider_selected();
void         red_slider_moved();
void         green_slider_moved();
void         blue_slider_moved();
void         set_current_color();
Widget       make_slider();
Widget       create_color_bar();
```

The global variable, **ncolors**, stores the total number of colors available to be edited. **MAXCOLORS** determines the maximum number of colors the program can edit. The variable

my_colormap stores the ID of an editable colormap, while **current_color** is an **XColor** structure used to set individual color cells.

6.2.2   The Source File, coloredit.c

The file coloredit.c contains the main body of the **coloredit** program. After initializing the Intrinsics, the program uses the Xlib macro **DisplayCells()** to determine the number of colors the screen supports. If the number of color cells supported by the screen exceeds **MAXCOLORS**, the variable **ncolors** is limited to **MAXCOLORS**. After creating the widgets used by the application, the program then initializes an array of **XColor** structures to represent each color cell in the default colormap. The color components in each cell of the default colormap are loaded into the **XColor** array using **XQueryColors()**. Then, we can make a copy of the default colormap by creating a new color map and storing the colors that were retrieved from the default colormap. The new colormap contains the same colors as the default colormap, but all colors are writeable by the **coloredit** program. Finally, **XSetWindow-Colormap()** sets the colormap of the editor's top level window to the new colormap.[2]

```
/*************************************************
 * coloredit.c: A simple color editor.
 *************************************************/
#include "coloredit.h"

main(argc, argv)
  int     argc;
  char    *argv[];
{
  Widget     toplevel, bb, sliders, rc;
  Colormap   def_colormap;
  XColor     Colors[MAXCOLORS];
  int        i;
  /*
   * Initialize the Intrinsics and save pointer to the display.
   */
  toplevel = XtInitialize(argv[0], "Coloredit", NULL, 0,
                          &argc, argv);
  dpy = XtDisplay(toplevel);
  /*
   * Determine the number of colors to be edited.
   */
  ncolors = DisplayCells(dpy, DefaultScreen(dpy));
```

---

2. Caution! This requires an ICCCM-compliant window manager, such as Motif's mwm. This program will not work without such a window manager.

```
if(ncolors > MAXCOLORS) ncolors = MAXCOLORS;
/*
 * Create a base to hold everything.
 */
rc = XtCreateManagedWidget("base",xmRowColumnWidgetClass,
                         toplevel, NULL, 0);
/*
 * Create a grid of buttons, one for each
 * color to be edited.
 */
create_color_bar(rc);
/*
 * A separator widget looks nice, between the colors
 * and the controls.
 */
XtCreateManagedWidget("sep", xmSeparatorWidgetClass,
                    rc, NULL, 0);
/*
 * Put the controls inside an XmBulletinBoard widget
 */
bb = XtCreateManagedWidget("controls",
                         xmBulletinBoardWidgetClass,
                         rc, NULL, 0);
/*
 * Use an XmLabel widget to display the current rgb values.
 */
color_display_panel =
      XtCreateManagedWidget("display",
                         xmLabelWidgetClass,
                         bb, NULL,0);
/*
 * Create a row column widget containing three sliders,
 * one for each color component.
 */
sliders = XtCreateManagedWidget("sliderpanel",
                            xmRowColumnWidgetClass,
                            bb, NULL, 0);
red_slider   = make_slider("red", sliders,
                            red_slider_moved);
green_slider = make_slider("green", sliders,
                            green_slider_moved);
blue_slider  = make_slider("blue",  sliders,
```

```
                        blue_slider_moved);
/*
 * Add a quit button.
 */
xs_create_quit_button(bb);
/*
 * Get the ID of the default colormap.
 */
def_colormap = DefaultColormap(dpy, DefaultScreen(dpy));
for( i = 0; i < ncolors; i++ ) {
  Colors[i].pixel = i;
  Colors[i].flags = DoRed|DoGreen|DoBlue;
}
XQueryColors(dpy, def_colormap, Colors, ncolors);
my_colormap =
    XCreateColormap(dpy, DefaultRootWindow(dpy),
                    DefaultVisual(dpy, DefaultScreen(dpy)),
                    AllocAll);
XStoreColors(dpy, my_colormap, Colors, ncolors);
/*
 * Initialize the pixel member of the global color struct
 * To the first editable color cell.
 */
current_color.pixel = 0;

XtRealizeWidget(toplevel);

XSetWindowColormap(dpy, XtWindow(toplevel), my_colormap);

XtMainLoop();
}
```

Fig. 6.3 shows the widget tree created by the **coloredit** program.

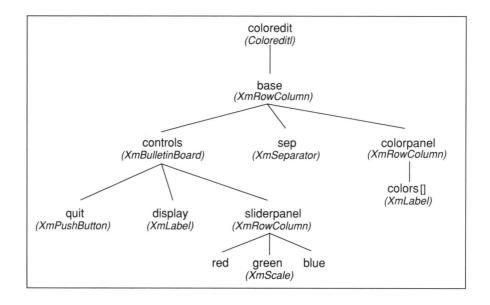

Figure 6.3 The coloredit widget tree.

The function **make_slider()** creates an XmScale widget used to control one color component and assigns the associated callbacks. The range between the minimum and maximum values of the slider allows the program to map directly between the position of a slider and the color component controlled by the slider. The minimum value of the slider, zero, corresponds to zero contribution from that color component, while the maximum valuator position (65535) corresponds to a one hundred percent contribution from that component. Functions on the **XmNvalueChangedCallback** list are invoked when the user clicks the mouse inside the XmScale widget, while functions registered as **XmNdragCallback** functions are invoked when the users drags the slider by holding a mouse button down while moving the sprite. The same function, **slider_moved()**, is registered for both of these callback lists.

```
Widget make_slider(name, parent, callback)
  char  *name;
  Widget parent;
  void (*callback)();
{
  Widget   w;
  int      n;
  Arg      wargs[10];
  /*
```

```
 * Create an XmScale widget.
 */
n = 0;
XtSetArg(wargs[n], XmNminimum, 0); n++;
XtSetArg(wargs[n], XmNmaximum, 65535); n++;

w = XtCreateManagedWidget(name, xmScaleWidgetClass,
                          parent, wargs, n);
/*
 * Add callbacks to be invoked when the slider moves.
 */
XtAddCallback(w, XmNvalueChangedCallback,callback,NULL);
XtAddCallback(w, XmNdragCallback, callback, NULL);

return (w);
}
```

The function **create_colorbar()** creates a row of XmLabel widgets, one for each color to be edited, managed by an XmRowColumn widget. This function sets the background color of each widget to one of the pixel values allocated for editing. An event handler is registered for **ButtonPress** events for each widget to set the current pixel index when a color is selected. It might seem as though it would be better to use XmPushButton widgets for the colors, since buttons provide a callback that allows them to be activated by a button press. However, Motif's automatic color generation gets in the way in this case. Because Xm-PushButton widgets have top and bottom shadow colors, and Motif generates these automatically from the foreground and background colors of each widget, we cannot create a widget for each color supported by the screen. Motif would automatically attempt to create up to three times as many colors as the screen supports. Using the XmLabel widget, which has no shadowing effect, is one way to get around this problem. Another way would be to specify the shadow colors to be the same as the background color of each widget, which would of course eliminate the three-dimensional look.

```
Widget create_color_bar(parent)
  Widget parent;
{
  Widget     panel;
  WidgetList colors;
  int        i, n;
  char       name[10];
  Arg        wargs[10];
  colors = (WidgetList) XtMalloc( ncolors * sizeof(Widget));

  /*
```

```
 * Create the row column manager to hold all
 * color buttons.
 */
n = 0;
panel = XtCreateManagedWidget("colorpanel",
                                xmRowColumnWidgetClass,
                                parent, wargs, n);
/*
 * Create ncolors widgets. Use the relative color
 * cell number as the name of each color. Add a
 * XmNactivateCallback for each cell with the color
 * index as client_data.
 */
for(i=0;i<ncolors;i++){
 n = 0;
 XtSetArg(wargs[n], XtNbackground, i); n++;
 sprintf(name,"%d",i);
 colors[i] = XtCreateWidget(name, xmLabelWidgetClass,
                                panel, wargs, n);
 XtAddEventHandler(colors[i], ButtonPressMask, FALSE,
                   set_current_color, i);
 }
 XtManageChildren(colors, ncolors);

 return panel;
}
```

Whenever the user moves a slider, the slider's corresponding callback function is invoked. These functions set the corresponding member of the global **XColor** structure, **current_color**, to the value indicated by the current position of the slider, extracted from the XmScale widget's call data. The **current_color** structure is used to update the color currently being edited and always contains the current value of each color component. When the user selects a color, the function **set_current_color()** sets the **pixel** member of **current_color**. Before each callback returns, the function **update_color()** is called to update the color components displayed in the XmLabel widget. Each slider has its own similar callback. The red slider's callback function is defined as:

```
void red_slider_moved(w, client_data, call_data)
    Widget    w;
    caddr_t   client_data;
    XmScaleCallbackStruct *call_data;
{
 /*
```

```
 * Set the red color components of  the global
 * current_color structure.
 */
current_color.red =  call_data->value;
/*
 * Update the digital rgb display and the current
 * color label.
 */
update_color();
}
```

The blue slider's callback function is the same, except that the blue component of the **XColor** structure is updated.

```
void blue_slider_moved(w, client_data, call_data)
    Widget   w;
    caddr_t  client_data;
    XmScaleCallbackStruct *call_data;
{
 /*
  * Set the blue color components of  the global
  * current_color structure.
  */
current_color.blue =  call_data->value;
/*
  * Update the digital rgb display and the current
  * color label.
  */
update_color();
}
```

The green slider's callback function is also similar:

```
void green_slider_moved(w, client_data, call_data)
    Widget   w;
    caddr_t  client_data;
    XmScaleCallbackStruct *call_data;
{
 /*
  * Set the green color components of  the global
  * current_color structure.
  */
current_color.green =  call_data->value;
/*
```

```
       * Update the digital rgb display and the current
       * color label.
       */
      update_color();
   }
```

The function **update_color()** displays the values of each color component of the current color in an XmLabel widget. It also uses **XStoreColor()** to update the current color in the application's colormap.

```
   update_color()
   {
     Arg  wargs[1];
     char str[25];

     /*
      * Update the digital display.
      */
      xs_wprintf(color_display_panel, "%3d %3d %3d",
                 current_color.red, current_color.green,
                 current_color.blue);
    /*
     * Update the current color.
     */
     XStoreColor(dpy, my_colormap, &current_color);
   }
```

The event handler **set_current_color()** is invoked when the user presses a mouse button in a widget in the color bar. This function sets the **pixel** member of the global **XColor** structure **current_color** to the pixel corresponding to the selected color. The **flags** member of the color structure is also set to the mask **DoRed|DoGreen|DoBlue**. The Xlib function **XQueryColor()** is used to initialize the **red**, **green**, and **blue** members of **current_color** to the components currently shown by the selected button. **XQueryColor()** fills in the existing RGB components of an **XColor** structure, given a pixel index. Finally, **set_current_color()** sets the position of each slider to correspond to the value of each color component.

```
   void set_current_color(w, number, event)
     Widget    w;
     int       number;
     XEvent    *event;
   {
     Arg wargs[10];
     current_color.flags = DoRed | DoGreen | DoBlue;
```

```
  /*
   * Get the current color components of the selected button.
   */
  current_color.pixel = number;
  XQueryColor(dpy, my_colormap, &current_color);
  /*
   * Use each color component to as the new
   * position of the corresponding slider.
   */
  XtSetArg(wargs[0], XmNvalue, current_color.red);
  XtSetValues(red_slider, wargs, 1);

  XtSetArg(wargs[0], XmNvalue, current_color.green);
  XtSetValues(green_slider, wargs, 1);

  XtSetArg(wargs[0], XmNvalue, current_color.blue);
  XtSetValues(blue_slider, wargs, 1);
}
```

6.2.3   The Class Resource File: Coloredit

Because the color editor uses the XmBulletinBoard widget to manage the colors editor's controls, we need to specify the position of each widget in a resource file. The class resource file corresponding to the layout shown in Fig. 6.2, contains:

```
!!!!!!!!!!!!!!!!!!!!!!!!!!!!!!!!!!!!!!!!!!!!!!!!!!!!!!!!!!!!
! Coloredit: Resources for the coloredit program
!!!!!!!!!!!!!!!!!!!!!!!!!!!!!!!!!!!!!!!!!!!!!!!!!!!!!!!!!!!!
!
*base.geometry: =400x400
!
! Set the location of the digital display
!
*display*x:          180
*display*y:           10
*display*height:      30
*display*width:      140
!
! Position color controls
!
*sliderpanel.x:       10
*sliderpanel.y:       10
```

```
*XmScale*orientation:          horizontal
*XmScale*processingDirection: max_on_right

*red*background:     red
*green*background:   green
*blue*background:    blue

*quit*x:             350
*quit*y:              50
```

Notice that the widgets in this program are organized so that the user can specify the location of functionally related groups of widgets, but cannot separate widgets that belong together. For example, all buttons used to select colors are grouped in a XmRowColumn widget. The user can control whether the buttons are arranged vertically in a single column, horizontally in a single row, or in a matrix. Similarly, the XmScale widgets can be oriented horizontally or vertically, in rows or columns, anywhere within the applications control area. However, they cannot be completely separated. This is one way the programmer can allow the user to achieve drastically different layouts, while maintaining some control over the layout of the program's widgets. It is also easier for the user to customize such a configuration than if each widget had to be placed individually.

6.3 SUMMARY

This chapter introduced the use of color in the X Window System. X provides a uniform color model that supports the design of applications that are portable across many types of displays, from monochrome to "true color" displays. It is important for programmers to be aware of the X color model and use it correctly so that their applications function properly on as many display types as possible.

The number of colors available, and also how colors can be used, depends on the visual type of the hardware. One common screen type is **PseudoColor**, which allows applications to choose from a large number of colors, although only a subset of the available colors can be used at once.

X associates a colormap with each window. A colormap contains the colors potentially available to an application. At any given time, one or more colormaps are installed into the hardware, so that the colors can be displayed. Applications refer to colors in the color map using an index, or pixel. The server maintains the contents of each colormap. Applications can request the server to allocate private, read-write color cells in a colormap, or sharable, read-only cells. Xlib provides many functions for allocating and manipulating the colors in a colormap.

7

MANIPULATING RASTER IMAGES

X provides many functions for creating and manipulating images stored in off-screen memory in addition to those displayed on the screen. These images fall into three categories: *pixmaps, bitmaps*, and *XImages*. This chapter introduces the Xlib functions for creating and manipulating these images and briefly describes how they are used.

7.1 PIXMAPS

A pixmap is a chunk of memory similar to a rectangular region of the screen, except that pixmaps are stored in *off-screen memory* and therefore are not visible to the user. Pixmaps have a depth, which is often, but not necessarily, the same as the depth of the screen with which it is associated. The function

XCreatePixmap(display, drawable, width, height, depth)

creates a pixmap **width** by **height** pixels in size. Each pixel contains **depth** bits. The new pixmap is associated with the same screen as the specified **drawable**. The pixmap can be used only on this screen, or on a screen with the same visual type. Applications can deallocate pixmaps when they are no longer needed using the Xlib function:

XFreePixmap(display, pixmap)

Pixmaps are drawables and can be used as destinations for text and graphics operations in the same way as windows. Because data can also be copied between drawables, pixmaps can be used to store off-screen representations of windows. Pixmaps can be used to specify clipping regions for graphics operations and can also be combined with other graphics operations to create patterns used by many Xlib graphics primitives.

Pixmaps are often referred to as *tiles*, because they are often used as a repeating background or fill pattern. A pixmap referred to as a tile is usually small (16 by 16 pixels) to facilitate rapid duplication.

7.2   BITMAPS

A pixmap with a depth of one is referred to as a bitmap. Applications can create a bitmap by specifying a depth of one when calling the function **XCreatePixmap()**. However, Xlib also provides functions used specifically to create bitmaps. The function

XCreateBitmapFromData(display, drawable, data, width, height)

creates a bitmap of **width** by **height** from the specified **data**, which must be a series of bits that represent the value of each pixel in the bitmap. One easy way to generate the data for a bitmap is to create it interactively using the standard editor, **bitmap**, usually distributed with X. This program creates a file that can be included directly in a program. The directory

/usr/include/X11/bitmaps/

also contains some predefined bitmap files. For example, the file

/usr/include/X11/bitmaps/xlogo64

defines the data for a bitmap of the X logo shown in Fig. 7.1.

Figure 7.1 A bitmap of the X logo.

7.3   COPYING BETWEEN DRAWABLES

The contents of a drawable (a window or a pixmap) may be copied to any other drawable that has the same depth using the function:

```
XCopyArea(display, src, dest, gc, src_x, src_y,
          width, height, dest_x, dest_y)
```

XCopyArea() copies the rectangular region of size **width** by **height**, starting at coordinate **(src_x, src_y)** in the **src** drawable, to **(dest_x, dest_y)** in the **dest** drawable. The graphics context, **gc**, controls how the bits from the source drawable are combined with the bits in the destination drawable. If the source and destination drawables do not have the same depth, the server generates a **BadMatch** error.

Applications can use the function

```
XCopyPlane(display, src, dest, gc, src_x, src_y,
           width, height, dest_x, dest_y, plane)
```

to copy data between drawables of different depths. **XCopyPlane()** copies the contents of a single plane of the specified region in the source drawable to the destination drawable. The graphics context determines the foreground and background color of the pattern in the destination drawable.

Let's examine a simple program named **xlogo** that uses bitmaps and pixmaps to display the X logo shown in Fig. 7.1. The header portion of the program includes the widget header files, the xlogo64 bitmap file, and declares a bitmap, a pixmap, and a graphics context used by the program. The body of the program creates an XmDrawingArea widget in which to display the pixmap and registers the function **redisplay()** as a callback to be invoked when the widget's window needs to be refreshed. It then calls the function **create_logo()** to create and initialize a pixmap containing the X logo. The pixmap is stored along with a graphics context and the size of the pixmap in a structure, which is passed as client data to the XmDrawingArea widget's expose and resize callbacks.

```
/**************************************************
 * xlogo.c: Display the X logo
 **************************************************/
#include <X11/StringDefs.h>
#include <X11/Intrinsic.h>
#include <Xm/Xm.h>
#include <Xm/DrawingA.h>
#include <X11/Xutil.h>
#include "xlogo64"

void     redisplay();
```

```
void       resize();
Pixmap     create_logo();

typedef struct {
   Pixmap      pix;
   GC          gc;
   Dimension   width, height;
} pixmap_data;

main(argc, argv)
   int    argc;
   char *argv[];
{
   Widget        toplevel, canvas;
   Arg           wargs[10];
   int           n;
   XGCValues     values;
   pixmap_data   data;

   toplevel = XtInitialize(argv[0], "Xlogo", NULL, 0,
                              &argc, argv);
   /*
    * Create a widget in which to display the logo.
    */
   canvas = XtCreateManagedWidget("canvas",
                                 xmDrawingAreaWidgetClass,
                                 toplevel, NULL, 0);
   /*
    * Use the foreground and background colors
    * of the canvas to create a graphics context.
    */
   n = 0;
   XtSetArg(wargs[n], XtNforeground, &values.foreground);n++;
   XtSetArg(wargs[n], XtNbackground, &values.background);n++;
   XtGetValues(canvas, wargs, n);
   data.gc = XtGetGC(canvas,GCForeground|GCBackground,&values);
   /*
    * Create the pixmap containing the X logo. Store the
    * pixmap, as well as the size of the pixmap in the struct.
    */
   data.width = xlogo64_width;
   data.height = xlogo64_height;
```

```
    data.pix = create_logo(canvas, data.gc, xlogo64_bits,
                           xlogo64_width, xlogo64_height );

    XtAddCallback(canvas, XmNexposeCallback, redisplay, &data);
    XtAddCallback(canvas, XmNresizeCallback, resize, &data);

    XtRealizeWidget(toplevel);
    XtMainLoop();
}
```

The function **create_logo()** creates and returns a pixmap representing the bit pattern passed to it. First, the function uses **XCreateBitmapFromData()** to create a bitmap from the data. Then, **XCreatePixmap()** creates a pixmap of the same width and height as the bitmap, but with the default depth of the screen used by the **given** widget. Finally, **XCopyPlane()** copies the contents of the bitmap from the single plane of the bitmap to the pixmap.[1] The graphics context determines the foreground and background colors of the pixmap. Since the bitmap is no longer needed, we can use **XFreePixmap()** to free it before returning the pixmap.

```
Pixmap create_logo(w, gc, bits, width, height)
    Widget    w;
    char      *bits;
    int       width, height;
{
  Pixmap    bitmap, pix;
 /*
  * Create a bitmap from the data.
  */
  bitmap=XCreateBitmapFromData(XtDisplay(w),
                               RootWindowOfScreen(XtScreen(w)),
                               bits, width, height);
 /*
  * Create a pixmap of the same depth as the default screen.
  */
  pix = XCreatePixmap(XtDisplay(w),
                      RootWindowOfScreen(XtScreen(w)),
                      width, height,
                      DefaultDepthOfScreen(XtScreen(w)));
 /*
```

---

1. This is an example of an area where many programmers introduce portability problems into their programs. A programmer using a single-plane system (black-and-white screen) can use XCopyArea() to copy the bitmap to the pixmap, or to a window, because both the bitmap and the destination drawable have the same depth. However, such a program will fail when run on a multiplane system.

```
 * Copy the contents of plane 1 of the bitmap to the
 * pixmap, using the widget's colors.
 */
XCopyPlane(XtDisplay(w), bitmap, pix, gc, 0, 0,
           xlogo64_width, xlogo64_height, 0, 0, 1);
/*
 * We don't need the bitmap anymore, so free it.
 */
XFreePixmap(XtDisplay(w), bitmap);
return pix;
}
```

The function **redisplay()** is registered as an **XmNexposeCallback** function. The
XmDrawingArea widget calls all callback functions on this list when the widget's window
needs to be redrawn. The **redisplay()** callback function checks the current width and
height of the widget and then uses **XCopyArea()** to transfer the contents of the pixmap
passed in the client data structure to the center of the XmDrawingArea widget's window.

```
void redisplay (w, data, call_data)
    Widget        w;
    pixmap_data   *data;
    XmDrawingAreaCallbackStruct *call_data;
{
  Arg        wargs[2];
  Dimension widget_width, widget_height;
  int        n;
  /*
   * Get the current size of the widget window.
   */
  n = 0;
  XtSetArg(wargs[n], XtNwidth,  &widget_width);n++;
  XtSetArg(wargs[n], XtNheight, &widget_height); n++;
  XtGetValues(w, wargs, n);
  /*
   * Copy the contents of the pixmap to the
   * center of the window.
   */
  XCopyArea(XtDisplay(w), data->pix, XtWindow(w), data->gc,
            0, 0, data->width, data->height,
            (widget_width  - data->width) / 2,
            (widget_height - data->height) / 2);
}
```

The **resize()** callback simply clears the XmDrawingArea widget's window, if it is realized. It is important to check whether or not the widget is realized, because the **XmNresizeCallback** can be called when the widget is resized, even if the window does not yet exist. This callback uses the Xlib function

XClearArea(display, window, x, y, width, height, exposures)

to clear the window. This function clears a rectangular area in a window. If the **width** is given as zero, it is replaced by the width of the window minus **x**. Similarly, if the **height** is given as zero, it is replaced by the height of the window minus **y**. The **exposures** parameter is a boolean value that indicates whether or not exposure events should be generated for the cleared area. Because the XmDrawingArea widget does not compress exposure events, we cannot guarantee that the **redisplay()** callback will be invoked every time the window is resized. However, by calling **XClearArea()** with **exposures** set to **TRUE**, we can trigger an **Expose** event for the entire window every time the window is resized.

```
void resize (w, data, call_data)
   Widget        w;
   caddr_t       data;
   XmDrawingAreaCallbackStruct *call_data;
   {
    if(XtIsRealized(w))
       XClearArea(XtDisplay(w), XtWindow(w), 0, 0, 0, 0, TRUE);
   }
```

This example illustrates many of the Xlib functions that create and initialize bitmaps and pixmaps, and also shows how data can be transferred between bitmaps, pixmaps, and windows. However, you may have noticed that one step in this example is unnecessary. The **redisplay()** callback could use **XCopyPlane()** to copy directly between the bitmap and the widget window, completely eliminating the need for the pixmap. Using this approach, we can define **create_logo()** as:

```
Pixmap create_logo(w, gc, bits, width, height)
   Widget   w;
   char     *bits;
   int      width, height;
{
  Pixmap bitmap;
 /*
  * Create a bitmap from the specified bit pattern.
  */
 bitmap=XCreateBitmapFromData(XtDisplay(w),
                              RootWindowOfScreen(XtScreen(w)),
                              bits, width, height);
  return bitmap;
}
```

Then, we can write the **redisplay()** callback as:

```
void redisplay (w, data, call_data)
    Widget         w;
    pixmap_data    *data;
    XmDrawingAreaCallbackStruct *call_data;
{
  Arg wargs[10];
  int n;
  Dimension widget_width, widget_height;
  /*
   * Get the current size of the widget window.
   */
  n = 0;
  XtSetArg(wargs[n], XtNwidth,  &widget_width);n++;
  XtSetArg(wargs[n], XtNheight, &widget_height);n++;
  XtGetValues(w, wargs, n);
  /*
   * Copy plane 1 of the bitmap to the center
   * of the window, using the widget's foreground
   * and background color.
   */
  XCopyPlane(XtDisplay(w), data->pix, XtWindow(w), data->gc,
             0, 0,  data->width, data->height,
             (widget_width - data->width)/ 2,
             (widget_height - data->height)/ 2, 1);
}
```

Another slight improvement in this example would be to have the **XmNresizeCall-back** function detect changes in the width and height of the widget. This would a be a much cleaner and more efficient way to handle changes in size because the server already notifies the application of any size changes, and we could eliminate the step of retrieving the widget's width and height every time the widget's window is exposed. However, to do this, we would have to resort to a global variable or extend the **pixmap_data** structure to make the size information (which would be set in the **resize()** callback) available to the **redisplay()** callback procedure, which is not as clean an approach as we might wish.

Also, it is important to realize that the purpose of the examples in this section is to demonstrate pixmaps and their related functions and not necessarily to show the easiest way to display the X logo. The easiest way to display a single pixmap such as the X logo, is to create the pixmap, as done by **create_logo()** and then use an XmLabel widget, with the **XmNlableType** resource set to **XmPIXMAP** to display the pixmap.

7.4   IMAGES

X provides a way to transfer images between applications and the server using an **XImage** data structure. This structure stores data in a device-dependent format; therefore, applications should never access the data directly. The server handles byte-swapping and other data transformations that are sometimes necessary when exchanging images between applications running on different machines . The **XImage** data structure contains the pixel data representing the image as well as information about the format of the image.

7.4.1   Creating Images

Applications can allocate an **XImage** using the function

```
XCreateImage(display, visual, depth, format, offset, data,
            width, height, bitmap_pad, bytes_per_line)
```

This function requires a pointer to the **Visual** structure used by the display. The **data** argument must specify an array of bits representing the image. The size of this data is specified by the **width**, **height** and **depth**. The **format** specifies the byte order of the data and must be one of the constants **XYPixmap**, **XYBitmap**, or **ZPixmap**. In **XYPixmap** format, each byte of data specifies the values of 8 pixels along one plane of a raster, with one bit of the data corresponding to each pixel. **ZPixmap** format specifies the data *depth-first*. For example, in **XYPixmap** format, on a display with eight bit planes, each byte of data represents one pixel. The argument **bytes_per_line** specifies the number of bytes in one raster and must be a multiple of 8, 16, or 32 bits.

Images may also be extracted from a drawable using the function:

```
XGetImage(display, drawable, x, y, width, height,
            plane_mask, format)
```

XGetImage() creates an **XImage** structure, copies a rectangular region of a drawable into the image, and returns a pointer to the **XImage** structure. The argument **plane_mask** determines which planes in the drawable are included in the image, while the **format** argument determines whether the image is created in **XYPixmap** or **ZPixmap** format.

X also provides several other functions for manipulating images:

- **XSubImage()** creates a new image and copies the contents of a rectangular sub-region of an old image into the new image.
- **XDestroyImage()** frees an image.
- **XPutPixel()** sets the pixel value of an *(x, y)* location in an **XImage**.
- **XGetPixel()** retrieves the value of a pixel at a particular *(x, y)* location with an **XImage**.
- **XPutImage()** transfers an image to a drawable.

7.5   CACHING PIXMAPS

Motif includes a pixmap caching facility usually used to store and retrieve common tiling patterns. Motif caches 10 built-in pixmaps, and applications can also store additional patterns. These cached pixmaps are often used as tiles. The function

XmGetPixmap (screen, name, foreground, background)

returns a named pixmap with the depth of the specified screen, using the given foreground and background colors. The pre-defined tiling patterns provided by Motif are:

`"background"`	`"25_foreground"`	`"50_foreground"`
`"75_foreground"`	`"horizontal"`	`"vertical"`
`"slant_right"`	`"slant_left"`	`"menu_cascade"`
`"menu_checkmark"`		

Since these pixmaps are cached and may be used in more than one place, applications should treat them as read only.

There are two ways to cache additional pixmaps. First, a program can register an **XImage** representing the desired pattern. This can be done using the function:

XmInstallImage(image, name)

The specified image must be in **XYBitmap** format and have a depth of 1. This approach has the advantage that it allows **XmGetPixmap()** to generate pixmaps of any color combinations from the image.

Let's see how we can use this approach to install a new bit pattern. We can write a simple function to register any bit pattern by simply creating an **XImage** from the bits and then registering the image, as follows:

```
xs_register_pattern(w, name, bits, width, height)
  Widget        w;
  char          *name;
  unsigned char *bits;
  int           width, height;
{
  XImage *image;
  image = XCreateImage(XtDisplay(w),
                       DefaultVisualOfScreen(XtScreen(w)),
                       1, XYBitmap, 0,
                       bits, width, height, 8, 2);
  XmInstallImage(image, name);
}
```

The second way to cache a pixmap is to use the function:

XmInstallPixmap (pixmap, screen, name, foreground, background)

Notice that in this case, the colors of the pixmap are specified at the time of registration.

Let's use the **xs_register_pattern()** function in a simple pattern browser. The browser allows the user to select from a list of patterns. For this example, the browser displays some of the Motif built-in images as well as an additional image registered by the browser, a "foreground" pixmap. Motif does not provide a "foreground" pixmap pattern, which is useful in some cases. We can define the bit pattern for a foreground tile as a 16 by 16 bit array of 1's.

First, let's look at the main body of a simple program to test the browser. The program defines the foreground bitmap, and a list of image names to be displayed in the browser. After registering the new pattern, the program calls **create_pixmap_browser()** with the list of pattern names.

```
/*******************************************************
 * browser.c : Display some tiling patterns
 *******************************************************/
#include <X11/StringDefs.h>
#include <X11/Intrinsic.h>
#include <Xm/Xm.h>
#include "libXs.h"

static unsigned char fg_bitmap[32] = {    /*  foreground */
      0xff, 0xff, 0xff, 0xff, 0xff, 0xff, 0xff, 0xff,
      0xff, 0xff, 0xff, 0xff, 0xff, 0xff, 0xff, 0xff,
      0xff, 0xff, 0xff, 0xff, 0xff, 0xff, 0xff, 0xff,
      0xff, 0xff, 0xff, 0xff, 0xff, 0xff, 0xff, 0xff
};

#define fg_width  16
#define fg_height 16

static char *patterns[] = {  "foreground",
                             "background",
                             "25_foreground",
                             "50_foreground",
                             "75_foreground",
                             "vertical",
                             "horizontal",
                             "slant_right",
                             "slant_left",
                          };
```

```
main(argc, argv)
   int   argc;
   char *argv[];
{
   Widget toplevel, browser;

   toplevel = XtInitialize(argv[0], "Browser", NULL, 0,
                          &argc, argv);
   /*
    * Register the "foreground" bit pattern with the
    * Motif pixmap cache.
    */
   xs_register_pattern(toplevel, "foreground",
                       fg_bitmap, fg_width, fg_height);
   /*
    * Create the browser.
    */
   browser = xs_create_pixmap_browser(toplevel,patterns,
                                      XtNumber(patterns),
                                      NULL, NULL);

   XtManageChild(browser);
   XtRealizeWidget(toplevel);
   XtMainLoop();
}
```

The function **xs_create_pixmap_browser()** creates a RadioBox widget containing an XmToggleButton widget for each pixmap in the browser. A RadioBox widget is just a form of the XmRowColumn widget that expects to manage a button-type widget or gadget. The RadioBox behavior of the XmRowColumn widget ensures that only one button is selected at any one time. The XmToggleButton widget is ideal in this situation, because it toggles between two states. The RadioBox widget ensures that only one XmToggleButton widget is in its "set" state at any one time.

```
/***************************************************************
 * xs_create_pixmap_browser(): let the user select from a set
 *                             of patterns.
 ***************************************************************/
#include <X11/Intrinsic.h>
#include <Xm/Xm.h>
#include <Xm/ToggleB.h>
#include <Xm/RowColumn.h>
#include "libXs.h"
```

```
Widget
xs_create_pixmap_browser (parent,tiles,n_tiles,callback,data)
    Widget     parent;        /* widget to manage the browser */
    char       *tiles[];       /* list of tile names           */
    int        n_tiles;        /* how many tiles               */
    void       (*callback)();  /* invoked when state changes   */
    caddr_t    data;           /* data to be passed to callback*/
{
  Widget      browser;
  WidgetList  buttons;
  int         i;
  Arg         wargs[10];
  /*
   * Malloc room for button widgets.
   */
  buttons = (WidgetList) XtMalloc(n_tiles * sizeof(Widget));
  /*
   * Create a "RadioBox" RowColumn widget. Set the entry class
   * so the RadioBox expects to manage XmToggleButton widgets.
   */
  XtSetArg(wargs[0],XmNentryClass,xmToggleButtonWidgetClass);
  browser = XmCreateRadioBox(parent, "browser", wargs, 1);
  /*
   * Create a button for each tile. If a callback function
   * has been given, register it as an XmNvalueChangedCallback
   */
  for(i=0;i< n_tiles;i++){
   buttons[i] = xs_create_pixmap_button(browser, tiles[i]);
   if(callback)
     XtAddCallback(buttons[i], XmNvalueChangedCallback,
                    callback, data);
  }
  /*
   * Manage all buttons and return the RadioBox widget, which
   * is still unmanaged
   */
  XtManageChildren(buttons, n_tiles);
  return browser;
}
```

The function **xs_create_pixmap_button()** creates an XmToggleButton widget to display the given pixmap pattern, which must be previously installed in the cached set of pixmaps. The pixmap is retrieved from the Motif pixmap cache, using the foreground and background colors of the widget in which the pixmap is to be displayed. To display a pixmap in an XmToggleButton widget, the widget's **XmNlabelType** resource must be set to **XmPIX-MAP**, and the **XmNlabelPixmap** resource set to the pixmap to be displayed. This function also sets the **XmNuserData** resource supported by all Motif widgets to the tile displayed in the widget. This resource can be used to store any data an application needs to associate with a widget. Storing the pixmap as user data allows an application to retrieve the pixmap from within a callback or event handler registered for the widget.

```
Widget xs_create_pixmap_button(parent, pattern)
     Widget          parent;
     char *          pattern;
{
    Pixmap    tile;
    Widget    button;
    Arg       wargs[10];
    Pixel     foreground, background;
    int       n;
    button = XtCreateWidget(pattern, xmToggleButtonWidgetClass,
                            parent, NULL, 0);
    /*
     * Retrieve the colors of the widget.
     */
    n = 0;
    XtSetArg(wargs[n], XtNforeground, &foreground);n++;
    XtSetArg(wargs[n], XtNbackground, &background);n++;
    XtGetValues(button, wargs, n);
    /*
     * Get a tile corresponding the given pattern.
     */
    tile = XmGetPixmap (XtScreen(button), pattern,
                        foreground, background);
    /*
     * Display the pixmap in the button and also store it
     * so it can be retrieved from the button later.
     */
    n = 0;
    XtSetArg(wargs[n], XmNlabelType,   XmPIXMAP); n++;
    XtSetArg(wargs[n], XmNlabelPixmap, tile); n++;
    XtSetArg(wargs[n], XmNuserData,    tile); n++;
    XtSetValues(button, wargs, n);

    return button;
}
```

Fig. 7.2 shows the pixmap browser created by this example. The functions described in this section are used again in Chapter 10, so they are placed in the libXs library for convenient reuse.

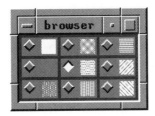

Figure 7.2 The pixmap browser.

7.6 SUMMARY

This chapter introduced the various types of raster images supported by X and the Xlib functions that manipulate them. X supports several types of image formats, bitmaps, pixmaps, and **XImage** structures. Pixmaps, bitmaps, and tiles are drawables, and can be used as destinations for Xlib graphics operations. Pixmaps are stored in off-screen memory, and are useful for storing and manipulating raster images without displaying them on the screen. A bitmap is simply a single-plane pixmap. Tile is another name for pixmap, usually used to refer to a pixmap containing a repeating pattern.

Applications can store images in the server using the Xlib **XImage** structure and its related functions. The primary reason for using **XImages** is to allow images to be transferred between clients running on different machines. Different machines sometimes store data in different formats, and the X server handles the byte swapping required to move images from one machine to another.

The following chapter discusses graphics contexts, a resource that controls how X graphics operations are performed. Graphics contexts affect how images are transferred between drawables such as pixmaps and bitmaps. Pixmaps are also used by graphics contexts as patterns to be combined with drawing operations.

8

GRAPHICS CONTEXTS

All graphics operations use attributes that determine the width of lines, foreground and background colors, fill patterns, fonts to be used when displaying text, and so on. X stores these attributes in an internal data structure known as a *graphics context*, often abbreviated as GC. This chapter discusses the attributes of GCs as well as the Xlib and Intrinsics functions that create and manipulate them. Chapters 9 and 10 show how to use graphics contexts with the X text and graphics functions.

8.1 CREATING GRAPHICS CONTEXTS

The Xlib function

```
XCreateGC(display, drawable, mask, &values)
```

creates a graphics context and returns a resource identifier that applications can use to refer to the GC. The X server maintains the data associated with the graphics context, and all clients must reference the graphics context by its ID. Graphics contexts are associated with a specific drawable, but can be used with any drawable of the same depth on a screen with the same visual type.

Applications can specify the initial value of each component of a graphics context in the **values** argument when calling **XCreateGC()**. This argument must be an **XGCValues** structure, which includes the following members:

```
int             function;   /* logical operation       */
unsigned long plane_mask;   /* plane mask              */
unsigned long foreground;   /* foreground pixel        */
unsigned long background;   /* background pixel        */
int             line_width; /* line width (in pixels)  */
int             line_style; /* LineSolid,
                               LineOnOffDash, or
                               LineDoubleDash           */
int             cap_style;  /* CapNotLast, CapButt,
                               CapRound, CapProjecting  */
int             join_style; /* JoinMiter, JoinRound,
                               or JoinBevel             */
int             fill_style; /* FillSolid, FillTiled,
                               FillStippled,
                               or FillOpaqueStippled    */
int             fill_rule;  /* EvenOddRule, WindingRule */
int             arc_mode;   /* ArcChord, ArcPieSlice    */
Pixmap          tile;       /* tile pixmap for tiling   */
Pixmap          stipple;    /* stipple 1 plane pixmap   */
int             ts_x_origin;/* tile and stipple offset  */
int             ts_y_origin;
Font            font;       /* default text font        */
int     subwindow_mode;     /* ClipByChildren, or
                               IncludeInferiors          */
Bool    graphics_exposures;/* report graphics exposures?*/
int     clip_x_origin;      /* clipping origin          */
int     clip_y_origin;
Pixmap clip_mask;           /* bitmap clipping          */
int     dash_offset;        /* line information         */
char    dashes;
```

The **mask** argument to **XCreateGC()** specifies which members of the **XGCValues** structure contain valid information. If this mask is zero, the GC will be created with default values for all attributes. To override the default value for a particular field, the mask must include a constant corresponding to that field. Fig. 8.1 lists the GC attribute masks, along with the default values of each attribute.

Mask	Default Value of GC
GCFunction	GXCopy
GCPlaneMask	AllPlanes
GCForeground	0
GCBackground	1
GCLineWidth	0
GCLineStyle	LineSolid

GCCapStyle	CapButt
GCJoinStyle	JoinMiter
GCFillStyle	FillSolid
GCFillRule	EvenOddRule
GCTile	Foreground
GCStipple	0
GCTileStipXOrigin	0
GCTileStipYOrigin	1
GCFont	Implementation-Dependent
GCSubwindowMode	ClipByChildren
GCGraphicsExposures	TRUE
GCClipXOrigin	0
GCClipYOrigin	0
GCClipMask	None
GCDashOffset	0
GCDashList	4
GCArcMode	ArcPieSlice

Figure 8.1 Masks used with graphics contexts.

For example, the following code segment creates a graphics context, specifying the foreground pixel, background pixel, and line style:

```
XGCValues gcv;
GC         gc;
gcv.foreground = 1;
gcv.background = 2;
gcv.line_style = LineOnOffDash;
gc = XCreateGC(display, window,
               GCForeground | GCBackground | GCLineStyle,
               &gcv);
```

The Xt Intrinsics also provides a function for creating graphics contexts:

```
XtGetGC(widget, mask, values)
```

This function caches graphics contexts to allow sharing of GCs within an application. Therefore, applications must not modify GCs created with **XGetGC()**.

8.2 MANIPULATING GRAPHICS CONTEXTS

After a GC is created, applications can use the function

```
XChangeGC(display, gc, mask, &values)
```

to modify any of the GCs attributes. The **mask** and **values** arguments serve the same function here as they do in **XCreateGC()**. Xlib also provides many convenience functions for modifying individual GC attributes. The following sections introduce many of these functions as we discuss the purpose of each of the attributes of a graphics context.

8.2.1   Display Functions

A graphics context's **GCFunction** attribute specifies a logical display function that determines how each pixel of a new image is combined with the current contents of a destination drawable. The new image, referred to as the *source*, could be copied from another drawable, or be generated by a graphics request. For example, when this attribute is set to **GXcopy**, the source image completely replaces the current contents of the affected region of the drawable. On the other hand, if the same figure is drawn using the **GXor** display function, the bits of the affected region of the drawable are set to the logical OR of the source and the previous contents of the destination. Fig. 8.2 shows the display functions defined in Xlib.h, along with their corresponding logical operations. The **src** parameter represents the bits being written and the **dst** parameter represents the current state of the bits in the drawable.

<u>Mask</u>	<u>Display Function</u>
GXclear	0
GXand	src AND dst
GXandReverse	src AND NOT dst
GXcopy	src
GXandInverted	(NOT src) AND dst
GXnoop	dst
GXxor	src XOR dst
GXor	src OR dst
GXnor	NOT (src OR dst)
GXequiv	(NOT src) XOR dst
GXinvert	NOT dst
GXorReverse	src OR (NOT dst)
GXcopyInverted	NOT src
GXorInverted	(NOT src) OR dst
GXnand	NOT (src AND dst)
GXset	1

Figure 8.2 Display functions.

On color screens, these logical operations are performed bit-wise on each pixel within the affected area. For example, let's see what happens if we draw a line using the **GXand** drawing function and a pixel index of 3 for the foreground color. If we draw the line in a drawable whose background color is pixel 10 on a display with 4 bit planes, the resulting line color is the represented by the pixel 2. This is easier to see if we examine the binary representation of these numbers:

$$3_{10} \text{ AND } 10_{10} = 2_{10}$$
$$0011_2 \text{ AND } 1010_2 = 0010_2$$

The *exclusive-OR* (XOR) function, specified by the constant **GXxor**, is a commonly used display function. The XOR function has the interesting property that drawing a figure twice in XOR mode restores the screen to its original state. This allows us to erase an image drawn in XOR mode simply by drawing it a second time. Contrast this with erasing an object on the screen by drawing the object in the background color of the window. In the latter case, the application must redraw the previous contents, if any, of the window. When an image is redrawn in XOR mode, the previous contents of the window are restored, as long as nothing else on the screen has changed. The most common use of the **XOR** display function is for *rubber banding* operations, where an object on the screen, often a line or rectangle, is moved and stretched in response to mouse motion. The **XOR** mode allows the rubber band object to move across other objects on the screen without disturbing them. Chapter 10 presents an example that illustrates rubber banding.

The function

```
XSetFunction(display, gc, function)
```

provides an easy way for applications to alter a graphics context's display function. The default value is **GXcopy**.

8.2.2   Plane Mask

The value of the **GCPlaneMask** attribute determines which bit planes of a drawable are affected by a graphics operation. The plane mask contains a one in each bit that can be modified. The function

```
XSetPlaneMask(display, gc, mask)
```

sets the plane mask of a graphics context. For example, a line drawn with foreground pixel 6 would normally affect bit planes 2 and 3 ($6_{10} = 0110_2$). However, if the plane mask of the graphics context is set to 5_{10} (0101_2), drawing a line with a foreground pixel 6 affects only plane 3, and the resulting line is displayed in the color indicated by the pixel index 4. Applications can use a macro

```
AllPlanes
```

to indicate all planes supported by a screen. The default value of the **GCPlaneMask** attribute is **AllPlanes**.

8.2.3   Foreground and Background

The **GCForeground** and **GCBackground** attributes of a graphics context indicate the pixels used as foreground and background colors for graphics operations. The pixel index must be an integer between zero and $n - 1$, where n is the number of colors supported by the display. This index is usually obtained using the color allocation functions discussed in Chapter 6. The function

   XSetForeground(display, gc, pixel)

sets the **GCForeground** attribute while the function

   XSetBackground(display, gc, pixel)

sets the **GCBackground** attribute. The default value of **GCForeground** is 0 and the default value of **GCBackground** is 1.

8.2.4   Line Attributes

Several GC attributes determine how a line is drawn. The **GCLineWidth** controls the width, in pixels, of the line. The default width is 0. The server draws zero width lines one pixel wide using an implementation-dependent algorithm. On displays that have hardware support for line drawing, this is often the fastest way to draw lines. The **GCLineStyle** attribute can be one of the constants:

   LineSolid   **LineOnOffDash**   **LineDoubleDash**

Fig. 8.3 shows each of these styles. The default value is **LineSolid**.

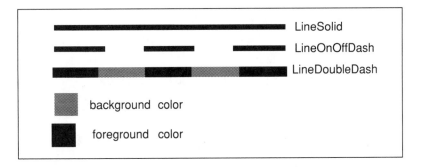

Figure 8.3 Line styles.

   Graphics contexts also control how the server draws the ends of wide lines. The **GCCapStyle** of a line can be one of the constants:

   CapNotLast   **CapButt**   **CapRound**   **CapProjecting**

The default value is **CapButt**. Fig. 8.4 shows how X draws each of these styles.

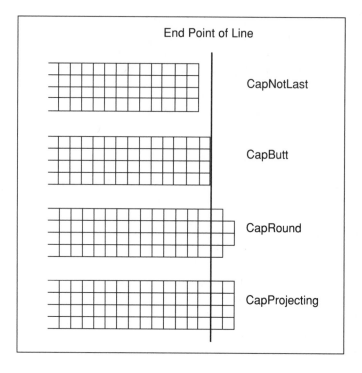

Figure 8.4 Line cap styles.

The graphics context also determines how the server draws connected lines. The style is determined by the **GCJoinStyle** attribute and can be one of the constants:

    JoinMiter   **JoinRound**   **JoinBevel**

Fig. 8.5 illustrates each of these styles. The default style is **JoinMiter**.

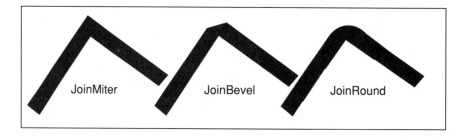

Figure 8.5 Line join styles.

The function

```
XSetLineAttributes(display, gc, width, style,
                   cap_style, join_style)
```

sets each of a GC's line attributes.

8.2.5   Fill Styles

X allows graphics figures to be *filled* by some color or pattern. The **GCFillStyle** attribute determines how figures are filled and must be one of the constants:

FillSolid   **FillTiled**   **FillStippled**   **FillOpaqueStippled**

Applications can use the function

```
XSetFillStyle(display, gc, style)
```

to set the fill style of a graphics context. The default fill style, **FillSolid**, specifies that figures are to be filled with the current foreground color. The **FillTiled** style indicates that figures are to be filled with the pixmap pattern specified in the **tile** attribute. This pixmap must have the same depth as the drawable with which the graphics context is used. The function

```
XSetTile(display, gc, tile)
```

sets a graphics context's **GCTile** attribute. Setting the **GCFillStyle** to **FillStippled** or **FillOpaqueStippled** specifies that regions be filled with a *stipple*. A stipple is a repeating pattern produced by using a bitmap (a pixmap of depth 1) as a mask in the drawing operation. When **FillStippled** is specified, graphics operations only operate on those bits of the stipple pattern that are set to 1. When **FillOpaqueStippled** is specified, bits in the stipple pattern that contain a 1 are drawn using the foreground color of the graphics context and those that contain a zero are drawn using the background color. The function

```
XSetStipple(display, gc, stipple)
```

sets a **GC**'s stipple pattern. Graphics contexts also use a fill rule attribute, **GCFillRule**, to determine the algorithm used to fill a region. The fill rule must be one of the constants **EvenOddRule** or **WindingRule**. The function

```
XSetFillRule(display, gc, rule)
```

sets the fill rule for a graphics context. Fig. 8.6 shows how the fill rule affects the appearance of a filled polygon. If **EvenOddRule** is specified, the server sets a pixel at a particular point if an imaginary line drawn between the point and the outside of the figure crosses the figure an odd number of times. If **WindingRule** is specified, the server determines whether a point should be filled using an imaginary line between the point and a vertex of the figure.

The line is rotated about the point so that it touches each vertex of the figure, in order, until it returns to the original position. If the line makes one or more complete rotations, the point is considered to be inside the figure, and the point is filled.

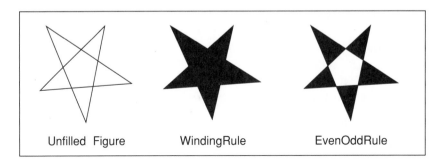

Figure 8.6 Comparison of EvenOddRule and WindingRule.

8.2.6   Fonts

The **GCFont** attribute of a graphics context determines the font used for all text operations. The function

    XSetFont(display, gc, font_id)

sets a graphics context's font attribute. The default font is implementation-dependent. Chapter 9 discusses fonts and how they are used to display text in a window.

8.2.7   Clip Masks

The **GCClipMask** attribute specifies a bitmap as a clip mask for all drawing operations. If a graphics context has a clip mask, drawing operations affect only those pixels in the drawable that correspond to a 1 in the clip mask. The function

    XSetClipMask(display, gc, bitmap)

sets the bitmap used as a clip mask. The default value is **None**, in which case no clipping is performed. The function

    XSetClipOrigon(display, gc, x, y)

alters the location of the clipmask relative to the origin of the drawable. A clipping region can also be specified as a list of rectangular areas, using the function:

    XSetClipRectangles(display, gc, xoffset, yoffset,
                        rect, nrect, ordering)

The arguments **xoffset** and **yoffset** indicate an offset to be added to the origin of all rectangles. The **rect** argument must be an array of **XRectangle** structures. This structure has the members:

```
short           x, y;
unsigned short width, height;
```

If the list of rectangles is given as **None**, no clipping is performed. Some X servers can perform clipping more efficiently if they know the order of the rectangles. The **order** argument must specify one of the constants **Unsorted, YSorted, YXSorted,** or **YXBanded** to indicate the order of the rectangles within the array.

8.3 GRAPHICS EXPOSURES

The server generates **GraphicsExpose** events when an **XCopyArea()** or **XCopyPlane()** function is unable to copy an area because the area is occluded by a window. The function

```
XSetGraphicsExposures(display, gc, flag)
```

enables or disables generation of these events for graphics operations that use the graphics context. **GraphicsExpose** events are enabled when **flag** is set to **TRUE**. The default value is **TRUE**.

8.4 REGIONS

X provides a set of utility routines for representing and manipulating non-rectangular areas. For example, applications often need to determine whether an exposed area intersects with the area occupied by a particular object on the screen. To deal with such situations, X provides an *opaque*[1] data, **Region**, and a set of functions that operate on regions. Internally, a region consists of an array of rectangles. Applications cannot access the region data structure directly, but must use functions provided by Xlib to manipulate **Region**s. Functions that manipulate regions do not make requests to the server; all calculations are done locally in the client. Applications that use regions must include the header file Xutil.h.

Some widgets use regions when reporting exposure events. Widgets that request the Intrinsics to compress exposure events are passed a **Region** that defines the sum of all exposed areas after all expose events are received. Some widgets choose to pass the region on to the application in callbacks.

---

1. An opaque data structure is one whose true definition is hidden using data abstraction techniques. The public definition of the structure is just a pointer to an undefined structure. The true definition and the procedures that operate on the data are kept in a private file. This same technique is used by the Xt Intrinsics to hide the implementation of widgets, and is discussed in more detail in Chapter 12.

The function

XCreateRegion()

creates and returns a new, empty **Region**. The function

XPolygonRegion(points_array, npoints, fill_rule)

creates a **Region** representing the polygonal area defined by an array of **XPoint** structures. This structure contains the members

short x, y;

The **fill_rule** argument to **XPolygonRegion()** determines the algorithm used to convert the polygon to a region and may be one of the constants **EvenOddRule** or **WindingRule**. Chapter 10 describes the meaning of these terms.

The function

XDestroyRegion(region)

destroys a **Region** and frees the memory used by the **Region**. The function

XEqualRegion(r1, r2)

compares two Regions and returns **TRUE** if they are equal, or **FALSE** if they are not.

The function

XEmptyRegion(region)

returns **TRUE** if the given **Region** is empty. A new **Region** defined by the intersection of two **Regions** can obtained using the function:

XIntersectRegion(region1, region2, result)

For example, we can use **XIntersectRegion()** to write a simple function that determines if two regions intersect:

```
does_intersect(region1, region2)
   Region region1, region2;
{
   int     is_empty;
   Region intersection;
   /*
    * Create the empty intersection region.
    */
   intersection = XCreateRegion();
   /*
    * Get the intersection of the two regions.
    */
```

```
    XIntersectRegion(region1, region2, intersection);
    /*
     * Check whether the result is an empty region.
     */
    is_empty = XEmptyRegion(intersection));
    /*
     * Free the region we created before returning the result.
     */
    XDestroyRegion(intersection);
    return (!is_empty);
}
```

The function

XPointInRegion(region, x, y)

returns **TRUE** if the given (x, y) point lies within the bounds of the region, while the function

XRectInRegion(region, x, y, width, height)

determines whether a rectangular area intersects a region. **XRectInRegion()** returns the constant **RectangleIn** if the rectangle is totally contained within the region, **RectangleOut** if the rectangle lies completely outside the region, and **RectanglePart** if the rectangle partially intersects the Region.

The smallest enclosing rectangle of a region can be obtained using the function:

XClipBox(region, &rect)

When this function returns, the **XRectangle** structure **rect** contains the bounding box of the specified region.

Applications can also use a **Region** as a clip mask in a graphics context. The function

XSetRegion(display, gc, region)

sets the clip mask of a graphics context to the given region. Xlib also includes many other useful functions that operate on **Region**s. These include functions that find the union of two regions, subtract regions, move regions, and so on.

The Xt Intrinsics also provides a useful function for converting the area reported in an **Expose** event to a region. The function

XtAddExposureToRegion(&event, region)

computes the union of the region and the rectangle contained in the **Expose** event and stores the result in the region.

8.5 SUMMARY

This chapter discussed graphics contexts and regions. Graphics contexts control color, style and other attributes used by the Xlib text and graphics primitives. Graphics contexts are maintained by the server and accessed by applications through a resource ID. Xlib provides functions to control the attributes of a graphics context, and the Xt Intrinsics provides a way to cache graphics contexts, so they can be shared within an application.

This chapter also discussed regions, which are often used by graphics applications to define clipping areas. Regions allow rectangular or non-rectangular areas to be represented, compared, and manipulated.

The following two chapters show how the topics discussed in this and the previous chapters (graphics contexts, raster images, regions, and color) are used in conjunction with the Xlib text and graphics operations.

9

TEXT AND FONTS

Xlib provides a set of primitive functions for drawing text in a window or pixmap. X draws characters on the screen using bitmaps that represent each character. A *font* is a collection of bitmapped characters. This chapter discusses fonts and presents the Xlib functions that draw text in a window. The chapter also presents examples that combine the elements of the last few chapters with the Xlib text-drawing functions.

In addition to the Xlib text facilities, Motif provides an abstraction known as a *compound string* for representing text in a language-independent manner. This chapter also discusses the functions provided by Motif for creating and manipulating compound strings.

9.1 FONTS

A font is a collection of *glyphs*, which are rectangular bitmaps representing an image. Although a glyph may contain any bit pattern, fonts usually contain textual characters. Before an application can use a font, it must load the font into the server. The function

    XLoadFont(display, font_name)

finds and loads the named font, and returns a resource ID that refers to the font. It is common, but not necessary, for fonts to be kept in a file. However, this is an implementation-dependent detail that application programmers do not need to be concerned with.

The function

    XQueryFont(display, font_ID)

returns an **XFontStruct** structure that contains detailed information about the font. The function

XLoadQueryFont(display, name)

performs the equivalent of an **XLoadFont()** followed by an **XQueryFont()** and returns the **XFontStruct** information with a single server request. The information in the **XFontStruct** structure includes:

- **fid**: The resource ID used to refer to the font.
- **direction**: A flag that indicates whether the characters in the font are defined left to right or right to left. X supports only horizontally drawn text.
- **min_bounds**: An **XCharStruct** structure that contains the bounding box of the smallest character in the font.
- **max_bounds**: An **XCharStruct** structure that contains the bounding box of the largest character in the font.
- **ascent**: An integer that indicates how far the font extends above the baseline.
- **descent**: An integer that indicates how far the font extends below the baseline.
- **per_char**: An array of **XCharStruct** structures for each character in the font. X fonts can be *mono-spaced* (having the same width) or *proportional* (varying widths among characters).

The **XCharStruct** structure is defined in Xlib.h and contains the following information:

```
short           lbearing;
short           rbearing;
short           width;
short           ascent;
short           descent;
unsigned short attributes;
```

This structure contains information about the size and location of a single character relative to the origin, as shown in Figure 9.1. When specifying the location of a character, the character's origin is the lower left corner of the bounding box.

Xlib provides functions that calculate the size, in pixels, of character strings based on the font used. The function

XTextWidth(fontstruct, string, string_length)

calculates the pixel length of a character string for a particular font. The function

XTextExtents(font, string, string_length, &direction, &ascent, &descent, &overall)

provides additional information. This function returns the **direction, ascent**, and **descent** for the entire string, and also returns an **XCharStruct, overall**, containing the width, left bearing, and right bearing of the entire string.

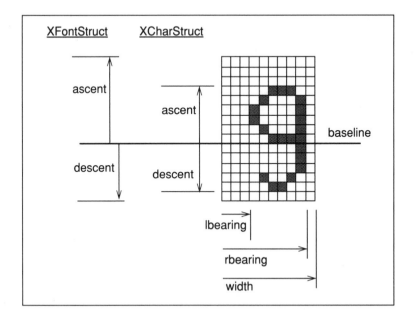

Figure 9.1 Bounding box of a character.

9.2 TEXT OPERATIONS

X displays text in a drawable by performing a fill operation on a region using the text font as a mask. Xlib provides two simple functions for displaying strings:

```
XDrawString(display, drawable, gc, x, y, str, length)
```

and

```
XDrawImageString(display, drawable, gc, x, y, str, length)
```

Both functions display a string in a drawable starting at the given position. The graphics context determines the foreground color, background color, the display function, the font, and the fill style. The graphics context also determines the stipple or tile pattern and clipping region used. **XDrawString()** draws only the foreground component of the text, while

XDrawImageString() also fills the background region within each character's bounding box.

Xlib also includes drawing functions that draw lines of text using multiple fonts in a single operation. The function

> **XDrawText(display, drawable, gc, x, y, items, nitems)**

draws **nitems** of text as specified in an array of type **XTextItem**. This structure contains the following members:

```
char    *chars;    /* Character array                 */
int      nchars;   /* number of characters in string  */
int      delta;    /* distance from previous string   */
Font     font;     /* Font for this string or None    */
```

XDrawText() processes each item in the array. If an entry in the array specifies the font as **None**, **XDrawText()** uses the font used by the previous item. The **delta** member of the structure specifies the distance along the x axis between the start of the current item and the end of the previous item.

9.3 EXAMPLE: A FILE VIEWER

This section uses some of the text and font functions discussed in the previous section to build a simple file viewer, called **fileview**. The viewer allows the user to view and scroll the contents of a text file in a window. The example uses an XmDrawingArea widget as a drawing surface on which to display the text, and demonstrates how the Xlib text functions can be used with the Xt Intrinsics and Motif widget set.[1]

The header of the **fileview** program includes the widget header files used by the program and defines the global variables and data structures used by the program.

```
/*************************************************************
 * fileview.h: declarations for fileview program
 *********************************************************/
#include <stdio.h>
#include <X11/Intrinsic.h>
#include <X11/StringDefs.h>
#include <X11/Xutil.h>
#include <Xm/Xm.h>
#include <Xm/DrawingA.h>
```

---

1. The approach used in this example is hardly the easiest way to write a file viewer. The most straightforward approach would simply use an XmText widget to display the file. The entire program would fit on a single page. However the point of this section is to demonstrate the Xlib text functions, so that we can use these functions when necessary (when writing a new widget that displays text, for example).

```
#include <Xm/ScrolledW.h>
#include <Xm/ScrollBar.h>
#include "libXs.h"

#define MAXLINESIZE   300
#define MAXLINES      2000
#define MIN(a,b)      (((a) < (b)) ? (a) : (b))
#define ABS(a)        (((a) >= 0) ? (a) : -(a))
#define MAX(a,b)      ((a > b) ? a : b)
#define MARGIN        5

typedef struct {
    char          *chars[MAXLINES];    /* Lines of text        */
    int           length[MAXLINES];    /* Length of each line */
    int           rbearing[MAXLINES];  /* right bearing of line*/
    int           descent;             /* descent below baseline*/
    XFontStruct   *font;               /* The font struct      */
    GC            gc;                   /* A read/write GC      */
    Widget        scrollbar;
    Widget        canvas;
    Dimension     canvas_height;       /* canvas dimensions    */
    Dimension     canvas_width;
    int           fontheight;          /* descent + ascent     */
    int           nitems;              /* number of text lines */
    int           top;                 /* line at top of window */
    } text_data, *text_data_ptr;

void          handle_exposures ();
void          scroll_bar_moved ();
void          resize ();

static XtResource resources[] = {
  {XtNfont, XtCFont, XtRFontStruct, sizeof (XFontStruct *),
     XtOffset(text_data_ptr, font), XtRString, "Fixed"       },
};
```

This example limits the size of the file to 2000 lines, as defined by the constant **MAXLINES**; a more realistic implementation would allocate space based on the size of the file. The **text_data** structure contains two arrays. The **chars** member is an array of character strings, while **length** is an array that caches the length of each line of the file. The **nitems** member records the number of lines in the file, and **top** contains the index of the line displayed at the top of the window. The structure also contains other useful information that needs to be passed to the event handlers and callbacks in this example, including the font, the graphics context used to draw the text, and the widgets used by the application.

The **resources** structure is used by the resource manager to load the font information into the buffer data structure. The default font is specified as "Fixed".

The file viewer window contains both an XmDrawingArea widget used to display the text and an XmScrollBar widget that scrolls the text in the XmDrawingArea widget. These widgets are managed by an XmScrolledWindow widget. In this example, the XmScrolled-Window widget simply provides a convenient layout for the scrollbar and the XmDrawingArea widgets. It is designed to manage a "workspace" and horizontal and verti-cal scrollbars. In this example, the XmScrolledWindow widget is created with the **XmNscrollingPolicy** resource set to **XmAPPLICATION_DEFINED**, which is the default policy. In this mode, the application must create the scrollbars and work areas and also han-dle the scrolling. The main body of the program creates all widgets, and calls other functions to load the file into the text buffer and initialize the global data structures de-fined in the header file.

```
/*******************************************************
 * fileview.c: A simple file viewer
 *******************************************************/
#include "fileview.h"

extern Widget create_scrollbar ();

main (argc, argv)
  int       argc;
  char      *argv[];
{
  Widget     toplevel, sb, sw;
  Arg        wargs[10];
  int        n;
  text_data  data;

  toplevel = XtInitialize (argv[0], "Fileview",
                           NULL, 0, &argc, argv);
  XtGetApplicationResources (toplevel, &data, resources,
                             XtNumber (resources), NULL, 0);
  /*
   * Read the file specified in argv[1] into the
   * text buffer.
   */
  load_file (&data, (argc == 2) ? argv[1] : NULL);
  /*
   * Create a ScrolledWindow widget as a base.
```

```
      */
      sw = XtCreateManagedWidget ("framework",
                                  xmScrolledWindowWidgetClass,
                                  toplevel, NULL, 0);
      /*
       * Create the drawing surface.
       */
      data.canvas= XtCreateManagedWidget("canvas",
                                         xmDrawingAreaWidgetClass,
                                         sw, NULL, 0);
      /*
       * Retrieve the initial size of the canvas widget.
       */
      XtSetArg (wargs[0], XtNheight, &data.canvas_height);
      XtSetArg (wargs[1], XtNwidth, &data.canvas_width);
      XtGetValues (data.canvas, wargs, 2);
      /*
       * Register callbacks for resizes and exposes.
       */
      XtAddCallback (data.canvas, XmNexposeCallback,
                     handle_exposures, &data);
      XtAddCallback (data.canvas, XmNresizeCallback,
                     resize, &data);
      /*
       * Create the scrollbar.
       */
      data.scrollbar = create_scrollbar (sw, &data);
      /*
       * Register the scrollbar and work area for the
       * ScrolledWindow widget.
       */
      n = 0;
      XtSetArg(wargs[n], XmNverticalScrollBar, data.scrollbar);n++;
      XtSetArg(wargs[n], XmNworkWindow, data.canvas); n++;
      XtSetValues(sw, wargs, n);

      XtRealizeWidget (toplevel);
      create_gc (&data);
      XtMainLoop ();
}
```

After calling **XtInitialize()**, the program retrieves the application resources that specify the font used to display the text. The function **load_file()** then reads the file into the text buffer. After creating the XmScrollBar and XmDrawingArea widgets, the program registers two callback functions with the XmDrawingArea widget. The **XmNresizeCallback** function updates the data in the text buffer when the widget is resized, while the **XmNexposeCallback** function redraws the text when necessary. The function **create_gc()** creates the graphics context used by the program. Notice that the graphics context is not created until after the widgets have been realized. This is because we need to create a modifiable graphics context using the Xlib function **XCreateGC()**, which requires a valid window ID.

The function **load_file()** attempts to open a file. If successful, the function uses **fgets()** to read each line of the file and load it into the text buffer. Because the contents of the buffer cannot change once the file has been read, we can use **XTextExtents()** to calculate the bounding box of each line of the file as it is read, and store this information with the text buffer. When the entire file has been read, the function stores the number of lines in the file and initializes the line to be displayed at the top of the window to zero.

```
load_file (data, filename)
  text_data     *data;
  char          *filename;
{
  int           foreground, background, i, dir, ascent, desc;
  XCharStruct   char_info;
  FILE          *fp, *fopen ();
  char          buf[MAXLINESIZE];
  /*
   * Open the file.
   */
  if ((fp = fopen (filename, "r")) == NULL) {
    fprintf (stderr, "Unable to open %s\n", filename);
    exit (1);
  }
  /*
   * Read each line of the file into the buffer,
   * calculating and caching the extents of
   * each line.
   */
  i = 0;
  data->fontheight = 0;
  while ((fgets (buf, MAXLINESIZE, fp)) != NULL &&
         i < MAXLINES) {
    data->chars[i] = XtMalloc (strlen (buf) + 1);
    buf[strlen (buf) - 1] = '\0';
    strcpy (data->chars[i], buf);
```

```
        data->length[i] = strlen (data->chars[i]);
        XTextExtents(data->font, data->chars[i],
                     data->length[i], &dir, &ascent,
                     &desc, &char_info);
        data->rbearing[i] = char_info.rbearing;
        data->descent    = desc;
        data->fontheight = ascent + desc;
        i++;
    }
    /*
     * Close the file.
     */
    fclose(fp);
    /*
     * Remember the number of lines, and initialize the
     * current line number to be 0.
     */
    data->nitems = i;
    data->top = 0;
}
```

The function **create_scrollbar()** creates an XmScrollBar widget and defines call-backs for the scroll bar's **XmNvalueChangedCallback** and **XmNdragCallback** lists. This function also sets the minimum position of the XmScrollBar widget to zero and the maximum position to the number of lines in the file. This allows the current position of the scroll bar to correspond directly to the line number of the first line of text in the window. The function also sets the size of the scrollbar slider so that ratio of the slider size to the canvas window size is equal to the ratio of the displayed text to the file size, and sets the **XmNpageIncrement** resource to the number of lines of text that can be displayed in the canvas widget's window. This allows the file viewer to scroll the correct number of lines when the user scrolls one page.

```
Widget create_scrollbar (parent, data)
    Widget       parent;
    text_data    *data;
{
    Arg     wargs[10];
    int     n;
    Widget  scrollbar;
    /*
     * Set the scrollbar so that movements are
     * reported in terms of lines of text. Set the
     * scrolling increment to a single line, and the page
```

```
 * increment to the number of lines the canvas widget
 * can hold. Also set the slider size to be proportional
 * to the part of the file displayed.
 */
n = 0;
XtSetArg (wargs[n], XmNminimum, 0);  n++;
XtSetArg (wargs[n], XmNmaximum, data->nitems);  n++;
XtSetArg (wargs[n], XmNincrement, 1);  n++;
XtSetArg (wargs[n], XmNsliderSize,
          data->canvas_height / data->fontheight);  n++;
XtSetArg (wargs[n], XmNpageIncrement,
          data->canvas_height/ data->fontheight);  n++;
scrollbar = XtCreateManagedWidget ("scrollbar",
                                    xmScrollBarWidgetClass,
                                    parent, wargs, n);
XtAddCallback (scrollbar, XmNvalueChangedCallback,
               scroll_bar_moved, data);
XtAddCallback (scrollbar, XmNdragCallback,
               scroll_bar_moved, data);
return scrollbar;
}
```

The XmScrollBar widget supports a large number of callbacks, which allow the application to easily determine things such as when the user has scrolled one page, or when the user has scrolled to the top or bottom of the page. If the application does not register any callbacks for these callback lists, the widget calls the **XmNvalueChangedCallback** and **XmNdragCallback** lists in all cases.

The function **create_gc()** creates a graphics context using the foreground and background colors retrieved from the **canvas** widget and the font retrieved from the resource data base.

```
create_gc (data)
  text_data  *data;
{
  XGCValues  gcv;
  Display    *dpy = XtDisplay(data->canvas);
  Window     w    = XtWindow(data->canvas);
  int        mask = GCFont | GCForeground | GCBackground;
  Arg        wargs[10];
  int        n;
  /*
   * Create a GC using the colors of the canvas widget.
   */
```

```
*/
n = 0;
XtSetArg(wargs[n], XtNforeground, &gcv.foreground); n++;
XtSetArg(wargs[n], XtNbackground, &gcv.background); n++;
XtGetValues(data->canvas, wargs, n);

gcv.font        = data->font->fid;
data->gc        = XCreateGC (dpy, w, mask, &gcv);
}
```

The XmDrawingArea widget passes a pointer to a structure of type **XmDrawing-AreaCallbackStruct** as call data to functions registered as **XmNexposeCallback** and **XmNresizeCallback** callback functions. This structure contains the following information:

```
int        reason;
XEvent     *event;
Window     window;
Region     region;
```

The callback **function handle_exposures()** draws as many lines of text as the XmDrawingArea widget's window can hold. This function uses the information contained in the call data structure to set the clip mask of the graphics context before redrawing the text to eliminate redrawing areas of the window outside the exposed region. To do this, the function creates a **Region** to represent the rectangular area reported by the **Expose** event. This allows us to use the Xlib region facilities to handle clipping. Once a valid region is available, this function uses **XSetRegion()** to set the clip mask of the GC to the area represented by the region.

Next, **handle_exposures()** draws each line in the text buffer, beginning with the line indexed by **data->top**, and continuing until either the text line lies outside the extent of the window, or the last line in the buffer has been drawn. The variable **yloc**, which determines the current *y* coordinate of the next line of text, is incremented by the height of the text each time through the while loop. Notice that **yloc** is incremented *before* each line is drawn, because **XDrawImageString()** draws text relative to the *lower* left corner of the bounding box. Therefore, the first line is drawn at **data->fontheight**.

Although setting the clipping region in the graphics contexts allows the server to clip the text to the region that needs to be redrawn, it is also somewhat inefficient to send the server requests for every line in the window, when only a few lines may need to be redrawn. A smart application should be able to redraw only those lines or portions of lines that are required, instead of relying on the server to do the clipping. The **fileview** example does this in a crude way, by using **XRectInRegion()** to determine whether or not a line intersects with the exposed region. By redrawing a line of text only if it intersects the exposed region, we can reduce the number of server requests and thereby improve the performance of the program. In this example, the performance gain is probably too small to be measured, but the basic principle of trying to reduce the number of server requests by drawing only what is necessary is applicable to more complex examples as well.

```
void handle_exposures (w, data, cb)
    Widget              w;
    text_data        *data;
    XmDrawingAreaCallbackStruct *cb;
{
    int      yloc = 0, index = data->top;
    Region   region;
    /*
     * Create a region and add the contents of the of the event
     */
    region = XCreateRegion();
    XtAddExposureToRegion(cb->event, region);
    /*
     * Set the clip mask of the GC.
     */
    XSetRegion (XtDisplay(w), data->gc, region);
    /*
     * Loop through each line until the bottom of the
     * window is reached, or we run out of lines. Redraw any
     * lines that intersect the exposed region.
     */
    while (index < data->nitems && yloc < data->canvas_height) {
        yloc += data->fontheight;
        if(XRectInRegion(region, MARGIN, yloc - data->fontheight,
                        data->rbearing[index],
                        data->fontheight) != RectangleOut)
            XDrawImageString(XtDisplay (w), XtWindow (w), data->gc,
                            MARGIN, yloc, data->chars[index],
                            data->length[index]);
        index++;
    }
    /*
     * Free the region.
     */
    XDestroyRegion(region);
}
```

To scroll the text in the window, all we have to do is change the value of **data->top** and redraw the entire buffer. The callback **scroll_bar_moved()** sets **data->top** to the current position of the scroll bar as reported in the **XmScrollBarCallbackStruct** and then calls **XClearArea()** to generate an **Expose** event for the entire window.

```
void scroll_bar_moved (w, data, call_data)
  Widget              w;
  text_data           *data;
  XmScrollBarCallbackStruct *call_data;
{
  data->top = call_data->value;
  XClearArea (XtDisplay (w), XtWindow (data->canvas),
              0, 0, 0, 0, TRUE);
}
```

The last function to discuss is the **resize()** callback function. This function simply updates the width and height information stored in the text buffer. We also must reset the XmScrollBar widget's size resources to reflect the new size of the canvas widget. Because the server generates an **Expose** event after a resizing a window, no further action is required to display the new text.

```
void resize (w, data, call_data)
  Widget              w;
  text_data           *data;
  caddr_t             call_data;
{
  Arg        wargs[2];
  int        n;
  /*
   * Determine the new widget of the canvas widget.
   */
  n = 0;
  XtSetArg (wargs[n], XtNheight, &data->canvas_height);n++;
  XtSetArg (wargs[n], XtNwidth,  &data->canvas_width); n++;
  XtGetValues (w, wargs, n);
  /*
   * Reset the scrollbar slider to indicate the relative
   * proportion of text displayed and also the new page size.
   */
  n = 0;
  XtSetArg (wargs[n], XmNsliderSize,
            data->canvas_height / data->fontheight);  n++;
```

```
   XtSetArg (wargs[n], XmNpageIncrement,
           data->canvas_height / data->fontheight);  n++;
   XtSetValues (data->scrollbar, wargs, n);
}
```

Figure 9.2 shows the fileview program.

```
╔══════════════════════ fileview ══════════════════════╗
║ main (argc, argv)                                     ║▲
║   int        argc;                                    ║
║   char       *argv[];                                 ║
║ {                                                     ║
║   Widget     toplevel, sb, sw;                        ║
║   Arg        wargs[10];                               ║
║   int        n;                                       ║
║   text_data  data;                                    ║
║                                                       ║
║   toplevel = XtInitialize (argv[0], "Fileview",       ║
║                            NULL, 0, &argc, argv);     ║
║   XtGetApplicationResources (toplevel, &data, resources,║
║                            XtNumber (resources), NULL, 0);║
║   /*                                                  ║
║    * Read the file specified in argv[1] into the      ║
║    * text buffer.                                     ║
║    */                                                 ║
║   load_file (&data, (argc == 2) ? argv[1] : NULL);    ║
║   /*                                                  ║
║    * Create a ScrolledWindow widget as a base.        ║
║    */                                                 ║
║   sw = XtCreateManagedWidget ("framework",            ║
║                            xmScrolledWindowWidgetClass,║
║                            toplevel, NULL, 0);        ║
║   /*                                                  ║
║    * Create the drawing surface.                      ║
║    */                                                 ║
║   data.canvas= XtCreateManagedWidget("canvas",        ║▼
╚═══════════════════════════════════════════════════════╝
```

Figure 9.2 The fileview program.

9.3.1   Adding Smooth Scrolling

There are many optimizations and improvements that we can make to the file viewer example. For example, in the version in the previous section, each time the text is scrolled by
even a single line, the entire window of text is redrawn. It is often better to copy the bitmapped image of some of the lines to their new location, and redraw only a few lines. Figure
9.3 illustrates this approach, which produces a smooth scrolling effect.

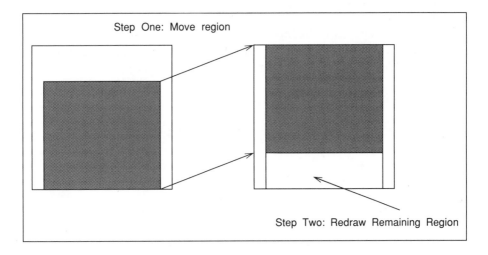

Figure 9.3 Using **XCopyArea()** to scroll the contents of a window.

To achieve a smooth scrolling effect, all we need to do is redesign the
scroll_bar_moved() callback function. All other parts of the program can remain the
same. The new **scroll_bar_moved()** function uses **XCopyArea()** to move as much text
as possible. It also calculates the remaining region of the window that must be redrawn and
clears that area. The server will generate **Expose** events to redraw the cleared area.

```
void scroll_bar_moved(w, data, call_data)
    Widget      w;
    text_data *data;
    XmScrollBarCallbackStruct *call_data;
{
    int      sliderpos = call_data->value;
    int      ysrc,  redraw_top, delta;

    /*
     * Compute the number of pixels the text must be moved.
     */
    delta = ABS((data->top - sliderpos) * data->fontheight);
    delta = MIN(delta, data->canvas_height);
    /*
     * If we are scrolling down, we start at zero and simply
     * move by the delta. The portion that must be redrawn
     * is simply between zero and delta.
     */
```

```
   ysrc = redraw_top = 0;
   /*
    * If we are scrolling up, we start at the delta and move
    * to zero. The part to redraw lies between the bottom
    * of the window and the bottom - delta.
    */
   if(sliderpos >= data->top){
     ysrc       =  delta;
     redraw_top =  data->canvas_height - delta;
   }
   /*
    * Set the top line of the text buffer.
    */
   data->top = sliderpos;
   /*
    * Move the existing text to its new position.
    * Turn off any clipping on the GC first.
    */
   XSetClipMask(XtDisplay(w), data->gc, None);
   XCopyArea(XtDisplay(data->canvas), XtWindow(data->canvas),
                       XtWindow(data->canvas), data->gc,
                       0, ysrc,
                       data->canvas_width,
                       data->canvas_height - delta,
                       0,  delta - ysrc);
   /*
    * Clear the remaining area of any old text,
    * Request server to generate Expose events for the
    * area by setting exposures to TRUE.
    */
   XClearArea(XtDisplay(w), XtWindow(data->canvas),
       0, redraw_top,
       0, delta, TRUE);
}
```

If the slider position is less than the top line in the window, then we need to scroll the window's contents down. The current contents of the window must be copied to the position determined by the difference between the old top and the new top of the window. Since the indexes are in terms of characters, we must multiply them by the font height to convert to pixel dimensions. If the scrollbar position is greater than the top line in the window, the text must be scrolled up. This can be done by moving the text from the computed delta to the top of the window.

After calculating the coordinates of the areas of text to be moved and redrawn, **scroll_bar_moved()** sets **data->top** to its new value, and calls **XCopyArea()** to shift the bitmapped image in the window to its new position. The remaining area of the window is cleared to remove the old text, and also to generate an **Expose** event on the cleared area. The **Expose** event then causes the **handle_exposures()** event handler to be invoked, which redraws the newly exposed area of text.

With this technique, only a small portion of the window is redrawn, producing a much smoother effect. An even smoother effect could be obtained by eliminating the server round trip that generates the **Expose** event when scrolling. One way to do this is to redraw the new portion of the text directly in the **scroll_bar_moved()** callback. In this case, the callback should not request exposures in the call to **XClearArea()**. In addition to reducing the number of server requests, this approach eliminates a race condition that can occur when scrolling rapidly. It is quite possible to scroll the window fast enough so that the contents of the window have already been scrolled a second time before the server generates the first **Expose** event. To use this approach, we must replace the call to **XClearArea()** in the previous version with the following lines:

```
/*
 * Clear the remaining area of any old text, and
 * redraw the area in that part of the window.
 */
{
  int  yloc = 0, index = data->top;
  XClearArea(XtDisplay(w), XtWindow(data->canvas),
                    0, redraw_top,
                    0, delta, FALSE);
  while (index < data->nitems && yloc < data->canvas_height){
    yloc += data->fontheight;
    if(yloc >= redraw_top  &&
       (yloc - data->fontheight)<= (redraw_top + delta))
      XDrawImageString(XtDisplay (w),
                    XtWindow (data->canvas), data->gc,
                    MARGIN, yloc, data->chars[index],
                    data->length[index]);
    index++;
  }
}
```

9.3.2   Reducing the Number of Redraws

There is one more interesting enhancement we can make to the file viewer to improve performance. You may have noticed that it seems somewhat wasteful to create a region and set the clip mask of graphics every time an **Expose** event occurs, particularly since the server often generates multiple **Expose** events when the window's visibility changes. However, we can use the technique of adding the exposures to the region to allow us to wait until all pending **Expose** events have been reported before drawing the text. This can potentially save many server requests. If the XmDrawingArea widget requested exposure events to be compressed, the Xt Intrinsics would do this automatically. However, it is straightforward to do it in the callback itself. As discussed in Chapter 5, the **count** member of an **XExposeEvent** structure reports the number of **Expose** events still pending in the event queue. We can modify the **handle_exposures()** callback to create a region when the first event is received, and add all **Expose** events to the region until an event is received with the **count** member set to zero. Only then does the function redraw the text, using the composite region as a clip mask. Once the window has been redrawn, **handle_exposures()** frees the region and sets it to **NULL** to prepare for the next set of **Expose** events. This variation of **handle_exposures()** is defined as:

```
void handle_exposures (w, data, cb)
   Widget          w;
   text_data       *data;
   XmDrawingAreaCallbackStruct *cb;
{
   int             yloc = 0, index = data->top;
   static Region region = NULL;
   /*
    * Create a region and add the rect reported in the event
    */
   if(!region)
     region = XCreateRegion();

   XtAddExposureToRegion(cb->event, region);
   /*
    * If there are more events pending, just return.
    */
   if(cb->event->xexpose.count != 0)
     return;
   /*
    * Set the clip mask of the GC.
    */
   XSetRegion (XtDisplay(w), data->gc, region);
   /*
    * Loop through each line until the bottom of the
    * window is reached, or we run out of lines. Redraw any
    * lines that intersect the exposed region.
```

```
  */
  while (index < data->nitems && yloc < data->canvas_height) {
    yloc += data->fontheight;
    if(XRectInRegion(region, MARGIN, yloc - data->fontheight,
                     data->rbearing[index],
                     data->fontheight) != RectangleOut)
      XDrawImageString(XtDisplay (w), XtWindow (w), data->gc,
                       MARGIN, yloc, data->chars[index],
                       data->length[index]);
    index++;
  }
  /*
   * Free the region, and reset it to NULL.
   */
  XDestroyRegion(region);
  region = NULL;
}
```

9.4 COMPOUND STRINGS

Motif provides an abstraction for representing text known as a *compound string*. The purpose of a compound string is to allow textual data to be encoded in a way that is independent of the underlying assumptions we often make about strings. For example, we often assume strings represent ASCII characters, which need not always be the case. For example, one character set that is important internationally is Kanji. Compound strings break text into several components:

- Character set: This attribute defines the mapping between a string of bits and the characters being represented. A character set is simply a character string (octets) that is used to match a font with a compound string.

- Direction: This attribute defines the relationship between the keystroke entry order and the order in which the characters in a string are seen on the screen. In English this display order goes from left to right, but in languages such as Hebrew the direction is right to left. The default direction is left-to-right.

- A text component which represents the actual data and is not interpreted.

Compound strings can consist of a single text component and its attributes, or a list of compound strings. A special type of compound string, a separator, is just a compound string with no value which is used to separate other segments.

9.4.1   Fontlists

Motif supports the concept of a *fontlist*, a list of fonts associated with a character set. Motif widgets uses an **XmNfontList** resource to determine the font with which text is to be displayed instead of the Intrinsics' **XtNfont** resource. The function

    `XmFontListCreate(font, charset)`

creates and returns a new fontlist with a single element specified by the **font** argument. The **charset** argument specifies an arbitrary character set identifier for the font list. Additional fonts can be added to an existing fontlist, using the function:

    `XmAddFontList(oldlist, font, charset)`

This function creates and returns a new fontlist. The **oldlist** argument specifies a pointer to the font list to which the specified font is to be added. The **oldlist** font list is destroyed after the required information is extracted and should not be accessed again.

Fontlists can be freed using the function:

    `XmFreeFontList(list)`

9.4.2   Creating and Manipulating Compound Strings

The simplest way to create a compound string is with the function:

    `XmStringCreate (text, charset)`

This function takes a character string and a character set and returns an equivalent compound string. The **xs_concat_words()** function from Chapter 2 provides an example of how this function can be used.

The function

    `XmStringLtoRCreate (text, charset)`

is similar to **XmStringCreate()** except that it searches for newline characters in the character string. All text up to the point where a newline is encountered is placed in a text segment. Successive segments are separated by separator components. This function is used by the **xs_wprintf()** function defined in Chapter 5.

Compound strings can be freed with the function:

    `XmStringFree(string)`

This function is also demonstrated in the **xs_concat_words()** function defined in Chapter 2.

The function

    `XmStringSeparatorCreate ()`

creates a separator component, which is basically equivalent to a newline character. Chapter 4 used a function, **xs_str_array_to_xmstr()**, without defining it. This function takes an array of character strings and returns an equivalent compound string, assuming each string in the array represents one line of a multi-line piece of text. We can now define this function as:

```
/*******************************************************
 * xs_str_array_to_xmstr(): convert char ** to
 *     compound string
 *******************************************************/
#include <X11/Intrinsic.h>
#include <Xm/Xm.h>

XmString xs_str_array_to_xmstr(cs, n)
      char      *cs[];
      int       n; {
      XmString  xmstr;
      int       i;
 /*
  * If the array is empty just return an empty string.
  */
 if (n <= 0)
    return (XmStringCreate("", XmSTRING_DEFAULT_CHARSET));

 xmstr = (XmString) NULL;

 for (i = 0; i < n; i++)  {
  if (i > 0)
   xmstr = XmStringConcat(xmstr, XmStringSeparatorCreate());
  xmstr = XmStringConcat(xmstr,
                         XmStringCreate(cs[i],
                         XmSTRING_DEFAULT_CHARSET));
 }
 return (xmstr);
 }
```

Motif also provides functions that allow the programmer to determine if two compound strings are equal, make copies of compound strings, append one string to another, and so on.

The function

XmStringByteCompare (s1, s2)

returns **TRUE** if the two given compound strings are identical, based on a byte-by-byte comparison of the two compound strings. Because a string may be stored in a compiled internal form, the byte-by-byte comparison of two seemingly identical strings may not succeed. The function

```
XmStringCompare (s1, s2)
```

can be used to determine whether or not two compound strings are semantically, but not necessarily byte-for-byte, equivalent.

The function

```
XmStringEmpty (s1)
```

returns **TRUE** if the compound string is empty.

The function

```
XmStringConcat (s1, s2)
```

appends **s2** to the end of **s1** and returns a new compound string. The original strings are unchanged.

Similarly, the function

```
XmStringNConcat (s1, s2, num_bytes)
```

returns a new compound string with **num_bytes** bytes from **s2** appended to **s1**. The original strings are unchanged.

The function

```
XmStringLength (s1)
```

returns the size in bytes of a compound string. The size includes all components of the string.

9.4.3   Displaying Compound Strings

Motif provides some additional functions for drawing compound strings in a X window. These functions are nearly identical to the corresponding Xlib text drawing functions. One important difference is that the (x, y) position specifies the top, left corner of the bounding box containing the string, rather than the lower left corner used by the Xlib drawing functions.

The function

```
XmStringDraw (d, w, fontlist, string, gc, x, y, width,
              alignment, layout_direction, clip);
```

draws a compound string in a window. The **layout_direction** argument specifies the direction in which the segments of the compound string are drawn. The **clip** argument allows the calling application to define a clipping rectangle that constrains the area in which text is drawn. If this argument is **NULL** no clipping will be done.

The function

```
XmStringDrawImage (d, w, fontlist, string, gc, x, y, width,
                        alignment, layout_direction, clip);
```

is similar to **XmStringDraw()**, except that it corresponds semantically to **XDrawImage-String()**.

9.4.4   Retrieving Segments from Compound Strings

Sometimes it is necessary to extract the contents of a compound string. Motif provides functions for retrieving segments and components of segments. To retrieve subsequent segments of a compound string, it is useful to have a simple means of remembering the state of the string. The functions that retrieve components from a compound string use a context of type

XmContext

to maintain this state. Motif does not make the definition of XmContext public, but it can be treated as an opaque data structure and simply declared as a untyped pointer.

Before using these functions, a context must be initialized using the function:

XmStringInitContext (&context, string)

When a context is no longer needed, it should be freed using the function:

XmStringFreeContext (context)

Successive segments of a string may be retrieved using the function:

```
XmStringGetNextSegment (context, &text, &charset,
                        &direction, &separator)
```

Each time this function is called, it returns the text, character set, and direction components of the next segment of a compound string. The boolean value **separator** is **TRUE** if the next component is a separator. The function returns **FALSE** if there are no more segments in the compound string.

We can use this function to write a routine that retrieves the character string from a compound string, assuming that we do not care about character sets (in this book we nearly always use the default character set), and assuming that the compound string consists of one or more segments created from ASCII characters. For example, this function can be used to retrieve an equivalent character string from a compound string created by the function **xs_concat_words()**, defined in Chapter 2. This function initializes a context and then calls **XmStringGetNextSegment()** repeatedly until there are no more segments in the string. The retrieved text is appended to a buffer after enlarging the buffer with **XtRealloc()**. When all segments have been processed, the function frees the context and returns the buffered text.

```
#include <X11/Intrinsic.h>
#include <Xm/Xm.h>

char * xs_get_string_from_xmstring (string)
    XmString string;
{
    caddr_t             context;
    char                *text;
    XmStringCharSet     charset;
    XmStringDirection   dir;
    Boolean             separator;
    char                *buf = NULL;

    int                 done = FALSE;
    XmStringInitContext (&context, string);
    while (!done)
      if(XmStringGetNextSegment (context, &text, &charset,
                                 &dir, &separator)){
        if(separator) /* Stop when next segment is a separator */
          done = TRUE;

        if(buf){
          buf = XtRealloc(buf, strlen(buf) + strlen(text) + 2);
          strcat(buf, text);
        }
         else {
          buf = (char *) XtMalloc(strlen(text) +1);
          strcpy(buf, text);
         }
        XtFree(text);
      }
      else
        done = TRUE;

  XmStringFreeContext (context);
  return buf;
}
```

9.4.5   Using Compound Strings

Now that we have described the functions that create and manipulate compound strings and font lists, let's look at an example that uses compound strings. This section re-implements the file viewer example from Section 9.3 using compound strings. Much of this example is identical to the earlier version, and only those functions that are new will be discussed.

First, we need to change the definition of the **text_data** structure defined in file-view.h to store an array of compound strings instead of an array of character strings. The new version of the structure is defined as:

```
typedef struct {
    XmString      chars[MAXLINES];
    Dimension     width[MAXLINES];
    int           descent;
    XFontStruct   *font;
    XmFontList    fontlist;
    GC            gc;
    Widget        scrollbar;
    Widget        canvas;
    Dimension     canvas_height;
    Dimension     canvas_width;
    int           fontheight;
    int           nitems;
    int           top;
} text_data, *text_data_ptr;
```

In addition to changing the text buffer to an array of compound strings, this structure also adds a fontlist, which needs to be defined by the application. We can do this by adding a call to the function **XmFontListCreate()** in the main program just after the application resources are retrieved. We can specify the name of the character set associated with this fontlist to be anything we like. The main part of this version of the fileview program is defined as:

```
/*******************************************************
 * fileview.c: A simple file viewer
 *******************************************************/
#include "fileview.h"

extern Widget create_scrollbar ();

main (argc, argv)
    int       argc;
    char      *argv[];
{
    Widget     toplevel, sb, sw;
    Arg        wargs[10];
    int        n;
    text_data  data;
```

```
    toplevel = XtInitialize (argv[0], "Fileview",
                             NULL, 0, &argc, argv);
    XtGetApplicationResources (toplevel, &data, resources,
                             XtNumber (resources), NULL, 0);
    data.fontlist=XmFontListCreate(data.font,
                             "Fileview_Charset");
/*
 * Read the file specified in argv[1] into the
 * text buffer.
 */
load_file (&data, (argc == 2) ? argv[1] : NULL);
/*
 * Create a ScrolledWindow widget as a base.
 */
sw = XtCreateManagedWidget ("framework",
                             xmScrolledWindowWidgetClass,
                             toplevel, NULL, 0);
/*
 * Create the drawing surface.
 */
data.canvas= XtCreateManagedWidget("canvas",
                                xmDrawingAreaWidgetClass,
                                sw, NULL, 0);
/*
 * Retrieve the initial size of the canvas widget.
 */
XtSetArg (wargs[0], XtNheight, &data.canvas_height);
XtSetArg (wargs[1], XtNwidth, &data.canvas_width);
XtGetValues (data.canvas, wargs, 2);
/*
 * Register callbacks for resizes and exposes.
 */
XtAddCallback (data.canvas, XmNexposeCallback,
                handle_exposures, &data);
XtAddCallback (data.canvas, XmNresizeCallback,
                resize, &data);
/*
 * Create the scrollbar.
 */
data.scrollbar = create_scrollbar (sw, &data);
/*
```

```
 * Register the scrollbar and work area for the
 * ScrolledWindow widget.
 */
n = 0;
XtSetArg(wargs[n], XmNverticalScrollBar, data.scrollbar);n++;
XtSetArg(wargs[n], XmNworkWindow, data.canvas); n++;
XtSetValues(sw, wargs, n);

XtRealizeWidget (toplevel);
create_gc (&data);
XtMainLoop ();
}
```

The only functions that must change are **load_file()**, which reads the file and stores the text in the **text_data** structure and the **XmNexposeCallback** function that draws the text. The function **load_file()** must now convert each line of text from the file to a compound string. It does this by calling **XmStringCreate()** using the charset created in the main program. This function also uses the Motif function **XmStringExtent()** to determine the size of each compound string.

```
load_file (data, filename)
  text_data       *data;
  char            *filename;
{
  XCharStruct      char_info;
  FILE             *fp, *fopen ();
  char             buf[MAXLINESIZE];
  int              height, i;
  /*
   * Open the file.
   */
  if ((fp = fopen (filename, "r")) == NULL) {
    fprintf (stderr, "Unable to open %s\n", filename);
    exit (1);
  }
  /*
   * Read each line of the file into the buffer,
   * calculating and caching the extents of each line.
   */
  i = 0;
  data->fontheight = 0;
  while ((fgets (buf, MAXLINESIZE, fp)) != NULL &&
          i < MAXLINES) {
```

```
        buf[strlen (buf) - 1] = ' ';
        data->chars[i]=XmStringCreate(buf,"Fileview_Charset");
        XmStringExtent (data->fontlist, data->chars[i],
                        &data->width[i], &height);
        data->fontheight = MAX(data->fontheight, height);
        i++;
    }
    /*
     * Close the file.
     */
    fclose(fp);
    /*
     * Set the number of lines, and initialize the
     * current line number to be 0.
     */
    data->nitems = i;
    data->top = 0;
}
```

Finally, the function **handle_exposures()** must be redefined to draw the compound strings using the function **XmStringDrawImage()**. Notice that the variable **yloc**, which keeps track of the vertical position of the next line of text, is now incremented after each line of text is drawn to account for the different interpretation of the origin used by Motif.

```
void handle_exposures (w, data, cb)
    Widget          w;
    text_data       *data;
    XmDrawingAreaCallbackStruct *cb;
{
    int         yloc = 0,
                index = data->top;
    Region   region;
    /*
     * Create a region and add the contents of the of the event
     */
    region = XCreateRegion();
    XtAddExposureToRegion(cb->event, region);
    /*
     * Set the clip mask of the GC.
     */
    XSetRegion (XtDisplay(w), data->gc, region);
    /*
```

```
 * Redraw each line until the bottom of the
 * window is reached, or we run out of lines.
 */
while (index < data->nitems && yloc < data->canvas_height) {
    XmStringDrawImage (XtDisplay (w), XtWindow (w),
                       data->fontlist,
                       data->chars[index],
                       data->gc,
                       MARGIN, yloc, data->width[index],
                       XmALIGNMENT_BEGINNING,
                       XmSTRING_DIRECTION_R_TO_L,
                       NULL);
    yloc += data->fontheight;
    index++;
}
/*
 * Free the region.
 */
XDestroyRegion(region);
}
```

9.5 SUMMARY

This chapter discussed the Xlib functions used to display text in a window as well as the fonts X uses to represent characters. X draws text by performing a fill operation on a rectangular region using a bitmap representing a character as a mask. A font is a collection of bitmapped characters. X provides several functions for drawing strings in windows or pixmaps. Because X treats text the same as any graphics operation, applications can combine Xlib text functions with clipping regions, graphics contexts, and raster operations.

The XmDrawingArea widget is useful when combining Xlib drawing functions with the widgets and architecture of the Xt Intrinsics. Using this widget, the programmer can let the Intrinsics handle the low-level details of the X protocol, but still directly control the contents of the widget's window.

Motif provides a high-level abstraction for text that is free of many of the assumptions often made about ASCII character strings. Compound strings can represent text that flows left to right or right to left and also supports different character sets.

The following chapter discusses the primitive graphics functions provided by Xlib and continues to explore graphics contexts, regions, and related functions.

10

USING THE X
GRAPHICS PRIMITIVES

Previous chapters examined the X color model, graphics contexts, and regions. This chapter presents the graphics primitives provided by Xlib and demonstrates some of these features in examples. Xlib provides a set of simple two-dimensional graphics functions for drawing points, lines, arcs and rectangles. These drawing functions use the same integer coordinate system as the functions that operate on windows. Applications that require more complex graphics functions for panning, scaling, or three-dimensional graphics must usually implement these as a layer above the Xlib graphics functions.[1] All graphics functions operate on a drawable, either a window or a pixmap.

10.1 DRAWING WITH POINTS

The simplest Xlib graphics function displays a single point in a drawable. The function

```
XDrawPoint(display, drawable, gc, x, y)
```

sets a single pixel at location x, y according to the specified GC. It is often more efficient to draw multiple points at once using the function:

---

1. An extension to the X protocol, known as PEX, defines a PHIGS three-dimensional interface for X. This extension has not been implemented at the time this book is being written, but is being considered by the X Consortium as a standard. Some X vendors also provide their own sophisticated graphics packages as extensions to X.

XDrawPoints(display, drawable, gc, points, npoints, mode)

This function draws **npoints** points with a single server request. The **points** argument must be an array of **XPoint** structures. The **mode** argument determines how the server interprets the coordinates in this array and must be one of the constants **CoordModeOrigin** or **CoordModePrevious**. If **CoordModeOrigin** is specified, the server interprets each coordinate relative to the origin of the drawable. The constant **CoordModePrevious** specifies that each coordinate should be interpreted relative to the preceding point. The server always interprets the first point relative to the drawable's origin.

Several attributes of the graphics context affect how points are drawn. These are:

GCFunction	**GCPlaneMask**	**GCForeground**	**GCClipYOrigin**
GCSubwindowMode	**GCClipMask**	**GCBackground**	**GCClipXOrigin**

Let's look at a simple example that uses **XDrawPoint()** to illustrate the basic use of graphics functions in X. The program computes and displays a *fractal* image. Fractals are mathematical expressions based on complex numbers that produce interesting images from simple equations. This example displays a fractal image generated by repeatedly evaluating the expression

$$z = (z + k)^2$$

where both z and k are complex numbers. The value of z is initially set to *(0, 0)*, while k is initialized to the value of each *(x, y)* position in the window. After evaluating the expression some number of times for each point, we test the value of z to see how far it has moved from the *(x, y)* plane. If it is within some predetermined distance of the plane, the pixel is said to be part of the *Mandelbrot Set* and the color of the pixel is set to the same color as all other pixels in the Mandelbrot Set. Otherwise, some other color is chosen for the pixel. This example program bases the color on the distance of the point from the (x, y) plane.

The header file of this program includes the necessary X header files and defines a few data structures. The fractal program defines a **complex** structure to represent complex numbers, and also defines an **image_data** structure to store a graphics context, a pixmap (used to save the image once it is drawn), and some auxiliary data needed for the image calculation.

```
/*****************************************************
 * fractal.h: declarations for the fractal program
 *****************************************************/
#include <X11/StringDefs.h>
#include <X11/Intrinsic.h>
#include <Xm/Xm.h>
#include <Xm/DrawingA.h>
#include <X11/Xutil.h>
#include "libXs.h"

void    resize();
```

```
void      redisplay();
void      create_image ();
/*
 * Structure to represent a complex number.
 */
typedef struct {
  float   real, imag;
} complex;
/*
 * Assorted information needed to generate and draw the image.
 */
typedef struct {
  int           depth, ncolors;
  float         range, max_distance;
  complex       origin;
  GC            gc;
  Pixmap        pix;
  Dimension     width, height;
} image_data, *image_data_ptr;
/*
 * Resource that affect the appearance of the fractal image.
 */
static XtResource resources[] = {
 {"depth", "Depth", XtRInt, sizeof (int),
   XtOffset(image_data_ptr, depth), XtRString, "20"            },
 {"real_origin", "RealOrigin", XtRFloat, sizeof (float),
   XtOffset(image_data_ptr, origin.real), XtRString, "-1.4" },
 {"imaginary_origin","ImaginaryOrigin",XtRFloat,sizeof(float),
   XtOffset(image_data_ptr, origin.imag), XtRString, "1.0"  },
 {"range", "Range", XtRFloat, sizeof(float),
   XtOffset(image_data_ptr,range), XtRString, "2.0"           },
 {"max_distance", "MaxDistance", XtRFloat, sizeof (float),
   XtOffset(image_data_ptr, max_distance),XtRString, "4.0"  }
 };
```

The header file also defines an **XtResources** array used by the resource manager to initialize some of the members of the **image_data** struct. The **depth** member determines how many times the fractal expression is evaluated for each pixel, while the **real_origin** and **imaginary_origin** members allow the image to be *panned* to view different parts of the image. These are floating point coordinates because the example calculates the image in normalized floating coordinates. This allows us to generate the same image regardless of the size of the window that displays the image. The **range** parameter determines the width and height of the real coordinates of the image, and can be altered to *zoom* the image in and out, while the **max_distance** parameter controls the *z* distance considered to be "close" to the *(x, y)* plane.

The main body of the program creates an XmDrawingArea widget used as a drawing canvas, and adds callbacks to handle exposures and resizes. The **xs_cvt_string_to_float** type converter, which we wrote in Chapter 3, is installed before calling **XtGetApplicationResources()** to retrieve the data specified in the **resources** array. Before entering the main event loop, the function **resize()** is called to trigger the creation of the initial image.

```
/****************************************************
 * fractal.c: A simple fractal generator
 ****************************************************/
#include "fractal.h"

main(argc, argv)
    int    argc;
    char *argv[];
{
  Widget      toplevel, canvas;
  image_data data;
  toplevel = XtInitialize(argv[0], "Fractal", NULL, 0,
                          &argc, argv);
  /*
   * Add the string to float type converter.
   */
  XtAddConverter(XtRString, XtRFloat, xs_cvt_str_to_float,
                 NULL, 0);
  XtGetApplicationResources(toplevel, &data, resources,
                            XtNumber(resources), NULL, 0);
  /*
   * Create the widget to display the fractal and register
   * callbacks for resize and refresh.
   */
  canvas = XtCreateManagedWidget("canvas",
                                 xmDrawingAreaWidgetClass,
                                 toplevel, NULL, 0);
  init_data(canvas, &data);
  XtAddCallback(canvas, XmNexposeCallback, redisplay, &data);
  XtAddCallback(canvas, XmNresizeCallback, resize, &data);
  XtRealizeWidget(toplevel);
  resize(canvas, &data, NULL);
  XtMainLoop();
}
```

The function **init_data()** creates a graphics context, determines how many colors are supported by the display, and initializes the **pixmap** member of the **image_data** structure to NULL.

```
init_data(w, data)
    Widget      w;
    image_data *data;
{
  int y;
  Arg wargs[2];
  /*
   * Get the size of the drawing area.
   */
  XtSetArg(wargs[0], XtNwidth,  &data->width);
  XtSetArg(wargs[1], XtNheight, &data->height);
  XtGetValues(w, wargs,2);
  /*
   * Find out how many colors we have to work with, and
   * create a default, writable, graphics context.
   */
  data->ncolors = XDisplayCells(XtDisplay(w),
                                XDefaultScreen(XtDisplay(w)));
  data->gc = XCreateGC(XtDisplay(w),
                       DefaultRootWindow(XtDisplay(w)),
                       NULL, NULL);
  /*
   *   Initialize the pixmap to NULL.
   */
  data->pix = NULL;
}
```

The fractal image is displayed when the window is exposed. However, the function **create_image()** actually generates the fractal. The function uses three nested **for** loops to evaluate the fractal expression. For each (x, y) coordinate, **create_image()** calculates the value of the expression repeatedly until either the maximum number of iterations are performed or until the z distance from the (x, y) plane exceeds the specified limit. If the point is still on the plane when all iterations are calculated, no point is drawn (which is equivalent to drawing the window's background color). If a point moves away from the plane before all iterations are calculated, the function draws a point on the screen. There are many ways to choose the color of each pixel. This example uses a straightforward method that achieves interesting results on color displays. The foreground color of the graphics context is determined by the z distance from the plane modulo the number of colors available.

Notice that **create_image()** draws each point twice: once in the XmDrawingArea widget and once in a pixmap. This creates a duplicate of the image in off-screen memory. Depending on the size of the window, this image can take considerable time to draw. Storing the image in off-screen memory allows us to use **XCopyArea()** to restore the image rather than recalculating the entire image each time the window is exposed.[2] However, we also have to be careful to draw the point in the window only if the widget has been realized. This is because **create_image()** is called from the widget's **XmNresizeCallback** list, and it is possible for this procedure to be called before the widget is realized.

```
void create_image (w, data)
      Widget       w;
      image_data   *data;
{
 int  x, y, iteration;
 /*
  * For each pixel on the window....
  */
 for (y = 0; y < data->height; y++) {
  for (x = 0; x < data->width; x++) {
    complex z, k;
   /*
    * Initialize K to the normalized, floating coordinate
    * in the x, y plane. Init Z to (0.0, 0.0).
    */
    z.real =  z.imag = 0.0;
    k.real =  data->origin.real + (float) x /
                 (float) data->width * data->range;
    k.imag =  data->origin.imag - (float) y /
                 (float) data->height * data->range;
   /*
    * Calculate z = (z + k) * (z + k) over and over.
    */
    for (iteration = 0; iteration < data->depth; iteration++){
       float   distance, real_part, imag_part;

       real_part = z.real + k.real;
       imag_part = z.imag + k.imag;
       z.real = real_part * real_part - imag_part * imag_part;
```

---

2. It isn't necessary to draw the point to the window at all. We could just store the image in the pixmap, then copy the image from the pixmap to the window. However, drawing the fractal image is time-consuming, and it is useful to provide some reassurance to the user that the program is making some progress by showing the preliminary image in the window as it is being created.

```
        z.imag = 2 * real_part * imag_part;
        distance  = z.real * z.real + z.imag * z.imag;
      /*
       * If the z point has moved off the plane, set the
       * current foreground color to the distance (coerced to
       * an int and modulo the number of colors available),
       * and draw a point in both the window and the pixmap.
       */
      if (distance  >= data->max_distance){
        int color = (int) distance % data->ncolors;
        XSetForeground(XtDisplay(w), data->gc, color);
        XDrawPoint (XtDisplay(w), data->pix, data->gc, x, y);
        if(XtIsRealized(w))
          XDrawPoint (XtDisplay(w), XtWindow(w), data->gc,x,y);
        break;
      }
    }
   }
  }
 }
}
```

The callback function **redisplay()** handles **Expose** events by copying the image from a region in the pixmap to the window. It uses **XCopyArea()** to copy the rectangular area defined by the **Expose** event in the call data from the pixmap to the window. Copying an image between a pixmap and a window is normally much faster than recomputing the image. This program is a good example of an application that could benefit from a server that provides backing store to automatically maintain a window's contents. However, using a pixmap to maintain the image works even with X servers that do not support this feature, as long as there is sufficient off-screen memory to support the pixmap.

```
    void redisplay (w, data, call_data)
        Widget          w;
        image_data      *data;
        XmDrawingAreaCallbackStruct    *call_data;
    {
     XExposeEvent  *event = (XExposeEvent *) call_data->event;
     /*
      * Extract the exposed area from the event and copy
      * from the saved pixmap to the window.
      */
      XCopyArea(XtDisplay(w), data->pix, XtWindow(w), data->gc,
                event->x, event->y, event->width, event->height,
                event->x, event->y);
    }
```

The remaining function to be discussed is the **XmNresizeCallback** function **resize()**. This function frees the current pixmap, which no longer corresponds to the size of the window, and creates a new pixmap the same size as the window. The pixmap is cleared by calling **XFillRectangle()** (see Section 10.3) with the default black pixel of the screen. It then calls **create_image()** to generate a new fractal scaled to the size of the new window.

```
void resize(w, data, call_data)
     Widget         w;
     image_data     *data;
     caddr_t        call_data;
{
  Arg wargs[10];
  /*
   *  Get the new window size.
   */
  XtSetArg(wargs[0], XtNwidth,  &data->width);
  XtSetArg(wargs[1], XtNheight, &data->height);
  XtGetValues(w, wargs, 2);
  /*
   * Clear the window and generate an Expose event for
   * the entire window.
   */
   if(XtIsRealized(w))
     XClearArea(XtDisplay(w), XtWindow(w), 0, 0, 0, 0, TRUE);
  /*
   *  Free the old pixmap and one the size of the window.
   */
  if(data->pix)
     XFreePixmap(XtDisplay(w), data->pix);
  data->pix= XCreatePixmap(XtDisplay(w),
                           DefaultRootWindow(XtDisplay(w)),
                           data->width, data->height,
                           DefaultDepthOfScreen(XtScreen(w)));
  XSetForeground(XtDisplay(w), data->gc,
                 BlackPixelOfScreen(XtScreen(w)));
  XFillRectangle(XtDisplay(w), data->pix, data->gc, 0, 0,
                 data->width,  data->height);
  /*
   * Generate a new image.
   */
  create_image(w, data);
}
```

Fig. 10.1 shows the fractal generated by this program.

Figure 10.1 The fractal program.

Although using a pixmap to store the fractal image in off-screen memory partially alle-viates the problem of handling **Expose** events for a graphics-intensive image application, the initial time required to compute and draw the image still leaves something to be desired. The calculation itself is time consuming, although there is little we can do about that because fractals are inherently expensive to compute. We can, however, optimize the drawing of the image by reducing the number of server requests. The function **XDrawPoints()** draws mul-tiple points with a single server request. All points use the same graphics context, but do not have to be contiguous. Using **XDrawPoints()** to reduce the number of server requests greatly increases the speed of the fractal program. The only part of the fractal program that must change is the function **create_image()**.

```
void create_image (w, data)
     Widget          w;
     image_data      *data;
{
  int x, y, iteration;
  /*
    * Start by zeroing all buffers.
```

```
    */
    init_buffer(data);
    /*
     * For each pixel on the window....
     */
    for (y = 0; y < data->height; y++) {
     for (x = 0; x < data->width; x++) {
      complex z, k;
      /*
       *   Initialize K to the normalized, floating coordinate in
       *   the x,y plane. Init Z to (0.0, 0.0).
       */
      z.real = z.imag = 0.0;
      k.real =  data->origin.real + (float) x /
                    (float) data->width * data->range;
      k.imag =  data->origin.imag - (float) y /
                    (float) data->height * data->range;
      /*
       * Calculate z = (z + k) * (z + k) over and over.
       */
      for (iteration = 0; iteration < data->depth; iteration++){
       float distance, real_part, imag_part;
       real_part = z.real + k.real;
       imag_part = z.imag + k.imag;
       z.real    = real_part * real_part - imag_part * imag_part;
       z.imag    = 2 * real_part * imag_part;
       distance  = z.real * z.real + z.imag * z.imag;
       /*
        * If the z point has moved off the plane, buffer the
        * point using the integerized distance as the color.
        */
       if (distance  >= data->max_distance){
         buffer_point(w,data,(int)distance % data->ncolors,x, y);
         break;
       }
      }
     }
    }
    /*
     * Display all remaining points.
     */
    flush_buffer(w, data);
    }
```

The primary difference between this version of **create_image()** and the previous version is that instead of calling **XDrawPoint()** directly, **create_image()** calls the function **buffer_point()**. This function stores points until they can be drawn as a group using **XDrawPoints()**. The function **init_buffer()** must be called before beginning the calculations to initialize the data structures used by the buffer routines and **flush_buffer()** must also be called to flush the buffer after all points are generated.

The buffering routines use a global data structure containing a two-dimensional array of **XPoint** structures. The array holds **MAXPOINTS** number of points for **MAXCOLOR** possible colors. The **points** structure also contains an array of integers that indicates how many points are stored in each of the point arrays.

```
#define MAXPOINTS 500
#define MAXCOLOR   256

struct{
   XPoint   data[MAXCOLOR][MAXPOINTS];
   int      npoints[MAXCOLOR];
} points;
```

The function **init_buffer()** initializes the number of points of each color to zero.

```
init_buffer(data)
     image_data *data;
{
  int i;
  if (data->ncolors > MAXCOLOR)
     XtError("This display has too many colors");
  for(i=0;i<MAXCOLOR;i++)
    points.npoints[i] = 0;
}
```

The **buffer_point()** routine first checks how many points of the given color are already stored in the buffer. If this number is equal to the maximum number that can be buffered, it uses **XDrawPoints()** to draw all points stored in the buffer in both the window and the pixmap. Then, it resets the number of points for the given color to zero, and stores the current point in the buffer.

```
buffer_point(w, data, color, x , y)
     Widget       w;
     image_data *data;
     int          color, x,y;
{
  if(points.npoints[color] == MAXPOINTS - 1){
    /*
```

```
 * If the buffer is full, set the foreground color
 * of the graphics context and draw the points in both
 * the window and the pixmap.
 */
XSetForeground(XtDisplay(w), data->gc, color);
if(XtIsRealized(w))
  XDrawPoints (XtDisplay(w), XtWindow(w), data->gc,
               points.data[color], points.npoints[color],
               CoordModeOrigin);
XDrawPoints (XtDisplay(w), data->pix, data->gc,
             points.data[color], points.npoints[color],
             CoordModeOrigin);
    /*
     * Reset the buffer.
     */
    points.npoints[color] = 0;
  }
  /*
   * Store the point in the buffer according to its color.
   */
  points.data[color][points.npoints[color]].x = x;
  points.data[color][points.npoints[color]].y = y;
  points.npoints[color] += 1;
}
```

The function **flush_buffer()** must be called when the image calculation is finished to draw any points remaining in the buffer. This function loops through all colors, drawing the remaining points in both the window and the pixmap.

```
flush_buffer(w, data)
     Widget      w;
     image_data *data;
{
  int i;
  /*
   * Check each buffer.
   */
  for(i=0;i<data->ncolors;i++)
    /*
     * If there are any points in this buffer, display them
     * in the window and the pixmap.
     */
    if(points.npoints[i]){
```

```
    XSetForeground(XtDisplay(w), data->gc, i);
    if(XtIsRealized(w))
      XDrawPoints (XtDisplay(w), XtWindow(w), data->gc,
                   points.data[i], points.npoints[i],
                   CoordModeOrigin);
      XDrawPoints (XtDisplay(w), data->pix, data->gc,
                   points.data[i], points.npoints[i],
                   CoordModeOrigin);
    points.npoints[i] = 0;
  }
}
```

Although the image calculation itself is still time consuming, buffering the points provides a significant speedup. In addition to reducing the time initially required to draw the image, buffering the drawing requests reduces the load on the server, which reduces the degree to which the fractal program interferes with other applications using the server while the image is being generated. This buffering example was more complex than many applications might be because the Xlib functions for drawing multiple points and lines use only a single GC. A black and white version of this program would be much simpler.

10.2 DRAWING WITH LINES

The Xlib function

XDrawLine(display, drawable, gc, x1, y1, x2, y2)

draws a single line between two points. The way in which **XDrawLine()** draws lines is determined by the following attributes of the graphics context:

GCFunction	GCPlaneMask	GCLineWidth
GCLineStyle	GCCapStyle	GCFillStyle
GCSubwindowMode	GCClipXOrigin	GCClipYOrigin
GCClipMask		

The function

XDrawSegments(display, drawable, gc, segments, nsegments)

draws multiple, discontiguous line segments with a single request. The line segments are specified by an array of type **XSegment**, which includes the members:

short x1, y1, x2, y2;

Although the line segments do not need to be connected, **XDrawSegments()** draws all segments using the same graphics context. This function uses the same graphics context members as **XDrawLine()**.

The function

XDrawLines(display, drawable, gc, points, npoints, mode)

draws multiple connected lines. This function draws **npoints − 1** lines between the points in the **points** array. **XDrawLines()** draws all lines in the order in which the points appear in the array. The **mode** argument determines whether the points are interpreted relative to the origin of the drawable or relative to the last point drawn, and must be one of **Coord-ModeOrigin** or **CoordModePrevious**. **XDrawLines()** uses the **GCJoinStyle** attribute of the graphics context, in addition to the graphics context members used by **XDrawLine()**.

We can demonstrate **XDrawLine()** in a simple program that uses a technique known as *rubber banding*. A rubber band line is usually drawn interactively by the user. The user first sets an initial endpoint, usually by pressing a mouse button. A line is then drawn between this endpoint and the current position of the sprite. As the user moves the sprite, the line appears to stretch as if it were a rubber band connected between the sprite and the initial position. The rubber banding ends in response to some user action, typically when the mouse button is released. This technique is commonly used to allow the user to define a beginning and ending coordinate for drawing lines or other figures interactively.

The example program, named **rubberband**, allows the user to draw rubber band lines in the window of an XmDrawingArea widget. The **rubberband** program begins by defining a data structure, **rubberband_data**, that contains information used by the event handlers that perform the rubber banding.

```
/*************************************************
 * rubberband.c: rubberband line example
 *************************************************/
#include <X11/StringDefs.h>
#include <X11/Intrinsic.h>
#include <X11/cursorfont.h>
#include <Xm/Xm.h>
#include <Xm/DrawingA.h>
#include "libXs.h"

typedef struct {
    int start_x, start_y, last_x, last_y;
    GC  gc;
  } rubber_band_data;

void start_rubber_band();
void end_rubber_band();
void track_rubber_band();
```

The body of the program simply creates an XmDrawingArea widget and adds event handlers for **ButtonPress**, **ButtonRelease** and pointer motion events which work together to implement the rubber banding.

```
main(argc, argv)
 int    argc;
 char *argv[];
{
  Widget              toplevel, canvas;
  rubber_band_data data;

  toplevel = XtInitialize(argv[0], "Rubberband", NULL, 0,
                          &argc, argv);
  /*
   * Create a drawing surface, and add event handlers for
   * ButtonPress, ButtonRelease and MotionNotify events.
   */
  canvas = XtCreateManagedWidget("canvas",
                                 xmDrawingAreaWidgetClass,
                                 toplevel, NULL, 0);
  XtAddEventHandler(canvas, ButtonPressMask, FALSE,
                    start_rubber_band, &data);
  XtAddEventHandler(canvas, ButtonMotionMask, FALSE,
                    track_rubber_band, &data);
  XtAddEventHandler(canvas, ButtonReleaseMask,
                    FALSE, end_rubber_band, &data);
  XtRealizeWidget(toplevel);
  /*
   * Establish a passive grab, for any button press.
   * Force the sprite to stay within the canvas window, and
   * change the sprite to a cross_hair.
   */
  XGrabButton(XtDisplay(canvas), AnyButton, AnyModifier,
              XtWindow(canvas), TRUE,
              ButtonPressMask | ButtonMotionMask |
              ButtonReleaseMask,
              GrabModeAsync, GrabModeAsync,
              XtWindow(canvas),
              XCreateFontCursor(XtDisplay(canvas),
                                XC_crosshair));
  /*
   * Create the GC used by the rubber banding functions.
   */
```

```
    data.gc = xs_create_xor_gc(canvas);
    XtMainLoop();
}
```

This example introduces some new Xlib and Intrinsics functions. The function

```
XGrabButton(display, button, modifiers, grab_window,
            owner_events, event_mask, pointer_mode,
            keyboard_mode, confine_to, cursor)
```

establishes a *passive grab* on the specified mouse button. A passive grab takes effect automatically when the user presses the specified mouse button. Once the pointer is grabbed, the
server reports all mouse events to the grabbing client, even if the sprite leaves the window.
This allows the server to track pointer motion more efficiently. **XGrabButton()** also allows us to constrain the sprite to stay within a particular window while the grab is in
effect. In this example, the sprite is constrained to the **canvas** window as long as the grab
is in effect. **XGrabButton()** also allows the programmer to specify the shape of the mouse
cursor while the grab is in effect. In this example, the mouse cursor changes to a crosshair
shape when the pointer is grabbed. The function

```
XCreateFontCursor(display, cursor_index)
```

retrieves a mouse cursor from a standard font. The file cursorfont.h defines a set of constants
used to as indexes into the cursor font. When the user releases the mouse button, the grab
automatically terminates and the mouse cursor returns to its previous shape.

The function **xs_create_xor_gc()** creates a graphics context set to exclusive-OR
mode which is used to draw the rubber band lines.

```
GC xs_create_xor_gc(w)
    Widget              w;
{
    XGCValues values;
    GC        gc;
    Arg       wargs[10];
    /*
     * Get the colors used by the widget.
     */
    XtSetArg(wargs[0], XtNforeground, &values.foreground);
    XtSetArg(wargs[1], XtNbackground, &values.background);
    XtGetValues(w, wargs,2);
    /*
     * Set the fg to the XOR of the fg and bg, so if it is
     * XOR'ed with bg, the result will be fg and vice-versa.
     * This effectively achieves inverse video for the line.
     */
```

```
values.foreground = values.foreground ^ values.background;
/*
 * Set the rubber band gc to use XOR mode and draw
 * a dashed line.
 */
values.line_style = LineOnOffDash;
values.function   = GXxor;
gc = XtGetGC(w, GCForeground | GCBackground |
               GCFunction | GCLineStyle, &values);
return gc;
}
```

The graphics context is created using the foreground and background colors obtained from the widget's resources. In addition, the line style is set to **LineOnOffDash** and the drawing function is set to XOR mode.

The task of drawing the rubber band line is performed by three cooperating event handlers. When the user presses a mouse button, the Intrinsics invokes the first event handler, **start_rubber_band()**. This function stores the position of the sprite when the **ButtonPress** event occurs as the initial position of the line, and also sets the last position of the line to the same point. The function **XDrawLine()** is called to draw the initial line, which is simply a point, because the start and end points are the same.

```
void start_rubber_band(w, data, event)
    Widget              w;
    rubber_band_data    *data;
    XEvent              *event;
{
  data->last_x = data->start_x = event->xbutton.x;
  data->last_y = data->start_y = event->xbutton.y;
    XDrawLine(XtDisplay(w), XtWindow(w),
            data->gc, data->start_x,
            data->start_y, data->last_x, data->last_y);
}
```

The function **track_rubber_band()** is called each time the sprite moves. It draws a line between the initial position at which the user pressed the mouse button and the last recorded position of the sprite. Because the line is drawn in XOR mode, this erases the current line and restores the previous contents of the screen. The end points of the line are then updated to reflect the new sprite position and the line is drawn again.

```
void track_rubber_band(w, data, event)
    Widget              w;
    rubber_band_data    *data;
    XEvent              *event;
```

```
{
  /*
   * Draw once to clear the previous line.
   */
  XDrawLine(XtDisplay(w), XtWindow(w), data->gc,
            data->start_x,data->start_y,
            data->last_x, data->last_y);
  /*
   * Update the endpoints.
   */
  data->last_x  =  event->xbutton.x;
  data->last_y  =  event->xbutton.y;
  /*
   * Draw the new line.
   */
  XDrawLine(XtDisplay(w), XtWindow(w), data->gc,
            data->start_x, data->start_y,
            data->last_x, data->last_y);
}
```

When the user releases the mouse button, the event handler **end_rubber_band()** is invoked. This function draws the line one last time in XOR mode to erase the line. The function also stores the current position of the sprite in the client data structure where any interested routine can retrieve it.

```
void end_rubber_band(w, data, event)
   Widget              w;
   rubber_band_data *data;
   XEvent              *event;
{
 /*
  * Clear the current line and update the endpoint info.
  */
  XDrawLine(XtDisplay(w), XtWindow(w), data->gc,
            data->start_x, data->start_y,
            data->last_x, data->last_y);
  data->last_x  =  event->xbutton.x;
  data->last_y  =  event->xbutton.y;
}
```

10.3   DRAWING POLYGONS AND ARCS

Xlib also provides functions for drawing more complex figures, including filled and un-filled polygons, arcs, and circles. The function

XDrawRectangle(display, drawable, gc, x, y, width, height)

draws the outline of a rectangle, while the function

XDrawRectangles(display, drawable, gc, rectangles,nrectangles)

draws multiple rectangles. The argument **rectangles** must be an array of type **XRectangle**, which includes the members:

short   x, y;
unsigned short width, height;

An arc can be drawn using the function:

XDrawArc(display, drawable, gc, x, y, width, height,
**   angle1, angle2)**

This function draws an arc starting from **angle1**, relative to a three o'clock position, to **angle2**, within the bounding rectangle specified by the parameters **x**, **y**, **width**, **height**, as shown in Fig. 10.2. The angles are specified in units of *(degrees * 64)*. For example, this function can be used to draw a circle or ellipse by specifying a starting angle of zero degrees and an ending angle of *(64 * 360)* degrees. Angles greater than *(64 * 360)* degrees are truncated.

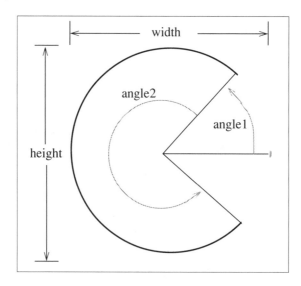

Figure 10.2 Dimensions of an Arc.

The function

```
XDrawArcs(display, drawable, gc, arcs, narcs)
```

draws multiple arcs with a single server request and uses an array of type **XArc** to define the parameters of each arc. The **XArc** structure contains the following members:

```
short          x, y;
unsigned short width, height;
short          angle1, angle2;
```

Xlib also provides functions for drawing polygons, rectangles, and arcs filled with a solid color or pattern. The function

```
XFillRectangle(display, drawable, gc, x, y, width, height)
```

draws a single rectangle filled as specified by the **GCForeground**, **GCBackground**, **GC-Tile**, and **GCStipple** attributes of the graphics context. The function

```
XFillRectangles(display, drawable, gc, rectangles,nrectangles)
```

draws multiple filled rectangles using an array of **XRectangle** structures. The function

```
XFillPolygon(display, drawable, gc, points, npoints,
             shape, mode)
```

draws a single polygon specified by an array of **XPoint** structures. If the path is not closed, **XFillPolygon()** automatically closes it before filling the figure. The shape parameter can be one of the constants **Complex**, **Convex**, or **Nonconvex**. The server can use this information to select the optimal drawing algorithm. The **mode** argument determines how the points are interpreted and must be one of the constants **CoordModeOrigin** or **CoordModePrevious**. The functions

```
XFillArc(display, drawable, gc, x, y, width, height,
         angle1, angle2)
```

and

```
XFillArcs(display, drawable, gc, arcs, narcs)
```

draw single and multiple filled arcs, respectively.

10.4 EXAMPLE: A SIMPLE DRAWING PROGRAM

This section concludes our discussion of the Xlib graphics functions by looking at a simple drawing program that uses many of the techniques and functions discussed in this chapter, as well as in the previous three chapters. The **draw** program shown in Fig. 10.3 allows the user to select from several possible shapes, and then position and size them using the rubber banding techniques discussed in Section 10.2. The user can also select fill patterns from the tiles provided by the Motif library for the shapes, using the pixmap browser functions we developed in Chapter 7.

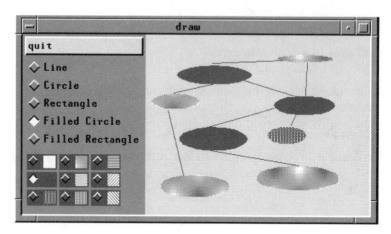

Figure 10.3   Using draw: A simple drawing program.

The header file, draw.h, includes the Motif widget header files used in this example, and also contains forward declarations of the callbacks and other procedures used in the program. The header file defines a "foreground" bitmap pattern and a list of patterns for the pixmap browser. It also includes definitions of three data structures used by the program. An array of type **GBUFFER** serves as a graphics buffer. Each position in the buffer stores a pair of *(x, y)* points, a graphics context and a pointer to a function that draws the object. The second data structure provides a central location for all client data used by the callback procedures. It is similar to the data structure used by the rubber banding function in Section 10.2, but is expanded to include a pointer to the graphics buffer and also a pointer to a function used to draw the graphical objects.

```
/************************************************
 * draw.h: declarations for the draw program
 ************************************************/
#include <X11/StringDefs.h>
#include <X11/cursorfont.h>
#include <X11/Intrinsic.h>
#include <X11/Xutil.h>
#include <Xm/Xm.h>
#include <Xm/DrawingA.h>
```

```
#include <Xm/RowColumn.h>
#include <Xm/Form.h>
#include <Xm/PushB.h>
#include <Xm/ToggleB.h>
#include <Xm/Label.h>
#include "libXs.h"

#define MAXOBJECTS 1000

static unsigned char fg_bitmap[32] = {   /* solid foreground */
      0xff, 0xff, 0xff, 0xff, 0xff, 0xff, 0xff, 0xff,
      0xff, 0xff, 0xff, 0xff, 0xff, 0xff, 0xff, 0xff,
      0xff, 0xff, 0xff, 0xff, 0xff, 0xff, 0xff, 0xff,
      0xff, 0xff, 0xff, 0xff, 0xff, 0xff, 0xff, 0xff
};

#define fg_width   16
#define fg_height 16

static char *patterns[] = {  "foreground",
                             "background",
                             "25_foreground",
                             "50_foreground",
                             "75_foreground",
                             "vertical",
                             "horizontal",
                             "slant_right",
                             "slant_left",
                          };

typedef struct {
  int   x1, y1, x2, y2;
  int   (*func) ();
  GC    gc;
} GBUFFER;

typedef struct {
  int           start_x, start_y, last_x, last_y;
  GC            xorgc;
  GC            gc;
  int           (*current_func)();
  int           foreground, background;
```

```
    GBUFFER         buffer[MAXOBJECTS];
    int             next_pos;
} graphics_data;

void  draw_line();
void  draw_circle();
void  draw_rectangle();
void  draw_filled_circle();
void  draw_filled_rectangle();

void  activate();
void  refresh();
void  set_stipple();
void  start_rubber_band();
void  track_rubber_band();
void  end_rubber_band();
void  set_fill_pattern();
```

The **draw** program uses an XmForm widget to manage a command pane built from an XmRowColumn widget and a drawing canvas (an XmDrawingArea widget). Fig. 10.4 shows the widget tree created by the **draw** program.

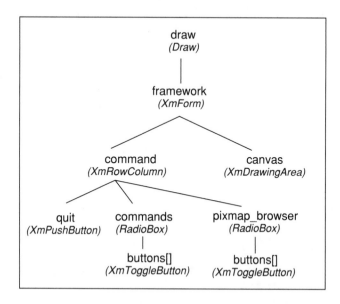

Figure 10.4 The draw widget tree.

The body of the program creates these widgets, initializes the graphics buffer and related data structures, and defines event handlers for the mouse buttons and pointer motion events.

```
/****************************************************
 * draw.c: a simple graphics drawing program.
 ****************************************************/
#include "draw.h"

main(argc, argv)
   int    argc;
   char *argv[];
{
  Widget         toplevel, canvas, framework, command, tiles;
  graphics_data data;
  int            n;
  Arg            wargs[10];

  toplevel = XtInitialize(argv[0], "Draw", NULL, 0,
                          &argc, argv);
  framework = XtCreateManagedWidget("framework",
                                    xmFormWidgetClass,
                                    toplevel, NULL, 0);
  /*
   * Create the column to hold the commands.
   */
  command = XtCreateManagedWidget("command",
                                  xmRowColumnWidgetClass,
                                  framework, NULL, 0);
  /*
   * Create the drawing surface and add the
   * rubber banding callbacks.
   */
  canvas = XtCreateManagedWidget("canvas",
                                 xmDrawingAreaWidgetClass,
                                 framework, NULL, 0);
  XtAddCallback(canvas, XmNexposeCallback, refresh, &data);

  XtAddEventHandler(canvas, ButtonPressMask, FALSE,
                    start_rubber_band, &data);
  XtAddEventHandler(canvas, ButtonMotionMask, FALSE,
                    track_rubber_band, &data);
  XtAddEventHandler(canvas, ButtonReleaseMask, FALSE,
```

```
                             end_rubber_band, &data);
    n = 0;
    XtSetArg(wargs[n], XmNtopAttachment,    XmATTACH_FORM);n++;
    XtSetArg(wargs[n], XmNbottomAttachment, XmATTACH_FORM);n++;
    XtSetArg(wargs[n], XmNleftAttachment,   XmATTACH_FORM);n++;
    XtSetValues(command, wargs, n);

    n = 0;
    XtSetArg(wargs[n], XmNtopAttachment,    XmATTACH_FORM);    n++;
    XtSetArg(wargs[n], XmNbottomAttachment, XmATTACH_FORM);    n++;
    XtSetArg(wargs[n], XmNleftAttachment,   XmATTACH_WIDGET);n++;
    XtSetArg(wargs[n], XmNleftWidget,       command);          n++;
    XtSetArg(wargs[n], XmNrightAttachment,  XmATTACH_FORM);  n++;
    XtSetValues(canvas, wargs, n);
    /*
     * Initialize the graphics buffer and other data.
     */
    init_data(canvas, &data);
    /*
     * Add a quit button.
     */
    xs_create_quit_button(command);
    /*
     * Add the drawing command panel.
     */
    create_drawing_commands(command, &data);
    /*
     * Add a palette of fill patterns.
     */
    xs_register_pattern(toplevel, "foreground", fg_bitmap,
                        fg_width, fg_height);
    tiles = xs_create_pixmap_browser(command,
                                     patterns,
                                     XtNumber(patterns),
                                     set_fill_pattern, &data);
    XtManageChild(tiles);
    XtRealizeWidget(toplevel);
    /*
     * Establish a passive grab on the drawing canvas window.
     */
    XGrabButton(XtDisplay(canvas), AnyButton, AnyModifier,
                XtWindow(canvas), TRUE,
```

```
                 ButtonPressMask | ButtonMotionMask |
                 ButtonReleaseMask,
                 GrabModeAsync, GrabModeAsync,
                 XtWindow(canvas),
                 XCreateFontCursor(XtDisplay(canvas),
                                   XC_crosshair));
     XtMainLoop();
 }
```

In addition to the quit button, the command panel contains a set of buttons used to set the current drawing function. The function **create_drawing_commands()** creates an XmRowColumn widget containing a set of XmToggleButton widgets, which the user can use to select the current drawing function. The selected function remains in effect until the user selects a new drawing function. Notice that each callback shares the **data** structure containing the graphics buffer through the callback functions' **client_data** argument.

```
 struct {
   char    *name;
   void    (*func)();
 } command_info[] = {
       "Line",               draw_line,
       "Circle",             draw_circle,
       "Rectangle",          draw_rectangle,
       "Filled Circle",      draw_filled_circle,
       "Filled Rectangle", draw_filled_rectangle
  };

 create_drawing_commands(parent, data)
       Widget          parent;
       graphics_data *data;
 {
   Widget  w, commands;
   Arg     wargs[2];
   int     i;
   /*
    * Group all commands in a RadioBox.
    */
   XtSetArg(wargs[0],XmNentryClass,xmToggleButtonWidgetClass);
   commands = XmCreateRadioBox(parent, "commands",
                               wargs, 1);
   XtManageChild(commands);
   /*
    * Create a button for each drawing function.
```

```
      */
    for(i=0;i < XtNumber(command_info); i++){
      XtSetArg(wargs[0], XmNuserData, command_info[i].func);
      w = XtCreateManagedWidget(command_info[i].name,
                                xmToggleButtonWidgetClass,
                                commands, wargs, 1);
      XtAddCallback(w, XmNvalueChangedCallback, activate, data);
    }
}
```

Often, we can use the client data passed to callbacks and event handlers to associate a piece of data with a particular widget. However, only one piece of client data can be passed to any one function. In this example, we are using the client data to pass the data structure containing the graphics buffer between functions. However, in addition, the **activate()** function requires a pointer to a function to be installed as the current drawing function. Since the graphics buffer and its associated data is passed as client data, we must find some other way to associate a drawing function with a particular button. Fortunately Motif allows us to attach an arbitrary data structure to any widget, using the **XmNuserData** resource. A pointer to the drawing function corresponding to each button is stored in the **XmNuserData** resource of each widget, where it can be retrieved by a callback function.

The next section of the command panel contains a menu of patterns that can be used as fill patterns for rectangles and circles. This pixmap browser is created by the functions described in Chapter 7. The callback function **set_fill_pattern()** is passed to the function **xs_create_pixmap_browser()**, to be invoked when one of the XmToggleButton widgets in the pixmap browser is selected. It sets the GC to the color and fill pattern of the selected button.

```
    void set_fill_pattern(w, data, call_data)
        Widget         w;
        graphics_data *data;
        XmToggleButtonCallbackStruct  *call_data;
    {
      Pixmap     tile;
      int        i;
      XGCValues  values;
      Arg        wargs[1];

      static int mask = GCForeground | GCBackground |
                        GCTile | GCFillStyle;
      if(call_data->reason==XmCR_VALUE_CHANGED && call_data->set){
        XtSetArg(wargs[0], XmNuserData, &tile);
        XtGetValues(w, wargs, 1);
        /*
```

```
    * Get a GC using this tile pattern
    */
   values.foreground = data->foreground;
   values.background = data->background;
   values.fill_style = FillTiled;
   values.tile       = tile;
   data->gc = XtGetGC(w, mask, &values);
 }
}
```

Now that we have seen how all the widgets used in this example are created, let's look at how the client data is initialized and used. The function **init_data()** initializes the current drawing function to NULL, sets the next available position in the graphics buffer to zero, and then creates two graphics contexts. One graphics context is used by the graphics objects, while the other graphics context is used by the rubber banding routines that position the objects.

```
init_data(w, data)
    Widget          w;
    graphics_data  *data;
{
  XGCValues values;
  Arg       wargs[5];
  data->current_func = NULL;
  data->next_pos     = 0;
  /*
   * Get the colors the user has set for the widget.
   */
  XtSetArg(wargs[0], XtNforeground, &data->foreground);
  XtSetArg(wargs[1], XtNbackground, &data->background);
  XtGetValues(w, wargs,2);
  /*
   * Fill in the values structure
   */
  values.foreground = data->foreground;
  values.background = data->background;
  values.fill_style = FillTiled;
  /*
   * Get the GC used for drawing.
   */
  data->gc= XtGetGC(w, GCForeground | GCBackground |
                       GCFillStyle, &values);
  /*
```

```
 * Get a second GC in XOR mode for rubber banding.
 */
data->xorgc = xs_create_xor_gc(w);
}
```

The three event handlers in this example draw objects using a rubber banding approach similar to that described in Section 10.2. However, instead of a hard-coded Xlib drawing function, these routines use the **current_function** member of the shared client data to draw the figures. This allows the same rubber banding functions to draw all types of figures. The function **start_rubber_band()** sets the initial anchor point of the rubber band figure when the user presses a mouse button.

```
void start_rubber_band(w, data, event)
        Widget            w;
        graphics_data    *data;
        XEvent            *event;
{
  if(data->current_func){
    /*
     * Store the starting point and draw the initial figure.
     */
    data->last_x = data->start_x = event->xbutton.x;
    data->last_y = data->start_y = event->xbutton.y;
    (*(data->current_func))(w, data->xorgc,
                                data->start_x, data->start_y,
                                data->last_x, data->last_y);
  }
}
```

The function **track_rubber_band()** erases the previous figure by drawing it in XOR mode, updates the position, and redraws the figure each time the sprite moves.

```
void track_rubber_band(w, data, event)
        Widget            w;
        graphics_data    *data;
        XEvent            *event;
{
 if(data->current_func){
    /*
     * Erase the previous figure.
     */
    (*(data->current_func))(w, data->xorgc,
                                data->start_x, data->start_y,
                                data->last_x, data->last_y);
```

```
    /*
     * Update the last point.
     */
    data->last_x  =  event->xbutton.x;
    data->last_y  =  event->xbutton.y;
    /*
     * Draw the figure in the new position.
     */
    (*(data->current_func))(w, data->xorgc,
                              data->start_x, data->start_y,
                              data->last_x, data->last_y);

  }
}
```

When the mouse button is released, the function **end_rubber_band()** erases the rubber banded figure, and redraws the figure using the current graphics context. After updating the position information in data, the function **store_object()** is called to record the new object in the graphics buffer.

```
void end_rubber_band(w, data, event)
        Widget          w;
        graphics_data   *data;
        XEvent          *event;
{
  if(data->current_func){
    /*
     * Erase the XOR image.
     */
    (*(data->current_func))(w, data->xorgc,
                              data->start_x, data->start_y,
                              data->last_x, data->last_y);
    /*
     * Draw the figure using the normal GC.
     */
    (*(data->current_func))(w, data->gc,
                              data->start_x, data->start_y,
                              event->xbutton.x,
                              event->xbutton.y);
    /*
     * Update the data, and store the object in
     * the graphics buffer.
     */
    data->last_x  =  event->xbutton.x;
    data->last_y  =  event->xbutton.y;
```

```
        store_object(data);
    }
}
```

The key to using the same rubber band functions for all figures is to find a way to draw all figures using the same parameters. Although the various Xlib graphics functions are similar, they are not exactly the same. However, it is easy to define functions that require the same parameters. Each of the following functions takes a widget, a graphics context, and a pair of *(x, y)* points. The function **draw_line()** draws a line between two points.

```
void draw_line(w, gc, x, y, x2, y2)
    Widget  w;
    GC      gc;
    int     x, y, x2, y2;
{
  Display *dpy = XtDisplay(w);
  Window   win = XtWindow(w);
  XDrawLine(dpy, win, gc, x, y, x2, y2);
}
```

The functions **draw_rectangle()** and **draw_filled_rectangle()** draw rectangles using the given points as the upper left and lower right corners of the rectangle. These functions are defined as:

```
void draw_rectangle(w, gc, x, y, x2, y2)
    Widget w;
    GC      gc;
    int     x, y, x2, y2;
{
  Display *dpy = XtDisplay(w);
  Window   win = XtWindow(w);

  check_points(&x, &y, &x2, &y2);
  XDrawRectangle(dpy, win, gc, x, y, x2 - x, y2 - y);
}

void draw_filled_rectangle(w, gc, x, y, x2, y2)
    Widget  w;
    GC      gc;
    int     x, y, x2, y2;
{
  Display *dpy = XtDisplay(w);
  Window   win = XtWindow(w);
```

```
     check_points(&x, &y, &x2, &y2);
     XFillRectangle(dpy, win, gc, x, y, x2 - x, y2 - y);
}
```

Some X servers do not draw polygonal figures correctly if the second point is less than the first in either direction. The auxiliary function **check_points()** checks for this case and reverses the coordinates if necessary.

```
check_points(x, y, x2, y2)
    int *x, *y, *x2, *y2;
{
  if(*x2 < *x){ int tmp = *x; *x = *x2; *x2 = tmp;}
  if(*y2 < *y){ int tmp = *y; *y = *y2; *y2 = tmp;}
}
```

The functions **draw_circle()** and **draw_filled_circle()** use the two points as the upper left and lower right corners of the bounding box of a circle. Theses functions are defined as:

```
void draw_circle(w, gc, x, y, x2, y2)
     Widget  w;
     GC      gc;
     int     x, y, x2, y2;
{
  Display *dpy = XtDisplay(w);
  Window   win = XtWindow(w);

  check_points(&x, &y, &x2, &y2);
  XDrawArc(dpy, win, gc, x, y, x2 - x, y2 - y, 0, 64 * 360);
}

void draw_filled_circle(w, gc, x, y, x2, y2)
     Widget  w;
     GC      gc;
     int     x, y, x2, y2;
{
  Display *dpy = XtDisplay(w);
  Window   win = XtWindow(w);

  check_points(&x, &y, &x2, &y2);
  XFillArc(dpy, win, gc, x, y, x2 - x, y2 - y, 0, 64 * 360);
}
```

These functions must be installed as the current drawing function when the user selects one of the drawing commands. Each XmToggleButton widget in the command pane has a call-

back function which activates the corresponding drawing function by setting the
current_func member of the shared client data structure. This function is retrieved from
the widget's **XmNuserData** resource. The **activate()** function is defined as:

```
void activate(w, data, call_data)
    Widget          w;
    graphics_data  *data;
    XmToggleButtonCallbackStruct  *call_data;
{
  int (*func)();
  Arg wargs[5];

  if(!call_data->set) return;

  XtSetArg(wargs[0], XmNuserData, &func);
  XtGetValues(w, wargs, 1);
  data->current_func = func;
}
```

We must save each figure the user draws in a buffer so we can redraw the image when
the XmDrawingArea widget is exposed. The function **store_object()** saves the size and
location of the figure, the graphics context, and a pointer to the function used to draw the
object in the next available slot of the graphics buffer array. It then increments the
next_pos counter. If the graphics buffer is full, the function issues a warning and returns
without storing the object.

```
store_object(data)
    graphics_data *data;
{
  /*
   * Check for space.
   */
  if(data->next_pos >= MAXOBJECTS){
   printf("Warning: Graphics buffer is full\n");
   return;
  }
  /*
   * Save everything we need to draw this object again.
   */
  data->buffer[data->next_pos].x1 = data->start_x;
  data->buffer[data->next_pos].y1 = data->start_y;
  data->buffer[data->next_pos].x2 = data->last_x;
  data->buffer[data->next_pos].y2 = data->last_y;
  data->buffer[data->next_pos].func = data->current_func;
```

```
        data->buffer[data->next_pos].gc = data->gc;
        /*
         * Increment the next position index.
         */
        data->next_pos++;
}
```

When the canvas widget is exposed, the Intrinsics invokes the callback functions on the **XmNexposeCallback** list, including the **refresh()** callback function. This function loops through the graphics buffer, redrawing each object.

```
void refresh(w, data, call_data)
    Widget          w;
    graphics_data   *data;
    caddr_t         call_data;
{
    int i;
    for(i=0;i<data->next_pos;i++)
        (* (data->buffer[i].func))(w, data->buffer[i].gc,
                                   data->buffer[i].x1,
                                   data->buffer[i].y1,
                                   data->buffer[i].x2,
                                   data->buffer[i].y2);
}
```

This function could be improved by applying the techniques discussed in Chapter 9 for compressing **Expose** events and using a region to set the clip mask in the graphics context.

10.5 SUMMARY

This chapter explored the graphics facilities provided by Xlib, and demonstrated how they can be used with the Xt Intrinsics and widgets. X provides simple two-dimensional graphics primitives, although efforts are underway to provide more sophisticated three-dimensional capabilities. Various attributes of a graphics context control how the Xlib drawing functions affect a drawable and allow the programmer to produce various special effects such as drawing rubber band lines.

Because each graphics operation makes a server request, complex images can be time consuming. It is often necessary to take extra steps to reduce the number of server requests, such as caching and combining requests, or saving complete or partial renditions of images in off-screen pixmaps.

The following chapter leaves the topic of graphics operations and discusses ways to provide communication and data sharing between applications.

11

INTERCLIENT COMMUNICATION

X provides many facilities that allow applications to communicate with each other and to exchange and share data. Interclient communication involves the use of *atoms*, *properties*, and *client messages*. This chapter first describes atoms and shows how atoms are used to identify names and types of properties. Then a short example demonstrates how properties can be used to store data in the server, where the data can be shared by multiple clients. Next we discuss how applications can use client message events to communicate with each other, and finally we look at the X *selection* mechanism for exchanging typed data between applications.

11.1 ATOMS

An atom is a unique resource ID used to represent a string. The relationship is stored in the X server so that all clients connected to that server share the same ID for any particular string. Atoms are primarily used for efficiency; it is faster to compare two atoms (using ==) than to compare two strings (using **strcmp()**).

Creating an atom is referred to as *interning*. The function

    XInternAtom(display, name, only_if_exists)

returns a unique atom corresponding to the string specified by name. When the boolean **only_if_exists** is **TRUE**, **XInternAtom()** returns an atom ID if the atom already exists. If the atom does not exist, the function returns the constant **None**. When **only_if_exists** is **FALSE**, **XInternAtom()** always returns an atom ID, creating a new atom unless the atom already exists. All applications that request an atom for the same string from the same server receive the same ID. The string must match exactly, including the case.

Applications can create new atoms to represent any arbitrary string. For example, the statement

```
Atom NEWATOM = XInternAtom(display, "A New Atom", FALSE);
```

creates an atom, **NEWATOM**, representing the string

```
"A New Atom"
```

Once an atom is interned, it exists until the server is reset, even if the client that created the atom exits. The function

```
XGetAtomName(display, atom)
```

returns the string corresponding to **atom**.

Atoms are useful whenever a unique identifier that must be shared and recognized by multiple applications is required. For example, atoms are used to identify the type of data stored in a property. X predefines a small set of atoms to identify common resource types such as **DRAWABLE**, **POINT**, **INTEGER**, **FONT**, and **PIXMAP**. The symbols for all predefined atoms are preceded by the letters "**XA_**" to avoid name clashes between client-defined atoms. For example, the atom that identifies the type **INTEGER** is defined by the symbol **XA_INTEGER**. X also predefines atoms intended for other uses, including selection types, property names, and font properties. Applications that use these predefined atoms must include the header file Xatom.h.

11.2   USING PROPERTIES

A property is a collection of named, typed data. Every property is associated with a window, and the data stored in the property is maintained by the server, where it can be accessed or altered by any client that has the window's ID and the name of the property. Properties are named and typed using atoms. The X server predefines some atoms commonly used as property names, including:

XA_CUT_BUFFER0	XA_RGB_RED_MAP	XA_WM_HINTS
XA_CUT_BUFFER1	XA_RESOURCE_MANAGER	XA_WM_ICON_NAME
XA_CUT_BUFFER2	XA_RGB_BEST_MAP	XA_WM_ICON_SIZE
XA_CUT_BUFFER3	XA_RGB_BLUE_MAP	XA_WM_NAME
XA_CUT_BUFFER4	XA_RGB_DEFAULT_MAP	XA_WM_NORMAL_HINTS
XA_CUT_BUFFER5	XA_RGB_GRAY_MAP	XA_WM_ZOOM_HINTS
XA_CUT_BUFFER6	XA_WM_CLASS	XA_WM_TRANSIENT_FOR
XA_CUT_BUFFER7	XA_WM_CLIENT_MACHINE	
XA_RGB_GREEN_MAP	XA_WM_COMMAND	

Although these property names are predefined by the server, the corresponding properties do not automatically exist, nor do they necessarily contain any data. Xlib predefines property names as a convenience so clients can use these properties without explicitly interning the atoms. Like all predefined atoms, predefined property names begin with the letters **XA_**. The data associated with a property is simply stored as a stream of bytes, and a second atom associated with the property identifies the type of the data. The server also predefines atoms to represent some common X data types, including:

XA_ARC	**XA_ATOM**	**XA_BITMAP**
XA_CARDINAL	**XA_COLORMAP**	**XA_CURSOR**
XA_DRAWABLE	**XA_FONT**	**XA_INTEGER**
XA_PIXMAP	**XA_POINT**	**XA_RGB_COLOR_MAP**
XA_RECTANGLE	**XA_STRING**	**XA_VISUALID**
XA_WINDOW	**XA_WM_HINTS**	**XA_WM_SIZE_HINTS**

Applications can create new atoms to represent any data type, including client-defined structures. The server attaches no particular meaning to any atom.

The function

```
XChangeProperty(display, window, name, type,
                format, mode, &data, nelements)
```

stores the given data in a property of the specified window. The third and fourth arguments to **XChangeProperty()** must be atoms that specify the name of the property and the type of the data stored in the property. The **format** argument specifies whether the data consists of multiples of 8, 16, or 32 bits. This information allows the server to do byte swapping, if necessary, when data is transferred between clients running on different machines. The **mode** argument indicates whether the data is to replace any data already stored in the property or be added to the beginning or the end of any existing contents, and must be one of the constants **PropModeReplace**, **PropModePrepend**, or **PropModeAppend**. The **data** argument provides the address of the data to be stored while **nelements** specifies the length of the data in multiples of the unit given by the **format** argument.

Window properties are normally used to share information with other clients. For example, most X window managers expect some basic properties to be stored in properties on every application's top level window. Programmers who use the Xt Intrinsics do not usually need to be aware of this, because the Intrinsics sets these properties automatically. One of these window manager properties, **XA_WM_NAME**, is expected to contain the name of a window. Xlib provides a convenient function,

```
XStoreName(display, window, name)
```

which stores a string, specified by the **name** argument, in the **XA_WM_NAME** property of the given window. This Xlib function provides an easy-to-use interface to the function **XChangeProperty()**, and is defined as:

```
XStoreName (dpy, w, name)
    Display  *dpy;
    Window   w;
    char     *name;
{
 XChangeProperty(dpy, w, XA_WM_NAME, XA_STRING,
                    8, PropModeReplace,
                    (unsigned char *)name,
                    name ? strlen(name) : 0);
}
```

Many other Xlib functions, including **XSetStandardProperties()** and **XSetWM-Hints()**, are implemented similarly.

A property exists until the window with which it is associated is destroyed, or until a client explicitly deletes the property. The lifetime of a property is not determined by the lifetime of the client that stores the property. The function

XDeleteProperty(display, window, property)

deletes a property from a window's property list.

Clients can retrieve the data stored in a property with the Xlib function:

XGetWindowProperty(display, window, name, offset, length, delete, requested_type, &actual_type, &actual_format, &nitems, &bytes_left, &data);

This function returns the constant **Success**, defined in Xlib.h, if no error condition is encountered while executing the function. This does not imply that the property was found, or that any data was retrieved. The **name** argument must be an atom identifying the property containing the desired data. The **offset** argument specifies the starting point within the data stored in the property from which data should be returned. The offset is measured in 32-bit quantities from the beginning of the stored data. The **length** argument specifies how many 32-bit multiples of the data should be returned. The boolean argument, **delete**, indicates whether or not the server should delete the data after it is retrieved. The **requested_type** must be either an atom identifying the desired type of the data or the constant **AnyPropertyType**. When **XGetWindowProperty()** returns, the argument **actual_type** is set to an atom representing the type of the data stored in the property, while **actual_format** contains the format of the stored data. If the property does not exist for the specified window, **actual_type** is set to **None**, and the **actual_format** is set to zero. The arguments **nitems** and **bytes_left** indicate the number of bytes retrieved and how many remaining bytes are stored in the property. This allows applications to retrieve large amounts of data by repeated calls to **XGetWindowProperty()**. If the function returns successfully, the **data** argument points to the bytes retrieved from the property. X allocates this data using **Xmalloc()**, and applications should free the data using **Xfree()** when the data is no longer needed.

The Xlib function

```
XFetchName(display, window, name)
```

uses **XGetProperty()** to retrieve the name of a window, stored in the **XA_WM_NAME** property. This function is the counterpart to **XStoreName()** and is defined by Xlib as:

```
Status XFetchName (dpy, w, name)
    Display *dpy;
    Window  w;
    char    **name;
{
  Atom              actual_type;
  int               actual_format;
  unsigned long     nitems;
  unsigned long     leftover;
  unsigned char *data = NULL;
  if (XGetWindowProperty(dpy, w, XA_WM_NAME, 0L, (long)BUFSIZ,
                         FALSE, XA_STRING, &actual_type,
                         &actual_format, &nitems,
                         &leftover, &data) != Success){
    *name = NULL;
    return (FALSE);
  }
  if ((actual_type == XA_STRING) && (actual_format == 8)){
    *name = (char *)data;
     return (TRUE);
  }
  if (data)
     Xfree ((char *)data);
  *name = NULL;
  return (FALSE);
}
```

If the call to **XGetWindowProperty()** is unsuccessful, **XFetchName()** returns **FALSE**, with **name** set to **NULL**. If the call is successful, **XGetWindowProperty()** returns **Success**, and **XFetchName()** checks whether the property type matches the requested type and also checks the format to ensure that the data is in 8-bit format. If these conditions are met, **XFetchName()** sets **name** to point to the retrieved data and returns **TRUE**. If the type and format of the data are incorrect, the function frees the retrieved data, using **Xfree()**, and returns **FALSE**.

11.2.1 Property Events

The X server notifies interested clients when any change occurs in a window's property list. The server generates a **PropertyNotify** event when the data stored in a property changes, when a property is initially created, or when a property is deleted. Clients must request **PropertyNotify** events using the event mask **PropertyChangedMask**. The server reports **PropertyNotify** events using an **XPropertyEvent** structure. In addition to the basic members included in all events, this structure contains the following members:

```
Atom      atom;
Time      time;
int       state;
```

The **atom** member contains the name of the modified property. The **state** member is set to the constant **NewValue** if the value of property has changed, or to **Deleted** if the property has been deleted. The **time** member is set to the server time when the property was modified.

11.2.2 Using Properties to Share Data

This section uses a simple example to demonstrate how properties and atoms can be used to allow two or more applications to share data. The first application, **controldata**, allows the user to control three parameters named **altitude**, **speed** and **direction**. The current values of these parameters are kept in a single data structure, stored in a property on the root window of the display. A second application, **monitordata**, displays the current value of this data. The monitoring application uses **PropertyNotify** events to detect changes in the data and update its display.

11.2.2.1 The controldata Program

First, let's examine the **controldata** program, which lets the user set some values using scroll bars. The program then stores these values in a property in the server.

Both **controldata** and **monitordata** use the same header file, data.h. This file includes the header files for the widgets used by both programs and also the definition of a data structure common to both programs. It also includes declarations of two new atoms used by both applications to identify a property and the data type stored in the property.

```
/****************************************************
 *  data.h: declarations for shared data example
 ****************************************************/
#include <X11/StringDefs.h>
#include <X11/Intrinsic.h>
#include <Xm/Xm.h>
```

```
#include <Xm/ScrollBar.h>
#include <Xm/RowColumn.h>
#include <Xm/Label.h>
#include "libXs.h"

/* Maximum settings */
#define MAX_SPEED 100
#define MAX_ANGLE 359
#define MAX_ALT   200
/*
 * Data structure to be stored in a property
 */
typedef struct {
    int         speed;
    int         angle;
    float       altitude;
} flight_data;
/*
 * Atoms representing the property name and data type.
 */
Atom        FLIGHT_DATA, FLIGHT_DATA_TYPE;
```

The **flight_data** structure contains three parameters shared by the two programs. The user can position a slider to set the value of each member of this structure between zero and the maximum value determined by corresponding constant: **MAX_ALT**, **MAX_ANGLE**, or **MAX_SPEED**.

The source file, controldata.c, includes the file data.h and globally defines the widgets used by the program. The main program initializes each member of the **flight_data** structure to zero, and creates the XmScrollBar widgets that control each parameter. An XmRowColumn manager widget manages three columns, each containing an XmScrollBar widget and an XmLabel widget. The XmLabel widget displays a label for the scroll bar.

```
/************************************************
 *  controldata.c: The data controller
 ************************************************/
#include "data.h"

void        slider_moved();
Widget      speed_ctl, angle_ctl, temp_ctl;
Widget      create_control();
Widget      make_controller();
```

```
main(argc, argv)
     int             argc;
     char            *argv[];
{
  Widget          toplevel, row_col;
  flight_data     data;

  data.speed = data.angle = data.altitude = 0;
  toplevel = XtInitialize(argv[0], "Controldata", NULL, 0,
                          &argc, argv);
  /*
   * Create the atoms to represent the properties
   * used to store the data.
   */
  create_atoms(toplevel);
  row_col = XtCreateManagedWidget("panel",
                                  xmRowColumnWidgetClass,
                                  toplevel, NULL, 0);
  /*
   *  Make three columns, each containing a label and a
   *  slider control to control: speed, direction,
   *  and altitude.
   */
  speed_ctl = make_controller("speed",     MAX_SPEED,
                              row_col, &data);
  angle_ctl = make_controller("direction", MAX_ANGLE,
                              row_col, &data);
  temp_ctl  = make_controller("altitude",  MAX_ALT,
                              row_col, &data);
  xs_create_quit_button(row_col);
  XtRealizeWidget(toplevel);
  XtMainLoop();
}
```

The function **create_atoms()** creates two new atoms. The first is the name of the property in which the data is stored and the other represents the type of the data.

```
create_atoms(w)
    Widget w;
{
 Display * dpy = XtDisplay(w);
 FLIGHT_DATA      = XInternAtom(dpy, "Flight Data",      0);
 FLIGHT_DATA_TYPE = XInternAtom(dpy, "Flight Data Type", 0);
}
```

The function **make_controller()** takes a name, a maximum value, a parent widget, and a pointer to some client data as arguments and creates an XmRowColumn widget containing a scroll bar and a label. It returns a pointer to the XmScrollBar widget.

```
Widget make_controller(name, max, parent, data)
    char          *name;
    int           max;
    Widget        parent;
    flight_data   *data;
{
 Widget rc, w;
 /*
  * Create an XmRowColumn widget to manage a single
  * control and a label.
  */
 rc = XtCreateManagedWidget(name, xmRowColumnWidgetClass,
                            parent, NULL, 0);
 XtCreateManagedWidget("label", xmLabelWidgetClass,
                        rc, NULL, 0);
 w = create_control(rc, "control", 0, max, data);

 return (w);
}
```

The function **create_control()** creates an XmScrollBar widget, defines minimum and maximum values for the scroll bar, and registers the callbacks that are invoked when the user moves the scroll bar slider.

```
Widget create_control(parent, name, minimum, maximum, data)
     Widget         parent;
     char           *name;
     int            minimum, maximum;
     flight_data *data;
{
  int    n;
  Arg    wargs[2];
  Widget w;
  /*
   * Create a scroll bar with range minimum to maximum.
   */
  n = 0;
  XtSetArg(wargs[n], XmNminimum, minimum); n++;
  XtSetArg(wargs[n], XmNmaximum, maximum); n++;
  w = XtCreateManagedWidget(name, xmScrollBarWidgetClass,
```

```
                            parent, wargs, n);
    /*
     * Register callback function for when the user moves the
     * scrollbar slider.
     */
    XtAddCallback(w,XmNvalueChangedCallback,slider_moved,data);
    XtAddCallback(w, XmNdragCallback, slider_moved, data);
    return (w);
}
```

The **XmNvalueChangedCallback** function **slider_moved()** updates the member of the **flight_data** structure corresponding to the slider that moved, and then calls **XChangeProperty()** to store the data in the **FLIGHT_DATA** property of the default root window of the display.

```
    void slider_moved(w, data, call_data)
        Widget          w;
        flight_data    *data;
        XmScaleCallbackStruct *call_data;
{
  /*
   * Set the member of the flight_data corresponding to
   * the slider that invoked this callback.
   */
  if(w == angle_ctl)
     data->angle = call_data->value;
  else if(w == speed_ctl)
     data->speed = call_data->value;
  else if(w == temp_ctl)
     data->altitude = (float) call_data->value / 10.0;
  /*
   * Replace the previous contents of the property
   * with the new data.
   */
  XChangeProperty(XtDisplay(w),
                  DefaultRootWindow(XtDisplay(w)),
                  FLIGHT_DATA, FLIGHT_DATA_TYPE,
                  32, PropModeReplace,
                  (unsigned char *) data,
                  sizeof(flight_data) / 4);
}
```

The class resource file contains the resources corresponding to the widget layout shown in Fig. 11.1.

```
!!!!!!!!!!!!!!!!!!!!!!!!!!!!!!!!!!!!!!!!!!!!!!!!!!!!!!
! Controldata: Resource File for controldata program
!!!!!!!!!!!!!!!!!!!!!!!!!!!!!!!!!!!!!!!!!!!!!!!!!!!!!!
Controldata*orientation:                 horizontal
Controldata*panel*RowColumn.orientation: vertical
Controldata*XmScrollbar*orientation:     horizontal
Controldata*speed*label*labelString:     Speed
Controldata*direction*label*labelString: Direction
Controldata*altitude*label*labelString:  Altitude
```

11.2.2.2 The monitordata Program

The **controldata** program allows a user to control the values represented by a complex data structure, and stores this data structure in a property of the root window. This section examines the **monitordata** program, which uses **PropertyNotify** events to retrieve and display the current value of this data whenever the program detects changes in the **FLIGHT_DATA** property.

The program includes the header file data.h, which contains the definition of the data structure used by both the **controldata** program and the **monitordata** program.

The first portion of the main program is similar to the **controldata** program, except that each of the three columns in the **monitordata** window consists of two XmLabel widgets. One of these displays the current value of a member of the shared data structure, while the other is used as a label. The function **create_atoms()** is identical to the function used by the **controldata** program, and is not repeated here.

```
/***********************************************************
 *  monitordata.c: display the data set by controldata
 ***********************************************************/
#include "data.h"

Widget    make_display();

main(argc, argv)
        int              argc;
        char             *argv[];
{
  Widget      toplevel, rc, speed, direction,  altitude;
  Window      root;
  XEvent      event;
  /*
   * Initialize the Intrinsics, saving the default root window
   */
```

```
toplevel = XtInitialize(argv[0], "Monitordata", NULL, 0,
                        &argc, argv);
root =  DefaultRootWindow(XtDisplay(toplevel));
/*
 * Initialize the Atoms used for the properties.
 */
create_atoms(toplevel);
rc = XtCreateManagedWidget("panel", xmRowColumnWidgetClass,
                           toplevel,  NULL, 0);
/*
 * Create the display widgets.
 */
speed       = make_display("speed",     rc);
direction   = make_display("direction", rc);
altitude    = make_display("altitude",  rc);
xs_create_quit_button(rc);

XtRealizeWidget(toplevel);
/*
 * Request property change event for the ROOT window.
 */
XSelectInput(XtDisplay(toplevel), root, PropertyChangeMask);
/*
 *   Get the initial value of the data.
 */
update_data(speed, direction, altitude);
/*
 * We must use our own event loop to get properties
 * events for the ROOT window.
 */
while(TRUE){
  XtNextEvent(&event);
  /*
   * Check for property change events on the ROOT window
   * before dispatching the event through the Intrinsics.
   */
  switch (event.type){
    case PropertyNotify:
      if(event.xproperty.window == root &&
         event.xproperty.atom == FLIGHT_DATA)
       update_data(speed, direction, altitude);
      else
```

```
            XtDispatchEvent(&event);
          break;
      default:
          XtDispatchEvent(&event);
    }
  }
}
```

The event loop for this program is quite different from previous examples. Because we are storing the property on the root window of the display, we cannot use **XtMainLoop()**. The Xt Intrinsics event handler mechanism allows applications to register event handlers to be invoked when a event occurs relative to a specific *widget*, but **monitordata** needs to be notified when an event occurs relative to the root window. Since the root window is not a widget, we cannot use the Intrinsics' dispatch mechanism to handle the event. Therefore, we must write our own event loop to intercept the event before it reaches the event dispatcher. Before entering the event loop, the program uses the Xlib function **XSelectInput()** to request **PropertyNotify** events for the root window. The default root window of the display is specified as the event window and the event mask is given as **PropertyChangeMask**. This requests the X server to send **PropertyNotify** events to **monitordata** when any property of the root window changes. The event loop uses **XtNextEvent()** to remove each event from the event queue. A switch statement checks the type of each event to determine if it is a **PropertyNotify** event. If it is, and the **property** member of the event is the atom **FLIGHT_DATA**, **update_data()** is called to retrieve the data stored in the property and update the values displayed in each XmLabel widget. Otherwise, the function **XtDispatchEvent()** is called to dispatch events to the appropriate widget. **XtDispatchEvent()** is also called for event types other that **PropertyNotify**.

The function **update_data()** uses **XGetWindowProperty()** to retrieve the contents of the **FLIGHT_DATA** property. The requested number of bytes is determined by the size of the **flight_data** structure. The length of the data actually retrieved is returned in the variable **nitems**, while **retdata** points to the contents of the property. If **XGetWindowProperty()** succeeds and the type of the property is **FLIGHT_DATA_TYPE**, the value of each field of the structure is converted to a string and displayed in the corresponding XmLabel widget.

```
    update_data(speed, direction, altitude)
        Widget speed, direction, altitude;
    {
      int             type, format, nitems, left;
      flight_data     *retdata;
      char            str[100];
      Arg             wargs[1];
```

```
    /*
     * Retrieve the data from the root window property.
     */
    if(XGetWindowProperty(XtDisplay(speed),
                          DefaultRootWindow(XtDisplay(speed)),
                          FLIGHT_DATA, 0, sizeof(flight_data),
                          FALSE, FLIGHT_DATA_TYPE,
                          &type, &format, &nitems, &left,
                          &retdata) == Success &&
        type ==FLIGHT_DATA_TYPE){
      /*
       * If the data exists, display it.
       */
      xs_wprintf(speed,      "%d",      retdata->speed);
      xs_wprintf(direction, "%d",      retdata->angle);
      xs_wprintf(altitude,  "%5.1f", retdata->altitude + 0.05);
      XFree(retdata);
    }
}
```

The only **monitordata** function we have not discussed, **make_display()**, creates one column of XmLabel widgets. One widget functions as a label for the data, while the other displays the value of the data.

```
Widget make_display(name, parent)
    char          *name;
    Widget        parent;
{
 Widget rc, w;
 /*
  * Create an XmRowColumn widget containing two
  * XmLabelwidgets.
  */
 rc = XtCreateManagedWidget(name, xmRowColumnWidgetClass,
                               parent, NULL, 0);
 XtCreateManagedWidget("label", xmLabelWidgetClass,
                           rc, NULL, 0);
 w = XtCreateManagedWidget("display", xmLabelWidgetClass,
                               rc, NULL, 0);
 return (w);
}
```

Fig. 11.1. shows both the **monitordata** and **controldata** programs

Figure 11.1 The monitordata and controldata programs.

This example illustrates how properties allow two separate applications to share data. **PropertyNotify** events allow multiple applications to be informed whenever a property changes. Properties and **PropertyNotify** events not only provide a way for applications to share data, but also provide a *trigger* mechanism that can be used to notify clients that data has changed and to synchronize multiple applications that use the data. Efficiency problems might arise if many applications use properties on the root window for such purposes, because **PropertyNotify** events cannot be requested for a particular property, only for all properties on a window's property list. However, the same effect can be achieved by having a set of related applications watch the properties on one common window instead of the root window.

The next section discusses a more direct way to provide communication between applications, using **ClientMessage** events.

11.3   COMMUNICATING WITH EVENTS

X allows applications to send events to any window. This feature can be used to forward events from one application to another, or to create and send new events. The function

        XSendEvent(display, window, propagate, mask, &event)

sends an event to clients that have selected any of the events in **mask** for the specified window. **XSendEvent()** can be used to send any valid X event type. The window argument must be either a valid window ID on the given display, or the constant **PointerWindow**, in which case the event is sent to the window currently containing the sprite. The **window** argument can also be the constant **InputFocus**, requesting that the event be sent to the current focus window. If **InputFocus** is specified and the sprite is contained within the focus window, the event is sent to the smallest window or subwindow of the focus window containing the sprite. The boolean flag, **propagate**, determines whether the server should propagate the event to ancestors if the specified window has not selected the event type. **XSendEvent()** returns a non-zero value if the function executes correctly. Successful execution does not imply that the intended window received the event, only that no error condition occurred during the process of sending the event.

11.3.1 Client Message Events

One common use of **XSendEvent()** is to send client messages. **ClientMessage** events are never generated by the server. They are used by applications to define new events and provide the basis for one form of interclient communication. **ClientMessage** events have no corresponding event mask and cannot be specifically selected. They are always received by the client that owns the window to which the event is sent.[1] The **XClientMessageEvent** structure is defined in Xlib.h as:

```
typedef struct {
        int             type;
        unsigned long serial;
        Bool            send_event;
        Display         *display;
        Window          window;
        Atom            message_type;
        int             format;
        union {
            char        b[20];
            short       s[10];
            long        l[5];
        } data;
} XClientMessageEvent;
```

In addition to the first five members, which are common to all event types, the **ClientMessage** event structure contains a **message_type** field that identifies the subtype of the event. The subtype is specified by an atom whose meaning must be recognized by both the sending and the receiving applications. The X server does not interpret the field. The **format** member specifies the data format of the bytes in the **data** field, and must be one of

---

1. The event is always received, in the sense that the server always places the event in the client's event queue. However, unless the client has defined an event handler for the event, the event will be ignored.

8, 16, or 32. The **data** field consists of 20 bytes, declared as a union of bytes, shorts, and longs. Clients are free to use this data field for any purpose.

Because **ClientMessage** events are *non-maskable* events, applications must specify **NoEventMask** (or 0) as the event mask when registering event handlers for **ClientMessage** events. For example, a function named **message_handler()** can be registered as an event handler for a widget with the statement:

```
XtAddEventHandler(w, NoEventMask, TRUE, message_handler, NULL);
```

The argument following the event mask must be **TRUE** to indicate that this is a non-maskable event.

11.3.2 An Example: xtalk

This section presents an example program that shows how **XSendEvent()** can be used to communicate between two applications. The program demonstrates **ClientMessage** events and also provides some additional examples of how properties and atoms can be used. The example, named **xtalk**, allows users on two different machines to communicate with each other, and is similar in spirit to the **talk** program found on most UNIX systems. First, let's look at Fig. 11.2 and discuss how the program works from the user's viewpoint.

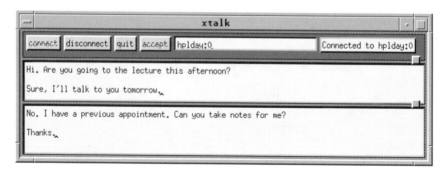

Figure 11.2 The xtalk program.

The main window of **xtalk** is divided into three primary areas: a command pane and two message panes. The user types into the top message pane, while messages from a remote **xtalk** program appear in the bottom message pane. The user can request a connection to another **xtalk** user by typing the name of the other user's display into the text field in the middle of the control pane, and then selecting the "connect" button. At this point, the message field on the right side of the command pane displays the message:

Waiting for a response

Assuming there is an **xtalk** program running on the requested display, the remote **xtalk** displays a message,

Connection requested from <machine>

where <machine> is the name of the first user's display.[2] If the user of the remote **xtalk** is willing to accept the **talk** request, he or she selects the "accept" button. Once a connection is established, the message field of each user's **xtalk** displays the message

Connected to <machine>

where <machine> is the name of the other user's machine. From this point on, until either user breaks the connection by selecting the disconnect button, everything typed in the top message pane of each **xtalk** is echoed in the bottom panel of the other **xtalk**.

The **xtalk** program uses **ClientMessage** events to make connection requests and to send "disconnect" and "accept" notifications between programs. In addition, the program uses **XSendEvent()** to forward each **KeyPress**, **ButtonPress**, and **MotionNotify** event that occurs in the top message pane of either **xtalk** to the lower text pane of the remote program. The **xtalk** program has several interesting aspects. First, the application must properly handle the atoms, properties, and window IDs on two different displays. Remembering when to use resources from the local display and when to use those of the remote display can be confusing, but interesting. This program also uses widget *sensitivity* to control what commands are available to the user at any given time, depending on the state of the program.[3] At any particular time, only the buttons that represent commands available to the user are sensitive to events. All other buttons are disabled.

The header file for **xtalk** includes the header files for each widget class used by the program. The header file also defines several atoms used as subtypes of **ClientMessage** events as well as some global variables used by the program. The file defines some strings as constants to eliminate the possibility of spelling the words differently in different parts of the program.

```
/**************************************************
 *   xtalk.h: declarations used by xtalk
 **********************************************/
#include <stdio.h>
#include <X11/Intrinsic.h>
#include <X11/StringDefs.h>
#include <X11/Xatom.h>
#include <Xm/Xm.h>
#include <Xm/RowColumn.h>
#include <Xm/PanedW.h>
```

---

2. For this program to work, each user must be able to open the display of the other user. Security in X is handled by the xhost program or the file /usr/lib/X0.hosts. Consult your local user's documentation for details.

3. Every widget has a XtNsensitive resource that determines whether a widget responds to events. If a widget is insensitive, the Intrinsics does not dispatch device events for it or any of its children. Most widgets change their appearance, and are "grayed out" when they are in an insensitive state.

```
#include <Xm/Text.h>
#include <Xm/Label.h>
#include <Xm/PushB.h>
#include "libXs.h"
/*
 *    Atoms used for communication
 */
Atom        XTALK_WINDOW, CONNECTION_REQUEST,
            CONNECTION_ACCEPT, DISCONNECT_NOTIFY;
Display  *remote_display = NULL;
Display  *my_display;
Window      remote_talker_window;
/*
 *   Various widgets
 */
Widget    name_field, msg_field,
          connect_button, disconnect_button,
          accept_button;
char      *othermachine[100];
char      *my_displayname;
int       connection_accepted = FALSE;
/*
 *   Define the strings used to create atoms
 */
#define XtNdisconnect          "Disconnect Notify"
#define XtNconnectionAccept    "Connection Accept"
#define XtNconnectionRequest "Connection Request"
#define XtNtalkWindow          "XTalk Window"
/*
 *  Declare the callbacks used in xtalk
 */
void    client_message_handler();
void    warn_wrong_pane();
void    accept_callback();
void    connect_callback();
void    disconnect_callback();
void    send_to_remote();
void    quit_callback();
```

The main body of the program uses **XtInitialize()** to initialize the toolkit and
open the local X display, and then saves both the display and the name of the display for later use. Fig. 11.3 shows the widget tree created by **xtalk**. An XmPanedWindow widget
manages the three panes of the **xtalk** window. The top pane, created by the function **cre-**

ate_command_panel(), contains a row of button widgets used to issue commands. The lower two panes each contain an XmText widget; The upper pane, referred to as the *talk* pane, allows the user to enter text. The lower pane, referred to as the *listen* pane, displays the text sent from remote **xtalk** programs. The event handler **send_to_remote()**, registered for the talk pane, is invoked when a **KeyPress** event, any button event, or a **MotionNotify** event occurs in the talk pane. The listen pane has two event handlers defined, one for **KeyPress** events and the other for events with no event mask, which includes **ClientMessage** events. We will examine the purpose of these event handlers shortly.

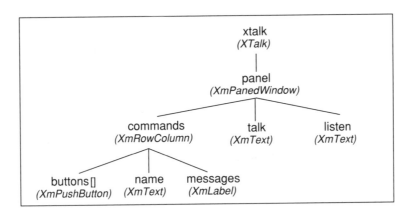

Figure 11.3 Widget tree for xtalk.

Finally, after realizing all widgets, the function **register_talker_window()** is called. This function stores the window ID of the listen pane in a property of the root window, where it can be accessed by other **xtalk** programs. This publicly announces the window ID to which remote **xtalk** programs can send connection requests. We cannot register the window ID until after the widget has been realized and the window actually exists.

```
/************************************************
 *   xtalk.c
 ***********************************************/
#include "xtalk.h"

main(argc, argv)
      int    argc;
      char *argv[];
{
  Widget toplevel, vpane, talk, listen;
  Arg     wargs[10];
  /*
```

```
     * Open display and save display and display name.
     */
    toplevel = XtInitialize(argv[0], "Xtalk", NULL, 0,
                            &argc, argv);

    my_display = XtDisplay(toplevel);
    my_displayname = XDisplayName(my_display);
    /*
     * Create a pane to hold all other widgets.
     */
    vpane = XtCreateManagedWidget("panel",
                                   xmPanedWindowWidgetClass,
                                   toplevel, NULL,0);
    create_command_panel(vpane);
    /*
     * Create the text panes used to talk.
     */
    XtSetArg(wargs[0], XmNeditMode, XmMULTI_LINE_EDIT);
    talk = XtCreateManagedWidget("talk",
                                  xmTextWidgetClass,
                                  vpane, wargs, 1);
    XtAddEventHandler(talk, KeyPressMask |
                            ButtonPressMask |
                            ButtonReleaseMask |
                            PointerMotionMask,
                      FALSE, send_to_remote, NULL);
    XtSetArg(wargs[0], XmNeditMode, XmMULTI_LINE_EDIT);
    listen = XtCreateManagedWidget("listen",
                                    xmTextWidgetClass,
                                    vpane, NULL, 0);
    XtAddEventHandler(listen, KeyPressMask, FALSE,
                      warn_wrong_pane, NULL);
    XtAddEventHandler(listen, NoEventMask, TRUE,
                      client_message_handler, NULL);
    XtRealizeWidget(toplevel);
    /*
     * Store the listen window ID in a public place.
     */
    register_talker_window(listen);
    XtMainLoop();
}
```

The function **create_command_panel()** creates a row of buttons and text widgets in the top pane of the **xtalk** window. Several of the buttons are initially made insensitive to input events. These buttons represent commands that are not currently available and are made sensitive when these commands can be issued. For example, the **accept_button** is enabled when a connection request is received and disabled again once the user has accepted a connection. The **disconnect_button** is enabled whenever a connection to another **xtalk** is established. The **name_field** widget provides a place where the user can enter the name of a remote display. Finally, an XmLabel widget serves as a status message area.

```
create_command_panel(parent)
    Widget parent;
{
 Widget   command, quit;
 Arg      wargs[3];
 int      n;
 /*
  * Create a row widget to hold the command buttons.
  */
 command = XtCreateManagedWidget("command",
                                 xmRowColumnWidgetClass,
                                 parent, NULL, 0);

 quit = xs_create_quit_button (command);
 XtAddCallback(quit, XmNactivateCallback, quit_callback,NULL);
 /*
  * Create the buttons.
  */
 connect_button=XtCreateManagedWidget("connect",
                                      xmPushButtonWidgetClass,
                                      command, NULL, 0);
 XtAddCallback(connect_button, XmNactivateCallback,
               connect_callback, NULL);

 XtSetArg(wargs[0], XtNsensitive, FALSE);
 disconnect_button =
   XtCreateManagedWidget("disconnect",xmPushButtonWidgetClass,
                         command, wargs, 1);
 XtAddCallback(disconnect_button, XmNactivateCallback,
               disconnect_callback, NULL);
 XtSetArg(wargs[0], XtNsensitive, FALSE);
 accept_button= XtCreateManagedWidget("accept",
                                      xmPushButtonWidgetClass,
                                      command, wargs, 1);
```

```
    XtAddCallback(accept_button, XmNactivateCallback,
                        accept_callback, NULL);
    /*
     * Create a text field in which the user can
     * enter new machine names.
     */
    name_field = XtCreateManagedWidget("name", xmTextWidgetClass,
                                            command, NULL, 0);
    /*
     * Create the message area.
     */
    msg_field = XtCreateManagedWidget("messages",
                                        xmLabelWidgetClass,
                                        command, NULL, 0);
    xs_wprintf(msg_field, "No Current Connection");
}
```

Before one **xtalk** program can send messages to another, it must have the window ID of the listen pane belonging to the other **xtalk**. The function **register_talker_window()** stores the window ID of the listen pane in a property of the root window, where it can be accessed by any other **xtalk** program. The function creates several atoms used by the program, and stores the listen window ID in the **XTALK_WINDOW** property.

```
register_talker_window(w)
      Widget w;
{
 Window    window = XtWindow(w);
 Display *dpy     = XtDisplay(w);
 /*
  * Intern the atoms used for communication.
  */
XTALK_WINDOW       = XInternAtom(dpy, XtNtalkWindow, 0);
CONNECTION_REQUEST = XInternAtom(dpy,XtNconnectionRequest,0);
CONNECTION_ACCEPT  = XInternAtom(dpy, XtNconnectionAccept,0);
DISCONNECT_NOTIFY  = XInternAtom(dpy, XtNdisconnect, 0);
  /*
   * Store the listen window ID on our root window.
   */
  XChangeProperty(dpy, DefaultRootWindow(dpy),
                  XTALK_WINDOW, XA_WINDOW,
                  32, PropModeReplace,
                  &window, 1);
}
```

To establish a connection with another **xtalk** program, the user must enter the name of a remote display in the **name_field** widget, and then select the **connect_button**. This action invokes the **connect_callback()** function, which attempts to open the display named by the string in the **name_field** widget. This function must make sure the string is not empty because **XOpenDisplay()** interprets an empty string as an instruction to open the display named by the environment variable **DISPLAY**, which is normally set to the local display. Therefore if the string is empty, **xtalk** would attempt to open a connection to itself. If the remote display is opened successfully, the function then retrieves the **XTALK_WINDOW** property from the remote display, and sends a connection request to the remote **xtalk** window.

```
void connect_callback(w, client_data, call_data)
   Widget    w;
   caddr_t   client_data, call_data;
{
   int         type, format, nitems, left, fail;
   Window      *retdata;
   Arg         wargs[2];
   char        *msg;
   Atom        REMOTE_XTALK_WINDOW;
   /*
    * Get the name of the display to connect to.
    */
   strcpy(othermachine, XmTextGetString(name_field));
   /*
    * Make sure the string isn't empty, so we don't connect
    * to ourselves.
    */
   if(strlen(othermachine) > 0){
     xs_wprintf(msg_field, "%s", "Trying To Open Connection");
     /*
      * Attempt to open the remote display.
      */
     if((remote_display = XOpenDisplay(othermachine)) == NULL){
        xs_wprintf(msg_field, "%s", "Connection Failed");
        return;
     }
     /*
      * Get the REMOTE property containing THEIR listen ID.
      */
     REMOTE_XTALK_WINDOW  =
            XInternAtom(remote_display, XtNtalkWindow, 0);
```

```
    if(XGetWindowProperty(remote_display,
                          DefaultRootWindow(remote_display),
                          REMOTE_XTALK_WINDOW,
                          0, 4, FALSE, XA_WINDOW,
                          &type, &format, &nitems, &left,
                          &retdata) == Success &&
        type == XA_WINDOW){
    remote_talker_window = *retdata;
    /*
     *  If all went well, request a connection.
     */
    xs_wprintf(msg_field, "Waiting for a response");
    connection_accepted = FALSE;
    xs_send_message(remote_display, remote_talker_window,
                    XtNconnectionRequest, my_displayname);
    }
    /*
     *  If something went wrong, disconnect.
     */
    else
      disconnect_callback(disconnect_button, NULL, NULL);
  }
}
```

Notice how atoms and properties on the remote display are accessed in this example. In previous sections we noted that an atom is a unique identifier for a string, shared by all applications connected to a server. Here, we are connected to two servers, and there is no guarantee that any two servers use the same atom to represent the same string. Therefore, we must obtain the **XTALK_WINDOW** atom defined by the remote server before retrieving the contents of the **XTALK_WINDOW** property from the remote display. Also notice that the first argument to **XGetWindowProperty()** refers to the *remote* display.

The function **xs_send_message()** is a general purpose routine that can be used to send a **ClientMessage** event to a window on any display. This function is used by **xtalk** to send various requests to remote **xtalk** programs. The name of the atom representing the message type must be given as the **msg_name** argument, while the **data** argument is expected to be a character string, which cannot exceed 19 characters.

This function first determines the atom ID that represents the **message type** on the given display. It then fills in the members of an **XClientMessageEvent** structure with the display and the ID of the destination window and copies the given **data** into the event's **data** field before using **XSendEvent()** to send the event. After sending the event, this function calls **XFlush()**, an Xlib function that forces the server to process all requests in the request queue. This is seldom necessary, because **XtNextEvent()** flushes the queue each time it is called. However, **XtNextEvent()** flushes the local display, and this function may be sending an event to a remote display. Without the call to **XFlush()**, the **ClientMessage** event would remain in the remote server's request queue until enough requests had accumulated to cause it to process the request. Explicitly flushing the remote request queue ensures that the remote server handles the **XSendEvent()** request in a timely manner.

```
/**********************************************************
 * xs_send_message(): send a client message
 **********************************************************/
#include <stdio.h>
#include <X11/Intrinsic.h>
#include <X11/StringDefs.h>
#include <X11/Xatom.h>
xs_send_message(display, window, msg_name, data)
     Display *display;
     Window   window;
     char    *msg_name;
     char    *data;
{
 XClientMessageEvent event;
 Atom                 MSG_ATOM;
 /*
  * Get the atom used
  * by the display.
  */
 MSG_ATOM = XInternAtom(display, msg_name, FALSE);
 /*
  * Fill out the client message event structure.
  */
 event.display = display;
 event.window  = window;
 event.type    = ClientMessage;
 event.format  = 8;
 event.message_type = MSG_ATOM;
 strncpy(event.data.b, data, 19);
 event.data.b[19] = '\0';
 /*
  * Send it and flush.
  */
 XSendEvent(display, window,
            TRUE, XtAllEvents, &event);
 XFlush(display);
}
```

When **xtalk** receives a client message, the Intrinsics invokes the event handler **client_message_handler()**, which looks at the subtype of each client message, and acts on those that it recognizes. Because the atoms used to identify subtypes are not constants, we cannot use a **switch** statement. Instead, we must check the subtype using a series of **if** statements.[4] If the subtype of the client message is **CONNECTION_REQUEST**, the **client_message_handler()** rings the terminal bell and displays a message to notify the user of the incoming connection request. It then saves a copy of the name of the machine making the connection request and enables the **accept_button** widget.

Other types of client messages are handled similarly. When a remote **xtalk** accepts a connection, it sends a client message of subtype **CONNECTION_ACCEPT**. After displaying a message for the user, the **client_message_handler()** disables the **disconnect_button** widget and enables the **connect_button** widget. The function also sets the global flag **connection_accepted** to **TRUE**.

If the client message is of subtype **DISCONNECT_NOTIFY**, **xtalk** closes the display connection, resets various parameters and buttons to their initial state, and displays the message "Disconnected".

Notice that because **client_message_handler()** is registered for a non-maskable event we must check the event type to be sure this event is a **ClientMessage** event. This event handler would also be called if the application receives any other type of non-maskable event.

```
void client_message_handler(w, client_data, event)
     Widget          w;
     caddr_t         client_data;
     XEvent          *event;
{
  Arg wargs[10];
  if(event->type != ClientMessage) return;
  if(event->xclient.message_type == CONNECTION_REQUEST){
   /*
    * Notify the user of the incoming request and
    * enable the "accept" button.
    */
   XBell(XtDisplay(w), 0);
   strcpy(othermachine, event->xclient.data.b);
   xs_wprintf(msg_field, "Connection Request from: %s",
              othermachine);
   XtSetSensitive(accept_button, TRUE);
  }
```

---

4. The atoms predefined by the X server are defined as constants, so this restriction applies only to atoms that are created by an application.

```
    else
      if(event->xclient.message_type == CONNECTION_ACCEPT){
        /*
         * Notify the user that the connection has
         * been accepted. Enable the "disconnect" button
         * and disable the "connect" button.
         */
        XBell(XtDisplay(w), 0);
        connection_accepted = TRUE;
        strcpy(othermachine, event->xclient.data.b);
        xs_wprintf(msg_field, "Connected to %s", othermachine);
        XtSetSensitive(connect_button, FALSE);
        XtSetSensitive(disconnect_button, TRUE);
      }
    else
      if(event->xclient.message_type == DISCONNECT_NOTIFY){
        /*
         * Close the remote display and reset
         * all command buttons to their initial state.
         */
        XBell(XtDisplay(w), 0);
        if(remote_display)
            XCloseDisplay(remote_display);
        remote_display = NULL;
        connection_accepted = FALSE;
        othermachine[0] = '\0';
        xs_wprintf(msg_field, "%s", "Disconnected");

        XtSetSensitive(connect_button, TRUE);
        XtSetSensitive(disconnect_button, FALSE);
      }
  }
```

When **xtalk** receives a connection request, the **accept_button** widget is enabled. If the user then selects the **accept_button** widget, the **accept_callback()** function is invoked. This function attempts to open the remote display and retrieve the window ID of the remote **xtalk**'s listen pane. If successful, the function sends an **XtNconnectionAccepted** client message to indicate that the connection has been accepted. The function also disables the **connect_button** and **accept_button** widgets and enables the **disconnect_button**.

```
void accept_callback(w, client_data, call_data)
     Widget     w;
     caddr_t    client_data, call_data;
{
  int       type, format, nitems, left, fail;
  Window    *retdata;
  Atom      REMOTE_XTALK_WINDOW;
  Arg       wargs[10];
  /*
   * Make sure there really is another machine.
   */
  if(strlen(othermachine) > 0 ){
   /*
    * Attempt to open the remote display.
    */
   if((remote_display = XOpenDisplay(othermachine)) == NULL){
      xs_wprintf(msg_field, "%s", "Connection Failed");
      return;
   }
   /*
    *  Get the window ID of the remote xtalk program
    */
   REMOTE_XTALK_WINDOW  =
                 XInternAtom(remote_display, XtNtalkWindow, 0);
   if(XGetWindowProperty(remote_display,
                     DefaultRootWindow(remote_display),
                     REMOTE_XTALK_WINDOW,
                     0, 4, FALSE, XA_WINDOW,
                     &type, &format, &nitems, &left,
                     &retdata) == Success &&
         type ==  XA_WINDOW) {
    connection_accepted = TRUE;
    remote_talker_window = *retdata;
    /*
     * Notify the remote xtalk that we accept the connection.
     */
    connection_accepted = TRUE;
    xs_send_message(remote_display, remote_talker_window,
                    XtNconnectionAccept, my_displayname);
    xs_wprintf(msg_field, "Connected to %s", othermachine);

    XtSetSensitive(accept_button, FALSE);
```

```
    XtSetSensitive(connect_button, FALSE);
    XtSetSensitive(disconnect_button, TRUE);
  }
  else
    disconnect_callback(disconnect_button, NULL, NULL);
  }
}
```

Once each program has established a connection to the other, each user can type into his or her talk pane. The event handler **send_to_remote()** is invoked when any key or mouse event occurs in the talk pane. This event handler uses **XSendEvent()** to send the event to the remote **xtalk** program, where it is treated just as if the remote user had typed the text into the window. The result is that everything typed in the talk pane of the local **xtalk** program is echoed in the listen pane of the remote **xtalk** program.

```
void send_to_remote(w, client_data, event)
   Widget     w;
   caddr_t    client_data;
   XEvent     *event;
{
  /*
   * Make sure that we have a valid connection
   * before sending the event.
   */
  if(remote_display && remote_talker_window &&
        connection_accepted){
    event->xany.display = remote_display;
    event->xany.window  = remote_talker_window;
    XSendEvent(remote_display, remote_talker_window,
            TRUE, XtAllEvents, event);
    XFlush(remote_display);
  }
}
```

The XmText widget does not provide a way to prevent the user from typing into the listen pane of the **xtalk** window. The XmText widget does not distinguish between events generated by the local keyboard and those sent by the remote **xtalk**. This could be confusing to the user, because text typed into the listen pane is echoed in the local listen pane, but is not sent to the remote **xtalk** program. Although we cannot intercept events generated by the keyboard, we can add an event handler that is called in addition to the one defined by the XmText widget. The event handler **warn_wrong_pane()** rings the terminal bell whenever the user types into the listen text pane to warn the user that he or she is using the wrong pane. This event handler examines the **send_event** member of each event to determine if the event was sent using **XSendEvent()**.

```
void warn_wrong_pane(w, client_data, event)
   Widget      w;
   caddr_t     client_data;
   XEvent      *event;
{
  /*
   * Just beep if the user types into the wrong pane.
   */
  if (!event->xany.send_event)
     XBell(XtDisplay(w), 0);
}
```

When a conversation has ended, either user can close the connection by activating the **disconnect_button**, invoking the callback function **disconnect_callback()**. This callback resets the state of the buttons and variables used by the program to their initial state, after sending an **XtNdisconnect** client message to notify the remote **xtalk** of the disconnection. Finally, **XCloseDisplay()** closes the connection to the remote display.

```
void disconnect_callback(w, client_data, call_data)
        Widget              w;
        caddr_t             client_data, call_data;
{
  Arg wargs[10];
  /*
   * Send a disconnect notice and close the display.
   */
  if(remote_display){
    connection_accepted = FALSE;
    xs_send_message(remote_display, remote_talker_window,
                    XtNdisconnect, my_displayname);
    XCloseDisplay(remote_display);
    xs_wprintf(msg_field, "%s", "Disconnected");
    othermachine[0] = '\0';
    remote_display = NULL;
    XtSetSensitive(connect_button, TRUE);
    XtSetSensitive(disconnect_button, FALSE);
  }
}
```

The connection is also broken when either user exits the **xtalk** program. Therefore the **quit_callback()** function, invoked when the user activates the quit button, also sends an

XtNdisconnect client message to notify the remote **xtalk** that the connection is about to be closed. This function also deletes the **XTALK_WINDOW** property, to prevent remote **xtalk**s from attempting to connect to a non-existent window.

```
void quit_callback(w, client_data, call_data)
        Widget          w;
        caddr_t         client_data, call_data;
{
  Display *dpy = XtDisplay(w);
  /*
   * Inform the remote connection that we are shutting down.
   */
  if(remote_display && remote_talker_window){
    connection_accepted = FALSE;
    xs_send_message(remote_display, remote_talker_window,
                  XtNdisconnect, my_displayname);
  }
  /*
   * Clean up.
   */
  XDeleteProperty(dpy, DefaultRootWindow(dpy), XTALK_WINDOW);
}
```

11.4 THE X SELECTION MECHANISM

Most window systems support some mechanism for transferring information between windows. This is often referred to as "cut and paste," because the user deletes ("cuts") an object or section of text from one window and then transfers ("pastes") it into another window.[5] Because all X applications in the user's environment do not necessarily run on the same machine, X implements "cut and paste" via an interclient communication mechanism, using the X server as a central communications point.

The client messages discussed in the previous section allow applications to define their own communication protocols and provides a flexible way to exchange information. These facilities are useful when two or more programs need to define a particular style of communication, as demonstrated by the **xtalk** example. However, for this approach to work, every application involved must respond to the same types of client messages. Requiring every application to define and decipher client messages to do a simple "copy and paste"

5. A variation on this technique is often used. Instead of deleting the object from the first window, it could just be copied. This should be referred to as "copy and paste," but often the phrase "cut and paste" is used loosely (although incorrectly) to apply to both techniques. This section actually describes "copy and paste."

data transfer places an unacceptable burden on application programmers. On the other hand, a flexible facility that allows arbitrary data types to be copied between applications is highly desirable.

X provides several events and functions that work together to implement a flexible "copy and paste" mechanism. This section first discusses the basic concepts of this mechanism as provided by Xlib, and then demonstrates the concepts with two simple examples using some higher-level functions provided by the Xt Intrinsics. Following this discussion, Section 11.5 presents the Motif clipboard facility, a higher level cut-and-paste mechanism built on the Xt Intrinsics selection facilities.

11.4.1 Basic Concepts

X supports data exchange between applications through the *selection* mechanism. Applications can define the contents of a selection and also request the contents of the selection from another application. Selections are owned and maintained by applications, but do not necessarily represent any existing data. Some applications may choose to generate the data represented by a selection only when another application requests a copy of the selection. Multiple selections can exist at once, each uniquely identified by different selection atoms. X predefines two selection atoms: **XA_PRIMARY**, and **XA_SECONDARY**; applications can also define additional selection atoms.

Any application can claim ownership of a selection by calling the Xlib function:

XSetSelectionOwner(display, atom, window, time)

This function informs the X server that the specified window claims ownership of the selection corresponding to the given atom. The **time** argument is used to eliminate potential race conditions and should be set to the current server time. Applications can obtain the current server time from most X events. Since most applications grab ownership in response to a user action, the timestamp in the corresponding event can be used to set the time. When an application claims ownership of a selection, the X server sends an **SelectionClear** event to the previous owner to notify it that it has lost the selection.

An application can ask for the ID of the window that currently owns a selection. The function

XGetSelectionOwner(display, atom)

returns the window ID of the current owner of the selection named by **atom**. Applications should call **XGetSelectionOwner()** after they request ownership of the selection to determine if the request succeeded. Once ownership of the selection is confirmed, most applications visually indicate the selection, often by displaying the region in inverse-video.

The function

XConvertSelection(display, atom, type, target_atom,
window, time)

allows applications to request the data corresponding to a selection. This function requests that the selection identified by the argument **atom** be stored in a property specified by the **target_atom** on the given window. In addition, the **type** argument is an atom that specifies the desired form of the selection. For example, one application might request a selection as a string, while another might request the bitmap image of the region containing the selection. When **XConvertSelection()** is called, the server sends a **SelectionRequest** event to the current owner of the selection. The owner of the selection is responsible for converting the contents of the selection to the requested type, and storing the result in the given property of the requestor's window. Afterwards, the selection owner is expected to send a **SelectionNotify** event to the requesting application to inform it that the data has been stored. The requestor is expected to retrieve the data and then delete the property.

The server reports **SelectionRequest** events using a **XSelectionRequestEvent** structure, which, in addition to the information included in all events, includes the members:

```
Window        owner;
Window        requestor;
Atom          selection;
Atom          target;
Atom          property;
Time          time;
```

This event reports the window ID of the owner of the selection and also the ID of the requestor. Three members of the event structure are atoms. The first, **selection**, identifies the name of the requested selection, while the second, **target**, specifies the data type desired by the requestor. The **property** atom contains the name of a property on the requestor's window where the data is to be stored.

After the owner of the selection converts the selection to the requested type and stores it on the given property of the requestor window, the selection owner is expected to send a **SelectionNotify** event back to the requestor. This event uses an **XSelectionEvent** structure, which includes the members:

```
Window        requestor;
Atom          selection;
Atom          target;
Atom          property;
Time          time;
```

If the selection owner is able to provide the requested type of data, the owner sets the **target** atom to the requested data type. Otherwise the owner sets the atom to the constant **None**. The **selection** member indicates the name of the selection and the **property** specifies the name of the property in which the selection is stored.

When a client requests ownership of a selection, the X server sends the current owner a **SelectionClear** event to notify the application that it has lost the selection. This event uses the **XSelectionClearEvent** event structure, which includes the members

```
Atom            selection;
Time            time;
```

The **selection** atom indicates the name of the selection that has been lost, while **time** indicates the server time at which the event occurred.

We can summarize the X selection process by looking at the sequence of steps that occur in a typical exchange. Assume there are two windows, "Window A" and "Window B," and that "Window A" currently owns a selection. If "Window B" requests the value of that selection, the sequence shown in Fig. 11.4 takes place.

Window B:	Calls **XConvertSelection()** to ask for selection contents.
Window A:	Receives a **SelectionRequest** event.
Window A:	Converts the selection data to the type requested by Window B.
Window A:	Stores data on a property of Window B.
Window A:	Sends a **SelectionNotify** event to Window B.
Window B:	Receives **SelectionNotify** event.
Window B:	Retrieves data from property.
Window B:	Deletes property.

Figure 11.4 Exchanging data using selections.

Now let's assume that Window B claims ownership of the selection currently owned by Window A. The sequence in Fig. 11.5 traces the steps that should occur when Window B calls **XSetSelectionOwner()**.[6]

Window B:	Calls **XSetSelectionOwner()** to grab the selection.
Window A:	Receives a **SelectionClear** event.
Window A:	Unhighlights selection.
Window B:	Calls **XGetSelectionOwner()**.
Window B:	Highlights selection if Window B is the owner.

Figure 11.5 Gaining ownership of a selection.

---

6. The word *should* should be emphasized. This protocol depends on cooperation between all applications. Every application must follow the same procedures for this approach to work. At the time this book is being written, very few X applications follow this protocol or use the selection mechanism at all.

11.4.2   Selections With The Xt Intrinsics

The discussion in Section 11.4.1 is a little simplistic and ignores several issues. For example, to transfer large amounts of data efficiently, applications must break up the transfer into several smaller transfers. The complete selection mechanism is defined by the InterClient Communications Conventions Manual (ICCCM). Implementing the selection mechanism as described in this manual can be quite complex. Fortunately the Xt Intrinsics provides several functions that handle most of the details and allow applications to use a much simpler interface. In addition to being simpler to use, the Xt Intrinsics allows application to view all selection transfers as being atomic. The Intrinsics breaks up large data transfers into smaller ones automatically and transparently.

The Intrinsics defines three primary selection functions. The first of these is used to claim ownership of a selection, and has the form:

```
XtOwnSelection(widget, selection, time, convert, lose, done)
```

The first argument to this function specifies the widget that claims ownership of the atom. The second argument is an atom that specifies the selection, usually **XA_PRIMARY** or **XA_SECONDARY**. The third argument is the current server time. As defined by the ICCCM, this time should not be the constant **CurrentTime,** but instead should be obtained from the user event responsible for claiming the selection. The last three arguments specify procedures that must be defined by the application. The first specifies a procedure that the Intrinsics can call when another application requests the value of the selection. The second is a procedure to be called when the application loses the selection. The third is a procedure to be called when a requesting application has actually received the data from a request. This procedure is optional and can be given as **NULL**. **XtOwnSelection()** returns **TRUE** if the caller has successfully gained ownership of the selection.

The **convert** procedure must have the form:

```
Boolean convert_proc(widget, selection, target,
                     type, value, length, format)
    Widget          widget;
    Atom            *selection;
    Atom            *target;
    Atom            *type;
    caddr_t         *value;
    unsigned long   *length;
    int             *format;
```

All parameters except the widget are pointers. The **selection** argument is a pointer to the requested selection atom. The **target** argument is a pointer to an atom that specifies the requested type, while **type** is a pointer to the type actually returned by this procedure. The **value** parameter is a pointer to the data returned by this procedure, while **length** and **format** indicate the size of the data pointed to by **value**. If the application registers a

done procedure, the application owns the data in **value**, and should use the **done** procedure to free it, if necessary. If the application does not register a **done** procedure, it does not own the storage associated with **value**. The **convert_proc()** callback must return **TRUE** if it successfully converted the selection and **FALSE** if it could not fulfill the request.

The **lose** procedure must have the form:

```
lose_proc(widget, selection)
    Widget   widget;
    Atom    *selection;
```

Here, **widget** is the widget that lost the selection, and **selection** points to an atom specifying the selection type.

The **done** procedure must have the form:

```
done_proc(widget, selection, target)
    Widget   widget;
    Atom    *selection;
    Atom    *target;
```

The **widget** argument is the widget that owns the selection, **selection** points to an atom indicating the selection, and **target** points to an atom indicating the type of the transferred selection.

To request a selection, an application can call the function:

```
XtGetSelectionValue(widget, selection, target, callback,
                    client_data, time)
```

Here, **widget** indicates the widget requesting the selection value, **selection** is an atom indicating the selection name, and **target** is an atom indicating the requested type of the data. The **callback** argument must specify a function defined by the application. The Intrinsics invokes this function when it obtains the selection value. The form of this function must be:

```
selection_callback(widget, client_data, selection, type,
                   value, length, format)
        Widget          widget;
        caddr_t         client_data;
        Atom           *selection;
        Atom           *type;
        caddr_t         value;
        unsigned long  *length;
        int            *format;
```

The **client_data** parameter contains the client data specified by the application when registering the callback. The other parameters correspond to the data returned by the selection owner.

11.4.3 Adding Selection Capability to memo

The next two sections demonstrate the X selection mechanism using two simple programs.
This section extends the **memo** program from Chapter 2 to grab ownership of the
XA_PRIMARY selection when the user presses a mouse button in the message window. This
version of memo uses an XmRowColumn widget to manage the message window and a quit
button. Like the earlier version, the message area is implemented using a XmLabel widget.
The application registers an event handler to claim ownership of the selection when a button
is pressed in the message widget.

```
/***********************************************
 *   memo.c: Selection Version
 ***********************************************/
#include <X11/Intrinsic.h>
#include <X11/StringDefs.h>
#include <Xm/Xm.h>
#include <Xm/PushB.h>
#include <Xm/RowColumn.h>
#include <Xm/Label.h>
#include <X11/Xatom.h>
#include "libXs.h"
void       grab_selection();
Boolean    convert_selection();
void       lose_selection();
Atom       COMPOUND_STRING;

main(argc, argv)
   int        argc;
   char       *argv[];
{
   Widget     toplevel, msg_widget, base;
   Arg        wargs[1];
   int        n;
   XmString   xmstr;
   toplevel = XtInitialize(argv[0],"Memo", NULL, 0,
                           &argc, argv);
   COMPOUND_STRING = XInternAtom(XtDisplay(toplevel),
                                 "Compound String", FALSE);
   /*
    *  Create a manager for the quit button and message window.
    */
   base = XtCreateManagedWidget("base", xmRowColumnWidgetClass,
                                toplevel, NULL, 0);

   xs_create_quit_button(base);
```

```
    /*
     * Get the contents of the command line and display it in
     * the message window.
     */
    n = 0;
    if((xmstr = xs_concat_words(argc - 1, &argv[1])) != NULL)
      XtSetArg(wargs[n], XmNlabelString, xmstr); n++;

    msg_widget = XtCreateManagedWidget("message",
                                       xmLabelWidgetClass,
                                       base, wargs, n);
    XtAddEventHandler(msg_widget, ButtonPressMask,
                      FALSE, grab_selection, NULL);
    /*
     * Realize all widgets and enter the event loop.
     */
    XtRealizeWidget(toplevel);
    XtMainLoop();
}
```

The **grab_selection()** event handler claims ownership of the **XA_PRIMARY** selection by calling **XtOwnSelection()**. It confirms that it owns the selection before calling **xs_invert_widget()** to highlight the selected text. Because **xs_invert_widget()** toggles the colors of the message widget when it is called, we must ensure that the widget is not accidently unhighlighted while we still own the selection. We can do this by setting the widget's sensitivity to **FALSE**, to prevent the user from selecting the widget again.

```
    void grab_selection(w, client_data, event)
        Widget     w;
        caddr_t    client_data;
        XEvent     *event;
    {
      /*
       * Claim ownership of the PRIMARY selection.
       */
      if(XtOwnSelection(w, XA_PRIMARY,
                        event->xbutton.time,
                        convert_selection,  /* handle requests */
                        lose_selection,     /* Give up selection*/
                        NULL)){
        xs_invert_widget(w);
        XtSetSensitive(w, FALSE);
      }
    }
```

The function **xs_invert_widget()** retrieves the current foreground and background colors of a widget and reverses them. This is a generally useful function that we can place in the libXs library.

```
/******************************************************************
 * invert.c: utility function for inverting a widget's color.
 ******************************************************************/
#include <X11/Intrinsic.h>
#include <X11/StringDefs.h>

xs_invert_widget(w)
    Widget   w;
{
  Arg      wargs[3];
  Pixel    fg, bg;
  /*
   * Get the widget's current colors.
   */
  XtSetArg(wargs[0], XtNforeground, &fg);
  XtSetArg(wargs[1], XtNbackground, &bg);
  XtGetValues(w, wargs, 2);
  /*
   * Reverse them and set the new colors.
   */
  XtSetArg(wargs[0], XtNforeground, bg);
  XtSetArg(wargs[1], XtNbackground, fg);
  XtSetValues(w, wargs, 2);
}
```

The Intrinsics calls the callback function **convert_selection()** whenever **memo** receives a request for the value of the selection. This callback function checks the requested type to be sure it is a type it can handle. In this example, **memo** can handle requests for either character strings or compound strings. If the selection is requested as type **COMPOUND_STRING**, this callback retrieves the compound string displayed in the message widget using **XtGetValues()** and returns **TRUE**. If the selection is requested as a character string, the callback function retrieves the compound string and uses the function **xs_get_string_from_xmstring()**, described in Chapter 9, to convert it to a character string before returning **TRUE**. If the requested selection type is unknown, the callback returns **FALSE**.

```
static Boolean convert_selection(w, selection, target,
                                   type, value, length, format)
    Widget        w;
    Atom          *selection, *target, *type;
    caddr_t       *value;
    unsigned long *length;
    int           *format;
{
   Arg wargs[10];

  if (*target == COMPOUND_STRING){
    XmString xmstr;
    XtSetArg(wargs[0], XmNlabelString, &xmstr);
    XtGetValues(w, wargs, 1);
    *type   = COMPOUND_STRING;
    *value  = xmstr;
    *length = XmStringLength(xmstr);
    *format = 8;
    return TRUE;
  }
  else if (*target == XA_STRING) {
    char      *str;
    XmString  xmstr;

    XtSetArg(wargs[0], XmNlabelString, &xmstr);
    XtGetValues(w, wargs, 1);

    *type   = XA_STRING;
    *value  = xs_get_string_from_xmstring (xmstr);
    *length = strlen(*value);
    *format = 8;
    return TRUE;
  }
   else   /* Requestor wants a type we can't handle */
     return FALSE;
}
```

The Intrinsics calls the callback function **lose_selection()** when the message widget loses the selection. This function simply inverts the widget to its normal state and then restores the message widget's sensitivity.

```
static void lose_selection(w, selection)
  Widget    w;
  Atom      *selection;
{
  xs_invert_widget(w);
  XtSetSensitive(w, TRUE);
}
```

We can use this version of **memo** to see how the selection mechanism allows applications to take ownership of a selection. Try running several instances of **memo** at once and click the mouse in each of the windows. As you select each window, the message changes to inverse-video, while the previously selected window reverts to normal video.

11.4.4 A Simple Clipboard

The second part of the selection example is a program named **clipboard** that copies and displays the value of the current **PRIMARY** selection upon request. A clipboard provides a temporary place to save data. The user can select the contents of the clipboard, in the same way as the **memo** program, to allow the data in the clipboard to be transferred to another client. The main portion of the program is similar to **memo**, but rather than extracting the message from the command line, the string displayed by the clipboard is obtained from the owner of the current selection. Like **memo** from the previous section, this program creates a XmRowColumn widget that manages the message window and a quit button. The user copies the contents of the current selection to the clipboard by selecting a second XmPushButton widget. The clipboard also uses an XmToggleButton widget to allow the user to select the type of the data to be transferred to the clipboard. The user can choose to copy the selection as either a compound string or a character string.

```
/*****************************************************
 * clipboard.c: A simple clipboard using X selections
 *****************************************************/
#include <X11/Intrinsic.h>
#include <X11/StringDefs.h>
#include <Xm/Xm.h>
#include <Xm/PushB.h>
#include <Xm/RowColumn.h>
#include <Xm/ToggleB.h>
#include <Xm/Label.h>
#include <X11/Xatom.h>
#include "libXs.h"

void       grab_selection();
void       request_selection();
```

```
Boolean    convert_selection();
void       lose_selection();
void       show_selection();
void       toggle_type();
Atom       COMPOUND_STRING;
Atom       current_type = XA_STRING;

main(argc, argv)
    int             argc;
    char            *argv[];
{
  Widget    toplevel, selection, request, row_col, toggle;

  toplevel = XtInitialize(argv[0], "Clipboard", NULL,
                          0, &argc, argv);
  COMPOUND_STRING = XInternAtom(XtDisplay(toplevel),
                               "Compound String", FALSE);

  row_col = XtCreateManagedWidget("commands",
                                  xmRowColumnWidgetClass,
                                  toplevel, NULL, 0);
  xs_create_quit_button(row_col);
  /*
   * Create a button used to request the selection and
   * a text widget to display it.
   */
  request = XtCreateManagedWidget("getselection",
                                  xmPushButtonWidgetClass,
                                  row_col, NULL, 0);
  toggle = XtCreateManagedWidget("type",
                                 xmToggleButtonWidgetClass,
                                 row_col, NULL, 0);
  xs_wprintf(toggle, "Type: Character String");
  selection = XtCreateManagedWidget("currentselection",
                                    xmLabelWidgetClass,
                                    row_col, NULL, 0);

  XtAddCallback(toggle, XmNvalueChangedCallback,
                toggle_type, NULL);
  XtAddCallback(request, XmNactivateCallback,
                request_selection, selection);
  XtAddEventHandler(selection, ButtonPressMask, FALSE,
```

```
                    grab_selection, NULL);

    XtRealizeWidget(toplevel);
    XtMainLoop();
}
```

This example defines an event handler and several callbacks. The **grab_selection()** function, registered as an **ButtonPress** event handler for the **selection** widget, is identical to the function of the same name defined for **memo** in the previous section. This function registers the functions **lose_selection()** and **convert_selection()**, also identical to those described in the previous section. Together, these functions claim ownership of the selection for the clipboard's selection widget and handle converting selection requests.

The **request_selection()** function requests the value of the **XA_PRIMARY** selection when the user clicks a mouse button in the **request** widget. This function simply calls **XtGetSelectionValue()** and is defined as:

```
    void request_selection(w, client_data, call_data)
        Widget          w;
        caddr_t         client_data;
        XmAnyCallbackStruct *call_data;
    {
      XtGetSelectionValue(w, XA_PRIMARY, current_type,
                          show_selection, client_data,
                          call_data->event->xbutton.time);
    }
```

This function requests selections according of the type specified by the atom **current_type**. Notice that the **time** argument to **XtGetSelectionValue()** is obtained from the event that caused this event handler to be called.

XtGetSelectionValue() registers a callback function, **show_selection()**, to be called when the Intrinsics obtains the value of the requested selection. It checks the type of the data received, and if it is a compound string, uses **XtSetValues()** to display it in the **selection** widget. If the type is a character string, the function uses **xs_wprintf()** to display the data. Notice that the **selection** widget is passed as client data.

```
    static void show_selection(w, client_data, selection, type,
                              value, length, format)
        Widget          w;
        Widget          client_data;
        Atom            *selection, *type;
        caddr_t         value;
        unsigned long   *length;
```

```
      int              *format;
{
  Arg wargs[2];
  if (*type == COMPOUND_STRING){
      XtSetArg(wargs[0], XmNlabelString, value);
      XtSetValues(client_data, wargs, 1);
  }
  else if (*type == XA_STRING){
      xs_wprintf(client_data, "%s", value);
  }
}
```

The callback function **toggle_type()** toggles the global variable **current_type** between the atoms **COMPOUND_STRING** and **XA_STRING**, and determines the type requested by the **request_selection()** callback function. The function also changes the label in the XmToggleButton widget to display the current type being requested.

```
void toggle_type (w, client_data, call_data)
     Widget          w;
     caddr_t         client_data;
     XmToggleButtonCallbackStruct *call_data;
{
   if(call_data->set){
     current_type = COMPOUND_STRING;
     xs_wprintf(w, "Type: Compound String");
   }
   else{
     current_type = XA_STRING;
     xs_wprintf(w, "Type: Character String");
   }
}
```

Now we can combine the clipboard program with the **memo** example to experiment with transferring selections between applications. Fig. 11.6 shows several instances of **memo**, and a **clipboard**. Clicking on any **memo** window causes that application to grab ownership of the selection. Selecting the **clipboard**'s "getselection" button retrieves and displays the contents of the selection. The contents of the **clipboard** can also be selected and transferred to other clipboards or any other X client that uses the selection mechanism.

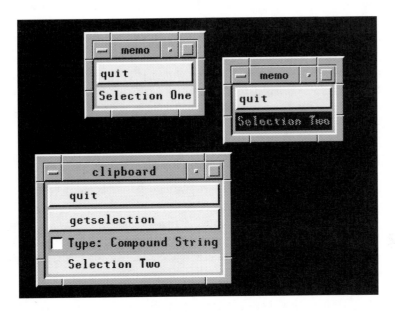

Figure 11.6 Retrieving a selection.

11.5   USING THE MOTIF CLIPBOARD

Motif builds on the selection mechanism provided by Xlib and the Xt Intrinsics to provide a clipboard mechanism for transferring data between applications. Basically, the Motif clipboard is an unseen location where applications can store and retrieve named, typed data. The following sections explain a few of the more common functions for manipulating the clipboard and provide a typical example.

11.5.1   STORING DATA IN THE CLIPBOARD

Transferring data to the clipboard requires three steps:

1. Initialize the clipboard. This step sets up some data structures in the clipboard and retrieves an identifier for this transaction.

2. Specify the data to be copied to the clipboard. Data can be transferred as bits of data, or it can be transferred by name. Transferring by name is similar to the model described in the previous section. The clipboard is informed that the application has some data to be copied to the clipboard, but no data is actually transferred until another application requests the data from the clipboard.

3. End the copy. In this step, the data (or the name of the data, if the transfer is by name only) is actually transferred to the clipboard. The clipboard is first locked to prevent any application from accessing the clipboard while the transfer is in progress. Then the data is transferred, and the clipboard unlocked.

Motif provides many functions for dealing with the clipboard, locking, unlocking, determining the type and size of the data stored on the clipboard, and so on. However, most applications can use a few simple functions that implement the steps described above.

To copy data to the clipboard, the application must first call the function:

```
XmClipboardStartCopy(display, window, label, time,
                     widget, callback, &item_id)
```

This function sets up storage and data structures within the clipboard. The **window** parameter specifies the window ID to be associated with the clipboard data. The **label** specifies a name to be associated with the clipboard. The **time** argument specifies the current server time and should be obtained from the event that triggered the copy. The **widget** argument indicates the widget that will receive messages requesting data previously passed by name, and can be any widget within the application. The clipboard assigns an identifier to this transaction and returns it to the application in the **item_id** argument. The application must use this ID in subsequent calls to **XmClipboardCopy()**, **XmClipboardEndCopy()**, and **Xm-ClipboardCancelCopy()**.

Applications can use the **callback** argument to specify a callback function to be invoked if the clipboard needs data stored by name. The form of this callback function is:

```
proc(widget, data_id, private, reason)
    Widget widget;
    int    *data_id;
    int    *private;
    int     reason;
```

Here, **widget** is the widget specified in the previous call to **XmClipboardStartCopy()**, **data_id** is the identifier for this transaction, **private** is a private identifier specified by the application in the function **XmClipboardCopy()**, and **reason** argument can be either **XmCRClipboardDataDelete** or **XmCRClipboardDataRequest**. The constant **XmCR-ClipboardDataDelete** indicates that an item passed by name has been deleted from the clipboard and the associated data is no longer needed. If the callback is invoked with the reason given as **XmCRClipboardDataRequest**, the application must transfer the data to the clipboard using the function:

```
XmClipboardCopyByName(display, window, data_id,
                      buffer, length, private)
```

Here, **data_id** is the clipboard's identifier for this transaction, **buffer** contains the data to be transferred and **length** indicates the number of bytes in the buffer. The **private** argument specifies an application-defined private ID to be associated with the data on the clipboard.

XmClipboardStartCopy() returns **ClipboardSuccess** if the function is successful, or **ClipboardLocked** if the clipboard is locked by another application.

The function

```
XmClipboardCopy(display, window, item_id, format, buffer,
                length, private, &dataid)
```

specifies the data, in **buffer**, to be copied to the clipboard. If **buffer** is given as **NULL**, the copy is assumed to be by name, and the callback specified in **XmClipboardStart-Copy()** will be invoked if the data is needed. Otherwise, the length of the buffer is specified by the **length** argument.

The window ID specified in the call should be the same window ID used for all clipboard functions. The **format** argument specifies the format of the data, for example, "STRING". This argument is not interpreted by the clipboard. The **item_id** must be the transaction identifier returned by **XmClipboardStartCopy()**. The **private** parameter allows the application to store a private identifier with the data. The clipboard assigns an identifier to this data and returns it to the application in the **data_id** parameter. This argument is required only for data that is passed by name.

The data in buffer is not actually entered in the clipboard data structure until the function **XmClipboardEndCopy()** is called. Additional calls to **XmClipboardCopy()** before a call to **XmClipboardEndCopy()** add additional formats to the data item or append data to an existing format.

XmClipboardCopy() returns **ClipboardSuccess** if the function is successful, or **ClipboardLocked** if the clipboard is locked by another application.

The function

```
XmClipboardEndCopy(display, window, item_id)
```

ends the data transfer and actually places the data on the clipboard. This function locks the clipboard, stores the data, and unlocks the clipboard. **XmClipboardEndCopy()** returns **ClipboardSuccess** if the function is successful, or **ClipboardLocked** if the clipboard is locked by another application.

11.5.2 RETRIEVING DATA FROM THE CLIPBOARD

The function

```
XmClipboardRetrieve(display, window, format_name, buffer,
                    length, num_bytes, &private_id)
```

retrieves an item from the clipboard. This function requests that **num_bytes** of data be copied into **buffer**. The size of the buffer, in bytes, is specified by the **length** argument. If the data is retrieved successfully, **XmClipboardRetrieve()** returns the constant **Clip-boardSuccess**. If the clipboard is locked by another application, the function returns **ClipboardLocked**. If desired, the application can continue to call the function again with the same parameters until the clipboard is no longer locked. If the data in the clipboard is larger than the size of the buffer provided, **XmClipboardRetrieve()** returns the value **ClipboardTruncate**, while if the clipboard is empty, **XmClipboardRetrieve()** returns **ClipboardNoData**.

11.5.3 A CLIPBOARD EXAMPLE

This section uses the functions described in the previous sections to implement a simple notepad that allows the user to enter and edit text. The user can select a region of text by highlighting it with the mouse, and copy it to the Motif clipboard. Text can also be retrieved from the clipboard and inserted into the notepad. The body of the program creates a XmPanedWindow widget, which manages two panes. The first pane contains three command buttons: "copy", "retrieve", and "quit". The second is a multi-line XmText widget which allows users to enter text or edit existing text. Two **XmNactivateCallback** callback functions, **copy_to_clipboard()** and **copy_from_clipboard()** handle transferring data between the text buffer and the clipboard.

```
/******************************************************
 * notepad.c: Copy text to and from the clipboard
 ******************************************************/
#include <stdio.h>
#include <X11/StringDefs.h>
#include <X11/Intrinsic.h>
#include <Xm/Xm.h>
#include <Xm/RowColumn.h>
#include <Xm/PanedW.h>
#include <Xm/Text.h>
#include <Xm/PushB.h>
#include <Xm/CutPaste.h>

extern void copy_to_clipboard ();
extern void copy_from_clipboard ();

main (argc, argv)
   int     argc;
   char *argv[];
{
  Widget toplevel, base, commands, text, copy, get;
  Arg     wargs[10];
```

```
/*
 * Initialize the Intrinsic and create a paned window
 * widget as the base of the application.
 */
toplevel = XtInitialize (argv[0], "Notepad", NULL, 0,
                         &argc, argv);
base = XtCreateManagedWidget("base",
                            xmPanedWindowWidgetClass,
                            toplevel, NULL, 0);
/*
 * Make a row of command buttons.
 */
commands = XtCreateManagedWidget("commands",
                                xmRowColumnWidgetClass,
                                base, NULL, 0);
copy = XtCreateManagedWidget("copy",
                            xmPushButtonWidgetClass,
                            commands, wargs, 0);
get = XtCreateManagedWidget("retrieve",
                            xmPushButtonWidgetClass,
                            commands, wargs, 0);
xs_create_quit_button(commands);
/*
 * Create a multi-line text edit pane to hold notes
 */
XtSetArg(wargs[0], XmNeditMode, XmMULTI_LINE_EDIT);
text = XtCreateManagedWidget("text", xmTextWidgetClass,
                            base, wargs, 1);
XtAddCallback (copy, XmNactivateCallback,
              copy_to_clipboard,  text);
XtAddCallback (get, XmNactivateCallback,
              copy_from_clipboard, text);
XtRealizeWidget(toplevel);
XtMainLoop();
}
```

The function **copy_to_clipboard()** checks to see if there is a valid selection in the text buffer. If there is, it uses **XmClipboardStartCopy()** to begin the transaction. Once this function succeeds, **XmClipboardCopy()** specifies the data to be transferred, and finally **XmClipboardEndCopy()** ends the transaction.

```
void copy_to_clipboard (w, text_w, call_data)
    Widget    w;
    Widget    text_w;
    XmAnyCallbackStruct *call_data;
{
   char     *selection = NULL;
   int      result;
   long     itemid, dataid;
   XButtonEvent *event = (XButtonEvent *) call_data->event;

  if ((selection = XmTextGetSelection (text_w)) != NULL) {
   /*
    * Begin the copy. If the clipboard is locked,
    * keep trying.
    */
   while ((result =
           XmClipboardStartCopy (XtDisplay(w),
                                 XtWindow(text_w),
                                 "Notepad", event->time,
                                 text_w, NULL,
                                 &itemid)) != ClipboardSuccess)
       ;
   /*
    * Copy the data.
    */
   while ((result =
           XmClipboardCopy (XtDisplay(w),
                            XtWindow(text_w), itemid,
                            XtRString, selection,
                            strlen(selection), 0,
                            &dataid)) != ClipboardSuccess)
       ;
   /*
    * End the transaction.
    */
   while ((result =
           XmClipboardEndCopy(XtDisplay(w),
                              XtWindow(text_w),
                              itemid)) != ClipboardSuccess)
       ;
   }
}
```

The function **copy_from_clipboard()** handles retrieving data from the clipboard and inserting it into the text buffer. This function calls **XmClipboardRetrieve()** to request the data from the clipboard. The value returned by this function is then tested. If the retrieval was successful, the data is inserted into the text buffer. If the clipboard was locked, **XmClipboardRetrieve()** is called repeatedly, until the lock is removed. Otherwise, the transfer is aborted.

```
void copy_from_clipboard (w, text_w, call_data)
     Widget  w;
     Widget  text_w;
     caddr_t call_data;
{
    char buffer[BUFSIZ];
    int  length, id, result;
    int  done = FALSE;
    /*
     * Retrieve the current contents of the clipboard.
     */
    while (!done){
      result = XmClipboardRetrieve (XtDisplay(w),
                                    XtWindow(text_w),
                                    XtRString, buffer,
                                    BUFSIZ, &length, &id);
    /*
     * Check the type. If locked, try again. If data is
     * retrieved successfully, append it to the buffer.
     */
    switch(result){
        case ClipboardSuccess:
          buffer[length] = '\0';
          xs_insert_string(text_w, buffer);
          done = TRUE;
          break;
        case  ClipboardTruncate:
          XtWarning("Insufficient space for clipboard data");
          done = TRUE;
        case  ClipboardNoData:
          done = TRUE;
          break;
        case  ClipboardLocked:
          break;
    }
  }
}
```

Fig. 11.7 shows the **notepad** program. You can run several notepads at once to try transferring data between them via the Motif clipboard. To copy to the clipboard highlight a section of text in the notepad's XmText widget and select the "copy" button. To retrieve text from the clipboard, just press the "retrieve" button.

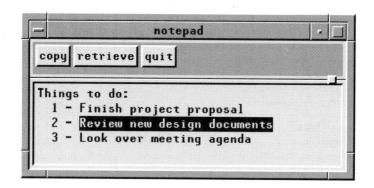

Figure 11.7 The notepad program.

11.6 SUMMARY

This chapter discussed several features of X that allow applications to communicate with each other. Atoms provide an efficient way to compare strings between applications. The server assigns an identifier to a string, which is shared by applications that use the same server. Among other things, atoms can be used to identify properties, property types, and types of client message.

Properties are collections of data, stored in the server. Every property has a name and also an associated atom that identifies the type of the data stored in the property. The X server does not interpret the data in a property, allowing applications to store and retrieve any series of bytes. Because properties are stored in the server, applications can retrieve data stored by other clients. This provides one way to shared typed data between applications.

Client messages allow applications to define new event types, which applications use to communicate directly with other applications. Client messages are typed using atoms, and applications that use client messages must agree on the format and meaning of the messages.

X also provides support for exchanging typed data, using selections. Applications can claim ownership of a selection or request the owner to convert the selection to a particular type and transfer it. The server automatically handles notifications between the owner of the selection and applications requesting its contents, or applications seeking to become the owner of the selection.

Motif provides a higher-level model for exchanging data which involves copying data to and from a clipboard. This model is implemented using the Xt Intrinsics selection functions, but hides many of the details from the programmer.

12

CREATING NEW WIDGETS

Earlier chapters discussed ways to build user interfaces by combining suitable widgets from the Motif widget set, defining a few callbacks and event handlers, and occasionally using Xlib functions. However, many programmers eventually find that they need a component not supplied by any existing widget set. In this case, the programmer can use the architecture defined by the Xt Intrinsics to create a new widget class.

After a brief overview of the internal architecture of a widget, this chapter presents some examples that illustrate how to create new widget classes. Widgets fall into three major categories. This chapter examines the simplest type of widget: those used primarily to display information. Chapter 13 presents an example of a composite widget that manages other widgets, and Chapter 14 discusses constraint widgets that control the geometry of their children according to some additional information associated with each child.

12.1 THE ARCHITECTURE OF A WIDGET

The Xt Intrinsics defines the basic architecture of a widget. This architecture allows widgets built by different programmers to work together smoothly. For example, the programs in this book mix the basic widgets provided by the Xt Intrinsics and the Motif widget set. These widgets can coexist peacefully in a single application because they share the same architecture. For the same reason, it is usually possible to mix widgets from other widget sets as well.[1]

The Xt Intrinsics defines an object-oriented architecture that organizes widgets into classes. From a widget programmer's viewpoint, a class consists of some private data structures and a set of procedures that operate on that data. Using object-oriented terminology, these procedures are referred to as *methods*.

Every widget consists of two basic components, a *class part* and an *instance-specific part*. Each of these components is implemented as a C structure containing data and pointers to methods. The Intrinsics defines the organization of each structure. All widgets belonging to the same class share a single copy of the data and methods in the class part, while each individual widget has its own copy of the data in the instance-specific part. The structure that contains the class part of a widget is known as the *class record*, while the structure that contains the instance-specific part is referred to as the *instance record*. A widget's class record is usually allocated and initialized statically at compile time, while a unique copy of the instance record is created at run time for each individual widget. The following sections discuss the organization and purpose of each of these widget components.

12.1.1   The Widget Class Record

A widget's class record contains data and methods that are common to all widgets of the class. Since all widgets belonging to the same class share the same class record, the class record must contain only static data that does not relate directly to the state of an individual widget. For example, every widget's class record includes a field containing the widget's class name. The class record also contains methods that define the appearance and behavior of all widgets in the class. Although most of these methods operate on the data in the widget's instance record, the methods themselves are shared by all widgets in a class.

All widget classes are subclasses of the Core widget class. This means, among other things, that the components of the Core widget's class record and instance record are included in the corresponding records of all other widget classes. The Core widget's class record is defined as

```
typedef struct{
    CoreClassPart   core_class;
} WidgetClassRec, *WidgetClass;
```

---

1. Although this is true in theory, conflicts may arise in practice because each widget set defines its own user interface style and policy. Although the programmer may be able to mix different widget sets without many *programmatic* problems, inconsistencies in the interaction style and appearance between widget sets may cause a problem for the user. Many widget sets, including the Motif widget set, define a particular style of user interface. Programmers should be aware of the human factors involved in designing a good user interface and mix widgets from different widget sets with caution.

where **CoreClassPart** is a structure defining the class data provided by the Core widget class. The widget class pointer for Core is declared as a pointer to the Core widget's class record:

```
WidgetClass widgetClass;
```

This is the class pointer that applications use as the **class** argument to **XtCreateWidget()** when creating a Core widget.

The Core widget's class record contains a single field, **core_class**, which is also a structure, **CoreClassPart**. The Core widget defines this structure as:

```
typedef struct _CoreClassPart {
        WidgetClass        superclass;
        String             class_name;
        Cardinal           widget_size;
        XtProc             class_initialize;
        XtWidgetClassProc  class_part_initialize;
        Boolean            class_inited;
        XtInitProc         initialize;
        XtArgsProc         initialize_hook;
        XtRealizeProc      realize;
        XtActionList       actions;
        Cardinal           num_actions;
        XtResourceList     resources;
        Cardinal           num_resources;
        XrmClass           xrm_class;
        Boolean            compress_motion;
        Boolean            compress_exposure;
        Boolean            compress_enterleave;
        Boolean            visible_interest;
        XtWidgetProc       destroy;
        XtWidgetProc       resize;
        XtExposeProc       expose;
        XtSetValuesFunc    set_values;
        XtArgsFunc         set_values_hook;
        XtAlmostProc       set_values_almost;
        XtArgsProc         get_values_hook;
        XtWidgetProc       accept_focus;
        XtVersionType      version;
        _XtOffsetList      *callback_private;
        String             tm_table;
        XtGeometryHandler  query_geometry;
```

```
    XtStringProc          display_accelerator;
    caddr_t               extension;
} CoreClassPart;
```

We can divide the fields in this structure into two basic categories: class data and pointers to methods. The data fields include:

- **superclass**. A pointer to the class record belonging to the widget's *superclass*.

- **class_name**. A string indicating the name of this class, used by the resource manager when retrieving a widget's resources. For the Core widget class, the **class_name** is initialized to "Core".

- **widget_size**. The size of the widget's instance record structure. This is usually determined using **sizeof()**.

- **class_inited**. A boolean that indicates whether this class structure has been initialized. A widget's class structure is initialized only once. The widget programmer must always initialize this flag to **FALSE**.

- **actions**. A list of actions supported by this widget class, used by the translation manager.

- **num_actions**. The length of the **actions** list.

- **resources**. The list of resources used by all widgets of this class. The resource manager uses this list to initialize each widget's instance record at run time.

- **num_resources**. The length of the resource list.

- **xrm_class**. A private data field containing a representation of the widget's class name used by the resource manager.

- **compress_motion**. A boolean that indicates whether the Intrinsics should compress mouse motion events for this widget.

- **compress_exposure**. A boolean that indicates whether the Intrinsics should compress **Expose** events for this widget.

- **compress_enterleave**. A boolean value indicating whether **EnterNotify** and **LeaveNotify** events should be reported to this widget if there are no other events between them.

- **visible_interest**. A boolean value that indicates whether the widget wants to know when it is visible.

- **version**. The version of the Xt Intrinsics. This is usually set to the constant **XtVersion**. The Intrinsics checks this field at run time to ensure that the widget's and the Intrinsics' versions match. Widget writers who are sure their widgets will work with multiple versions of the Intrinsics can set this field to **XtVersionDontCheck**.

Section 12.2.3 discusses the initialization of the data in this structure in more detail, as we discuss the implementation of an example widget. The remaining members of the Core class record are pointers to the methods that determine the behavior of the Core widget class. These members include:

`class_initialize`	`class_part_initialize`
`initialize`	`initialize_hook`
`realize`	`destroy`
`resize`	`expose`
`set_values`	`set_values_hook`
`set_values_almost`	`get_values_hook`
`accept_focus`	`query_geometry`

Every widget class must define these methods in one way or another. They are often inherited from the widget's superclass, and some may also be specified as **NULL** if the widget class does not require the particular method. We will discuss each of these methods in Section 12.2.3 as we build a simple widget.

12.1.2 The Instance Record

Each individual widget has its own copy of a structure known as an instance record. The instance record contains the current state of the widget. For example, every widget's instance record contains the window ID of the widget's window, and also the size and location of the window. The instance record also contains a pointer to the widget's class record. Fig 12.1 illustrates this architecture, showing the relationship between the class record and instance records of several widgets belonging to the Core widget class.

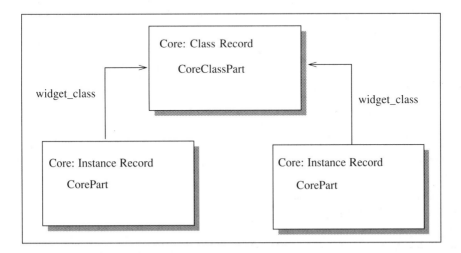

Figure 12.1 Class architecture of a widget.

The Core widget's instance record is defined as:

```
typedef struct{
    CorePart core;
} WidgetRec, *Widget;
```

From this definition, we might guess that when an application declares a variable of type **Widget**, it is declaring the variable as a pointer to the widget's instance record. This is true, but applications do not have access to this exact definition, because the Intrinsics uses the data abstraction techniques discussed in Section 12.1.4. The **Widget** type used by applications is declared as a pointer to an undefined structure:

```
typedef struct _WidgetRec *Widget;
```

The function **XtCreateWidget()** returns a pointer to an instance record allocated based on the **widget_size** field of the class record. The Core widget's instance record contains one member, whose type is **CorePart**. Every widget contains its own copy of this **CorePart** data structure in its instance record. In addition to general information needed by the Intrinsics to manipulate the widget, this structure caches some information about the widget's window, to reduce the need to query the server for this information. The information in the **CorePart** structure includes:

- **self**. A pointer to this instance record. The **self** member is of type **Widget**.
- **widget_class**. A pointer to the class record for this widget class.
- **parent**. A pointer to the instance record of this widget's parent.
- **name**. A string containing the name of this particular widget.
- **screen**. The **Screen** structure used by this widget.
- **colormap**. The ID of the colormap associated with the widget's window.
- **window**. The ID of the X window used by the widget.
- **x, y, width, height**. The position and dimensions of the widget's window. The type of **x** and **y** is **Position**, while the type of **width** and **height** is **Dimension**.
- **depth**. The depth of the window.
- **border_width**. The width of the window's border, declared as type **Dimension**.
- **border_pixel** and **border_pixmap**. The pixel index and tiling pattern used for the window border.
- **background_pixel** and **background_pixmap**. The pixel index and tiling pattern used for the window background.
- **event_table**. A private structure used to maintain the event mask and event handlers used by the window.

- **constraints**. A pointer to a constraints structure. This field is NULL unless the widget is a child of a constraint widget. If so, the contents of the **constraints** structure is defined by the widget's parent. (See Chapter 14).

- **visible**. If the **visible_interest** member of the widget's class record is set to **TRUE**, this flag is guaranteed to be **TRUE** when the widget's window is visible. The flag may be **FALSE** if the window is not visible, but this is not guaranteed.

- **sensitive**. If this flag is **TRUE**, the widget responds to events (i.e., the Intrinsics invokes its event handlers). If it is **FALSE**, device events are ignored, although **Expose**, **ConfigureNotify** and some other events are still processed.

- **ancestor_sensitive**. **TRUE** if the widget's parent is sensitive to events. If a widget is insensitive, its children are also insensitive.

- **managed**. **TRUE** if the widget is managed by another widget.

- **mapped_when_managed**. If **TRUE**, the Intrinsics automatically maps the widget's window whenever the widget is managed and unmaps it when it is unmanaged.

- **being_destroyed**. Widgets are destroyed in two phases. The first phase sets the **being_destroyed** flag to prevent other functions from operating on the widget while it is being destroyed.

- **destroy_callbacks**. A pointer to a list of callbacks to be invoked when the widget is destroyed.

- **popup_list**. The Xt Intrinsics allows popups to be attached to any widget. If a widget has a popup associated with it, the popup widget is listed here.

- **num_popups**. The length of the **popup_list**.

12.1.3   Inheritance

Inheritance is a powerful feature of many object-oriented systems, including the Xt Intrinsics. Inheritance allows new classes to be created that automatically have most or all the characteristics of another class, but with a few additional or different features. Inheritance allows a programmer to create a new widget class without having to program every detail of the new widget. Often, a widget programmer can design a new widget class by specifying only how the new class differs from its superclass.

Many object-oriented languages provide inheritance as part of the language. However, the Xt Intrinsics is written in the C language, which does not directly support object-oriented programming. In the Xt Intrinsics, inheritance is implemented by including the components of the class record and the instance record from each of the widget's superclasses in the new widget's class and instance records. Each widget class in the inheritance hierarchy contributes one component to these structures.

For example, suppose we want to create a new widget class whose class name is Basic. Assume that we would like this new Basic widget class to be identical to the Core widget class except that we need the Basic widget class to support a foreground pixel and a graphics context, neither of which are provided by the Core widget class. To create this new widget class, we must first define a class record for the new widget class.

```
typedef struct{
    CoreClassPart    core_class;
    BasicClassPart    basic_class;
} BasicClassRec, *BasicWidgetClass;
```

The new widget class record contains two members. The first is the same **CoreClassPart** structure used by the Core widget class. The second is the additional class part for the new widget class. The Basic widget class doesn't require any additional class resources and therefore the structure **BasicClassPart** is defined as an dummy structure:

```
typedef struct{
    int     ignore;
} BasicClassPart;
```

Next, we can define the Basic widget's class pointer as:

```
BasicWidgetClass basicWidgetClass;
```

The Basic widget's instance record consists of the **CorePart** structure defined by the Core widget class, followed by a structure defined by the Basic widget. The instance record is defined as:

```
typedef struct{
    CorePart     core;
    BasicPart    basic;
} BasicRec, *BasicWidget;
```

The structure **BasicPart** defines the new instance-specific resources needed by the Basic widget:

```
typedef struct{
    int    foreground;
    GC     gc;
} BasicPart;
```

Internally, the Basic widget's methods can refer to the **foreground** and **gc** members by accessing the **basic** field of the widget's instance record, for example:

```
w->basic.foreground
```

These methods can also access the resources defined by the Core widget class through the **core** member of the instance record, for example:

```
w->core.background_pixel
```

Fig. 12.2 shows the architecture of the new Basic widget class, including the superclass pointer to the Core widget class.

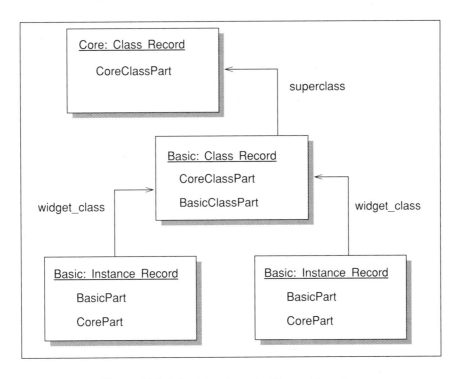

Figure 12.2 Inheriting from the Core widget class.

New widget classes inherit the resources defined by their superclass by specifically including the definition of the superclass structure in the definition of the new class. However, the Xt Intrinsics also provides a mechanism for inheriting the methods defined by a superclass. This is done in two ways. The first mechanism is referred to as *chaining*. When a method is chained, the Intrinsics invokes the method defined by each of the widget's superclasses first, before invoking the widget's method. This allows a widget to inherit part of the behavior of its superclass. The Core widget methods that are chained are:

```
ClassInitialize()        ClassPartInitialize()
InitializeHook()         SetValuesHook()
GetValuesHook()          Initialize()
SetValues()
```

For example, if an application were to create an instance of the Basic widget described in the previous section, the Intrinsics would invoke the Core widget's `Initialize()` method first, and then the Basic widget's `Initialize()` method. If needed, the Basic widget's

Initialize() method can override any resources in the **CorePart** set by the Core widget's **Initialize()** method. If the Basic widget class requires no initialization beyond that done by the Core **Initialize()** method, the widget programmer can set the **initialize** field of its class record to NULL. In this example, the Basic widget's **Initialize()** method must create a graphics context based on the foreground color in the **BasicPart** structure and the background color found in the **CorePart** structure.

The Xt Intrinsics also provides a mechanism for inheriting methods that are not chained. This is done by using special symbols to specify the methods in the widget's class record. Each symbol is defined by the superclass that adds the method to the widget's class record. For example, the Core widget class defines the following symbols for its methods:

XtInheritTranslations	**XtInheritRealize**
XtInheritResize	**XtInheritExpose**
XtInheritSetValuesAlmost	**XtInheritAcceptFocus**
XtInheritQueryGeometry	

These symbols can be used by any subclass of the Core widget class. They do not have to be redefined by each widget class. Only those classes that contribute new methods to the class record need to define new symbols. For example, the Composite widget class defines symbols for its new methods, including:

XtInheritGeometryManager	**XtInheritChangeManaged**
XtInheritInsertChild	**XtInheritDeleteChild**

When a widget class specifies one of these symbols in the class record, the Intrinsics copies the corresponding method used by the widget's superclass into the widget's class structure at class initialization time.[2]

12.1.4   Data Abstraction

The Xt Intrinsics uses a data abstraction technique to hide the implementation of a widget from applications that use the widget. This technique involves maintaining both a private, complete definition of each widget structure, and a public, incomplete definition. Applications that use a widget see only the incomplete definition of the widget, and therefore cannot directly access fields in the widget structure. Applications declare all widgets as type **Widget**, which is known as an *opaque type*. This means the application has a pointer to the widget structure, but does not have access to the real definition of the data that it represents. Therefore it cannot access the contents of the data structure.[3]

To implement this style of data abstraction, the widget programmer must organize the widget implementation into several different files. Each widget implementation consists of one or more private header files, a public header file, and one or more C source files. The pri-

---

2. These symbols are actually just macros that coerce the symbol _XtInherit to the appropriate procedure type.

3. To say that the contents of the structure cannot be accessed is really wishful thinking. In C, it is always possible to compromise the integrity of such schemes using pointer arithmetic.

vate header file contains the real definitions used internally by the widget, while the public header file contains only those definitions required by applications that use the widget.

12.1.4.1   The Private Header File

Every widget class has at least one private header file containing the complete definitions of the widget class record and instance record. Most widget classes have only a single private header file whose name, by convention, ends with the letter "P". For example, the name of the Core widget's private header file is CoreP.h. This file contains the true definitions of the **CoreClassPart** structure and the **CorePart** structure. Finally, the private header file can contain definitions of any other private data structures or variables used by the widget.

It is customary to enclose widget header files within pairs of **#ifdef** statements to prevent problems if the header file is included in an application more than once. Using this convention, the Basic widget's private header file would have the form:

```
#ifndef BASICP_H
#define BASICP_H

/* Declarations go here */

#endif BASICP_H
```

12.1.4.2   The Public Header File

The public header file for most widget classes is very simple and declares any public information exported by the widget. At a minimum, it contains an external declaration of a pointer to the widget class record, used by applications as an argument to **XtCreateWidget()**. For example, the Core widget class's public file, Core.h, contains only the declaration of a pointer to the widget class:

```
extern WidgetClass widgetClass;
```

The public header also often contains definitions of resource strings used by the program. Like the private header file, a widget's public header should also be enclosed within **#ifdef** statements to prevent multiple definitions. By convention, the Basic widget's public header file would have the form:

```
#ifndef BASIC_H
#define BASIC_H

/* Declarations go here */

#endif BASIC_H
```

12.1.4.3   The Widget Source File

The source files for most widgets have a similar structure. Each file includes both the widget class's public and private header files as well as the public and private Intrinsic header files. The file then declares forward references to the methods and other internal functions used by the widget, followed by a resource list used by the resource manager to initialize the widget's resources and a list of the actions used by the translation manager. Next, the widget's class record is statically initialized, and finally the widget's methods are defined. These methods are usually declared as static so that they are not visible to applications.

12.2   A SIMPLE WIDGET: THE DIAL WIDGET

Although at first exposure the widget architecture may seem to be complex and confusing, it is simple to use in practice. Much of the code for a widget class is "boiler plate", and is quite similar from class to class. This section provides a practical look at the widget architecture by creating a new widget class, which we will name the Dial widget class. A Dial widget displays a rotary dial, similar in appearance to an analog clock, that can be used as a gauge or valuator. An indicator, similar to a clock hand, indicates the relative value displayed by the dial. The Dial widget can display information between a range specified by any two integers. The Dial widget defines resources that allow users and applications to control the number of markers between the minimum and maximum values, and also the position of the indicator. The Dial widget also defines a callback list that allows an application to register a function which the widget invokes when the user "selects" the widget. The widget is "selected" by invoking an action procedure through the translation manager. Fig. 12.3 shows the physical appearance of a Dial widget.

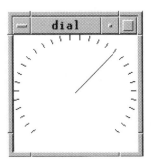

Figure 12.3 A Dial widget.

The widgets described in this and the following chapters are simple examples of typical widgets, designed specifically for this book. They are not part of the Motif widget set nor any vendor's widget set. To avoid confusion, the names of all widgets presented in Chapter

12, 13, and 14 begin with the prefix "Xs" to indicate the X-sample widget set. Otherwise, the naming and capitalization used in the examples follow the conventions normally used by the Xt Intrinsics and Motif widgets, as described in Chapter 2. Following widget conventions, names of widget methods have the same names as the corresponding member of the widget class record, except that the method name uses mixed case. For example, the method corresponding to the **set_values** member of a widget's core part is usually named **SetValues()**.

12.2.1   The Private Header File: DialP.h

We will begin the discussion of the Dial widget class by examining the contents of the private header file, DialP.h. We must first define a structure containing the Dial widget's contribution to the class record.

```
typedef struct _XsDialClassPart{
        int ignore;
} XsDialClassPart;
```

Even when a widget class has nothing significant to add to the class record, each widget class is expected to add a member to the class record. The Dial widget inherits directly from the Core widget class. Therefore, we can define the Dial widget's full class record as:

```
typedef struct _XsDialClassRec{
   CoreClassPart     core_class;
   XsDialClassPart   dial_class;
} XsDialClassRec;

extern XsDialClassRec XsdialClassRec;
```

The resources used by the Dial widget class are defined in the instance record. The structure **XsDialPart** defines the resources added by the Dial widget.

```
typedef struct _XsDialPart {
    Pixel     indicator_color;  /* Color of the             */
    Pixel     foreground;       /*  indicator and markers   */
    int       minimum;          /* minimum value            */
    int       maximum;          /* maximum value            */
    int       markers;          /* number of marks          */
    Dimension marker_length;    /* in pixels                */
    Position  position;         /* indicator position       */
    Position  indicator_x;      /* x,y position of tip      */
    Position  indicator_y;      /*    of the indicator      */
    Position  center_x;         /* coordinates of the       */
    Position  center_y;         /*    dial center           */
    Position  inner_diam;       /* inside of markers        */
```

```
    Position    outer_diam;          /* outside of markers    */
    GC          dial_GC;             /* assorted gc's         */
    GC          indicator_GC;
    GC          inverse_GC;
    XPoint      segments[MAXSEGMENTS];
    XtCallbackList select;           /* callback list         */
} XsDialPart;
```

This structure maintains the current state of each Dial widget, and includes such things as the relative position of the indicator and the color of the markers. Some of the members of this structure (the maximum and minimum dial settings, for example) can be accessed by an application using the Intrinsics functions **XtSetValues()** and **XtGetValues()**. The widget programmer must define corresponding resources in the widget's resource list. Other fields in the **XsDialPart** are strictly for internal use. The widget's **Initialize()** method derives some of these fields from other resource values. For example, the graphics contexts are derived from the widget's foreground and background colors. The **segments** member is an array of points that define the line segments used to draw the face of the dial. The size of this array must be defined earlier in the file. For example, here it is defined as:

#define MAXSEGMENTS 200

Having defined the **XsDialPart** data structure, we can define the Dial widget's instance record by combining the **CorePart** structure defined by the Core widget class and the **XsDialPart**.

```
typedef struct _XsDialRec {
    CorePart            core;
    XsDialPart          dial;
} XsDialRec;
```

This completes the Dial widget class's private header file.

12.2.2   The Public Header File: Dial.h

The Dial widget's public header file defines the Dial widget's class pointer and also defines some strings used to specify resources. Widgets that define new resource names should make these names available to applications by including them in the public header file.

```
/*******************************************************
 * Dial.h: Public header file for Dial Widget Class
 *******************************************************/
#ifndef  DIAL_H
#define  DIAL_H
extern WidgetClass XsdialWidgetClass;
typedef struct _XsDialClassRec *XsDialWidgetClass;
```

```
typedef struct _XsDialRec        *XsDialWidget;
/*
 * Define resource strings for the Dial widget.
 */
#define XtNselectCallback "selectCallback"
#define XtNmarkers        "markers"
#define XtNminimum        "minimum"
#define XtNmaximum        "maximum"
#define XtNindicatorColor "indicatorColor"
#define XtNposition       "position"
#define XtNmarkerLength   "markerLength"

#define XtCMarkers        "Markers"
#define XtCMin            "Min"
#define XtCMax            "Max"
#define Xs_SELECTED       1

typedef struct {
  int      reason;
  XEvent *event;
  int      position;
}  xsdialCallbackStruct;
             /* Possible  reasons */

#endif DIAL_H
```

12.2.3   The Dial Widget Source File: Dial.c

The file Dial.c contains the declaration and static initialization of the Dial widget's class record, and also contains the widget's methods. Dial.c begins by including the Intrinsics's private header file, IntrinsicP.h, the private header file of the Dial widget's superclass, CoreP.h, and the Dial widget's public and private header files. In addition, the first part of the file defines several convenient macros used by the widget, and declares the widget's methods. Notice that these methods are declared as static, making them private to this file and effectively hiding them from applications that use the widget.

```
/**********************************************************
 * Dial.c: The Dial Widget Methods
 **********************************************************/
#include <stdio.h>
#include <math.h>
#include <X11/IntrinsicP.h>
```

```
#include <X11/Intrinsic.h>
#include <X11/StringDefs.h>
#include <X11/CoreP.h>
#include "DialP.h"
#include "Dial.h"

#define   RADIANS(x)   (M_PI * 2.0 * (x) / 360.0)
#define   DEGREES(x)   ((x) / (M_PI * 2.0) * 360.0)
#define   MIN_ANGLE    225.0
#define   MAX_ANGLE    270.0
#define   MIN(a,b)     (((a) < (b)) ? (a) :   (b))

static void     select_dial ();
static void     Initialize();
static void     Redisplay();
static void     Resize();
static void     Destroy();
static Boolean SetValues();
```

The next section of the source file defines an action list and a translations list used by the translation manager to map between a user action and a function to be invoked when the action occurs. These statements specify that, by default, the "**select()**" action is invoked in response to a **<Btn1Down>** action. An array of type **XtActionsRec** maps the "**select()**" action to a function, **select_dial()**, defined later:

```
static char defaultTranslations[] = "<Btn1Down>: select()";
static XtActionsRec actionsList[] = {
  { "select",    (XtActionProc) select_dial},
};
```

Next, we must define a resource list used by the resource manager to initialize the widget's instance record when an application creates a Dial widget. The resources are automatically stored in the appropriate fields of the instance record. The Dial widget's resource list is defined as:

```
static XtResource resources[] = {
  {XtNmarkers, XtCMarkers, XtRInt, sizeof (int),
    XtOffset(XsDialWidget, dial.markers), XtRString, "10"  },
  {XtNminimum, XtCMin, XtRInt, sizeof (int),
    XtOffset(XsDialWidget, dial.minimum), XtRString, "0"   },
  {XtNmaximum, XtCMax, XtRInt, sizeof (int),
    XtOffset(XsDialWidget, dial.maximum), XtRString, "100" },
  {XtNindicatorColor, XtCColor, XtRPixel, sizeof (Pixel),
    XtOffset(XsDialWidget, dial.indicator_color),
```

```
        XtRString, "Black"                                       },
    {XtNposition, XtCPosition, XtRPosition, sizeof (Position),
      XtOffset(XsDialWidget, dial.position), XtRString, "0"   },
    {XtNmarkerLength,XtCLength,XtRDimension,sizeof (Dimension),
      XtOffset(XsDialWidget, dial.marker_length),
      XtRString, "5"                                           },
    {XtNforeground, XtCForeground, XtRPixel, sizeof (Pixel),
      XtOffset(XsDialWidget, dial.foreground),
      XtRString, "Black"},
    {XtNselectCallback,XtCCallback,XtRCallback,sizeof(caddr_t),
      XtOffset (XsDialWidget, dial.select), XtRCallback, NULL },
    };
```

Notice that only new resources added by the Dial widget class are included in this list.
The Dial widget also inherits the resources defined by the **CorePart** of the widget's instance record from the Core widget class. The resource manager initializes the resources
inherited from the Core widget class before retrieving the resources defined by the Dial widget. A widget can override the default values for resources defined by its superclass if
necessary. However, the Dial widget does not need to override any Core resources.

12.2.3.1   The Class Record

The next step is to define the contents of the Dial widget's class record, which is initialized
at compile time by declaring the contents of the structure statically in the source code.

```
XsDialClassRec  XsdialClassRec = {
    /* CoreClassPart */
  {
   (WidgetClass) &widgetClassRec,     /* superclass              */
   "Dial",                            /* class_name              */
   sizeof(XsDialRec),                 /* widget_size             */
   NULL,                              /* class_initialize        */
   NULL,                              /* class_part_initialize   */
   FALSE,                             /* class_inited            */
   Initialize,                        /* initialize              */
   NULL,                              /* initialize_hook         */
   XtInheritRealize,                  /* realize                 */
   actionsList,                       /* actions                 */
   XtNumber(actionsList),             /* num_actions             */
   resources,                         /* resources               */
   XtNumber(resources),               /* num_resources           */
   NULLQUARK,                         /* xrm_class               */
   TRUE,                              /* compress_motion         */
   TRUE,                              /* compress_exposure       */
```

```
    TRUE,                               /* compress_enterleave    */
    TRUE,                               /* visible_interest       */
    Destroy,                            /* destroy                */
    Resize,                             /* resize                 */
    Redisplay,                          /* expose                 */
    SetValues,                          /* set_values             */
    NULL,                               /* set_values_hook        */
    XtInheritSetValuesAlmost,           /* set_values_almost      */
    NULL,                               /* get_values_hook        */
    NULL,                               /* accept_focus           */
    XtVersion,                          /* version                */
    NULL,                               /* callback private       */
    defaultTranslations,                /* tm_table               */
    NULL,                               /* query_geometry         */
    NULL,                               /* display_accelerator    */
    NULL,                               /* extension              */
    },
        /* Dial class fields */
    {
    0,                                  /* ignore                 */
    }
};
```

WidgetClass XsdialWidgetClass = (WidgetClass) &XsdialClassRec;

Writing a new widget primarily consists of filling in this structure with appropriate values and then writing the methods that define the appearance and behavior of the widget. The following section examines the purpose of each member of the class record in the context of the Dial example, and discusses each of the Dial widget's methods.

The structure of the first part of the Dial class record is inherited from the Core widget class. However, the Dial widget is responsible for initializing this data. The first line indicates that the Dial widget inherits from the Core widget class by specifying a pointer to the Core class record. The next line specifies the class name of the widget, "Dial". **XtCreateWidget()** uses the **widget_size** member of the class record to allocate a new instance of the widget. The **widget_size** member must be set to the size, in bytes, of the Dial widget's instance record.

In addition to the static initialization of the class record, some classes must be initialized dynamically when the first widget belonging to the class is created. The **class_initialize()** and **class_part_initialize()** members allow the widget programmer to define methods to initialize the widget's class record at run time. Because the Dial widget's class record requires no run-time initialization, these members are set to **NULL**. Regardless of whether or not the widget requires dynamic initialization, every widget must initialize the **class_inited** field to **FALSE**.

The next member of the Dial class structure points to the widget's actions list, followed by the length of the actions list. If the widget adds no actions to those defined by its superclasses, the **actions** member can be set to **NULL**, and the **num_actions** field can be set to zero.

Similarly, the **resource** member points to the widget's resource list, if the widget has one, and **num_resource** indicates the length of the list. The translation manager merges the actions list and the resources of a widget with those supplied by its superclasses.

The next four fields of the class structure define how the widget wishes to have events reported to it. The Dial widget specifies that the Intrinsics should compress all events.

The Dial widget must compute the location of the indicator on the face of the dial and draw the indicator whenever its position changes. It is therefore useful to know if the widget is visible, to avoid redrawing the indicator unnecessarily. Therefore we will set the **visible_interest** field to **TRUE**, requesting the Intrinsics to keep the **visible** member of the Dial widget's instance record up to date.

The Dial widget does not use the **dial** part of the class record and initializes its dummy member to **NULL**.

12.2.3.2   Methods

A widget's methods determine its behavior. All methods are private to the Dial widget, and the application programmer can not invoke them directly. Instead, the Intrinsics invokes a widget's methods when events occur or when an application calls the interface functions provided by the Intrinsics. For example, applications use the function **XtCreateWidget()** to create a Dial widget, the function **XtRealizeWidget()** to realize the widget, **XtManageWidget()** and **XtUnmanageWidget()** to manage and unmanage the widget, and so on. Users can also customize the Dial widget using the resource manager, and applications can use the functions **XtSetValues()** and **XtGetValues()** to set and retrieve the widget's resources. These Intrinsics functions call the appropriate methods based on the class of each particular widget.

Not every widget class defines every method in the class structure. For example, the Dial widget does not define several methods in the class record, including:

ClassInitialize()	ClassPartInitialize()
InitializeHook()	SetValuesHook()
GetValuesHook()	QueryGeometry()

The Dial widget initializes the members of the class record corresponding to these methods to **NULL**.

The Dial widget class inherits the **Realize()** and **SetValuesAlmost()** methods from its superclass by specifying **XtInheritRealize** and **XtInheritSetValues-Almost** for these methods. The remaining methods are defined by the Dial widget class. These methods are:

```
Initialize()                    Destroy()
Resize()                        Redisplay() (expose)
SetValues()
```

The following sections present each of the methods used by the Dial widget.

The Initialize() Method

While the class record of most widgets can be initialized at compile time, the instance record of each widget must be initialized at run time. When a new widget is created, the Intrinsics invokes the widget's **Initialize()** method specified in the widget's class record. This method requires two parameters, each of which are versions of the widget's instance record. The **new** parameter is the real widget, the other is a copy. Every **Initialize()** method has the form:

```
static void Initialize (request, new)
    Widget request, new;
```

Each resource in the **request** widget is set to the original value obtained from defaults in the widgets resource list, taken from values specified by the application when creating the widget, or taken from the user's resource files. By the time this method is called, the **new** structure has potentially been modified by each of the widget's superclasses' **Initial-ize()** methods. In this example, the Intrinsics calls the Core widget's **Initialize()** method before it calls the Dial widget's **Initialize()** method. A widget's **Initialize()** method may therefore rely on the widget's superclasses to initialize the inherited resources in the instance record. Each widget class needs to initialize only those resources it adds. The **Initialize()** method can also check any of the resources defined by its superclasses that it cares about and recalculate them if necessary. For example, the Dial widget's **Initialize()** method checks the size of the widget and adjusts the values if they are not acceptable. Unless the application or the user sets the size of the widget's window, it will have zero height and width at this point. The X server will generate an error if a widget attempts to create a zero width or height window, so every widget should make sure its window will have acceptable dimensions.

When changing values set by a superclass, the widget must consider both the values in **new** widget structure and the original values provided by the resource manager, found in the **request** parameter, and resolve any differences. All changes must be made to the **new** structure.

The Dial widget's **Initialize()** method is defined as:

```
static void Initialize (request, new)
    XsDialWidget request, new;
{
  XGCValues values;
  XtGCMask  valueMask;
```

```
Window    root   = RootWindowOfScreen(XtScreen(new));
Display *dpy   = XtDisplay(new);
/*
 * Make sure the window size is not zero. The Core
 * Initialize() method doesn't do this.
 */
if (request->core.width == 0)
  new->core.width = 100;
if (request->core.height == 0)
  new->core.height = 100;
/*
 * Make sure the min and max dial settings are valid.
 */
if (new->dial.minimum >= new->dial.maximum) {
  XtWarning ("Maximum must be greater than the Minimum");
  new->dial.minimum = new->dial.maximum - 1;
}
if (new->dial.position > new->dial.maximum) {
  XtWarning ("Position exceeds the Dial Maximum");
  new->dial.position =  new->dial.maximum;
}
if (new->dial.position < new->dial.minimum) {
  XtWarning ("Position is less than the Minimum");
  new->dial.position =  new->dial.minimum;
}
/*
 * Allow only MAXSEGMENTS / 2 markers
 */
if(new->dial.markers > MAXSEGMENTS / 2){
  XtWarning ("Too many markers");
  new->dial.markers = MAXSEGMENTS / 2;
}
/*
 * Create the graphics contexts used for the dial face
 * and the indicator.
 */
valueMask = GCForeground | GCBackground;
values.foreground = new->dial.foreground;
values.background = new->core.background_pixel;
new->dial.dial_GC = XtGetGC(new,valueMask,&values);

values.foreground = new->dial.indicator_color;
```

```
    new->dial.indicator_GC = XtGetGC(new, valueMask, &values);

    valueMask = GCForeground | GCBackground;
    values.foreground = new->core.background_pixel;
    values.background = new->dial.indicator_color;
    new->dial.inverse_GC = XtGetGC (new, valueMask, &values);

    Resize (new);
}
```

This method begins by checking the size of the widget's window. If the user or the application specifies a size, the resource manager sets the window size before this method is called. Otherwise, we must ensure that the window width and height are greater than zero. The **Initialize()** method also checks the value of other parameters, such as the maximum and minimum dial settings, to be sure they are reasonable, and initializes derived data fields, such as the graphics contexts used by the widget. The resource manager initializes the widget structure, using the widget's resource list, before the **Initialize()** method is called. Therefore, we can base the graphics contexts on the foreground color in the **dial_part** of the instance record, and the background color in the **core_part** of the instance record. The Dial widget's **Initialize()** method also calls the widget's **Resize()** method, which calculates the initial position of the dial markers and indicator.

The Realize() Method

The function **XtRealizeWidget()** invokes a widget's **Realize()** method, which is responsible for creating the window used by the widget. Since this method is almost always the same for each widget class, most widget classes inherit their superclass's **Realize()** method. Unlike the **Initialize()** method, the **Realize()** method is not chained. The Dial widget inherits its superclass's **Realize()** method by specifying the symbol **XtInheritRealize** in the class record. The **realize** field of the widget's class record cannot be set to **NULL** unless the widget class is never realized. Realizing a widget whose **Realize()** method is **NULL** generates a fatal error.

The Destroy() Method

Before a widget is destroyed, the Intrinsics invokes the widget's **Destroy()** method. This method is chained, although the calling order is reversed with respect to other chained methods. The function **XtDestroyWidget()** calls each widget's **Destroy()** method before its superclass's **Destroy()** method. Each widget class is expected to clean up the resources it has created. For example, the Dial widget class creates three graphics contexts and also defines a callback list that should be removed before the widget is destroyed. A widget's **Destroy()** method must not free the widget structure itself; this is done by the Intrinsics. The Dial widget's **Destroy()** method is defined as:

```
static void Destroy (w)
    XsDialWidget w;
{
  XtReleaseGC (w, w->dial.indicator_GC);
  XtReleaseGC (w, w->dial.dial_GC);
  XtReleaseGC (w, w->dial.inverse_GC);
  XtRemoveAllCallbacks (w, XtNselectCallback,
                           w->dial.select);
}
```

The Resize() Method

The Intrinsics invokes a widget's **Resize()** method whenever the widget's window is reconfigured in any way. The **Resize()** method should examine the members of the widget structure and recalculate any derived data that is dependent on the configuration of the widget's window. The Dial widget must recalculate the center of the window, the size of the indicator, and the line segments used to draw the face of the dial. Because the X server generates an **Expose** event if the contents of a window are lost because of resize, the **Resize()** method only updates the data needed to allow the **Redisplay()** method to redraw the widget correctly and does not actually redraw the window. This method generates a set of line segments that defines the circular face of the dial, centered in the widget window. The Dial widget's **Resize()** method is defined as:

```
static void Resize (w)
    XsDialWidget w;
{
  double    angle, cosine, sine, increment;
  int       i;
  XPoint    *ptr;
  /*
   * Get the address of the first line segment.
   */
  ptr = w->dial.segments;
  /*
   * calculate the center of the widget
   */
  w->dial.center_x = w->core.width/2;
  w->dial.center_y = w->core.height/2;
  /*
   *  Generate the segment array containing the
   *  face of the dial.
   */
  increment = RADIANS(MAX_ANGLE) /(float)(w->dial.markers -1);
```

```
    w->dial.outer_diam = MIN(w->core.width, w->core.height) / 2;
    w->dial.inner_diam=w->dial.outer_diam-w->dial.marker_length;
    angle = RADIANS(MIN_ANGLE);
    for (i = 0; i < w->dial.markers;i++){
      cosine = cos(angle);
      sine   = sin(angle);
      ptr->x   = w->dial.center_x + w->dial.outer_diam * sine;
      ptr++->y = w->dial.center_y - w->dial.outer_diam * cosine;
      ptr->x   = w->dial.center_x + w->dial.inner_diam * sine;
      ptr++->y = w->dial.center_y - w->dial.inner_diam * cosine;
      angle += increment;
    }
  calculate_indicator_pos(w);
}
```

The auxiliary function **calculate_indicator_pos()** calculates the coordinates of the end point of the indicator, based on the indicator position and the size of the window. It is defined as

```
    static calculate_indicator_pos(w)
        XsDialWidget w;
    {
      double   normalized_pos, angle;
      Position indicator_length;
      /*
       * Make the indicator two pixels shorter than the
       * inner edge of the markers.
       */
      indicator_length=w->dial.outer_diam-w->dial.marker_length-2;
      /*
       * Normalize the indicator position to lie between zero
       * and 1, and then convert it to an angle.
       */
      normalized_pos = (w->dial.position - w->dial.minimum)/
                   (float)(w->dial.maximum - w->dial.minimum);
      angle = RADIANS(MIN_ANGLE + MAX_ANGLE  * normalized_pos);
       /*
        * Find the x,y coordinates of the tip of the indicator.
        */
      w->dial.indicator_x = w->dial.center_x +
                                   indicator_length * sin(angle);
      w->dial.indicator_y = w->dial.center_y -
                                   indicator_length  * cos(angle);
    }
```

The Redisplay() Method

A widget's **Redisplay()** method is responsible for redrawing any information in the widget's window when an **Expose** event occurs.[4] A widget's **expose** member can be set to **NULL** if the widget does not need to display anything. The Dial widget's **Redisplay()** method draws the face of the dial, using the line segments calculated by the **Resize()** method, and draws the dial indicator at its current position. The **Redisplay()** method is invoked with three parameters: the widget instance to be redisplayed, a pointer to an **Expose** event, and a **Region**. If the **compress_exposures** member of the widget's class structure is **TRUE**, the **Region** contains the sum of the rectangles reported in all **Expose** events, and the **event** parameter contains the bounding box of the region. If **compress_exposures** is **FALSE**, the **region** parameter is always **NULL**. The Dial widget requests that **Expose** events be compressed, so we could use the **region** argument as a clip mask for the graphics contexts to eliminate redrawing the dial face unnecessarily. However, in this example, the graphics contexts have been created using **XtGetGC()**, which creates GCs that may be shared by others. Therefore we must not alter the GC in any way, or at least we must undo any changes immediately. For this example we will take the easy way out and simply not use the information in the **region** argument, redrawing the entire face of the dial instead. Notice that the **Redisplay()** checks the **visible** member of the **CorePart** of the widget's instance record and redraws the dial face only if the widget is visible.

```
static void Redisplay (w, event, region)
    XsDialWidget   w;
    XEvent         *event;
    Region         region;
{
  if(w->core.visible){
    /*
     * Draw the markers used for the dial face.
     */
    XDrawSegments(XtDisplay(w), XtWindow(w),
                  w->dial.dial_GC,
                  w->dial.segments,
                  w->dial.markers);
    /*
     * Draw the indicator at its current position.
     */
```

4. Notice that this is one case where we cannot simply use a mixed case version of the name of the class record member as the method name. The symbol Expose is defined in X.h as an event type, using a C #define statement:

    #define Expose 12

Therefore, the C pre-processor would replace any method named Expose() by 12().

```
        XDrawLine(XtDisplay(w), XtWindow(w),
                w->dial.indicator_GC,
                w->dial.center_x,
                w->dial.center_y,
                w->dial.indicator_x,
                w->dial.indicator_y);
    }
}
```

The SetValues() Method

The **SetValues()** method allows a widget to be notified when one of its resources is set or changed. This can occur when the resource manager initializes the widget's resources, or when an application calls **XtSetValues()**. The **SetValues()** methods are chained, and are invoked in superclass to subclass order.

The **SetValues()** method takes three arguments, each a version of the widget's instance record. The form of every **SetValues()** method is:

```
static Boolean SetValues (current, request, new)
    Widget current, request, new;
```

The **current** parameter contains the previous, unaltered state of the widget. The **request** parameter contains the values requested for the widget by a combination of the user's resource files, the widget default resources and the application. The **new** parameter contains the state of the widget after all superclass's **SetValues()** methods have been called. Like the **Initialize()** method, the **SetValues()** method must resolve any differences between these parameters and may override any values that it wishes. All changes must be made to the **new** widget. Notice that at this point the Intrinsics layer has already changed the requested values in the **new** widget. The **SetValues()** method's primary task is to generate any data derived from parameters that have changed and check that all requested values are acceptable.

The **SetValues()** method returns a boolean value indicating whether the widget should be redrawn. If this value is **TRUE**, the Intrinsics causes an **Expose** event to be generated for the entire window. Because the **SetValues()** method can be invoked at any time, it must not assume that the widget is realized. Therefore, this method must not perform any graphics operations on the widget's window (which might not exist yet) unless the widget is realized.

The Dial widget's **SetValues()** method checks the minimum and maximum values of the dial to ensure that they are reasonable, and resets the values if they are out of range. If the foreground or background colors have changed, we must create new graphics contexts. Last, if the dial position has changed, the method calls the auxiliary function **calculate_indicator_pos()** to calculate the new position of the indicator. If only the position of the indicator has changed, and the redraw flag is still **FALSE**, the old indicator is erased by drawing it with the inverse GC, and then displayed at the new position by drawing it with the normal GC. Notice that when erasing the indicator both the old position and the old graphics context are obtained from the **current** widget, in case the indicator moves and changes color at the same time.

The Dial widget's **SetValues()** method is defined as:

```
static Boolean SetValues (current, request, new)
     XsDialWidget current, request, new;
{
  XGCValues   values;
  XtGCMask    valueMask;
  Boolean     redraw = FALSE;
  Boolean     redraw_indicator = FALSE;
  /*
   * Make sure the new dial values are reasonable.
   */
  if (new->dial.minimum >= new->dial.maximum) {
    XtWarning ("Minimum must be less than Maximum");
    new->dial.minimum = 0;
    new->dial.maximum = 100;
  }
  if (new->dial.position > new->dial.maximum) {
    XtWarning("Dial position is greater than the Maximum");
    new->dial.position = new->dial.maximum;
  }
  if (new->dial.position < new->dial.minimum) {
    XtWarning("Dial position is less than the Minimum");
    new->dial.position = new->dial.minimum;
  }
  /*
   * If the indicator color or background color
   * has changed, generate the GC's.
   */
  if(new->dial.indicator_color!=current->dial.indicator_color||
    new->core.background_pixel !=current->core.background_pixel){
      valueMask = GCForeground | GCBackground;
      values.foreground = new->dial.indicator_color;
      values.background = new->core.background_pixel;
      XtReleaseGC(new, new->dial.indicator_GC);
      new->dial.indicator_GC = XtGetGC(new, valueMask,&values);
      values.foreground = new->core.background_pixel;
      values.background = new->dial.indicator_color;
```

```
      XtReleaseGC(new, new->dial.inverse_GC);
      new->dial.inverse_GC = XtGetGC(new, valueMask, &values);
      redraw_indicator = TRUE;
  }
  /*
   * If the marker color has changed, generate the GC.
   */
  if (new->dial.foreground != current->dial.foreground){
      valueMask = GCForeground | GCBackground;
      values.foreground = new->dial.foreground;
      values.background = new->core.background_pixel;
      XtReleaseGC(new, new->dial.dial_GC);
      new->dial.dial_GC = XtGetGC (new, valueMask, &values);
      redraw = TRUE;
  }
  /*
   * If the indicator position has changed, or if the min/max
   * values have changed, recompute the indicator coordinates.
   */
  if (new->dial.position != current->dial.position ||
        new->dial.minimum != current->dial.minimum ||
        new->dial.maximum != current->dial.maximum){
      calculate_indicator_pos(new);
      redraw_indicator = TRUE;
  }
  /*
   * If only the indicator needs to be redrawn and
   * the widget is realized, erase the current indicator
   * and draw the new one.
   */
  if(redraw_indicator && ! redraw &&
     XtIsRealized(new) && new->core.visible){
      XDrawLine(XtDisplay(current), XtWindow(current),
                current->dial.inverse_GC,
                current->dial.center_x,
                current->dial.center_y,
                current->dial.indicator_x,
                current->dial.indicator_y);
      XDrawLine(XtDisplay(new), XtWindow(new),
                new->dial.indicator_GC,
                new->dial.center_x,
                new->dial.center_y,
```

```
                  new->dial.indicator_x,
                  new->dial.indicator_y);
        }
     return (redraw);
  }
```

12.2.3.3   Defining Action Procedures

The last procedure defined by the Dial widget is not a method, but is specified in the list of actions defined at the beginning of the file. This list associates an action named "**select()**" with a function **select_dial()**. By default, the "**select()**" action is bound to the user event **<Btn1Down>**. The actions provided by a widget are entirely up to the widget programmer. The Dial widget assumes that the "**select()**" action is the result of a mouse button event, and calculates the position of the indicator based on the coordinates of the mouse event. The position is then used in the **call_data** argument to the **XtNselectCallback** list. This callback list is defined in the Dial widget's instance record. The **select_dial()** procedure uses **XtCallCallbacks()** to invoke any **XtNselectCallback** functions registered by the application programmer. The **select_dial()** function is defined as:

```
static void select_dial (w, event, args, n_args)
      XsDialWidget    w;
      XEvent          *event;
      char            *args[];
      int             n_args;
{
  Position    pos;
  double      angle;
  xsdialCallbackStruct cb;

  pos = w->dial.position;
  if(event->type == ButtonPress ||
         event->type == MotionNotify){
    /*
     * Get the angle in radians.
     */
    angle=atan2((double)(event->xbutton.y - w->dial.center_y),
               (double)(event->xbutton.x - w->dial.center_x));
    /*
     * Convert to degrees from the MIN_ANGLE.
     */
    angle = DEGREES(angle) - (MIN_ANGLE - 90.0);
```

```
    if (angle < 0)
      angle = 360.0 + angle;
    /*
     * Convert the angle to a position.
     */
    pos = w->dial.minimum + (angle /
            MAX_ANGLE * (w->dial.maximum - w->dial.minimum));
  }
  /*
    * Invoke the callback, report the position in the call_data
    * structure
    */
  cb.reason   = Xs_SELECTED;
  cb.event    = event;
  cb.position = pos;
  XtCallCallbacks (w, XtNselectCallback, &cb);
}
```

This concludes the implementation of our first widget. Because the Dial widget uses the architecture and follows the basic conventions of the Xt Intrinsics, it can be combined freely with other widgets in applications. The following section looks at an example program that exercises the Dial widget.

12.2.4   Using The Dial Widget

In this section, we will look at an application of the Dial widget described in the previous section. This simple example creates a single Dial widget and defines a callback that moves the dial indicator to the position of the sprite when the user clicks the mouse within the Dial window.

Every application that uses the Dial widget must include the Intrinsic.h header file and also the Dial widget's public header file, Dial.h. After initializing the Intrinsics, the program creates a Dial widget using **XtCreateManagedWidget()**, and adds a function to the widget's **XtNselectCallback** list. After realizing the toplevel widget, the application enters the main event loop. At this point, a single Dial widget, similar to the image in Fig. 12.3, should appear on the screen.

```
/*****************************************************
 * dial.c : test the Dial widget class
 *****************************************************/
#include <X11/Intrinsic.h>
#include "Dial.h"

void select_callback();
```

```
main(argc, argv)
  int     argc;
  char *argv[];
{
  Widget toplevel, dial;
  /*
   * Initialize the Intrinsics.
   */
  toplevel = XtInitialize(argv[0], "DialTest", NULL,
                          0, &argc, argv);
  /*
   * Create a dial widget and add a select callback.
   */
  dial = XtCreateManagedWidget("dial", XsdialWidgetClass,
                               toplevel, NULL, 0);
  XtAddCallback(dial, XtNselectCallback,
                select_callback, NULL);
  XtRealizeWidget(toplevel);
  XtMainLoop();
}
```

The callback function **select_callback()** uses **XtSetValues()** to reposition the dial indicator. The Dial widget's **XtNselectCallback** provides the position of the indicator corresponding to the location of the sprite in the **call_data** argument, but does not move the indicator. The application can use **XtSetValues()** to move the Dial widget's indicator to the position reported in the call data, if desired. The **select_callback()** function is defined as:

```
void select_callback(w, client_data, call_data)
  Widget      w;
  caddr_t     client_data;
  xsdialCallbackStruct *call_data;
{
  Arg wargs[1];

  XtSetArg(wargs[0], XtNposition, call_data->position);
  XtSetValues(w, wargs, 1);
}
```

12.2.5   Compiling the Dial Widget Example

Since we may want to use the Dial widget in many applications, it is useful to place the widget in the libXs library where it can be linked with applications that use it. We can add the Dial widget to the library in the same way as any other functions.

```
cc −c Dial.c
ar ruv libXs.a Dial.o
```

Then the **dial** example can be compiled and linked with the command:

```
cc −o dial dial.c −lXs −lXt −lX11 −lm
```

12.3   USING INHERITANCE: THE SQUAREDIAL WIDGET

Programmers often find that they need a widget similar to, but not exactly like, an existing widget. In this case, it is often easiest to create a new widget class by inheriting from the existing, similar widget class. We used inheritance in the previous section (the Dial widget class inherits from the Core widget class), but it is possible to go further and inherit from any widget that meets our needs, not just the meta classes provided by the Xt Intrinsics and Motif.

Let's illustrate this with a simple example. Suppose the Dial example of this chapter is almost what we need, except that we would like markers on the dial face to be square instead of round. We could, of course, write a whole new widget class that creates the square dial face. This new class would also have to duplicate everything the Dial class already does. It is much faster and simpler to inherit from the Dial class and reuse some of the work we did in the Dial widget.

12.3.1   The Private Header File: SquareDialP.h

As with any widget class, we must create a new private header file containing the definition of the SquareDial widget's class record and instance record. The file SquareDialP.h defines a dummy SquareDial class part.

```
typedef struct _XsSquareDialClassPart{
    int ignore;
} XsSquareDialClassPart;
```

The class record for the new class is defined by adding the SquareDial class part to the Core and Dial widget class parts.

```
typedef struct _XsSquareDialClassRec {
    CoreClassPart           core_class;
    XsDialClassPart         dial_class;
```

```
    XsSquareDialClassPart     square_dial_class;
} XsSquareDialClassRec;

extern XsSquareDialClassRec XssquareDialClassRec;
```

The SquareDial widget class's contribution to the instance record is also a dummy structure, because we are only going to change the way the new widget displays information and no new resources are required. This dummy structure is added to the instance record after the Dial widget's contribution to the instance record.

```
typedef struct _XsSquareDialPart{
   int ignore;
} XsSquareDialPart;

typedef struct _XsSquareDialRec{
   CorePart          core;
   XsDialPart        dial;
   XsSquareDialPart  squaredial;
} XsSquareDialRec;
```

12.3.2   The Public Header File: SquareDial.h

The public header file contains the public declarations of the SquareDial widget class, and defines the same strings used by the Dial widget class. If we were creating a entire set of widgets, we could define these resources in a header file shared by all widgets in the set. For now, it is easier to just include the file Dial.h.

```
/***********************************************************
 * SquareDial.h:The SquareDial widget public header file.
 ***********************************************************/
#ifndef  SQUAREDIAL_H
#define  SQUAREDIAL_H
#include "Dial.h"

extern WidgetClass XssquareDialWidgetClass;

typedef struct _XsSquareDialClassRec * XsSquareDialWidgetClass;
typedef struct _XsSquareDialRec       * XsSquareDialWidget;

#endif  SQUAREDIAL_H
```

12.3.3   The Source File: SquareDial.c

The source file of the new widget class must initialize the class record of the new widget class and define any new methods used by the widget. The SquareDial widget class only defines two methods, the **Initialize()**, and **Resize()** methods. The **Initialize()** method is called in addition to the Dial widget's **Initialize()** method, while the **Resize()** method is called instead of the Dial widget's **Resize()** method. The SquareDial class inherits the Dial widget class's **Redisplay()** method and also its translations. Notice that SquareDial.c includes the Dial widget's private header file. The initial declarations and class initialization of the SquareDial widget class is done as follows:

```
/********************************************************
 * SquareDial.c: A subclass of the Dial widget class
 ********************************************************/
#include <stdio.h>
#include <X11/IntrinsicP.h>
#include <X11/Intrinsic.h>
#include <X11/StringDefs.h>
#include <X11/CoreP.h>
#include "DialP.h"
#include "Dial.h"
#include "SquareDialP.h"
#include "SquareDial.h"

#define  MIN(a,b)     (((a) < (b)) ? (a) :  (b))

static void Resize();
static void Initialize();

XsSquareDialClassRec  XssquareDialClassRec = {
/* CoreClassPart */
  {
    (WidgetClass) &XsdialClassRec,    /* superclass          */
    "SquareDial",                     /* class_name          */
    sizeof(XsSquareDialRec),          /* widget_size         */
    NULL,                             /* class_initialize    */
    NULL,                             /* class_part_initialize */
    FALSE,                            /* class_inited        */
    (XtWidgetProc) Initialize,        /* initialize          */
    NULL,                             /* initialize_hook     */
    XtInheritRealize,                 /* realize             */
    NULL,                             /* actions             */
    0,                                /* num_actions         */
```

```
    NULL,                           /* resources             */
    0,                              /* num_resources         */
    NULLQUARK,                      /* xrm_class             */
    TRUE,                           /* compress_motion       */
    TRUE,                           /* compress_exposure     */
    TRUE,                           /* compress_enterleave   */
    TRUE,                           /* visible_interest      */
    NULL,                           /* destroy               */
    (XtWidgetProc) Resize,          /* resize                */
    XtInheritExpose,                /* expose                */
    NULL,                           /* set_values            */
    NULL,                           /* set_values_hook       */
    XtInheritSetValuesAlmost,       /* set_values_almost     */
    NULL,                           /* get_values_hook       */
    XtInheritAcceptFocus,           /* accept_focus          */
    XtVersion,                      /* version               */
    NULL,                           /* callback private      */
    XtInheritTranslations,          /* tm_table              */
    NULL,                           /* query_geometry        */
    NULL,                           /* display_accelerator   */
    NULL                            /* extension             */
    },
        /* Dial class fields */
    {
      0,                            /* ignore                */
    },
        /* Square Dial class fields */
    {
      0,                            /* ignore                */
    }
};

WidgetClass XssquareDialWidgetClass =
        (WidgetClass) &XssquareDialClassRec;
```

The SquareDial **Initialize()** method simply calls the SquareDial widget's **Resize()** method to override some of the calculations done by the Dial widget class's **Initialize()** method.

```
static void Initialize(request, new)
  XsSquareDialWidget     request, new;
{
  Resize(new);
}
```

Finally, the SquareDial widget class defines its own **Resize()** method. **Resize()** re-computes the line segments that represent the face of the dial as a square rather than a circle. We can rely on the inherited **Redisplay()** method to actually draw the segments.

```
static void Resize(w)
  XsSquareDialWidget     w;
{
  int        marks_per_side, h_increment, v_increment, i;
  XPoint  *ptr;
  /*
   * Get the address of the segment array.
   */
  ptr = w->dial.segments;
  /*
   * Calculate the center of the window.
   */
  w->dial.center_x = w->core.width / 2;
  w->dial.center_y = w->core.height / 2;

  w->dial.outer_diam = MIN(w->core.width, w->core.height) / 2;
  w->dial.inner_diam=w->dial.outer_diam-w->dial.marker_length;
  /*
   * Position the marks up the left side, across the top,
   * and down the right side of the window.
   */
  marks_per_side  = w->dial.markers / 3;
  w->dial.markers = marks_per_side * 3;
  h_increment = w->core.width / (marks_per_side + 1);
  v_increment = w->core.height / (marks_per_side + 1);
  /*
   * Do the left side.
   */
  for(i=0;i<marks_per_side;i++){
    ptr->x   = 0;
    ptr++->y = w->core.height - i * v_increment -v_increment;
    ptr->x   = w->dial.marker_length;
    ptr++->y = w->core.height - i * v_increment - v_increment;
```

```
    }
    /*
     * Do the top.
     */
    for(i=0;i<marks_per_side;i++){
      ptr->x    = h_increment + i * h_increment;
      ptr++->y  = 0;
      ptr->x    = h_increment + i * h_increment;
      ptr++->y  = w->dial.marker_length;
    }
    /*
     * Do the right side.
     */
    for(i=0;i<marks_per_side;i++){
      ptr->x    = w->core.width - w->dial.marker_length;
      ptr++->y  = w->core.height - i * v_increment -v_increment;
      ptr->x    = w->core.width;
      ptr++->y  = w->core.height - i * v_increment -v_increment;
    }
}
```

This completes the implementation of the SquareDial widget class. By inheriting the behavior of the Dial class, we were able to create the new SquareDial class by writing fewer lines of code than if we had designed the new widget class from scratch. The Dial widget class consists of 336 uncommented lines of code, while the SquareDial widget class required only 121. In addition, it is not necessary (in theory) to have access to the Dial widget's source code in order to inherit from it. In practice, we were able to create a new class easily because we had detailed information about how the Dial class works. Because we know how the dial face was drawn, and that the line segments used for the dial are computed in the Dial widget's **Resize()** method, we were able to make the desired changes by redefining only that method. This would be more difficult without access to the source code.

12.3.4   Using The SquareDial Widget Class

The new SquareDial class is used in exactly the same way as the Dial widget class. We can simply change the header file and the widget class specified to **XtCreateWidget()** in the **dial** test program we used earlier to produce the file sqdial.c.

```
/********************************************************
 * sqdial.c : Test of the Square Dial widget class
 ********************************************************/
#include <X11/Intrinsic.h>
#include "SquareDial.h"
```

```
void select_callback();

main(argc, argv)
    int    argc;
    char *argv[];
  {
    Widget toplevel, dial;
    /*
     * Initialize the Intrinsics.
     */
    toplevel = XtInitialize(argv[0], "DialTest", NULL,
                            0, &argc, argv);
    /*
     * Create a square dial widget and assign a callback.
     */
    dial = XtCreateManagedWidget("dial",
                                 XssquareDialWidgetClass,
                                 toplevel, NULL, 0);
    XtAddCallback(dial, XtNselectCallback,
                  select_callback, NULL);
    XtRealizeWidget(toplevel);
    XtMainLoop();
  }
```

The callback function, **select_callback()**, is defined exactly as in the earlier example. This program produces the display shown in Fig. 12.5.

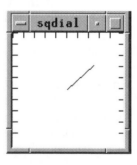

Figure 12.4 A SquareDial widget.

12.4   META-CLASSES

In the previous section we saw how inheritance can simplify the task of writing a new widget. Often this task can be made even easier by carefully structuring new widget classes. It is often possible to extract some general functionality from two or more new widget classes and create a meta-class. Remember that in the Xt Intrinsics, a meta-class is a class that is not intended to be instantiated directly, but serves as a superclass for other similar widgets. For example, in addition to the two types of dials discussed in this chapter, we can probably think of other types of dials or gauges that share some of the characteristics of the Dial and SquareDial widget classes. Therefore, we might consider restructuring the widget classes in this chapter by defining a Gauge meta-class that includes those components common to all dials and gauges. This meta-class might include the creation of graphics contexts, the management of minimum and maximum values, and so on. Using this approach, the two widget classes discussed in this chapter might become the RoundDial and SquareDial classes, which could both be subclasses of the Gauge widget class. Fig. 12.6 shows how this widget hierarchy might look.

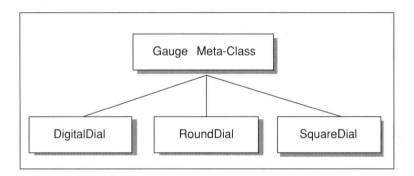

Figure 12.5 Organization of a Gauge meta-class.

When creating a complete new widget set, it is often useful to create a hierarchy of meta-classes. With this approach, the top meta-class in the hierarchy defines elements that all widget classes in the set have in common, while each subclass becomes more and more specialized. Such an organization allows the widget programmer to create new widget classes with the least amount of effort, although there is some extra initial effort required to design and create the meta classes. For example, this approach is used by the Motif widget set, where all display widgets inherit from the XmPrimitive meta-class and all composite widgets inherit from the XmManager widget class. Had we chosen to make the Dial widget a subclass of the XmPrimitive widget class, basic resources such as a foreground color, and various graphics contexts for producing the three dimensional shading used by Motif would have been provided for us automatically.

12.5 SUMMARY

This chapter discussed the architecture of a widget class and created a simple widget class that inherits from the Core widget class. Widgets consist of two basic parts, a class record and an instance record. The class record contains components shared by all widgets of a class, for example, the widget's class name, resource list and methods. Methods are private procedures that operate on the data in the widget's instance record. Each widget has its own copy of the instance record. This structure records the state of the specific widget: the size and position of the widget's window, the colors it uses, and so on.

The implementation of a widget uses a data abstraction technique that uses a private header file containing the true definition of the widget and a public file containing an incomplete definition. Applications see only the incomplete definition, and use Intrinsics functions to create and manipulate the widget.

When creating a new widget, programmers can often reuse parts of a similar widget by inheriting from that widget. To do this, the programmer includes the superclass's class record and instance record in the new widget's definition. Special symbols also allow the programmer to specify that the Intrinsics should copy some of the superclass's methods into the new widget's class record. Other methods are chained, so that the superclass's methods are called first. This provides another way to inherit part of the behavior of another widget.

13

CREATING COMPOSITE WIDGETS

In the previous chapter, we built some simple widgets that defined their own appearance and style of interaction. This chapter presents a more complex type of widget known as a composite widget. These widgets are subclasses of the Composite meta-class, which is defined by the Xt Intrinsics and is a subclass of the Core widget class. The Composite class inherits all the characteristics of the Core widget class, and adds the ability to manage child widgets. Widgets belonging to subclasses of the Composite widget class are referred to as composite widgets. Composite widgets are used primarily as containers for other widgets and are responsible for managing the geometry of their children. A managed widget is never permitted to resize or move itself directly. Instead, it must request its parent to make the changes. The parent widget considers the request and allows the change, disallows the change, or suggests a compromise, depending on its management policy. Although they do not usually have display semantics, composite widgets are an important part of any widget set because they allow the application programmer to combine other widgets to create a complete user interface.

Motif container widget classes never inherit directly from the Composite widget class, but rather are subclasses of XmManager. The XmManager widget class provides several important features that are used by all Motif container classes. However, it is easier to discuss the features provided by each meta-class if we examine the class individually. So, the widget discussed in this chapter is not completely representative of the way Motif does a container widget, but is similar in principle. This chapter first discusses the general architecture of the Composite widget class, and then presents an example composite widget.

13.1   ARCHITECTURE OF A COMPOSITE WIDGET

The Composite widget class, along with the Xt Intrinsics, defines the basic mechanism for managing children. Every composite widget's class record contains the methods that implement the widget's management policy. The first two members of every composite widget's class record includes both the Core widget class's **CoreClassPart** structure and a new **CompositeClassPart** structure. For example, the Composite widget class's class record is defined as:

```
typedef struct _CompositeClassRec {
    CoreClassPart        core_class;
    CompositeClassPart   composite_class;
} CompositeClassRec;
```

The **CompositeClassPart** structure contains pointers to the methods that manage children. This structure is defined as:

```
typedef struct _CompositeClassPart {
    XtGeometryHandler geometry_manager;
    XtWidgetProc      change_managed;
    XtWidgetProc      insert_child;
    XtWidgetProc      delete_child;
    caddr_t           extension;
} CompositeClassPart;
```

Each composite widget class must supply these methods in one form or another. Section 13.2.3 discusses each of these methods in the context of an example composite widget.

Each composite widget's instance record includes the **CorePart** structure defined by the Core widget class, followed by a **CompositePart** structure. The Composite widget class's instance record is defined as:

```
typedef struct _CompositeRec {
    CorePart      core;
    CompositePart composite;
} CompositeRec;
```

The **CompositePart** structure is defined in the Composite widget's private header file as:

```
typedef struct _CompositePart {
    WidgetList  children;
    Cardinal    num_children;
    Cardinal    num_slots;
    XtOrderProc insert_position;
} CompositePart;
```

The first member of this structure, **children**, is a list of all widgets managed by the composite widget, while the second member, **num_children**, indicates the number of children on this list. The field **num_slots** is set to the maximum size of the list, and is used by the widget to alter the size of the children list dynamically. The last member of the **CompositePart** structure is a pointer to a method that must return an integer index into the **children** array. This index determines the position in the **children** list where the next child is to be inserted. Most widget classes inherit this method from the Composite widget class, but they can choose to redefine this method to control the order in which widgets are kept on the **children** list.

13.2 A COMPOSITE WIDGET: THE ROW WIDGET

The easiest way to understand how a composite widget works is to look at an example. This section creates a new composite widget class, which we will name the Row widget class.

Every composite widget implements its own management policy that determines how its children are positioned. The Row widget's management policy is simple. It places all managed children in a single row, evenly separated by any remaining space. The Row widget determines the position of each child widget; children may not move themselves. The Row widget honors all resize requests from children as long as there is enough room or if the Row widget itself can grow to accommodate the request. The Row widget serves only as a container for other widgets and therefore has no display semantics itself. Fig. 13.1 shows a Row widget managing several button widgets.

Figure 13.1 The Row widget.

Like all widgets, composite widgets consist of private header files, a public header file, and one or more source files. The following sections describe the contents of each of the Row widget's files.

13.2.1 The Private Header File: RowP.h

The Row widget's private header file contains the definitions of the Row widget's class record and the instance record. The Row widget inherits directly from the Composite widget class. It defines its class record by adding its own class part structure to the class parts defined by the Core and Composite widget classes. Because the Row widget uses no additional class data, its class part is a dummy structure.

```
typedef struct _XsRowClassPart {
         int    ignore;
} XsRowClassPart;
```

The Row widget's complete class record can now be defined as:

```
typedef struct _XsRowClassRec {
    CoreClassPart          core_class;
    CompositeClassPart     composite_class;
    XsRowClassPart         row_class;
} XsRowClassRec;


extern XsRowClassRec XsrowClassRec;
```

The next step in creating a widget is to define the instance record. The Row widget requires no additional data in its instance record, so its contribution to the instance record is also a dummy structure, defined as:

```
typedef struct {
     int ignore;
} XsRowPart;
```

The Row widget's complete instance record is defined as:

```
typedef struct _XsRowRec {
    CorePart          core;
    CompositePart     composite;
    XsRowPart         row;
}   XsRowRec;
```

13.2.2   The Public Header File: Row.h

The Row widget's public header file is similar to the public header file for all widgets and consists of only a few public definitions:

```
#ifndef ROW_H
#define ROW_H
extern WidgetClass XsrowWidgetClass;
typedef struct _XsRowClassRec *XsRowWidgetClass;
typedef struct _XsRowRec      *XsRowWidget;
#endif ROW_H
```

Applications use the class pointer, **XsrowWidgetClass**, as an argument to **XtCreateWidget()** to create a Row widget.

13.2.3   The Source File: Row.c

The file Row.c contains the static definition of the Row widget class record, as well as the Row widget's methods. The source file includes the Composite widget class's header files in addition to the private and public Intrinsic header files. It also includes the private and public Row widget header files.

```
/***************************************************
 * Row.c: Methods for the Row widget
 ***************************************************/
#include     <X11/IntrinsicP.h>
#include     <X11/Intrinsic.h>
#include     <X11/Composite.h>
#include     <X11/CompositeP.h>
#include     "RowP.h"
#include     "Row.h"
```

Next, the methods and other functions used by the Row widget are declared as static, making these functions private to the file. **MAX()** and **MIN()** are useful macros that determine the larger and smaller of two numbers, respectively.

```
#define MAX(a,b) ((a) > (b) ? (a) : (b))
#define MIN(a,b) ((a) < (b) ? (a) : (b))

static void              Initialize();
static void              Resize();
static void              ChangeManaged();
static Boolean           SetValues();
static XtGeometryResult  GeometryManager();
static XtGeometryResult  PreferredSize();
static XtGeometryResult  try_layout();
```

13.2.3.1   The Class Record

The Row widget's class record is initialized entirely at compile time. Because the Row widget has no display semantics of its own and provides no actions or resources, it does not use many of the methods defined by the Core class part. For example, there is no need for a **SetValues()** method or an **Expose()** method. However, we must define several new methods that allow the Row widget to manage its children. The class record is initialized as:

```
XsRowClassRec XsrowClassRec = {
  {
    /* core_class members       */
    (WidgetClass) &compositeClassRec, /* superclass       */
```

```
    "Row",                              /* class_name            */
    sizeof(XsRowRec),                   /* widget_size           */
    NULL,                               /* class_initialize      */
    NULL,                               /* class_part_init       */
    FALSE,                              /* class_inited          */
    Initialize,                         /* initialize            */
    NULL,                               /* initialize_hook       */
    XtInheritRealize,                   /* realize               */
    NULL,                               /* actions               */
    0,                                  /* num_actions           */
    NULL,                               /* resources             */
    0,                                  /* num_resources         */
    NULLQUARK,                          /* xrm_class             */
    TRUE,                               /* compress_motion       */
    TRUE,                               /* compress_exposure     */
    TRUE,                               /* compress_enterleave*/
    FALSE,                              /* visible_interest      */
    NULL,                               /* destroy               */
    Resize,                             /* resize                */
    NULL,                               /* expose                */
    NULL,                               /* set_values            */
    NULL,                               /* set_values_hook       */
    XtInheritSetValuesAlmost,           /* set_values_almost     */
    NULL,                               /* get_values_hook       */
    NULL,                               /* accept_focus          */
    XtVersion,                          /* version               */
    NULL,                               /* callback_private      */
    NULL,                               /* tm_table              */
    PreferredSize,                      /* query_geometry        */
    NULL,                               /* display_accelerator*/
    NULL,                               /* extension             */
  },
  {
    /* composite_class members */
    GeometryManager,                    /* geometry_manager      */
    ChangeManaged,                      /* change_managed        */
    XtInheritInsertChild,               /* insert_child          */
    XtInheritDeleteChild,               /* delete_child          */
    NULL,                               /* extension             */
  },
  {
    /* Row class members */
```

```
    0,                              /* ignore              */
  }
};
WidgetClass XsrowWidgetClass = (WidgetClass) &XsrowClassRec;
```

The superclass member of the class record specifies a pointer to **compositeClassRec**, the Composite widget class's class structure. The Row widget requires no run time initialization of the class structure, so the **class_initialize** and **class_part_initialize** members are set to **NULL**. Because there are no actions or settable resources, the **actions** and **resource** members are also set to **NULL**. The Row widget sets the **visible_interest** member of the class record to **FALSE** because it does not display anything itself, and does not care if it is visible.

13.2.3.2 Methods

The Row widget defines three core part methods similar to those defined by the simple Dial widget in Chapter 12. However, the most interesting aspect of any composite widget class is the way it manages its children. The Row widget defines several methods and auxiliary functions that allow the Row widget to control the geometry of its children and also negotiate the geometry of the Row widget with its parent. The following sections discuss each of the Row widget's methods, beginning with the basic methods that all widget classes must provide before discussing the methods added by the Composite widget class.

The Initialize() Method

Because the Row widget defines no additional resources of its own, the Row widget's **Initialize()** method is simple. Every widget's **Initialize()** method should check that the width and height of its window are greater than zero. The **Initialize()** method is defined as:

```
    static void Initialize(request, new)
        XsRowWidget request, new;
    {
      if (request -> core.width <= 0)
        new -> core.width = 5;
      if (request -> core.height <= 0)
        new -> core.height = 5;
    }
```

The Realize() Method

Like most widgets, the Row widget class inherits the basic method defined by the Core widget class to create its window. The Row widget sets the **realize** member of its class record to the symbol **XtInheritRealize** to inherit the **Realize()** method used by the

Composite widget class. In turn, the Composite widget class inherits its **Realize()** method from the Core widget class.

The InsertChild() Method

Every composite widget must have an **InsertChild()** method, which is responsible for adding new child widgets to the composite widget's list of children. **XtCreateWidget()** calls this method when it creates a widget as a child of a composite widget. Most composite widgets inherit the basic method defined by the Composite widget by specifying the symbol **XtInheritInsertChild** for the **insert_child** member of the class record. The Composite widget's **InsertChild()** method adds new children to the children list, enlarging the list using **XtRealloc()**, if needed. It calls the widget's **InsertPosition()** method to determine the next available position in the **children** array. If this procedure is not defined, the default is to append the child to the end of the list. The list of children contains all widgets created as a child of the composite widget, regardless of whether or not they are currently managed. A composite widget can discover whether a particular child widget is managed by examining the **managed** field of the child's core part.

The DeleteChild() Method

Every composite widget must provide a method to remove widgets from its list of children. Most widgets, including the Row widget, inherit this method from the Composite class, by setting the **delete_child** member of the widget's class record to the symbol **XtInheritDeleteChild**.

The Resize() Method

The Row widget bases the layout of its children on its own size. When a widget's size changes, the Intrinsics invokes its **Resize()** method. The Row widget's **Resize()** method simply calls an auxiliary function, **do_layout()**, to recalculate the layout of its children.

```
static void Resize(w)
     XsRowWidget     w;
{
  do_layout(w);
}
```

The function **do_layout()** determines the position of each managed child. It iterates twice over the list of children found in the composite part of the instance record. On the first pass it computes the sum of the widths of all managed children, to determine how much space, if any, it can place between each widget. The second pass positions each managed child, evenly separated, in a single row.

```
do_layout(parent)
     XsRowWidget parent;
{
  Widget      child;
  int         i;
  Dimension   childwidth = 0;
  Position    xpos = 0;
  Dimension   pad = 0;
  int     n_managed_children = 0;
 /*
  * Compute the total width of all managed children and
  * determine how many children are managed.
  */
  for (i = 0; i < parent -> composite.num_children; i++){
    child = parent -> composite.children[i];
    if(child->core.managed){
      n_managed_children++;
      childwidth += child->core.width +
                        child->core.border_width * 2;
    }
  }
  /*
   *   Divide any remaining space by the number
   *   of children.
   */
  if((n_managed_children > 1) &&
         (parent->core.width > childwidth))
    pad = (parent->core.width - childwidth) /
                                (n_managed_children - 1);
  /*
   * Position all children.
   */
  for (i = 0; i < parent -> composite.num_children; i++){
    child = parent -> composite.children[i];
    if(child->core.managed){
      XtMoveWidget (child, xpos, 0);
      xpos += pad + child->core.width +
                          child->core.border_width * 2;
    }
  }
}
```

The QueryGeometry() Method

Managing the geometry of a widget's children often requires a series of negotiations between the composite widget, its parent and its children. While a composite widget has complete control over the geometry of its children, it has no control over its own geometry. Often, a widget that manages the layout of multiple children must alter the size or position of one or more widgets to fulfill its particular layout policy within the constraints mandated by its own size. In this situation, it is often useful for the widget to be able to determine the preferred size of each of its children.

Every widget contains a pointer to a **QueryGeometry()** method in its Core class part. This method is invoked by the Intrinsics function:

```
XtQueryGeometry(widget, &intended, &preferred)
```

A composite widget that intends to change the size or position of one of its children can call this function to determine the child's preferred geometry. The **intended** and **preferred** parameters are structures of type **XtWidgetGeometry**, which contains the members:

```
XtGeometryMask  request_mode;
Position        x, y;
Dimension       width, height, border_width;
Widget          sibling;
int             stack_mode;
```

The **request_mode** member of this structure indicates which members of the structure contain valid information and must be set using the masks:

```
CWX                     CWY                    CWWidth
CWHeight                CWBorderWidth          CWSibling
CWStackMode
```

Before calling **XtQueryGeometry()**, the parent widget indicates the changes it plans to make in an **XtWidgetGeometry** structure and uses it as the **intended** argument. If the child widget has no **QueryGeometry()** method, **XtQueryGeometry()** fills in the **preferred** geometry structure with the child widget's current geometry. Otherwise it invokes the child's **QueryGeometry()** method. If the proposed changes are acceptable to the child widget, its **QueryGeometry()** method should return the constant **XtGeometryYes**. If the changes are unacceptable, or if the child's current geometry is identical to the child's preferred geometry, the method should return **XtGeometryNo**. If some of the proposed changes are acceptable, but others are not, the method can fill in the **preferred** structure with its preferred geometry and return the constant **XtGeometryAlmost**.

A parent widget is under no obligation to a child to maintain the child's preferred geometry, and may choose to ignore the information returned by **XtQueryGeometry()**. The Row widget bases its preferred geometry on the maximum height and the total width of its managed children. Although this is simple in principle, the method that computes the Row widget's preferred geometry is a bit long because there are many cases to test. The Row widget's **QueryGeometry()** method is defined as:

```
static XtGeometryResult PreferredSize(w, request, preferred)
  XsRowWidget         w;
  XtWidgetGeometry *request, *preferred;
{
  Widget child;
  int i;
  /*
   * If no changes are being made to width or
   * height, just agree.
   */
  if(!(request->request_mode & CWWidth) &&
     !(request->request_mode & CWHeight))
    return (XtGeometryYes);
  /*
   * Calculate our minimum size.
   */
  preferred->width = 0;
  preferred->height = 0;
  for (i = 0; i < w -> composite.num_children; i++){
    child = w -> composite.children[i];
    if(child->core.managed){
      preferred->width += child->core.width +
                             child->core.border_width * 2;
      if(preferred->height < child->core.height +
              child->core.border_width * 2)
        preferred->height = child->core.height +
                             child->core.border_width * 2;
    }
  }
  preferred->request_mode = CWWidth | CWHeight;
  /*
   * If both width and height are requested.
   */
  if((request->request_mode & CWWidth) &&
     (request->request_mode & CWHeight)){
    /*
     * If we are to be the same or bigger, say ok.
     */
    if(preferred->width <= request->width &&
            preferred->height <= request->height){
```

```
        preferred->width = request->width;
        preferred->height = request->height;
        return (XtGeometryYes);
    }
    /*
     * If both dimensions are unacceptable, say no.
     */
    else
      if(preferred->width < request->width &&
         preferred->height < request->height)
        return (XtGeometryNo);
    /*
     * Otherwise one must be right, so say almost.
     */
      else
         return (XtGeometryAlmost);
}
/*
 * If only the width is requested, either it's
 * OK or it isn't. Same for height.
 */
else
  if(request->request_mode & CWWidth){
    if(preferred->width <= request->width){
       preferred->width = request->width;
       return (XtGeometryYes);
    }
    else
       return (XtGeometryNo);
  }
  else
   if(request->request_mode & CWHeight){
    if(preferred->height <= request->height){
       preferred->height = request->height;
       return (XtGeometryYes);
    }
    else
       return (XtGeometryNo);
  }
  return (XtGeometryYes);
}
```

Notice that this method does not help the Row widget manage its children, but rather assists the parent of a Row widget in managing the Row widget itself. Ideally, every widget should define this method to make it easier for its parent to manage the widget's geometry. Geometry management of multiple widgets is a process of negotiation that requires some give and take between all widgets involved. This negotiation is more likely to succeed if every widget defines a **QueryGeometry()** method that provides accurate information about the best size of the widget. Widgets that always claim that their current geometry is the preferred geometry (by specifying the **query_geometry** member as **NULL**) do little to help the negotiation process.

The GeometryManager() Method

As mentioned previously, a widget should never attempt to alter its size or location directly, because the geometry of every widget is the responsibility of the widget's parent. Geometry requests are made using the function:

```
XtMakeGeometryRequest(widget, &request, &reply)
```

This function takes a **XtWidgetGeometry** structure as an argument and returns one of the constants:

XtGeometryYes	**XtGeometryNo**
XtGeometryAlmost	**XtGeometryDone**

XtMakeGeometryRequest() invokes the **GeometryManager()** method belonging to the parent of the given widget. If the parent allows the request, this method returns the constant **XtGeometryYes**, and **XtMakeGeometryRequest()** makes the requested changes. If the **GeometryManager()** method fulfills the request itself, it should return **XtGeometryDone**. The parent's **GeometryManager()** method can also disallow the request by returning **XtGeometryNo** or suggest a compromise by returning the constant **XtGeometryAlmost**.

The Row widget's **GeometryManager()** method begins by checking for and rejecting any changes to the position of a child widget. If the request involves a change in width or height, the method saves the child widget's original size and temporarily sets the widget to the requested size. Next, the Row widget's **GeometryManager()** method calls the auxiliary function **try_layout()** to determine if the new size is acceptable. The **try_layout()** function returns a result of type **XtGeometryResult**, and also a mask containing information about which dimension, if any, is unacceptable. If the result of **try_layout()** is XtGeometryNo, the **GeometryManager()** method restores the widget's original dimensions and returns **XtGeometryNo**. If the result of **try_layout()** is **XtGeometryAlmost**, the **GeometryManager()** method restores the original values for the unacceptable dimensions and returns **XtGeometryAlmost**. In this case, the child widget can choose to use the compromise suggested by the Row widget and call **XtMakeGeometryRequest()** a second time using the suggested values, or it can abort the request and keep its original geometry. Finally, if **try_layout()** returns **XtGeometryYes**, **GeometryManager()** calls **do_layout()** to reposition the children before returning the value **XtGeometryYes**.

```
static XtGeometryResult GeometryManager(w, request, reply)
    Widget             w;
    XtWidgetGeometry   *request;
    XtWidgetGeometry   *reply;
{
  XsRowWidget        rw = (XsRowWidget) w -> core.parent;
  Mask               mask;
  XtGeometryResult   result;
  Dimension          wdelta, hdelta;
  /*
   * Say no.  We control the vertical....
   */
  if ((request->request_mode & CWX &&
                  request->x != w->core.x)||
      (request->request_mode & CWY &&
                  request->y != w->core.y))
    return (XtGeometryNo);
  /*
   *  Otherwise, grant all requests if they fit.
   */
  if (request->request_mode &
                  (CWWidth | CWHeight | CWBorderWidth)){
    /*
     * Save the original widget size, and set the
     * corresponding widget fields to the requested sizes.
     */
    Dimension savewidth       = w->core.width;
    Dimension saveheight      = w->core.height;
    Dimension saveborderwidth = w->core.border_width;

    if (request->request_mode & CWWidth)
      w->core.width = request->width;
    if (request->request_mode & CWHeight)
      w->core.height = request->height;
    if (request->request_mode & CWBorderWidth)
      w->core.border_width = request->border_width;
    /*
     * See if we can still handle all the children
     * if the request is granted.
```

```
    */
    result = try_layout(rw, &mask, &wdelta, &hdelta);
    /*
     * If the children won't fit, restore the widget to its
     * original size, and return no.
     */
    if(result == XtGeometryNo){
      w->core.width  = savewidth;
      w->core.height = saveheight;
      w->core.border_width = saveborderwidth;
      return (XtGeometryNo);
    }
    /*
     * If only one dimension fits, restore the one that
     * doesn't fit and return "almost".
     */
    if(result == XtGeometryAlmost){
      reply->request_mode = request->request_mode;
      if(!(mask & CWWidth)){
        reply->width = w->core.width = savewidth;
        reply->border_width = saveborderwidth;
        w->core.border_width = saveborderwidth;
      }
      if(!(mask & CWHeight))
        reply->height = w->core.height = saveheight;

      return (XtGeometryAlmost);
    }
    /*
     *  If we got here, everything must fit, so reposition
     *  all children based on the new size, and return "yes".
     */
    do_layout(rw);
    return (XtGeometryYes);
  }
  return (XtGeometryYes);
}
```

The function **try_layout()** calculates the Row widget's minimum width and height, based on the current size of its managed children. If all children fit, the function returns **XtGeometryYes**. Otherwise, the Row widget issues a resize request to its parent in an attempt to accommodate the new size of its children. In this case, **try_layout()** returns the value returned by this request. If the Row widget's parent suggests a compromise geometry, **do_layout()** sets the **mask** argument to indicate which dimension was disallowed and calculates the difference between the requested width and height and the allowed width and height. This information is used by the **ChangeManaged()** method described in the next section.

```
static XtGeometryResult
try_layout(parent, mask, w_delta, h_delta)
    XsRowWidget parent;
    Mask        *mask;
    Dimension   *w_delta, *h_delta;
{
  int  i;
  Dimension total_width = 0, max_height = 0;
  /*
   * Get the bounding width and height of all children.
   */
  for (i = 0; i < parent -> composite.num_children; i++){
  Widget      child;
  Dimension width, height;

  child  = parent -> composite.children[i];
  if(child->core.managed){
    height =child->core.height + child->core.border_width * 2;
    width  =child->core.width + child->core.border_width * 2;
    total_width += width;
    max_height = MAX(max_height, height);
  }
}
/*
 *  If everyone doesn't fit, ask if we can grow. Return the
 *  result, after setting the mask to indicate which (if
 *  any) dimension is ok.
 */
if(total_width > parent->core.width ||
    max_height > parent->core.height){
  XtGeometryResult result;
  Dimension replyWidth, replyHeight;
  Dimension width  =  MAX(total_width, parent->core.width);
  Dimension height = MAX(max_height, parent->core.height);

  result = XtMakeResizeRequest (parent, width, height,
                                    &replyWidth, &replyHeight);
  *mask = NULL;
```

```
    if(total_width == replyWidth)
      *mask  = CWWidth;
    if(max_height == replyHeight)
     *mask |= CWHeight;

    if(result == XtGeometryAlmost)
      XtMakeResizeRequest (parent, replyWidth, replyHeight,
                           NULL, NULL);
    *w_delta = total_width - parent->core.width;
    *h_delta = max_height - parent->core.height;
    return (result);
  }
  /*
   * If everybody fits, just return yes.
   */
  *mask = CWWidth | CWHeight;
  return (XtGeometryYes);
}
```

These two functions, **GeometryManager()** and **try_layout()**, illustrate several aspects of the process of negotiating geometry. The Row widget completely controls the geometry of its children and tries its best to accommodate their preferred sizes. However, the Row widget cannot control its own size; that is controlled by its parent. The Row bases its preferred size on the sum of its children's sizes, and attempts to grow if necessary to contain its managed children. If all widgets cooperate, this negotiation process works smoothly. However, this process fails if any widget in an application's widget tree does not negotiate.

The ChangeManaged() Method

A composite widget's **ChangeManaged()** method is invoked whenever one of its children changes between being managed or unmanaged. Composite widgets generally use this method to recalculate the layout of their children when the set of managed widgets changes. The Row widget's **ChangeManaged()** method first calls **try_layout()** to determine whether all children still fit. Remember that **try_layout()** attempts to increase the size of the Row widget if all children do not fit. If **try_layout()** fails, it returns a delta indicating the difference between the size of the Row widget and the size needed to contain all the children. In this case, **ChangeManaged()** reduces the width of each widget by its share of the width delta, and reduces each widget's height to the height of the Row widget if necessary. Once the children's sizes have been adjusted, **ChangeManaged()** calls **do_layout()** to position each child.

```
static void ChangeManaged(w)
    XsRowWidget w;
{
  XtGeometryResult result;
  Dimension        width, height, delta;
  int              i;
  Mask             mask;
  Widget           child;
  /*
   * See if all children fit.
   */
  result = try_layout(w, &mask, &width, &height);
  /*
   * If they don't, resize all children to be smaller.
   */
  if(result != XtGeometryYes){
    if(w->composite.num_children > 0){
      delta = width / w->composite.num_children;
      for(i=0;i<w->composite.num_children;i++){
        child = w->composite.children[i];
        height = MIN(child->core.height,
                     w->core.height -child->core.border_width);
        if(child->core.managed)
          XtResizeWidget(child,
                         child->core.width - delta,
                         height,
                         child->core.border_width);
      }
    }
  }
  /*
   * Move all children to their new positions.
   */
  do_layout(w);
}
```

Notice that this method resizes all children equally if the total size of all managed children exceeds the available space. This method could be improved by adding calls to **XtQueryGeometry()** to check each child's preferred geometry, in case one child is more willing than others to have its size reduced.

13.2.4   USING THE ROW WIDGET

This section describes a simple program, **rowtest**, that tests the Row widget's management capabilities. The program uses a Row widget to manage four button widgets. Several callbacks allow the buttons to request size changes, and also to add and delete buttons.

```
/************************************************
 * rowtest.c: Program to test the Row widget
 ************************************************/
#include <X11/StringDefs.h>
#include <X11/Intrinsic.h>
#include <Xm/Xm.h>
#include <Xm/PushB.h>
#include "Row.h"

void    grow();
void    unmanage();
void    manage();

char *names[] = {"Button1", "Button2", "Button3", "Button4"};

main(argc, argv)
  int     argc;
  char    *argv[];
{
  Widget toplevel, row, buttons[4];
  Arg    wargs[2];
  int    i;
  /*
   * Initialize the Intrinsics.
   */
  toplevel = XtInitialize(argv[0], "Rowtest", NULL,
                          0, &argc, argv);
  /*
   * Create a Row widget.
   */
  row = XtCreateManagedWidget("row", XsrowWidgetClass,
                              toplevel, NULL, 0);
  /*
   * Add children to the Row widget.
   */
  for(i=0;i<XtNumber(names);i++)
    buttons[i] = XtCreateWidget(names[i],
```

```
                                   xmPushButtonWidgetClass,
                                   row, NULL, 0);

   XtAddCallback(buttons[0], XmNactivateCallback,
                 grow , NULL);
   XtAddCallback(buttons[1], XmNactivateCallback,
                 unmanage, NULL);
   XtAddCallback(buttons[2], XmNactivateCallback,
                 manage, buttons[1]);
   XtAddCallback(buttons[3], XmNactivateCallback,
                 grow , NULL);

   XtManageChildren(buttons, XtNumber(buttons));
   XtRealizeWidget(toplevel);
   XtMainLoop();
}
```

Fig. 13.1 in Section 13.2 shows the initial layout of the buttons produced by this program.

The **rowtest** program defines three callback functions that demonstrate and test the Row widget's geometry manager. The first callback, **grow()**, is registered as a **XmNactivateCallback** function for the widgets **Button1** and **Button4**. Each time the user activates one of these buttons, this callback function requests the Row widget to increase the width and height of the button by 10 pixels.

```
   void grow (w, client_data, call_data)
     Widget      w;
     caddr_t     client_data;
     caddr_t     call_data;
   {
     Arg         wargs[2];
     Dimension   width, height;
     /*
      *  Get the current width and height of the widget.
      */
     XtSetArg(wargs[0], XtNwidth,  &width);
     XtSetArg(wargs[1], XtNheight, &height);
     XtGetValues(w, wargs, 2);
     /*
      * Increment the width and height by 10 pixels before
      * setting the size.
      */
     width  +=10;
```

```
height +=10;
XtSetArg(wargs[0], XtNwidth, width);
XtSetArg(wargs[1], XtNheight, height);
XtSetValues(w, wargs, 2);
}
```

Fig. 13.2 shows the layout of the **rowtest** example after this function has been called several times.

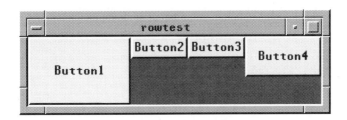

Figure 13.2 Handling resize requests.

A second **XmNactivateCallback** function is registered for **Button2**. The **unmanage()** function calls **XtUnmanageChild()**, and causes the Row widget's **ChangeManaged()** method to be invoked to recompute the widget layout. This function is defined as:

```
void unmanage(w, client_data, call_data)
   Widget     w;
   caddr_t    client_data;
   caddr_t    call_data;
{
  XtUnmanageChild(w);
}
```

The last **XmNactivateCallback** function is registered with **Button3**. This function calls **XtManageChild()** to add **Button2** back to the Row widget's managed list.

```
void manage(w, button, call_data)
   Widget     w;
   Widget     button;
   caddr_t    call_data;
{
  XtManageChild(button);
}
```

Fig. 13.3 shows the how the Row widget adjusts the layout when **Button2** is unmanaged.

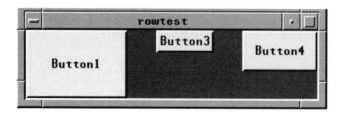

Figure 13.3 Row widget after unmanaging Button2.

13.3 SUMMARY

This chapter introduced the architecture of a composite widget. All composite widgets are subclasses of the Composite widget class. The distinguishing feature of a composite widget is that it can manage other widgets. Composite widgets are primarily responsible for managing the geometry of its children. Widgets can never resize or move themselves directly; instead, they must request their parent to do it for them. Composite widgets define several methods solely for the purpose of managing children.

An understanding of how composite widgets are implemented and how they negotiate and control widget geometries can help an application programmer to choose the best widget for a given task. This chapter explored composite widgets by building a simple example, the Row widget class. We can see from this example that the widget programmer has a large amount of latitude in determining the management policy of its children. The layout policy used by the Row widget is completely arbitrary, and others can easily be imagined. For example, instead of denying resize requests when no more room is available, the Row widget could allow the request, but reduce the size of all other children to create the extra space. Different policies regarding spacing between children are also possible. Many manager widgets provide resources that allow the application programmer to alter the layout policy of a composite widget. This makes the widget much more flexible, but increases the complexity of the widget.

The next chapter discusses the Constraint widget class, a powerful subclass of the Composite widget class.

14

CREATING CONSTRAINT WIDGETS

In the last chapter, we saw how composite widgets manage the layout of other widgets. Composite widgets usually apply their management policy uniformly without regard to any special characteristics of their children. The Constraint widget class is a subclass of the Composite widget class that manages its children based on additional information associated with each child. The class name comes from the fact that this information often takes the form of some constraint. For example, one might like to impose the constraint, "The ScrollBar widget must always be to the left of the Text widget."

A constraint widget has all the responsibilities of a composite widget, but must also manage the constraints imposed on each widget. This chapter discusses the Constraint widget class and presents an example of a constraint widget whose children represent nodes of an acyclic hierarchical graph.

14.1 ARCHITECTURE OF CONSTRAINT WIDGETS

The Constraint widget class's architecture is similar to that of the Composite widget class. However, the Constraint widget class adds methods and resources used to handle constraints. Every constraint widget includes the **CoreClassPart**, the **CompositeClassPart**, and the **ConstraintClassPart** as the first components of its class record.

```
typedef struct _ConstraintClassRec {
    CoreClassPart         core_class;
    CompositeClassPart    composite_class;
    ConstraintClassPart   constraint_class;
} ConstraintClassRec;
```

The **ConstraintClassPart** structure contains information and methods used by every constraint widget.

```
typedef struct _ConstraintClassPart {
    XtResourceList    resources;
    Cardinal          num_resources;
    Cardinal          constraint_size;
    XtInitProc        initialize;
    XtWidgetProc      destroy;
    XtSetValuesFunc   set_values;
    caddr_t           extension;
} ConstraintClassPart;
```

In addition to the basic resource list contained in the Core class part of every widget class, the **ConstraintClassPart** of a constraint widget's class record contains a constraint resource list. The resource manager uses this resource list to initialize the constraints structure attached to each child widget. Every widget has a pointer to a constraint structure in the **CorePart** of its instance record (See Chapter 12). This pointer is set to **NULL** unless the child is managed by a constraint widget. When a widget is managed by a constraint widget, the Intrinsics allocates space for a constraint structure, the size of which is determined by the **constraint_size** member of the parent's **ConstraintClassPart** structure. The **ConstraintClassPart** structure also contains pointers to three new methods that initialize and manage the constraints of the composite widget's children.

   The Constraint widget class's instance record is defined as:

```
typedef struct _ConstraintRec {
    CorePart        core;
    CompositePart   composite;
    ConstraintPart  constraint;
} ConstraintRec, *ConstraintWidget;
```

The Constraint widget class requires no additional fields in its instance record, so **ConstraintPart** is defined as a dummy structure.

```
typedef struct _ConstraintPart {
    int    ignore;
} ConstraintPart;
```

Each constraint widget must also define the constraint structure attached to each of its children. This structure is specific to each particular type of constraint widget and the policy it supports. The example in the following section shows how this is done.

14.2   A CONSTRAINT WIDGET: THE TREE WIDGET

The rest of this chapter presents an example of a constraint widget, the Tree widget class. A Tree widget organizes its children as a hierarchical graph according to a constraint that specifies each child widget's position in the tree.[1] Applications can use the resource manager to specify this constraint when the widget is created. The following sections look at the public and private header files used by the Tree widget and then discuss the Tree widget's methods.

14.2.1 The Tree Private Header File: TreeP.h

The Tree widget's private header file defines the class record, the instance record, and the constraint record attached to each widget managed by the Tree widget. The Tree widget does not require any additional resources in the class record, so its contribution is a dummy structure.

```
typedef struct _XsTreeClassPart {
    int           ignore;
} XsTreeClassPart;
```

The Tree widget's complete class record is defined as:

```
typedef struct _XsTreeClassRec {
    CoreClassPart       core_class;
    CompositeClassPart  composite_class;
    ConstraintClassPart constraint_class;
    XsTreeClassPart     tree_class;
} XsTreeClassRec;

extern XsTreeClassRec XstreeClassRec;
```

The Tree widget's instance record contains auxiliary information used to position the nodes in the tree and draw connecting lines. This information includes the minimum and maximum spacing between nodes of the tree, the foreground color and graphics context used to draw lines connecting the nodes, and some auxiliary data used by the methods that calculate the position of each widget. The instance record also includes a member that points to a widget used as the root of the tree. The tree widget creates this **tree_root** widget to

---

1. We have already used many of the terms associated with trees to refer to the X window and widget hierarchies, as well as the inheritance relationship between widget classes. Therefore, in the following discussion each element of the tree is referred to as a node. Each node, except for the root of the tree, has a super node and can also have subnodes.

guarantee that every child widget has a super node. This simplifies the tree layout calculations. The **XsTreePart** structure is defined as:

```
typedef struct {
    Dimension       h_min_space;
    Dimension       v_min_space;
    Pixel           foreground;
    GC              gc;
    TreeOffsetPtr   horizontal;
    TreeOffsetPtr   vertical;
    Widget          tree_root;
} XsTreePart;
```

The type **TreeOffsetPtr** is a pointer to an auxiliary structure used by the functions that compute the tree layout. This structure is defined as:

```
typedef struct {
    Dimension   *array;
    int         size;
}  TreeOffset, *TreeOffsetPtr;
```

The Tree widget's complete instance record is defined as:

```
typedef struct _XsTreeRec {
    CorePart        core;
    CompositePart   composite;
    ConstraintPart  constraint;
    XsTreePart      tree;
}  XsTreeRec;
```

We must also define the constraint structure that the Tree widget attaches to its children. This structure is defined as

```
typedef struct _TreeConstraintsRec {
    TreeConstraintsPart tree;
} TreeConstraintsRec, *TreeConstraints;
```

where the **TreeConstraintsPart** structure is defined as:

```
typedef struct _TreeConstraintsPart {
    Widget      super_node;
    WidgetList  sub_nodes;
    long        n_sub_nodes;
    long        max_sub_nodes;
    Position    x, y;
} TreeConstraintsPart;
```

This structure contains the child's super node, a list of the child's subnodes, and also records the current length and maximum size of the subnode list. The tree layout algorithm uses the **x** and **y** members when calculating each widget's position. Defining the constraint record as a structure within a structure allows us to inherit constraints by adding in each superclasses constraint part, in the same way as we inherit the class parts and instance record parts.

Since we will often be retrieving the constraint record from a child of the Tree widget, it is convenient to define a macro to extract the **constraints** member of the child widget and coerce it to the proper type. This can be done as:

```
#define TREE_CONSTRAINT(w) \
                 ((TreeConstraints)((w)->core.constraints))
```

14.2.2 The Tree Public Header File: Tree.h

The Tree widget's public header file is straightforward and similar to the examples in previous chapters. In addition to the type declarations, the header file defines the resource strings that refer to resources defined by the Tree widget.

```
/**********************************************************
 * Tree.h: Public header file for the Tree widget
 **********************************************************/
#ifndef TREE_H
#define TREE_H
extern WidgetClass  XstreeWidgetClass;

typedef struct _XsTreeClassRec *XsTreeWidgetClass;
typedef struct _XsTreeRec       *XsTreeWidget;

#define XtNhorizontalSpace      "horizontalSpace"
#define XtNverticalSpace        "verticalSpace"
#define XtCPad                  "Pad"
#define XtNsuperNode            "superNode"
#define XtCSuperNode            "SuperNode"
#endif TREE_H
```

14.2.3 The Tree Widget Source File: Tree.c

The file Tree.c contains the declaration of the class record and the Tree widget's private methods. The file begins by including the Xt Intrinsics private header file, the Core, Composite, and Constraint widget's private header files, and also the public and private Tree widget header files.

```
/*******************************************************
 * Tree.c: The Tree Widget Source File
 *******************************************************/

#include   <X11/Intrinsic.h>
#include   <X11/IntrinsicP.h>
#include   <X11/StringDefs.h>
#include   <X11/CoreP.h>
#include   <X11/CompositeP.h>
#include   <X11/ConstrainP.h>
#include   "Tree.h"
#include   "TreeP.h"
#define    MAX(a,b) ((a) > (b) ? (a) : (b))
```

Forward declarations of the methods and other functions used by the Tree widget come next, followed by the Tree widget's resource lists. This resource list allows applications and users to use the resource manager to control the minimum horizontal and vertical space between nodes and also the foreground color used to draw lines between nodes.

```
static void                Initialize();
static void                ConstraintInitialize();
static void                ConstraintDestroy();
static Boolean             ConstraintSetValues();
static Boolean             SetValues();
static XtGeometryResult    GeometryManager();
static void                ChangeManaged();
static void                insert_new_node();
static void                delete_node();
static void                new_layout();
static void                Redisplay();
static TreeOffsetPtr       create_offset();
static int                 compute_positions();
static void                shift_subtree();
static void                set_positions();
static void                reset();
static Position            current_position();
static void                set_current_position();
static Position            sum_of_positions();

static XtResource resources[] = {
  {XtNhorizontalSpace,XtCSpace,XtRDimension,sizeof(Dimension),
    XtOffset(XsTreeWidget, tree.h_min_space), XtRString,"15" },
  {XtNverticalSpace,XtCSpace, XtRDimension,sizeof (Dimension),
```

```
    XtOffset(XsTreeWidget, tree.v_min_space), XtRString,"5"  },
  {XtNforeground, XtCForeground, XtRPixel, sizeof (Pixel),
   XtOffset(XsTreeWidget, tree.foreground), XtRString,"Black"},
};
```

Constraint widgets usually specify an additional resource list used by the resource manager to set the values in the constraint part of each child widget. The Tree widget's constraint resource list allows applications to use **XtSetValues()** to specify each widget's super node.

```
static XtResource treeConstraintResources[] = {
  {XtNsuperNode, XtCSuperNode, XtRPointer, sizeof(Widget),
   XtOffset(TreeConstraints, tree.super_node),
   XtRPointer, NULL},
};
```

14.2.3.1 The Class Record

Like each of the examples in previous chapters, the Tree widget's class record is initialized entirely at compile time, as follows:

```
XsTreeClassRec XstreeClassRec = {
  {
    /* core_class fields  */
    (WidgetClass) &constraintClassRec,/* superclass        */
    "Tree",                           /* class_name        */
    sizeof(XsTreeRec),                /* widget_size       */
    NULL,                             /* class_init        */
    NULL,                             /* class_part_init   */
    FALSE,                            /* class_inited      */
    Initialize,                       /* initialize        */
    NULL,                             /* initialize_hook   */
    XtInheritRealize,                 /* realize           */
    NULL,                             /* actions           */
    0,                                /* num_actions       */
    resources,                        /* resources         */
    XtNumber(resources),              /* num_resources     */
    NULLQUARK,                        /* xrm_class         */
    TRUE,                             /* compress_motion   */
    TRUE,                             /* compress_exposure */
    TRUE,                             /* compress_enterleave*/
    TRUE,                             /* visible_interest  */
    NULL,                             /* destroy           */
    NULL,                             /* resize            */
```

```
            Redisplay,                              /* expose              */
            SetValues,                              /* set_values          */
            NULL,                                   /* set_values_hook     */
            XtInheritSetValuesAlmost,               /* set_values_almost   */
            NULL,                                   /* get_values_hook     */
            NULL,                                   /* accept_focus        */
            XtVersion,                              /* version             */
            NULL,                                   /* callback_private    */
            NULL,                                   /* tm_table            */
            NULL,                                   /* query_geometry      */
            NULL,                                   /* display_accelerator*/
            NULL,                                   /* extension           */
        },
        {
            /* composite_class fields */
            GeometryManager,                        /* geometry_manager    */
            ChangeManaged,                          /* change_managed      */
            XtInheritInsertChild,                   /* insert_child        */
            XtInheritDeleteChild,                   /* delete_child        */
            NULL,                                   /* extension           */
        },
        {
            /* constraint_class fields */
            treeConstraintResources,                /* subresources        */
            XtNumber(treeConstraintResources),      /* subresource_count   */
            sizeof(TreeConstraintsRec),             /* constraint_size     */
            ConstraintInitialize,                   /* initialize          */
            ConstraintDestroy,                      /* destroy             */
            ConstraintSetValues,                    /* set_values          */
            NULL,                                   /* extension           */
        },
        {
            /* Tree class fields */
            0,                                      /* ignore              */
        }
    };
```

The Tree class pointer is declared internally as a pointer to this **XstreeClassRec** structure:

```
WidgetClass XstreeWidgetClass = (WidgetClass) &XstreeClassRec;
```

14.2.3.2   Methods

The primary difference between a constraint widget and a composite widget is the additional methods that initialize and set the values of the resources in each child widget's constraint record. The **Initialize()** and **SetValues()** methods manage the constraint widget's resources, while the **ConstraintInitialize()** and **ConstraintSetValues()** methods manage the constraints attached to each child widget.

The Initialize() Method

The Intrinsics invokes the Tree widget's **Initialize()** method when the Tree widget is created. The **Initialize()** method first checks that the width and height of the widget are greater than zero, and then creates a graphics context used to draw the lines connecting the nodes of the tree. Next it creates a widget that serves as the root of the tree. This widget is created, but never managed. It is not visible to the user and only exists to simplify the tree layout calculations. Finally, the horizontal and vertical fields of the Tree widget's instance record are initialized. We will discuss the use of these fields and the function **create_offset()** along with the tree layout algorithm.

```
static void Initialize(request, new)
    XsTreeWidget request, new;
{
  Arg        wargs[2];
  XGCValues values;
  XtGCMask   valueMask;
  /*
   * Make sure the widget's width and height are
   * greater than zero.
   */
  if (request->core.width <= 0)
    new->core.width = 5;
  if (request->core.height <= 0)
    new->core.height = 5;
  /*
   * Create a graphics context for the connecting lines.
   */
  valueMask = GCForeground | GCBackground;
  values.foreground = new->tree.foreground;
  values.background = new->core.background_pixel;
  new->tree.gc = XtGetGC (new, valueMask, &values);
  /*
   * Create the hidden root widget.
   */
  new->tree.tree_root = (Widget) NULL;
```

```
    XtSetArg(wargs[0], XtNwidth, 1);
    XtSetArg(wargs[1], XtNheight, 1);
    new->tree.tree_root =
            XtCreateWidget("root", widgetClass, new, wargs, 2);
    /*
     * Allocate the tables used by the layout
     * algorithm.
     */
    new->tree.horizontal = create_offset(10);
    new->tree.vertical   = create_offset(10);
}
```

The ConstraintInitialize() Method

Every constraint widget also has a **ConstraintInitialize()** method. The Intrinsics invokes this method each time a child of the Tree widget is created, to initialize the child's constraint record. The arguments **request** and **new** are versions of a child of the Tree widget, not the Tree widget itself. The **request** parameter is copy of the widget with all resources as originally requested by a combination of command line arguments, the contents of the resource database and widget defaults. The **new** parameter is the widget after it has been processed by all superclasses's **ConstraintInitialize()** methods. The Tree widget's **ConstraintInitialize()** method sets the **n_sub_nodes** and **sub_nodes** members of each child's constraint record to zero and **NULL**, respectively, and checks to see if the widget has a super node. If so, the child widget is added to the super node widget's list of subnodes. Otherwise, the widget becomes a subnode of the **tree_root** widget created by the Tree widget. Notice the test to determine whether the **tree_root** widget exists. This prevents the **tree_root** widget from attempting to add itself recursively to its own list of subnodes when it is created.

```
    static void ConstraintInitialize(request, new)
        Widget request, new;
    {
      TreeConstraints tree_const = TREE_CONSTRAINT(new);
      XsTreeWidget tw = (XsTreeWidget) new->core.parent;
      /*
       * Initialize the widget to have no sub-nodes.
       */
      tree_const->tree.n_sub_nodes = 0;
      tree_const->tree.max_sub_nodes = 0;
      tree_const->tree.sub_nodes = (WidgetList) NULL;
      tree_const->tree.x = tree_const->tree.y = 0;
      /*
```

```
 * If this widget has a super-node, add it to that
 * widget' sub-nodes list. Otherwise make it a sub-node of
 * the tree_root widget.
 */
if(tree_const->tree.super_node)
  insert_new_node(tree_const->tree.super_node, new);
else
  if(tw->tree.tree_root)
    insert_new_node(tw->tree.tree_root, new);
}
```

The SetValues() Method

The **SetValues()** method is called when a Tree widget resource is altered. The Tree widget's **SetValues()** method must check the values of three resources. If the Tree widget's foreground color is altered, a new graphics context is created and the **redraw** flag is set to **TRUE**. If either of the horizontal or vertical space resources is modified, **SetValues()** calls the auxiliary functions **new_layout()** to reposition all children. Finally, **SetValues()** returns the value of the **redraw** flag, which indicates whether or not the Intrinsics should force the window to be redrawn.

```
static Boolean SetValues(current, request, new)
    XsTreeWidget current, request, new;
{
 Boolean    redraw = FALSE;
 XGCValues values;
 XtGCMask   valueMask;
 /*
  * If the foreground color has changed, redo the GC's
  * and indicate a redraw.
  */
 if (new->tree.foreground != current->tree.foreground ||
     new->core.background_pixel !=
                           current->core.background_pixel){
   valueMask          = GCForeground | GCBackground;
   values.foreground = new->tree.foreground;
   values.background = new->core.background_pixel;
   XtReleaseGC(new, new->tree.gc);
   new->tree.gc     = XtGetGC (new, valueMask, &values);
   redraw = TRUE;
 }
 /*
```

```
       * If the minimum spacing has changed, recalculate the
       * tree layout. new_layout() does a redraw, so we don't
       * need SetValues to do another one.
       */
      if (new->tree.v_min_space != current->tree.v_min_space ||
          new->tree.h_min_space != current->tree.h_min_space){
        new_layout(new);
        redraw = FALSE;
      }
      return (redraw);
    }
```

The ConstraintSetValues() Method

The Intrinsics invokes a widget's **ConstraintSetValues()** method when a child's constraint resource is altered. The only resource in the Tree widget's constraint resource list is the **XtNsuperNode** resource. If this resource has changed, the Tree widget calls the function **delete_node()** to remove the affected child widget from the subnode list of the widget's current super node. Then the method **insert_node()** is called to add the widget to the new super node's list of subnodes. Notice that the **new** widget structure is passed to both of these methods. This is important because each of these methods stores a pointer to the widget in a list. The **new** structure is the actual widget. The other arguments are temporary copies of the widget's instance record, created by the Intrinsics before calling the **ConstraintSetValues()** method. Finally, **ConstraintSetValues()** calls the auxiliary function **new_layout()** to recalculate the position of each child widget.

```
    static Boolean ConstraintSetValues(current, request, new)
        Widget current, request, new;
    {
     TreeConstraints newconst = TREE_CONSTRAINT(new);
     TreeConstraints current_const = TREE_CONSTRAINT(current);
     XsTreeWidget tw = (XsTreeWidget) new->core.parent;
     /*
      * If the super_node field has changed, remove the widget
      * from the old widget's sub_nodes list and add it to the
      * new one.
      */
     if(current_const->tree.super_node !=
                                    newconst->tree.super_node){
       if(current_const->tree.super_node)
         delete_node(current_const->tree.super_node, new);
       if(newconst->tree.super_node)
```

```
      insert_new_node(newconst->tree.super_node, new);
    /*
     * If the Tree widget has been realized,
     * compute new layout.
     */
    if(XtIsRealized(tw))
      new_layout(tw);
    }
    return (FALSE);
}
```

The auxiliary functions **insert_node()** and **delete_node()** are responsible for
managing the **sub_nodes** list in each child's constraint record. Each time a new subnode is
added, the **insert_node()** function checks whether the list is large enough to contain another widget. If not, the list must be enlarged using **XtRealloc()**. Then the function adds
the widget to the end of the list and increments the **n_sub_nodes** index.

```
static void insert_new_node(super_node, node)
    Widget super_node, node;
{
  TreeConstraints super_const = TREE_CONSTRAINT(super_node);
  TreeConstraints node_const = TREE_CONSTRAINT(node);
  int index = super_const->tree.n_sub_nodes;

  node_const->tree.super_node = super_node;
  /*
   * If there is no more room in the sub_nodes array,
   * allocate additional space.
   */
  if(super_const->tree.n_sub_nodes ==
                            super_const->tree.max_sub_nodes){
    super_const->tree.max_sub_nodes +=
                    (super_const->tree.max_sub_nodes / 2) + 2;
    super_const->tree.sub_nodes =
      (WidgetList) XtRealloc(super_const->tree.sub_nodes,
                            (super_const->tree.max_sub_nodes) *
                            sizeof(Widget));
  }
  /*
   * Add the sub_node in the next available slot and
   * increment the counter.
   */
```

```
    super_const->tree.sub_nodes[index] = node;
    super_const->tree.n_sub_nodes++;
}
```

The function **delete_node()** performs the opposite operation, removing a widget from the list of subnodes, closing any gap in the list caused by the removal of an entry, and decrementing the **n_sub_nodes** counter.

```
static void delete_node(super_node, node)
    Widget  super_node, node;
{
  TreeConstraints node_const = TREE_CONSTRAINT(node);
  TreeConstraints super_const;
  int             pos, i;
  /*
   * Make sure the super_node exists.
   */
  if(!super_node) return;

  super_const = TREE_CONSTRAINT(super_node);
  /*
   * Find the sub_node on its super_node's list.
   */
  for (pos = 0; pos < super_const->tree.n_sub_nodes; pos++)
    if (super_const->tree.sub_nodes[pos] == node)
      break;
  if (pos == super_const->tree.n_sub_nodes) return;
  /*
   * Decrement the number of sub_nodes
   */
  super_const->tree.n_sub_nodes--;
  /*
   * Fill in the gap left by the sub_node.
   * Zero the last slot for good luck.
   */
  for (i = pos; i < super_const->tree.n_sub_nodes; i++)
    super_const->tree.sub_nodes[i] =
                          super_const->tree.sub_nodes[i+1];
 super_const->tree.sub_nodes[super_const->tree.n_sub_nodes]=0;
}
```

The ConstraintDestroy() Method

The **ConstraintDestroy()** method is called whenever a managed child of a constraint widget is destroyed. It provides the constraint widget the opportunity to make any adjustments required by the deletion of a child widget. The method is called with only one argument, which indicates the widget being destroyed. For example, the Tree widget needs to remove any pointers to the widget from other children's constraint records, and relocate any subnodes of the widget being destroyed. The tree widget simply moves these subnodes to the **sub_nodes** list of the super node of the widget being destroyed, and triggers a new layout.

```
static void ConstraintDestroy(w)
     Widget w;
{
  TreeConstraints tree_const = TREE_CONSTRAINT(w);
  int i;
 /*
  * Remove the widget from its parent's sub-nodes list and
  * make all this widget's sub-nodes sub-nodes of the parent.
  */
  if(tree_const->tree.super_node) {
    delete_node(tree_const->tree.super_node, w);
    for(i=0;i< tree_const->tree.n_sub_nodes; i++)
      insert_new_node(tree_const->tree.super_node,
                      tree_const->tree.sub_nodes[i]);
  }
  new_layout(w->core.parent);
}
```

The Constraint Tree

Now that we have introduced the functions used to initialize and modify the constraint records of the Tree widget's children, let's pause and look closer at the structure created by these constraints. The following small code segment creates a Tree widget that manages three children.

```
tree = XtCreateManagedWidget("TreeTest", XstreeWidgetClass,
                             toplevel, NULL, 0);
widg1 =  XtCreateManagedWidget("One", widgetClass,
                               tree, NULL, 0);
XtSetArg(wargs[0], XtNsuperNode, widg1);
widg2 =  XtCreateManagedWidget("Two", widgetClass,
                               tree, wargs, 1);
XtSetArg(wargs[0], XtNsuperNode, widg1);
widg3 =  XtCreateManagedWidget("Three", widgetClass,
                               tree, wargs, 1);
```

Let's consider the contents of the constraint record of each of these widgets and also the dummy **tree_root** widget created by the Tree widget at the point after **widg3** has been created. The **tree_root** widget's **super_node** field is **NULL**, and its **sub_nodes** list contains a single widget, **widg1**. The **super_node** field of **widg2**'s constraint record contains a pointer to the **tree_root** widget, and its **sub_nodes** list contains two widgets, **widg2**, and **widg3**. The **sub_nodes** fields of **widg2** and **widg3** contain a pointer to **widg1**, and their **sub_nodes** list is empty. Fig. 14.1 shows how these pointers create a hierarchical graph.

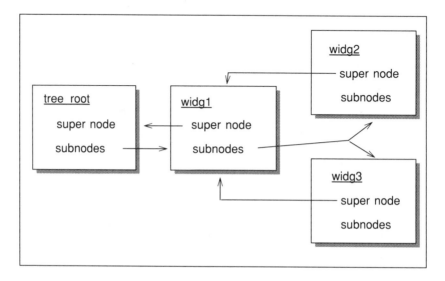

Figure 14.1 A hierarchical constraints structure.

The GeometryManager() Method

The Intrinsics invokes the Tree widget's **GeometryManager()** method when a child of the Tree widget makes a geometry request. The Tree widget's management policy does not allow a child to change its position, because the tree layout algorithm determines the position of every widget. However, the geometry manager grants all size requests without question. **GeometryManager()** calls the auxiliary function, **new_layout()**, to recompute and redraw the tree layout before returning **XtGeometryYes**.

```
static XtGeometryResult GeometryManager(w, request, reply)
    Widget              w;
    XtWidgetGeometry    *request;
    XtWidgetGeometry    *reply;
{
```

```
XsTreeWidget tw = (XsTreeWidget) w->core.parent;
/*
 * No position changes allowed!.
 */
if ((request->request_mode & CWX && request->x!=w->core.x)
    ||(request->request_mode & CWY && request->y!=w->core.y))
  return (XtGeometryNo);
/*
 * Allow all resize requests.
 */
if (request->request_mode & CWWidth)
  w->core.width = request->width;
if (request->request_mode & CWHeight)
  w->core.height = request->height;
if (request->request_mode & CWBorderWidth)
  w->core.border_width = request->border_width;
/*
 *  Compute the new layout based on the new widget sizes;
 */
new_layout(tw);
return (XtGeometryYes);
}
```

The ChangeManaged() Method

The Intrinsics invokes the Tree widget's **ChangeManaged()** method whenever the Tree widget's set of managed children changes. **ChangeManaged()** simply calls **new_layout()** to calculate the desired position of all children.[2]

```
static void ChangeManaged(tw)
    XsTreeWidget tw;
{
  new_layout(tw);
}
```

---

2. In most constraint widgets, this method should also update the constraint records of all affected widgets when a widget is managed or unmanaged. However, this brings up several sticky issues in the Tree widget (for example, what should be done with a widget's subnodes when the widget is unmanaged, but the subnodes are still managed?), and complicates the Tree widget example beyond the scope of this example. Therefore, this example treats managed and unmanaged children in exactly the same way.

The Redisplay() Method

The **Redisplay()** method is called whenever an **Expose** event occurs within in Tree widget's window. This method is also called by some other Tree widget methods to redraw the lines connecting the nodes of the tree. This method loops through each child on the Tree widget's list of children, drawing a line from the right edge to the left edge of each of the widget's subnodes.

```
static void Redisplay (w, event, region)
      XsTreeWidget    w;
      XEvent          *event;
      Region          region;
{
  int               i, j;
  TreeConstraints tree_const;
  Widget            child;
  /*
   * If the Tree widget is visible, visit each managed child.
   */
  if(w->core.visible)
    for (i = 0; i < w -> composite.num_children; i++){
      child = w -> composite.children[i];
      tree_const = TREE_CONSTRAINT(child);
      /*
       * Draw a line between the right edge of each widget
       * and the left edge of each of its sub_nodes. Don't
       * draw lines from the fake tree_root.
       */
      if(child != w->tree.tree_root &&
        tree_const->tree.n_sub_nodes)
        for (j = 0; j < tree_const->tree.n_sub_nodes; j++)
          XDrawLine(XtDisplay(w), XtWindow(w),
                    w->tree.gc,
                    child->core.x + child->core.width,
                    child->core.y + child->core.height / 2,
                    tree_const->tree.sub_nodes[j]->core.x,
                    tree_const->tree.sub_nodes[j]->core.y +
                  tree_const->tree.sub_nodes[j]->core.height/2);
    }
}
```

14.2.3.3   The Tree Layout Procedures

The previous sections presented each of the Tree widget's methods. The remaining functions are auxiliary functions used to determine the position of each child widget. The layout algorithm uses a few simple rules of thumb, intended to produce an aesthetically pleasing tree layout. The basic rules, worded to apply to trees that are laid out horizontally, are:

*   The overall tree should be as narrow, top to bottom, as possible.
*   Each node should be placed as close as possible to its siblings.
*   Each node should be centered to the left of its subnodes.
*   Nodes at the same level should begin at the same horizontal position.
*   The shape of any given subtree should be independent of its position in the tree.

The concept of the tree layout algorithm is simple. The first node of each level is initially positioned at y coordinate 0, and each successive node on the same level is placed below its neighbor. After the positions of all nodes within a particular branch are determined, the super node of the branch is centered to the left of its subnodes. If this position is less than the next available position on the super node's level, we must shift the entire subtree. The offset necessary to move the super node to the next available position at its level is calculated and the entire sub-tree is shifted. This function establishes the y coordinate of each widget. To determine the x position of each widget, we store the maximum width of all nodes at each level. Once the y position of each widget has been computed, this information is used to determine the final x position of each widget.

The function **new_layout()** provides the top-level interface to the layout algorithm. The function resets the auxiliary tables used to store temporary information, then calls other functions to do the real work.

```
static void new_layout(tw)
    XsTreeWidget    tw;
{
  /*
   *  Reset the auxiliary tables.
   */
  reset(tw->tree.vertical);
  reset(tw->tree.horizontal);
  /*
   * Compute each widget's x,y position
   */
  compute_positions(tw, tw->tree.tree_root, 0);
  /*
   * Move each widget into place.
   */
  set_positions(tw, tw->tree.tree_root, 0, 0);
  /*
```

```
 * If realized, clear the Tree widget's window.
 * The resulting Expose event will result in a
 * call to the widget's Redisplay() method.
 */
if(XtIsRealized(tw))
   XClearArea(XtDisplay(tw), XtWindow(tw), 0, 0, 0, 0, TRUE);
}
```

The function **reset()** initializes two data structures that store the next available position in the vertical direction and the maximum width of the widgets on each level in the horizontal direction. We will look at this data structure and its related functions shortly.

The main portion of the tree layout algorithm is handled by the auxiliary function **compute_positions()**.

```
static int compute_positions(tw, w, level)
    XsTreeWidget tw;
    Widget       w;
    long         level;
{
 Position          current_hpos, current_vpos;
 int               i, depth = 0;
 TreeConstraints tree_const = TREE_CONSTRAINT(w);
 /*
  * Get the current positions for this level.
  */
 current_hpos = current_position(tw->tree.horizontal, level);
 current_vpos = current_position(tw->tree.vertical, level);
 /*
  * Set the current horizontal width to the max widths of all
  * widgets at this level.
  */
 set_current_position(tw->tree.horizontal, level,
                    MAX(current_hpos, w->core.width));
 /*
  * If the node has no sub_nodes, just set the vertical
  * position to the next available space.
  */
 if(tree_const->tree.n_sub_nodes == 0){
   tree_const->tree.y = current_vpos;
 }
 else {
   Widget            first_kid, last_kid;
   TreeConstraints const1, const2;
```

```
    Position          top, bottom;
/*
 * If the node has sub_nodes, recursively figure the
 * positions of each sub_node.
 */
    for(i = 0; i < tree_const->tree.n_sub_nodes; i++)
      depth = compute_positions(tw,
                                tree_const->tree.sub_nodes[i],
                                level + 1);
/*
 * Now that the vertical positions of all children are
 * known, find the vertical extent of all sub_nodes.
 */
    first_kid= tree_const->tree.sub_nodes[0];
    last_kid =
      tree_const->tree.sub_nodes[tree_const->tree.n_sub_nodes-1];
    const1   = TREE_CONSTRAINT(first_kid);
    const2   = TREE_CONSTRAINT(last_kid);
    top      = const1->tree.y + first_kid->core.height / 2;
    bottom   = const2->tree.y + last_kid->core.height / 2;
/*
 * Set the node's position to the center of its sub_nodes.
 */
    tree_const->tree.y = (top + bottom)/2 - (w->core.height/ 2);
/*
 * If this position is less than the next available
 * position, correct it to be the next available
 * position, calculate the amount by which all sub_nodes
 * must be shifted, and shift the entire sub-tree.
 */
    if(tree_const->tree.y < current_vpos){
      Dimension offset = current_vpos - tree_const->tree.y;
      for(i = 0; i < tree_const->tree.n_sub_nodes; i++)
        shift_subtree(tree_const->tree.sub_nodes[i], offset);
     /*
      * Adjust the next available space at all levels below
      * the current level.
      */
      for(i = level + 1; i <= depth; i++){
        Position pos = current_position(tw->tree.vertical, i);
        set_current_position(tw->tree.vertical, i, pos+offset);
      }
```

```
            tree_const->tree.y = current_vpos;
          }
       }
    /*
     * Record the current vertical position at this level.
     */
    set_current_position(tw->tree.vertical, level,
                         tw->tree.v_min_space +
                         tree_const->tree.y + w->core.height);
    return (MAX(depth, level));
  }
```

The function **shift_subtree()** moves the given widget's entire subtree by an integer offset.

```
    static void shift_subtree(w, offset)
        Widget      w;
        Dimension   offset;
    {
      int               i;
      TreeConstraints tree_const = TREE_CONSTRAINT(w);
      /*
       * Shift the node by the offset.
       */
      tree_const->tree.y += offset;
      /*
       * Shift each sub-node into place.
       */
      for(i=0; i< tree_const->tree.n_sub_nodes; i++)
        shift_subtree(tree_const->tree.sub_nodes[i], offset);
    }
```

Once the layout of all widgets has been determined, the function **set_positions()** sets the x position of each widget and calls **XtMoveWidget()** to move each widget into place. If all children don't fit in the Tree widget, this function makes a geometry request to the Tree widget's parent to attempt to enlarge the Tree widget.

```
    static void set_positions(tw, w, level)
        XsTreeWidget tw;
        Widget       w;
        int          level;
    {
     int               i;
     Dimension         replyWidth = 0, replyHeight = 0;
```

```
    XtGeometryResult   result;

    if(w){
     TreeConstraints tree_const = TREE_CONSTRAINT(w);
     /*
      * Add up the sum of the width's of all nodes to this
      * depth, and use it as the x position.
      */
     tree_const->tree.x = (level * tw->tree.h_min_space) +
                    sum_of_positions(tw->tree.horizontal, level);
     /*
      * Move the widget into position.
      */
     XtMoveWidget (w, tree_const->tree.x, tree_const->tree.y);
     /*
      * If the widget position plus its width or height doesn't
      * fit in the tree, ask if the tree can be resized.
      */
     if(tw->core.width < tree_const->tree.x + w->core.width ||
        tw->core.height < tree_const->tree.y + w->core.height){
        result =
          XtMakeResizeRequest(tw, MAX(tw->core.width,
                                      tree_const->tree.x +
                                      w->core.width),
                                  MAX(tw->core.height,
                                      tree_const->tree.y +
                                      w->core.height),
                              &replyWidth, &replyHeight);
        /*
         * Accept any compromise.
         */
        if (result == XtGeometryAlmost)
          XtMakeResizeRequest (tw, replyWidth, replyHeight,
                               NULL, NULL);
     }
     /*
      * Set the positions of all sub_nodes.
      */
     for(i=0; i< tree_const->tree.n_sub_nodes;i++)
        set_positions(tw, tree_const->tree.sub_nodes[i], level+1);
    }
}
```

The remaining functions store and retrieve a value from a dynamically resizable array. The layout functions use these functions to store the next available position and the maximum width of each level. The function **create_offset()** allocates an array of the given size.

```
static TreeOffsetPtr create_offset(size)
    long size;
{
 TreeOffsetPtr  offset =
                    (TreeOffsetPtr) XtMalloc(sizeof(TreeOffset));
 offset->size = size;
 offset->array =
                (Dimension *) XtMalloc(size * sizeof(Dimension));
 return (offset);
}
```

The **reset()** function zeroes all entries in a table.

```
static void reset(offset)
    TreeOffsetPtr offset;
{
  long i;
  for(i=0; i< offset->size; i++)
    offset->array[i] = 0;
}
```

The function **current_position()** returns the value in an given position in a table. If the requested position is greater than the size of the table, the function returns zero.

```
static Position current_position(offset, position)
    TreeOffsetPtr  offset;
    long           position;
{
  if(position >= offset->size)
    return (0);
  return (offset->array[position]);
 }
```

The function **set_current_position()** stores a value in a table at a given index position. If the index is larger than the size of the table, the table is enlarged using **XtRealloc()**.

```
static void set_current_position(offset, index, value)
    TreeOffsetPtr offset;
    int           index;
    Dimension     value;
```

```
{
  if(index >= offset->size){
    offset->size = index + index / 2;
    offset->array =
      (Dimension *) XtRealloc(offset->array,
                              offset->size * sizeof(Dimension));
  }
  offset->array[index] = value;
}
```

The **sum_of_positions()** function returns the sum of all values in a table up to the given position.

```
static Position sum_of_positions(offset, index)
    TreeOffsetPtr   offset;
    long            index;
{
  int     i;

  Position  sum  = 0;
  long      stop = index;
  if(index > offset->size)
    stop = offset->size;
  for (i=0;i < stop; i++)
    sum += offset->array[i];
  return (sum);
}
```

This completes the implementation of the Tree widget. The next section discusses an example that uses the Tree widget.

14.2.4 Using The Tree Widget

This section shows how an application can use the Tree widget to display a tree. In this example, the Tree widget is managed by an XmScrolledWindow widget to allow the tree to display an area larger than the screen if necessary. The program, named **sort**, reads a list of integers from standard input and displays them in a binary sort tree.[3] A binary sort tree is a tree in which the value of the key in each left subnode is less than the value of its super node's key, and the value of the key in each right subnode is greater than its super node's key. The header includes the various header files and defines a structure used to store the sorted tree.

---

3. Notice that although this example uses the Tree widget to display a binary tree, the Tree widget is not limited to binary trees.

```
/*****************************************************************
 * sort.c: Display a binary sort tree using the tree widget.
 *****************************************************************/
#include <stdio.h>
#include <X11/StringDefs.h>
#include <X11/Intrinsic.h>
#include <Xm/Xm.h>
#include <Xm/Label.h>
#include <Xm/ScrolledW.h>
#include "Tree.h"
/*
 * Define the structure for a node in the binary sort tree.
 */
typedef struct _node {
  int          key;
  struct _node *left;
  struct _node *right;
} node;

extern node *insert_node();
extern node *make_node();
```

The body of the program creates the Tree widget, and then inserts numbers read from standard input into a binary sorted tree of **node** structures. Once the tree is built, the function **show_tree()** creates a widget for each node of the tree.

```
main(argc, argv)
    int     argc;
    char    *argv[];
{
  Widget    toplevel, sw, tree;
  int       i;
  node      *head = NULL;
  int       digit;
  Arg       wargs[10];
  toplevel = XtInitialize(argv[0], "Sort", NULL, 0,
                          &argc, argv);
  /*
   * Put the tree in a scrolled window, to handle
   * large trees.
   */
  XtSetArg(wargs[0], XmNscrollingPolicy, XmAUTOMATIC);
  sw = XtCreateManagedWidget("swindow",
```

```
                              xmScrolledWindowWidgetClass,
                              toplevel, wargs, 1);
    /*
     * Create the tree widget.
     */
    tree = XtCreateManagedWidget("tree", XstreeWidgetClass,
                              sw, NULL, 0);
    /*
     * Create a binary sort tree from data read from stdin.
     */
    while(scanf("%d", &digit) != EOF)
        head = insert_node(digit, head);
    /*
     * Create the widgets representing the tree.
     */
    show_tree(tree, head, NULL);

    XtRealizeWidget(toplevel);
    XtMainLoop();
}
```

The function **insert_node()** inserts an integer into the appropriate node of a tree. If the tree doesn't exist, an initial node is allocated and the given key becomes the root of the sort tree. Otherwise, this function follows the branches of the tree until a leaf is found. The new key is inserted at the leaf. At each node, the branch that is followed depends on whether the key in that node is less than or greater than the new key.

```
node *insert_node(key, head)
    int    key;
    node *head;
{
    node *prev, *ptr  = head;
    /*
     * If the tree doesn't exist, just create and
     * return a new node.
     */
    if(!head)
        return (make_node(key));
    /*
     * Otherwise, find a leaf node, always following the
     * left branches if the key is less than the value in each
     * node, and the right branch otherwise.
     */
```

```
    while(ptr != NULL){
      prev = ptr;
      ptr = (key < ptr->key) ? ptr->left : ptr->right;
    }
    /*
     * Make a new node and attach it to the appropriate branch.
     */
    if (key < prev->key)
      prev->left = make_node(key);
    else
      prev->right = make_node(key);
    return (head);
}
```

The function **make_node()** creates a new node structure, stores the integer key, and initializes the node's subnode pointers to **NULL**.

```
node *make_node(key)
    int   key;
{
  node  *ptr = (node *) malloc(sizeof(node));

  ptr->key  = key;
  ptr->left = ptr->right = NULL;
  return (ptr);
}
```

Once the tree has been sorted, the function **show_tree()** performs a pre-order traversal of the nodes, and creates widgets for each node. The function also sets the **XtNsuperNode** constraint for each widget to point to the widget previously created for the super node in the binary tree.

```
show_tree(parent, branch, super_node)
    Widget    parent;
    node      *branch;
    Widget    super_node;
{
  Widget    w;
  Arg       wargs[3];
  int       n = 0;
  /*
   * If we've hit a leaf, return.
   */
  if(!branch) return;
```

```
/*
 * Create a widget for the node, specifying the
 * given super_node constraint.
 */
n = 0;
XtSetArg(wargs[n], XtNsuperNode, super_node); n++;
w  =  XtCreateManagedWidget("node", xmLabelWidgetClass,
                            parent, wargs, n);
xs_wprintf(w, "%d", branch->key);
/*
 * Recursively create the subnodes, giving this node's
 * widget as the super_node.
 */
show_tree(parent, branch->left,  w);
show_tree(parent, branch->right, w);
}
```

We can try this program by creating a sample data file containing some numbers.

```
% cat tree.data
50 21 72 10 15 17 19 11 14 80 60
90 83 91 65 52 79 25 67 63 68 66
```

Then we can run the sort program with this data to produce the tree in Fig. 14.2.

```
% sort < tree.data
```

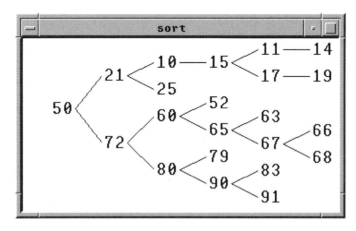

Figure 14.2 A binary sort tree.

14.3 SUMMARY

This chapter presented the architecture and construction of a Constraint widget. The Constraint widget class is a subclass of the Composite widget class that uses additional information attached to its children to determine how the children are managed. Each constraint widget attaches a constraint record to its children to store this additional information, and often provides additional resources for the child widget. The constraint resources allow the application programmer or the user to specify the corresponding values in the constraint record, and influence the layout of each individual widget. Constraint widgets define additional methods to initialize and manage changes to its children's constraint record.

The Tree widget presented in this chapter provides one example of the type of constraint information that can be attached to a widget. Each widget position is constrained by its hierarchical relationship to other widgets in a tree. The actual positions are determined by heuristics that specify the desirable shape of a tree.

The widgets presented in Chapters 12, 13, and 14 were designed to be direct subclasses of the Core, Composite and Constraint widget classes. Although these widgets will work in conjunction with Motif widgets, they do not support the unique features of Motif widgets. All Motif widgets are subclasses of either the XmPrimitive or XmManager widget classes. The XmPrimitive class provides support for the Motif shadowing effect and also support for keyboard traversal. The Tree widget suffers the most from not inheriting from a Motif widget class. All Motif container widgets support Motif's keyboard traversal mechanism and also can manage gadgets. The Tree widget cannot manage gadgets as children. The mechanisms used by the Motif widget set to implement these features rely on internal functions which have not been publicly documented as this book goes to press, and which do not appear to be stable enough to describe here. However, creating a subclass of a Motif widget is much the same as creating a subclass of any widget. The programmer should first understand the capabilities of all potential superclasses and choose the closest match to the desired new widget class. The programmer than creates the new class using the techniques discussed in this and the previous chapters, using inheritance to reuse as much of the functionality of the superclass as possible.

APPENDIX A

THE MOTIF CLASS TREE

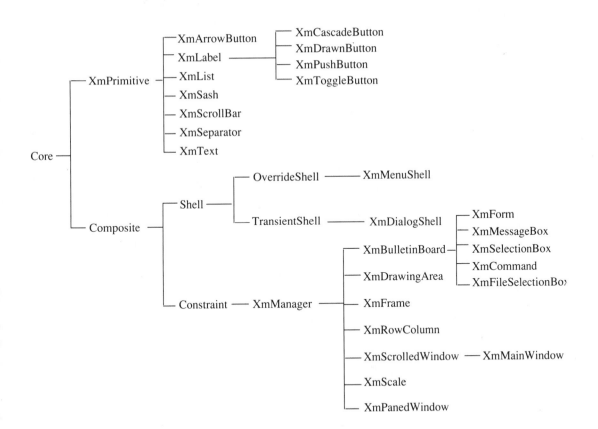

APPENDIX B

QUICK WIDGET REFERENCE

This appendix is a mini-reference guide to the widget classes in the Xt Intrinsics and the Motif widget set. The following sections briefly describe each widget class and lists each widget's class pointer, class name, the header file to include when using the widget class, and the widget's superclass. Each entry also lists the resources added by the widget class as well as the translations and callback lists provided by the widget class. To determine the complete list of resources supported by a particular widget class, also refer to the resources supported by each of the widget's superclasses. Not every widget class inherits all the resources of all superclasses, but usually this is correct.

Many of the default values of resources used by the Motif widget set depend on the value of some other resource. In these cases, the tables list each case, if possible. The Motif widget set also supports some resources whose default values can only be determined dynamically at run time. An example is the shadow colors that produce the three-dimensional effect used by many Motif widgets. These are computed at run time based on the other colors of the widget. Resources whose default values can only be determined at run time are listed in this appendix as "dynamic." For more information, or examples of how a widget is used, refer to the chapter or section listed in each entry.

Xt INTRINSICS META-CLASSES

Composite

Class Pointer:	`compositeWidgetClass`
Class Name:	`Composite`
Include File:	`<X11/Composite.h>`
Superclass:	`Core`

426

Description:

The Composite widget class is a meta-class defined by the Xt Intrinsics. Composite widgets are used as containers for other widgets.

Refer To: Section 4.2.2, Chapter 13

Constraint

Class Pointer: `constraintWidgetClass`
Class Name: `Constraint`
Include File: `<X11/Constraint.h>`
Superclass: `Composite`
Description:

The Constraint widget class is a meta-class defined by the Xt Intrinsics. A constraint widget attaches additional resources to its children. Constraint widgets normally use these additional resources to manage the geometry of its children.

Refer To: Section 4.2.3, Chapter 14

Core

Class Pointer: `widgetClass`
Class Name: `Core`
Include File: `<X11/Core.h>`
Superclass: `None`
Description:

The Core widget class is a meta-class provided by the Xt Intrinsics. It serves as the superclass of all widgets.

Refer To: Section 4.2.1, Chapter 12
Resources:

Name	Type	Default
XtNscreen	XtRPointer	copy from parent
XtNcolormap	XtRPointer	copy from parent
XtNancestorSensitive	XtRBoolean	TRUE
XtNx	XtRPosition	0
XtNy	XtRPosition	0
XtNwidth	XtRDimension	0
XtNheight	XtRDimension	0
XtNdepth	XtRInt	0
XtNbackground	XtRPixel	1
XtNbackgroundPixmap	XtRPixmap	None
XtNborderWidth	XtRDimension	1
XtNborderColor	XtRPixel	0
XtNborderPixmap	XtRPixmap	None

XtNsensitive	XtRBoolean	TRUE
XtNmappedWhenManaged	XtRBoolean	TRUE
XtNtranslations	XtRTranslationTable	NULL
XtNaccelerators	XtRAcceleratorTable	NULL

Callbacks:

Callback	Call Data
XtNdestroyCallback	NULL

Notes:

The default values of the **XtNwidth** and **XtNheight** resources are set by the Core widget class to be zero. However, most subclasses of Core override this default at initialization time, usually to a small value such as 5 or 10 pixels.

Shell

Class Pointer:	**shellWidgetClass**
Class Name:	**Shell**
Include File:	**<X11/Shell.h>**
Superclass:	**Composite**

Description:

The Shell widget class is defined by the Xt Intrinsics and provides an interface between applications and the window manager. Every application uses a Shell widget or a subclass of Shell as its top level widget.

Refer To: Section 4.2.4

Resources:

Name	Type	Default
XtNdepth	XtRInt	default screen depth
XtNcolormap	XtRPointer	default colormap
XtNallowShellResize	XtRBoolean	FALSE
XtNancestorSensitive	XtRBoolean	FALSE
XtNgeometry	XtRString	NULL
XtNcreatePopupChildProc	XtRFunction	NULL
XtNsaveUnder	XtRBoolean	FALSE
XtNoverrideRedirect	XtRBoolean	FALSE

Callbacks:

Callback	Call Data
XtNpopupCallback	NULL
XtNpopdownCallback	NULL

MOTIF WIDGET CLASSES

ArrowButton

Class Pointer: **xmArrowButtonWidgetClass**
Class Name: **XmArrowButton**
Include File: **<Xm/ArrowB.h>**
Superclass: **XmPrimitive**
Description:

An XmArrowButton widget provides the functionality of an XmPushButton widget, but displays an arrow.

Resources:

Name	Type	Default
XmNarrowDirection	XmRArrowDirection	XmARROW_UP

Callbacks:

Callback List	Call Data Type	Reason
XmNactivateCallback	XmNAnyCallbackStruct	XmCR_ACTIVATE
XmNarmCallback	XmNAnyCallbackStruct	XmCR_ARM
XmNdisarmCallback	XmNAnyCallbackStruct	XmCR_DISARM

Translations:

<Btn1Down>:	Arm()
<Btn1Up>:	Activate(), Disarm()
<EnterWindow>:	Enter()
<LeaveWindow>:	Leave()

ArrowButtonGadget

Class Pointer: **xmArrowButtonGadgetClass**
Class Name: **XmArrowButtonGadget**
Include File: **<Xm/ArrowBG.h>**
Superclass: **XmGadget**
Description:

The XmArrowButtonGadget widget is the gadget version of the XmArrowButton widget.

Resources:

Name	Type	Default
XmNarrowDirection	XmRArrowDirection	XmARROW_UP

Callbacks:

Callback List	Call Data Type	Reason
XmNactivateCallback	XmNAnyCallbackStruct	XmCR_ACTIVATE
XmNarmCallback	XmNAnyCallbackStruct	XmCR_ARM
XmNdisarmCallback	XmNAnyCallbackStruct	XmCR_DISARM

BulletinBoard

Class Pointer:	**xmBulletinBoardWidgetClass**
Class Name:	**XmBulletinBoard**
Include File:	**<Xm/BulletinB.h>**
Superclass:	**XmManager**

Description:

The XmBulletinBoard widget class is a container widget class that does not enforce any particular position or size on its children.

Refer To: Section 4.3.4.1

Resources:

Name	Type	Default
XmNshadowType	XmRShadowType	XmSHADOW_OUT
XmNshadowThickness	XmRShort	0
XmNmarginWidth	XmRShort	10
XmNmarginHeight	XmRShort	10
XmNdefaultButton	XmRWindow	NULL
XmNcancelButton	XmRWindow	NULL
XmNstringDirection	XmRStringDirection	XmSTRING_DIRECTION_L_TO_R
XmNbuttonFontList	XmRFontList	NULL
XmNlabelFontList	XmRFontList	NULL
XmNtextFontList	XmRFontList	NULL
XmNtextTranslations	XmRTranslationTable	NULL
XmNallowOverlap	XmRBoolean	TRUE
XmNautoUnmanage	XmRBoolean	TRUE
XmNdefaultPosition	XmRBoolean	TRUE
XmNresizePolicy	XmRResizePolicy	XmRESIZE_ANY
XmNnoResize	XmRBoolean	FALSE
XmNdialogStyle	XmRDialogStyle	DialogStyleDefault
XmNdialogTitle	XmRXmString	NULL

Callbacks:

Callback List	Call Data Type	Reason
XmNfocusCallback	XmAnyCallbackStruct	XmCR_FOCUS
XmNmapCallback	XmAnyCallbackStruct	XmCR_MAP
XmNunmapCallback	XmAnyCallbackStruct	XmCR_UNMAP

Translations:

<EnterWindow>:	Enter()
<FocusIn>:	FocusIn()
<Btn1Down>:	Arm()
<Btn1Up>:	Activate()
<Key>F1:	Help()
<Key>Return:	Return()
<Key>KP_Enter:	Return()

CascadeButton

Class Pointer:	`xmCascadeButtonWidgetClass`
Class Name:	`XmCascadeButton`
Include File:	`<Xm/CascadeB.h>`
Superclass:	`XmLabel`

Description:

The XmCascadeButton is used in menus as an attachment point for pulldown or cascading menu panes.

Refer To: Section 4.4.4.5

Resources:

Name	Type	Default
XmNsubMenuId	XmRMenuWidget	0
XmNcascadePixmap	XmRPrimForegroundPixmap	menu_cascade
XmNmappingDelay	XmRInt	100
XmNshadowThickness	XmRShort	2

Callbacks:

Callback List	Call Data Type	Reason
XmNactivateCallback	XmAnyCallbackStruct	XmCR_ACTIVATE
XmNcascadingCallback	XmAnyCallbackStruct	XmCR_CASCADING

Translations:

When used in a menubar:

<BtnDown>:	CheckArmAndPost()
<Key>Return:	KeySelect()

When used in a popup or pulldown menu:

<BtnDown>:	StartDrag()
<EnterWindow>:	DelayedArm()
<LeaveWindow>:	CheckDisarm()
<BtnUp>:	DoSelect()
<Key>Return:	KeySelect()
<Key>Escape:	MenuShellPopdownDone()

Otherwise:

\<BtnDown\>:	MenuBarSelect()
\<EnterWindow\>:	MenuBarEnter()
\<LeaveWindow\>:	MenuBarLeave()
\<BtnUp\>:	DoSelect()
\<Key\>Return:	KeySelect()
\<Key\>Escape:	CleanupMenuBar()

CascadeButtonGadget

Class Pointer:	`xmCascadeButtonGadgetClass`
Class Name:	`XmCascadeButtonGadget`
Include File:	`<Xm/CascadeBG.h>`
Superclass:	`XmLabelGadget`
Description:	

The XmCascadeButtonGadget performs the same function as the XmCascadeButton widget, but is a gadget.

Resources:

Name	Type	Default
XmNactivateCallback	XmRCallback	NULL
XmNcascadingCallback	XmRCallback	NULL
XmNsubMenuId	XmRMenuWidget	0
XmNcascadePixmap	XmRManForegroundPixmap	menu_cascade
XmNmappingDelay	XmRInt	100
XmNshadowThickness	XmRShort	2

Callbacks:

Callback List	Call Data Type	Reason
XmNactivateCallback	XmAnyCallbackStruct	XmCR_ACTIVATE
XmNcascadingCallback	XmAnyCallbackStruct	XmCR_CASCADING

Command

Class Pointer:	`xmCommandWidgetClass`
Class Name:	`XmCommand`
Include File:	`<Xm/Command.h>`
Superclass:	`XmSelectionBox`
Description:	

The XmCommand widget provides a text field for command entry, a prompt area and a scrollable command history list. The history list allows the user to browse and select commands previously entered in the command entry area.

Resources:

Name	Type	Default
XmNpromptString	XmRXmString	">"
XmNcommand	XmRXmString	NULL
XmNhistoryItems	XmRXmStringTable	NULL
XmNhistoryItemCount	XmRInt	0
XmNhistoryMaxItems	XmRInt	100
XmNhistoryVisibleItemCount	XmRInt	8
XmNdialogType	XmRDialogType	XmDIALOG_COMMAND
XmNdefaultPosition	XmRBoolean	FALSE
XmNautoUnmanage	XmRBoolean	FALSE

Callbacks:

Callback List	Call Data Type	Reason
XmNcommandEnteredCallback	XmCommandCallbackStruct	XmCR_COMMAND_ENTERED
XmNcommandChangedCallback	XmCommandCallbackStruct	XmCR_COMMAND_CHANGED

DialogShell

Class Pointer: `xmDialogShellWidgetClass`
Class Name: `XmDialogShell`
Include File: `<Xm/DialogS.h>`
Superclass: `transientShell`
Description:

The XmDialogShell widget forms the basis of many types of popup dialogs. The programmer seldom deals with the XmDialogShell widget directly and instead interacts with the managed child of the XmDialogShell widget. Managing the child causes the dialog to appear on the screen.

Refer To: Section 4.4.1
Resources:

Name	Type	Default
XmNdeleteResponse	XmRDeleteResponse	XmUNMAP

DrawingArea

Class Pointer: `xmDrawingAreaWidgetClass`
Class Name: `XmDrawingArea`
Include File: `<Xm/DrawingA.h>`
Superclass: `XmManager`

Description:

> The XmDrawingArea widget provides an empty window in which an application can draw graphics or text.

Refer To: Sections 5.4.1, 9.3, 10.1, 10.2, 10.4

Resources:

Name	Type	Default
XmNmarginWidth	XmRShort	10
XmNmarginHeight	XmRShort	10
XmNresizePolicy	XmRResizePolicy	XmRESIZE_ANY

Callbacks:

Callback List	Call Data Type	Reason
XmNresizeCallback	XmDrawingAreaCallbackStruct	XmCR_RESIZE
XmNexposeCallback	XmDrawingAreaCallbackStruct	XmCR_EXPOSE
XmNinputCallback	XmDrawingAreaCallbackStruct	XmCR_INPUT

Translations:

<KeyDown>:	Input()
<KeyUp>:	Input()
<Btn1Down>:	Arm()
<Btn1Up>:	Activate()
<BtnDown>:	Input()
<BtnUp>:	Input()
<EnterWindow>:	Enter()
<FocusIn>:	FocusIn()

DrawnButton

Class Pointer:	`xmDrawnButtonWidgetClass`
Class Name:	`XmDrawnButton`
Include File:	`<Xm/DrawnB.h>`
Superclass:	`XmLabel`

Description:

> The XmDrawnButton widget has the semantics of an XmPushButton widget, but allows the programmer to display arbitrary text or graphics in the widget's window.

Resources:

Name	Type	Default
XmNpushButtonEnabled	XmRBoolean	FALSE
XmNshadowType	XmRShadowType	XmSHADOW_ETCHED_IN
XmNshadowThickness	XmRShort	2
XmNlabelString	XmRXmString	NULL

Callbacks:

Callback List	Call Data Type	Reason
XmNactivateCallback	XmDrawnButtonCallbackStruct	XmCR_ACTIVATE
XmNarmCallback	XmDrawnButtonCallbackStruct	XmCR_ARM
XmNdisarmCallback	XmDrawnButtonCallbackStruct	XmCR_DISARM
XmNexposeCallback	XmDrawnButtonCallbackStruct	XmCR_EXPOSE
XmNresizeCallback	XmDrawnButtonCallbackStruct	XmCR_RESIZE

Translations:

<Btn1Down>:	Arm()
<Btn1Up>:	Activate() Disarm()
<Key>Return:	ArmAndActivate()
<Key>space:	ArmAndActivate()
<EnterWindow>:	Enter()
<LeaveWindow>:	Leave()

ErrorDialog

Class Pointer:	`xmMessageBoxWidgetClass`
Class Name:	`XmMessageBox`
Include File:	`<Xm/MessageB.h>`
Superclass:	`XmBulletinBoard`

Description:

An ErrorDialog consists of an XmMessageBox widget managed by an XmDialogShell widget. It is intended to be used to display error messages, and can be created with the convenience function:

```
XmCreateErorDialog(parent, name, args, nargs)
```

FileSelectionBox

Class Pointer:	`xmFileSelectionWidgetClass`
Class Name:	`XmFileSelectionBox`
Include File:	`<XmFileSB.h>`
Superclass:	`XmSelectionBox`

Description:

The XmFileSelectionBox widget allows the user to browse through files and directories.

Resources:

Name	Type	Default
XmNautoUnmanage	XmRBoolean	FALSE
XmNlistLabelString	XmRXmString	"Files"

XmNapplyLabelString	XmRXmString	"Filter"
XmNdirSpec	XmRXmString	NULL
XmNdialogType	XmRDialogType	XmDIALOG_FILE_SELECTION
XmNfilterLabelString	XmRXmString	FileFilter
XmNdirMask	XmRXmString	"*"
XmNfileSearchProc	XmRProc	DoFileSearch
XmNlistUpdated	XmRBoolean	TRUE

FileSelectionBoxDialog

Class Pointer: `xmFileSelectionWidgetClass`
Class Name: `XmFileSelectionBox`
Include File: `<Xm/FileSB.h>`
Superclass: `XmSelectionBox`
Description:

The FileSelectionBoxDialog combines an XmFileSelectionBox widget and a Xm-DialogShell widget. It can be created using the convenience function:

`XmCreateFileSelectionDialog (parent, name, args, nargs)`

Form

Class Pointer: `xmFormWidgetClass`
Class Name: `XmForm`
Include File: `<Xm/Form.h>`
Superclass: `XmBulletinBoard`
Description:

The XmForm widget is a constraint widget that allows children to specify various types of attachments. Children may be attached to each other, to the Xm-Form widget, or to a relative position within the XmForm widget

Refer To: Section 4.3.4.3

Constraint Resources:

Name	Type	Default
XmNtopAttachment	XmRAttachment	XmATTACH_NONE
XmNbottomAttachment	XmRAttachment	XmATTACH_NONE
XmNleftAttachment	XmRAttachment	XmATTACH_NONE
XmNrightAttachment	XmRAttachment	XmATTACH_NONE
XmNtopWidget	XmRWindow	NULL
XmNbottomWidget	XmRWindow	NULL
XmNleftWidget	XmRWindow	NULL
XmNrightWidget	XmRWindow	NULL
XmNtopPosition	XmRInt	0

XmNbottomPosition	XmRInt	0
XmNleftPosition	XmRInt	0
XmNrightPosition	XmRInt	0
XmNtopOffset	XmRInt	dynamic
XmNbottomOffset	XmRInt	dynamic
XmNleftOffset	XmRInt	dynamic
XmNrightOffset	XmRInt	dynamic
XmNresizable	XmRBoolean	TRUE

Resources:

Name	Type	Default
XmNhorizontalSpacing	XmRInt	0
XmNverticalSpacing	XmRInt	0
XmNfractionBase	XmRInt	100
XmNrubberPositioning	XmRBoolean	FALSE

Notes:

The various offset resources, marked here as dynamic, are initialized to an improbable value designed to force a recomputation of these values at run time.

FormDialog

Class Pointer: `xmFormWidgetClass`
Class Name: `XmForm`
Include File: `<Xm/Form.h>`
Superclass: `XmBulletinBoard`
Description:

The FormDialog combines an XmForm widget and a XmDialogShell widget. It can be created using the convenience function:

`XmCreateFileSelectionDialog (parent, name, args, nargs)`

Refer To: Section 4.4.1

Frame

Class Pointer: `xmFrameWidgetClass`
Class Name: `XmFrame`
Include File: `<Xm/Frame.h>`
Superclass: `XmManager`
Description:

The XmFrame widget class is a manager widget that encloses a single child in a three-dimensional frame. It can be used to give a three-dimensional appearance to widgets that do not provide this look.

Resources:

Name	Type	Default
XmNmarginWidth	XmRShort	0
XmNmarginHeight	XmRShort	0
XmNshadowType	XmRShadowType	XmSHADOW_ETCHED_IN

Translations:

<EnterWindow>:	Enter()
<FocusIn>:	FocusIn()
<Btn1Down>:	Arm()
<Btn1Up>:	Activate()

Notes:

If the widget is a child of a Shell widget, the default value of the **XmNshadow-Type** resource is **XmSHADOW_OUT**.

Gadget

Class Pointer:	**xmGadgetClass**
Class Name:	**XmGadget**
Include File:	**<Xm/Gadget.h>**
Superclass:	**rectObj**

Description:

The XmGadget class is the meta-class for all gadgets. A gadget is a window-less widget which displays itself in its parent's window.

Refer To: Section 4.5

Resources:

Name	Type	Default
XmNborderWidth	XmRDimension	0
XmNtraversalOn	XmRBoolean	FALSE
XmNhighlightOnEnter	XmRBoolean	FALSE
XmNhighlightThickness	XmRShort	0
XmNshadowThickness	XmRShort	2
XmNunitType	XmRUnitType	XmPIXELS
XmNuserData	XmRPointer	NULL

Callbacks:

Callback List	Call Data Type	Reason
XmNhelpCallback	XmAnyCallbackStruct	XmCR_HELP

Notes:

If the gadget is a child of a subclass of XmManager, the default value of **XmN-unitType** is copied from the parent.

InformationDialog

Class Pointer:	**xmMessageBoxWidgetClass**
Class Name:	**XmMessageBox**
Include File:	**<Xm/MessageB.h>**
Superclass:	**XmBulletinBoard**

Description:

An InformationDialog combines an XmMessageBox widget and an XmDialogShell widget to display information to the user. It can be created using the convenience function:

XmCreateInformationDialog (parent, name, args, nargs)

Refer To: Section 4.4.1

Label

Class Pointer:	**xmLabelWidgetClass**
Class Name:	**XmLabel**
Include File:	**<Xm/Label.h>**
Superclass:	**XmPrimitive**

Description:

The XmLabel widget class displays a compound string or a pixmap.

Refer To: Section 2.4, 4.3.3.1

Resources:

Name	Type	Default
XmNshadowThickness	XmRShort	0
XmNalignment	XmRAlignment	XmALIGNMENT_CENTER
XmNlabelType	XmRLabelType	XmSTRING
XmNmarginWidth	XmRShort	2
XmNmarginHeight	XmRShort	2
XmNmarginLeft	XmRShort	0
XmNmarginRight	XmRShort	0
XmNmarginTop	XmRShort	0
XmNmarginBottom	XmRShort	0
XmNfontList	XmRFontList	Fixed

XmNlabelPixmap	XmRPrimForegroundPixmap	XmUNSPECIFIED_PIXMAP
XmNlabelInsensitivePixmap	XmRPixmap	XmUNSPECIFIED_PIXMAP
XmNlabelString	XmRXmString	NULL
XmNmnemonic	XmRChar	NULL
XmNaccelerator	XmRString	NULL
XmNacceleratorText	XmRXmString	NULL
XmNrecomputeSize	XmRBoolean	TRUE
XmNstringDirection	XmRStringDirection	XmSTRING_DIRECTION_L_TO_R

Translations:

<EnterWindow>:	Enter()
<leave>:	Leave()

Translations defined for subclasses of Label

<Unmap>:	Unmap()
<FocusOut>:	FocusOut()
<FocusIn>:	FocusIn()
<Key>space:	Noop()
<Key>Left:	MenuTraverseLeft()
<Key>Right:	MenuTraverseRight()
<Key>Up:	MenuTraverseUp()
<Key>Down:	MenuTraverseDown()
<Key>Home:	Noop()

LabelGadget

Class Pointer:	**xmLabelGadgetClass**
Class Name:	**XmLabelGadget**
Include File:	**<Xm/LabelG.h>**
Superclass:	**XmGadget**
Description:	

Similar to an XmLabel widget, but a gadget.

Resources:

Name	Type	Default
XmNshadowThickness	XmRShort	0
XmNalignment	XmRAlignment	XmALIGNMENT_CENTER
XmNlabelType	XmRLabelType	XmSTRING
XmNmarginWidth	XmRShort	2
XmNmarginHeight	XmRShort	2
XmNmarginLeft	XmRShort	0
XmNmarginRight	XmRShort	0
XmNmarginTop	XmRShort	0
XmNmarginBottom	XmRShort	0
XmNfontList	XmRFontList	Fixed
XmNlabelPixmap	XmRManForegroundPixmap	XmUNSPECIFIED_PIXMAP
XmNlabelInsensitivePixmap	XmRPixmap	XmUNSPECIFIED_PIXMAP
XmNlabelString	XmRXmString	NULL

XmNmnemonic	XmRChar	NULL
XmNaccelerator	XmRString	NULL
XmNacceleratorText	XmRXmString	NULL
XmNrecomputeSize	XmRBoolean	TRUE
XmNstringDirection	XmRStringDirection	XmSTRING_DIRECTION_L_TO_R

List

Class Pointer:	**xmListWidgetClass**
Class Name:	**XmList**
Include File:	**<Xm/List.h>**
Superclass:	**XmPrimitive**
Description:	

   The XmList widget allows the user to choose from a list of items.

Refer To: Section 4.3.4.4
Resources:

Name	Type	Default
XmNlistSpacing	XmRShort	0
XmNlistMarginWidth	XmRShort	0
XmNlistMarginHeight	XmRShort	0
XmNfontList	XmRFontList	"Fixed "
XmNstringDirection	XmRStringDirection	XmSTRING_DIRECTION_L_TO_R
XmNitems	XmRXmStringTable	NULL
XmNitemCount	XmRInt	0
XmNselectedItems	XmRXmStringTable	NULL
XmNselectedItemCount	XmRInt	0
XmNvisibleItemCount	XmRInt	1
XmNselectionPolicy	XmRSelectionPolicy	XmBROWSE_SELECT
XmNlistSizePolicy	XmRListSizePolicy	XmRESIZE_IF_POSSIBLE
XmNscrollBarDisplayPolicy	XmRScrollBarDisplayPolicy	XmAS_NEEDED
XmNautomaticSelection	XmRBoolean	FALSE
XmNdoubleClickInterval	XmRInt	250
XmNhorizontalScrollBar	XmRWindow	NULL
XmNverticalScrollBar	XmRWindow	NULL

Callbacks:

Callback List	Call Data Type	Reason
XmNsingleSelectionCallback	XmListCallbackStruct	XmCR_SINGLE_SELECT
XmNmultipleSelectionCallback	XmListCallbackStruct	XmCR_MULTIPLE_SELECT
XmNextendedSelectionCallback	XmListCallbackStruct	XmCR_EXTENDED_SELECT
XmNbrowseSelectionCallback	XmListCallbackStruct	XmCR_BROWSE_SELECT
XmNdefaultActionCallback	XmListCallbackStruct	XmCR_DEFAULT_ACTION

Translations:

Button1<Motion>:	ListButtonMotion()
~Shift ~Ctrl Meta<Btn1Down>:	ListMetaSelect()
~Shift ~Ctrl Meta<Btn1Up>:	ListMetaUnSelect()
~Shift ~Ctrl Meta<KeyDown>space:	ListKbdMetaSelect()
~Shift ~Ctrl Meta<KeyUp>space:	ListKbdMetaUnSelect()
Shift ~Ctrl ~Meta<Btn1Down>:	ListShiftSelect()
Shift ~Ctrl ~Meta<Btn1Up>:	ListShiftUnSelect()
Shift ~Ctrl ~Meta<KeyDown>space:	ListKbdShiftSelect()
Shift ~Ctrl ~Meta<KeyUp>space:	ListKbdShiftUnSelect()
Ctrl ~Shift ~Meta<Btn1Down>:	ListCtrlSelect()
Ctrl ~Shift ~Meta<Btn1Up>:	ListCtrlUnSelect()
Ctrl ~Shift ~Meta<KeyDown>space:	ListKbdCtrlSelect()
Ctrl ~Shift ~Meta<KeyUp>space:	ListKbdCtrlUnSelect()
~Shift ~Ctrl ~Meta<Btn1Down>:	ListElementSelect()
~Shift ~Ctrl ~Meta<Btn1Up>:	ListElementUnSelect()
~Shift ~Ctrl ~Meta<KeyDown>space:	ListKbdSelect()
~Shift ~Ctrl ~Meta<KeyUp>space:	ListKbdUnSelect()
~Shift ~Ctrl Meta<Key>Up:	ListMetaPrevElement()
~Shift ~Ctrl Meta<Key>Down:	ListMetaNextElement()
Shift ~Ctrl ~Meta<Key>Up:	ListShiftPrevElement()
Shift ~Ctrl ~Meta<Key>Down:	ListShiftNextElement()
~Shift Ctrl ~Meta<Key>Up:	ListCtrlPrevElement()
~Shift Ctrl ~Meta<Key>Down:	ListCtrlNextElement()
~Shift ~Ctrl ~Meta<Key>Up:	ListPrevElement()
~Shift ~Ctrl ~Meta<Key>Down:	ListNextElement()
<Enter>:	ListEnter()
<Leave>:	ListLeave()
<FocusIn>:	ListFocusIn()
<FocusOut>:	ListFocusOut()
<Unmap>:	PrimitiveUnmap()
Shift<Key>Tab:	PrimitivePrevTabGroup()
<Key>Tab:	PrimitiveNextTabGroup()
<Key>F6:	PrimitiveNextTabGroup()
<Key>Home:	PrimitiveTraverseHome()

MainWindow

Class Pointer:	`xmMainWindowWidgetClass`
Class Name:	`XmMainWindow`
Include File:	`<Xm/MainW.h>`
Superclass:	`XmScrolledWindow`

Description:

The XmMainWindow widget provides a convenient layout for a common configuration of widgets. The widget can manage any of a MenuBar, a CommandWindow, a work area, and scrollbars.

Resources:

Name	Type	Default
XmNcommandWindow	XmRWindow	NULL
XmNmenuBar	XmRWindow	NULL
XmNmainWindowMarginWidth	XmRShort	0
XmNmainWindowMarginHeight	XmRShort	0
XmNshowSeparator	XmRBoolean	FALSE

Manager

Class Pointer:	`xmManagerWidgetClass`
Class Name:	`XmManager`
Superclass:	`Constraint`

Description:

The XmManager widget is a meta-class for all other Motif container widgets.

Refer To: Section 4.3.2

Resources:

Name	Type	Default
XmNforeground	XmRPixel	dynamic
XmNbackground	XmRPixel	dynamic
XmNbackgroundPixmap	XmRPixmap	XmUNSPECIFIED_PIXMAP
XmNborderWidth	XmRDimension	0
XmNhighlightColor	XmRPixel	Black
XmNhighlightPixmap	XmRManHighlightPixmap	dynamic
XmNunitType	XmRUnitType	XmPIXELS
XmNshadowThickness	XmRShort	2
XmNtopShadowColor	XmRPixel	dynamic
XmNtopShadowPixmap	XmRManTopShadowPixmap	dynamic
XmNbottomShadowColor	XmRPixel	dynamic
XmNbottomShadowPixmap	XmRManBottomShadowPixmap	dynamic
XmNuserData	XmRPointer	NULL

Callbacks:

Callback List	Call Data Type	Reason
XmNhelpCallback	XmRCallback	NULL

Translations:

<EnterWindow>:	ManagerEnter()

<FocusOut>:	ManagerFocusOut()
<FocusIn>:	ManagerFocusIn()
<Key>space:	ManagerGadgetSelect()
<Key>Return:	ManagerGadgetSelect()
Shift<Key>Tab:	ManagerGadgetPrevTabGroup()
<Key>Tab:	ManagerGadgetNextTabGroup()
<Key>F6:	ManagerGadgetNextTabGroup()
<Key>Up:	ManagerGadgetTraversePrev()
<Key>Down:	ManagerGadgetTraverseNext()
<Key>Left:	ManagerGadgetTraversePrev()
<Key>Right:	ManagerGadgetTraverseNext()
<Key>Home:	ManagerGadgetTraverseHome()

Notes:

If the widget is a managed by a subclass of XmManager, the default **XmNunit-Type** is copied from the parent. The default values of the various color and pixmap resources are computed dynamically based on the other colors and the visual type of the screen.

MenuBar

Class Pointer: `xmRowColumnWidgetClass`
Class Name: `XmRowColumn`
Include File: `<Xm/RowColumn.h>`
Superclass: `XmManager`
Description:

A MenuBar is a convenience form of an XmRowColumn, configured to act as a menu bar for pulldown menus. A MenuBar can be created using the convenience function:

```
XmCreateMenuBar (parent, name, args, nargs)
```

Refer To: Section 4.3.4.5, RowColumn widget

MenuShell

Class Pointer: `xmMenuShellWidgetClass`
Class Name: `XmMenuShell`
Include File: `<Xm/MenuShell.h>`
Superclass: `overrideShell`
Description:

The XmMenuShell widget forms the basis of popup and pulldown menu panes. It is seldom used directly. Instead, the programmer should use the convenience functions provided by Motif to create menus.

Refer To: Section 4.3.4.5
Resources:

Name	Type	Default
XmNsaveUnder	XmRBoolean	TRUE
XmNallowShellResize	XmRBoolean	TRUE

Translations:

<BtnDown>:	ClearTraversal()
<Key>Escape:	MenuShellPopdownDone()
<BtnUp>:	MenuShellPopdownDone()

MessageBox

Class Pointer:	**xmMessageBoxWidgetClass**
Class Name:	**XmMessageBox**
Include File:	**<Xm/MessageB.h>**
Superclass:	**XmBulletinBoard**

Description:

The XmMessageBox is a dialog widget used to display a message.

Refer To: Section 4.4.1
Resources:

Name	Type	Defaulkt
XmNdialogType	XmRDialogType	XmDIALOG_MESSAGE
XmNminimizeButton	XmRBoolean	FALSE
XmNdefaultButtonType	XmRDefaultButtonType	XmDIALOG_OK_BUTTON
XmNmessageString	XmRXmString	NULL
XmNmessageAlignment	XmRAlignment	XmALIGNMENT_BEGINNING
XmNsymbolPixmap	XmRManForegroundPixmap	XmUNSPECIFIED_PIXMAP
XmNokLabelString	XmRXmString	"OK"
XmNcancelLabelString	XmRXmString	"Cancel"
XmNhelpLabelString	XmRXmString	"Help"

Callbacks:

Callback List	Call Data Type	Reason
XmNokCallback	XmAnyCallbackStruct	XmCR_OK
XmNcancelCallback	XmAnyCallbackStruct	XmCR_CANCEL

MessageDialog

Class Pointer:	**xmMessageBoxWidgetClass**
Class Name:	**XmMessageBox**
Include File:	**<Xm/MessageB.h>**
Superclass:	**XmBulletinBoard**

Description:

The MessageDialog combines an XmMessageBox widget with an XmDialogShell widget. It can be created using the convenience function:

`XmCreateMessageDialog (parent, name, args, nargs)`

Refer To: Section 4.4.1

OptionMenu

Class Pointer: **`xmRowColumnWidgetClass`**
Class Name: **`XmRowColumn`**
Include File: **`<Xm/RowColumn.h>`**
Superclass: **`XmManager`**
Description:

An OptionMenu is a convenience form of an XmRowColumn. An OptionMenu can be created using the convenience function:

`XmCreateOptionMenu (parent, name, args, nargs)`

Refer To: RowColumn widget

PanedWindow

Class Pointer: **`xmPanedWindowWidgetClass`**
Class Name: **`XmPanedWindow`**
Include File: **`<Xm/PanedW.h>`**
Superclass: **`XmManager`**
Description:

The XmPanedWindow widget arranges it children in vertical tiled panes. The user can adjust the size of each pane using a Sash attached to each pane.

Refer To: Section 5.4.1

Constraint Resources:

Name	Type	Default
XmNallowResize	XmRBoolean	FALSE
XmNminimum	XmRInt	1
XmNmaximum	XmRInt	1000
XmNskipAdjust	XmRBoolean	FALSE

Resources:

Name	Type	Default
XmNmarginWidth	XmRShort	3
XmNmarginHeight	XmRShort	3

XmNspacing	XmRInt	8
XmNrefigureMode	XmRBoolean	TRUE,
XmNseparatorOn	XmRBoolean	TRUE,
XmNsashIndent	XmRPosition	-10
XmNsashWidth	XmRDimension	10
XmNsashHeight	XmRDimension	10
XmNsashShadowThickness	XmRInt	2

Translations:

~Shift ~Ctrl ~Alt <Key>F1:	help()
<Btn1Down>:	arm()
<Btn1Up>:	activate()

PopupMenu

Class Pointer: `xmRowColumnWidgetClass`
Class Name: `XmRowColumn`
Include File: `<Xm/RowColumn.h>`
Superclass: `XmManager`
Description:

A PopupMenu is a form of an XmRowColumn, configured to act as a menu pane for popup menus. A PopupMenu can be created using the convenience function:

`XmCreatePopupMenu(parent, name, args, nargs)`

Refer To: Section 4.3.4.5, RowColumn widget

Primitive

Class Pointer: `xmPrimitiveWidgetClass`
Class Name: `XmPrimitive`
Superclass: `Core`
Description:

The XmPrimitive class is a meta-class that is used as the superclass for all Motif display widgets.

Refer To: Section 4.3.2
Resources:

Name	Type	Default
XmNforeground	XmRPixel	dynamic
XmNbackground	XmRPixel	dynamic
XmNbackgroundPixmap	XmRPixmap	XmUNSPECIFIED_PIXMAP
XmNborderWidth	XmRDimension	0
XmNtraversalOn	XmRBoolean	FALSE

XmNhighlightOnEnter	XmRBoolean	FALSE
XmNunitType	XmRUnitType	XmPIXELS
XmNhighlightThickness	XmRShort	0
XmNhighlightColor	XmRPixel	Black
XmNhighlightPixmap	XmRPrimHighlightPixmap	dynamic
XmNshadowThickness	XmRShort	2
XmNtopShadowColor	XmRPixel	dynamic
XmNtopShadowPixmap	XmRPrimTopShadowPixmap	dynamic
XmNbottomShadowColor	XmRPixel	dynamic
XmNbottomShadowPixmap	XmRPrimBottomShadowPixmap	XmUNSPECIFIED_PIXMAP
XmNuserData	XmRPointer	NULL

Callbacks:

Callback List	**Call Data Type**	**Reason**
XmNhelpCallback	XmAnyCallbackStruct	XmCR_HELP

Translations:

\<FocusIn\>:	PrimitiveFocusIn()
\<FocusOut\>:	PrimitiveFocusOut()
\<Unmap\>:	PrimitiveUnmap()
Shift\<Key\>Tab:	PrimitivePrevTabGroup()
\<Key\>Tab:	PrimitiveNextTabGroup()
\<Key\>F6:	PrimitiveNextTabGroup()
\<Key\>Up:	PrimitiveTraversePrev()
\<Key\>Down:	PrimitiveTraverseNext()
\<Key\>Left:	PrimitiveTraversePrev()
\<Key\>Right:	PrimitiveTraverseNext()
\<Key\>Home:	PrimitiveTraverseHome()

Notes:

If the widget is a managed by a subclass of XmManager, the default **XmNunit-Type** is copied from the parent. The default values of the various color and pixmap resources are computed dynamically based on the other colors and the visual type of the screen.

PromptDialog

Class Pointer:	**xmMessageBoxWidgetClass**
Class Name:	**XmMessageBox**
Include File:	**\<Xm/MessageB.h\>**
Superclass:	**XmBulletinBoard**
Refer To:	Section 4.4.1

PulldownMenu

Class Pointer:	`xmRowColumnWidgetClass`
Class Name:	`XmRowColumn`
Include File:	`<Xm/RowColumn.h>`
Superclass:	`XmManager`

Description:

A PulldownMenu is an XmRowColumn, configured to act as a menu pane for pulldown menus. A PulldownMenu can be created using the convenience function:

`XmCreatePulldownMenu(parent, name, args, nargs)`

Refer To: Section 4.3.4.5, RowColumn widget

PushButton

Class Pointer:	`xmPushButtonWidgetClass`
Class Name:	`XmPushButton`
Include File:	`<Xm/PushB.h>`
Superclass:	`XmLabel`

Description:

The XmPushButton widget allows the user to issue a command by "pushing" the button.

Refer To: Section 4.3.3.2

Resources:

Name	Type	Default
XmNfillOnArm	XmRBoolean	TRUE
XmNarmColor	XmRPixel	dynamic
XmNarmPixmap	XmRPrimForegroundPixmap	XmUNSPECIFIED_PIXMAP
XmNshowAsDefault	XmRShort	0
XmNshadowThickness	XmRShort	2

Callbacks:

Callback List	Call Data Type	Reason
XmNactivateCallback	XmAnyCallbackStruct	XmCR_DISARM
XmNarmCallback	XmAnyCallbackStruct	XmCR_ARM
XmNdisarmCallback	XmAnyCallbackStruct	XmCR_DISARM

Translations:

<Btn1Down>:	Arm()
<Btn1Up>:	Activate(), Disarm()
<Key>Return:	ArmAndActivate()
<Key>space:	ArmAndActivate()

<EnterWindow>:	Enter()
<LeaveWindow>:	Leave();

If used in a menu

<BtnDown>:	BtnDown()
<BtnUp>:	BtnUp()
<EnterWindow>:	Enter()
<LeaveWindow>:	Leave()
<Key>Return:	KeySelect()
<Key>Escape:	MenuShellPopdownDone()

QuestionDialog

Class Pointer:	`xmMessageBoxWidgetClass`
Class Name:	`XmMessageBox`
Include File:	`<XmMessageB.h>`
Superclass:	`XmBulletinBoard`
Refer To:	Section 4.4.1

RadioBox

Class Pointer:	`xmRowColumnWidgetClass`
Class Name:	`XmRowColumn`
Include File:	`<Xm/RowColumn.h>`
Superclass:	`XmManager`
Description:	

A RadioBox is an XmRowColumn widget configured to force RadioBox style behavior on its children. By default a RadioBox widget expects to manage Xm-ToggleButtonGadget. A RadioBox can be created using the convenience function:

```
XmCreateRadioBox (parent, name, args, nargs)
```

Refer To:	Section 4.3.1, 7.5

RowColumn

Class Pointer:	`xmRowColumnWidgetClass`
Class Name:	`XmRowColumn`
Include File:	`<Xm/RowColumn.h>`
Superclass:	`XmManager`
Description:	

The XmRowColumn widget arranges its children in rows and columns. This widget can be configured as a general work area, a menu bar, a popup menu pane, or a pulldown menu pane.

Refer To: Section 4.3.4.2, 4.3.4.5
Resources:

<u>Name</u>	<u>Type</u>	<u>Default</u>
XmNresizeWidth	XmRBoolean	TRUE
XmNresizeHeight	XmRBoolean	TRUE
XmNadjustLast	XmRBoolean	TRUE,
XmNmarginWidth	XmRDimension	3
XmNmarginHeight	XmRDimension	3
XmNspacing	XmRDimension	0
XmNisAligned	XmRBoolean	TRUE
XmNadjustMargin	XmRBoolean	TRUE
XmNradioBehavior	XmRBoolean	FALSE
XmNradioAlwaysOne	XmRBoolean	TRUE
XmNisHomogeneous	XmRBoolean	FALSE
XmNentryClass	XmRInt	NULL
XmNmenuHelpWidget	XmRMenuWidget	NULL
XmNlabelString	XmRXmString	NULL
XmNsubMenuId	XmRMenuWidget	NULL
XmNmenuHistory	XmRMenuWidget	NULL
XmNpopupEnabled	XmRBoolean	TRUE
XmNnumColumns	XmRShort	1
XmNentryAlignment	XmRAlignment	XmALIGNMENT_BEGINNING
XmNrowColumnType	XmRRowColumnType	XmWORK_AREA
XmNpacking	XmRPacking	XmPACK_TIGHT
XmNmnemonic	XmRChar	FALSE

When XmNrowColumnType is MENU_POPUP

XmNwhichButton	XmRWhichButton	Button2
XmNorientation	XmROrientation	XmVERTICAL
XmNentryBorder	XmRDimension	0
XmNmenuAccelerator	XmRString	<Key>F4

When XmNrowColumnType is MENU_OPTION

XmNwhichButton	XmRWhichButton	Button2
XmNorientation	XmROrientation	XmHORIZONTAL
XmNspacing	XmRDimension	3
XmNentryBorder	XmRDimension	0
XmNmenuAccelerator	XmRString	NULL

When XmNrowColumnType is MENU_BAR

XmNisHomogeneous	XmRBoolean	TRUE
XmNwhichButton	XmRWhichButton	Button1
XmNorientation	XmROrientation	XmHORIZONTAL
XmNspacing	XmRDimension	0
XmNentryBorder	XmRDimension	0
XmNmenuAccelerator	XmRString	<Key>F10
XmNentryClass	XmRInt	xmCascadeButtonWidgetClass

When XmNrowColumnType is WORK_AREA

XmNwhichButton	XmRWhichButton	Button1
XmNorientation	XmROrientation	XmVERTICAL
XmNspacing	XmRDimension	3
XmNentryBorder	XmRDimension	0
XmNmenuAccelerator	XmRString	NULL

When XmNrowColumnType is MENU_PULLDOWN

XmNorientation	XmROrientation	XmVERTICAL
XmNspacing	XmRDimension	0
XmNentryBorder	XmRDimension	0
XmNmenuAccelerator	XmRString	NULL

When XmNRadioBehavior is TRUE

XmNentryClass	XmRInt	xmToggleButtonGadgetClass

Callbacks:

Callback List	Call Data Type	Reason
XmNentryCallback	XmRowColumnCallbackStruct	XmCR_ACTIVATE
XmNmapCallback	XmAnyCallbackStruct	XmCR_MAP
XmNunmapCallback	XmAnyCallbackStruct	XmCR_UNMAP

Translations:

When XmNrowColumnType is a MENU type

<Unmap>:	MenuUnmap()
<FocusIn>:	MenuFocusIn()
<FocusOut>:	MenuFocusOut()
<EnterWindow>:	MenuEnter()
<Key>Left:	MenuGadgetTraverseLeft()
<Key>Right:	MenuGadgetTraverseRight()
<Key>Up:	MenuGadgetTraverseUp()
<Key>Down:	MenuGadgetTraverseDown()

When XmNrowColumnType is MENU_OPTION

<Key>Return:	MenuGadgetReturn()
<BtnDown>:	PopupBtnDown()
<BtnUp>:	PopupBtnUp()

When XmNrowColumnType is MENU_POPUP

<Key>Return:	MenuGadgetReturn()
<Key>Escape:	MenuGadgetEscape()
<BtnDown>:	PopupBtnDown()
<BtnUp>:	PopupBtnUp()

When XmNrowColumnType is MENU_PULLDOWN

<Key>Return:	MenuGadgetReturn()
<Key>Escape:	MenuGadgetEscape()
<BtnDown>:	PulldownBtnDown()
<BtnUp>:	PulldownBtnUp()

When XmNrowColumnType is WORK_AREA

<Btn1Down>:	WorkAreaBtnDown()
<Btn1Up>:	WorkAreaBtnUp()

When XmNrowColumnType is MENU_BAR

<BtnDown>:	MenuBarBtnDown()
<Key>Return:	MenuGadgetReturn()
<Key>Escape:	MenuGadgetEscape()
<BtnUp>:	MenuBarBtnUp()

Sash

Class Pointer:	`xmSashWidgetClass`
Class Name:	`XmSash`
Superclass:	`XmPrimitive`

Description:

The XmSash is used by the XmPaneWindow widget to allow the user to adjust the size of a pane. This widget is designed to be used only by the XmPanedWindow widget.

Resources:

Name	Type	Default
XmNborderWidth	XmRDimension	0
XmNcallback	XmRCallback	NULL

Translations:

Shift <Btn1Down>:	SashAction(Start, UpperPane)
Ctrl <Btn1Down>:	SashAction(Start, LowerPane)
<Btn1Down>:	SashAction(Start, ThisBorderOnly)
Shift <Btn1Motion>:	SashAction(Move, Upper)
Ctrl <Btn1Motion>:	SashAction(Move, Lower)
<Btn1Motion>:	SashAction(Move, ThisBorder)
<Btn1Up>:	SashAction(Commit)
<EnterWindow>:	enter()
<LeaveWindow>:	leave()

Scale

Class Pointer:	`xmScaleWidgetClass`
Class Name:	`XmScale`
Include File:	`<Xm/Scale.h>`
Superclass:	`XmManager`

Description:

The XmScale widget displays a value or allows the user to enter a value between a range of integers by positioning a slider.

Refer To: Section 6.2.2
Resources:

<u>Name</u>	<u>Type</u>	<u>Default</u>
XmNvalue	XmRInt	0
XmNmaximum	XmRInt	100
XmNminimum	XmRInt	0
XmNorientation	XmROrientation	XmVERTICAL
XmNprocessingDirection	XmRProcessingDirection	XmMAX_ON_TOP
XmNtitleString	XmRXmString	NULL
XmNfontList	XmRFontList	Fixed
XmNshowValue	XmRBoolean	FALSE
XmNdecimalPoints	XmRShort	0
XmNscaleWidth	XmRDimension	0
XmNscaleHeight	XmRDimension	0
XmNhighlightOnEnter	XmRBoolean	FALSE
XmNhighlightThickness	XmRShort	0

Callbacks:

<u>Callback List</u>	<u>Call Data Type</u>	<u>Reason</u>
XmNvalueChangedCallback	XmScaleCallbackStruct	XmCR_VALUE_CHANGED
XmNdragCallback	XmScaleCallbackStruct	XmCR_DRAG

<u>ScrollBar</u>

Class Pointer: `xmScrollBarWidgetClass`
Class Name: `XmScrollBar`
Include File: `<Xm/ScrollBar.h>`
Superclass: `XmPrimitive`
Description:

The XmScrollBar widget allows the user to scroll an area that is too large to be view at once.

Refer To: Section 9.3
Resources:

<u>Name</u>	<u>Type</u>	<u>Default</u>
XmNvalue	XmRInt	0
XmNminimum	XmRInt	0
XmNmaximum	XmRInt	100
XmNsliderSize	XmRInt	10
XmNshowArrows	XmRBoolean	TRUE
XmNorientation	XmROrientation	XmVERTICAL
XmNprocessingDirection	XmRProcessingDirection	XmMAX_ON_BOTTOM
XmNincrement	XmRInt	1
XmNpageIncrement	XmRInt	10

| XmNinitialDelay | XmRInt | 250 |
| XmNrepeatDelay | XmRInt | 50 |

Callbacks:

Callback List	Call Data Type	Reason
XmNvalueChangedCallback	XmScrollBarCallbackStruct	XmCR_VALUE_CHANGED
XmNincrementCallback	XmScrollBarCallbackStruct	XmCR_INCREMENT
XmNdecrementCallback	XmScrollBarCallbackStruct	XmCR_DECREMENT
XmNpageIncrementCallback	XmScrollBarCallbackStruct	XmCR_PAGE_INCREMENT
XmNpageDecrementCallback	XmScrollBarCallbackStruct	XmCR_PAGE_DECREMENT
XmNtoTopCallback	XmScrollBarCallbackStruct	XmCR_TO_TOP
XmNtoBottomCallback	XmScrollBarCallbackStruct	XmCR_TO_BOTTOM
XmNdragCallback	XmScrollBarCallbackStruct	XmCR_DRAG

Translations:

~Shift ~Ctrl ~Meta ~Alt <Btn1Down>:	Select()
~Shift ~Ctrl ~Meta ~Alt <Btn1Up>:	Release()
~Shift ~Ctrl ~Meta ~Alt Button1<PtrMoved>:	Moved()
Shift ~Ctrl ~Meta ~Alt <Btn1Down>:	GoToTop()
~Shift Ctrl ~Meta ~Alt <Btn1Down>:	GoToBottom()
~Shift ~Ctrl ~Meta ~Alt <Key>Up:	UpOrLeft(0)
~Shift ~Ctrl ~Meta ~Alt <Key>Down:	DownOrRight(0)
~Shift ~Ctrl ~Meta ~Alt <Key>Left:	UpOrLeft(1)
~Shift ~Ctrl ~Meta ~Alt <Key>Right:	DownOrRight(1)
<EnterWindow>:	Enter()
<LeaveWindow>:	Leave()
<FocusIn>:	PrimitiveFocusIn()
<FocusOut>:	PrimitiveFocusOut()
<Unmap>:	PrimitiveUnmap()
Shift<Key>Tab:	PrimitivePrevTabGroup()
<Key>Tab:	PrimitiveNextTabGroup()
<Key>F6:	PrimitiveNextTabGroup()

ScrolledList

Class Pointer:	`xmListWidgetClass`
Class Name:	`XmList`
Include File:	`<Xm/List.h>`
Superclass:	`XmPrimitive`

Description:

The ScrolledList component combines an XmList widget and an XmScrolled-Window widget to provide scrollable lists. The ScrolledList widget can be created by the convenience function:

```
XmCreateScrolledList(parent, name, args, nargs)
```

Refer To: Section 4.3.4.4

ScrolledText

Class Pointer:	`xmTextWidgetClass`
Class Name:	`XmText`
Include File:	`<Xm/Text.h>`
Superclass:	`XmPrimitive`

Description:

The ScrolledText component consists of an XmScrolledWindow widget and an XmText widget. The ScrolledText widget can be created using the convenience fuction:

`XmCreateScrolledText(parent, name, args, nargs)`

ScrolledWindow

Class Pointer:	`xmScrolledWindowWidgetClass`
Class Name:	`XmScrolledWindow`
Include File:	`<Xm/ScrolledW.h>`
Superclass:	`XmManager`

Description:

The XmScrolledWindow widget manages a work area and two scrollbars. The scrollbars can be used to scroll a large work area within the visible clipping area of the widget. The scrolling behavior can be handled automatically or defined entirely by the application.

Refer To: Section 9.3

Resources:

Name	Type	Default
XmNhorizontalScrollBar	XmRWindow	NULL
XmNverticalScrollBar	XmRWindow	NULL
XmNworkWindow	XmRWindow	NULL
XmNclipWindow	XmRWindow	NULL
XmNscrollingPolicy	XmRScrollingPolicy	XmAPPLICATION_DEFINED
XmNvisualPolicy	XmRVisualPolicy	XmVARIABLE
XmNscrollBarDisplayPolicy	XmRScrollBarDisplayPolicy	XmSTATIC
XmNscrollBarPlacement	XmRScrollBarPlacement	XmBOTTOM_RIGHT
XmNscrolledWindowMarginWidth	XmRShort	0
XmNscrolledWindowMarginHeight	XmRShort	0
XmNspacing	XmRInt	4
XmNshadowThickness	XmRShort	0

Notes:

If **XmNscrollingPolicy** is **XmAUTOMATIC**, the default value for **XmN-scrollBarDisplayPolicy** is **XmAS_NEEDED** and the default value of the **XmNshadowThickness** resource is 2.

SelectionBox

Class Pointer:	**xmSelectionBoxWidgetClass**
Class Name:	**XmSelectionBox**
Include File:	**<Xm/SelectioB.h>**
Superclass:	**XmBulletinBoard**

Description:

The XmSelectionBox widget allows the user to select an item from a list. The widget combines an XmList widget with a label, a text area for editing an item, and "OK", "cancel", and "help" buttons.

Resources:

Name	Type	Default
XmNtextAccelerators	XmRAcceleratorTable	NULL
XmNselectionLabelString	XmRXmString	"Selection"
XmNlistLabelString	XmRXmString	NULL
XmNtextColumns	XmRInt	20
XmNtextString	XmRXmString	NULL
XmNlistItems	XmRXmStringTable	NULL
XmNlistItemCount	XmRInt	0
XmNlistVisibleItemCount	XmRInt	8
XmNokLabelString	XmRXmString	"OK"
XmNapplyLabelString	XmRXmString	"Apply"
XmNcancelLabelString	XmRXmString	"Cancel"
XmNhelpLabelString	XmRXmString	"Help"
XmNmustMatch	XmRBoolean	FALSE
XmNminimizeButtons	XmRBoolean	FALSE
XmNdialogType	XmRDialogType	XmDIALOG_WORK_AREA

Notes:

If the XmSelectionBox widget is a child of a DialogShell widget, the default value for the **XmNdialogType** resource is **XmDIALOG_SELECTION**

Callbacks:

Callback List	Call Data Type	Reason
XmNokCallback	XmAnyCallbackStruct	XmCR_OK
XmNapplyCallback	XmAnyCallbackStruct	XmCR_APPLY
XmNcancelCallback	XmAnyCallbackStruct	XmCR_CANCEL

XmNnoMatchCallback	XmAnyCallbackStruct	XmCR_NO_MATCH

Translations:

<Key>Up:	UpOrDown(0)
<Key>Down:	UpOrDown(1)
<Key>F1:	Help()
<Key>Return:	Return()
<Key>KP_Enter:	Return()

SelectionDialog

Class Pointer:	**xmSelectionBoxWidgetClass**
Class Name:	**XmSelectionBox**
Include File:	**<Xm/SelectioB.h>**
Superclass:	**XmBulletinBoard**
Description:	

This compoenent combines an XmSelectionBox widget with a DialogShell widget. It can be created with the function:

XmCreateSelectionDialog (parent, name, args,nargs)

Refer To:	Section 4.4.1

Separator

Class Pointer:	**xmSeparatorWidgetClass**
Class Name:	**XmSeparator**
Include File:	**<Xm/Separator.h>**
Superclass:	**XmPrimitive**
Description:	

The XmSeparator widget draws a thin horizontal or vertical line with a three dimensional appearance. It is useful for visually separating different functional areas of a window.

Refer To:	Section 4.3.4.5

Resources:

Name	Type	Default
XmNseparatorType	XmRSeparatorType	XmSHADOW_ETCHED_IN
XmNmargin	XmRShort	0
XmNorientation	XmROrientation	XmHORIZONTAL

SeparatorGadget

Class Pointer:	**xmSeparatorGadgetClass**

Class Name: `XmSeparatorGadget`
Include File: `<Xm/SeparatoG.h>`
Superclass: `XmGadget`
Description:

A gadet version of an XmSeparator widget.

Resources:

Name	Type	Default
XmNseparatorType	XmRSeparatorType	XmSHADOW_ETCHED_IN
XmNmargin	XmRShort	0
XmNorientation	XmROrientation	XmHORIZONTAL

Text

Class Pointer: `xmTextWidgetClass`
Class Name: `XmText`
Include File: `<Xm/Text.h>`
Superclass: `XmPrimitive`
Description:

The XmText widget provides single-line or multi-line text editing capabilities.

Refer To: Section 4.3.3.3
Resources:

Name	Type	Default
XmNsource	XmRPointer	NULL
XmNvalue	XmRString	NULL
XmNmaxLength	XmRInt	MAXINT
XmNmarginHeight	XmRShort	3
XmNmarginWidth	XmRShort	3
XmNoutputCreate	XmRFunction	NULL
XmNinputCreate	XmRFunction	NULL
XmNtopPosition	XmRInt	0
XmNcursorPosition	XmRInt	0
XmNeditMode	XmREditMode	XmSINGLE_LINE_EDIT
XmNautoShowCursorPosition	XmRBoolean	TRUE
XmNeditable	XmRBoolean	TRUE
XmNpendingDelete	XmRBoolean	TRUE
XmNselectThreshold	XmRInt	5
XmNfontList	XmRFontList	fixed
XmNwordWrap	XmRBoolean	FALSE
XmNblinkRate	XmRInt	500
XmNcolumns	XmRShort	20
XmNrows	XmRShort	1
XmNresizeWidth	XmRBoolean	TRUE

XmNresizeHeight	XmRBoolean	TRUE
XmNscrollVertical	XmRBoolean	TRUE
XmNscrollHorizontal	XmRBoolean	TRUE
XmNscrollLeftSide	XmRBoolean	FALSE
XmNscrollTopSide	XmRBoolean	FALSE
XmNcursorPositionVisible	XmRBoolean	TRUE

Callbacks:

Callback List	Call Data Type	Reason
XmNactivateCallback	XmAnyCallbackStruct	XmCR_ACTIVATE
XmNfocusCallback	XmAnyCallbackStruct	XmCR_FOCU
XmNlosingFocusCallback	XmTextVerifyCallbackStruct	XmCR_LOSING_FOCUS
XmNvalueChangedCallback	XmAnyCallbackStruct	XmCR_VALUE_CHANGED
XmNmodifyVerifyCallback	XmTextVerifyCallbackStruct	XmCR_MODIFYING_TEXT_VALUE
XmNmotionVerifyCallback	XmTextVerifyCallbackStruct	XmCR_MOVING_INSERT_CURSOR

Translations:

Shift<Key>Tab:	prev-tab-group()
<Key>Tab:	next-tab-group()
<Key>F6:	next-tab-group()
<Key>Up:	traverse-prev()
<Key>Down:	traverse-next()
<Key>Home:	traverse-home()
Ctrl<Key>Right:	end-of-line()
Shift<Key>Right:	key-select(right)
<Key>Right:	forward-character()
Ctrl<Key>Left:	beginning-of-line()
Shift<Key>Left:	key-select(left)
<Key>Left:	backward-character()
Shift<Key>Delete:	delete-next-word()
<Key>Delete:	delete-next-character()
Shift<Key>BackSpace:	delete-previous-word()
<Key>BackSpace:	delete-previous-character()
<Key>Return:	activate()
~Ctrl <Key>:	self-insert()
Shift<Btn1Down>:	extend-start()
<Btn1Down>:	grab-focus()
Button1<PtrMoved>:	extend-adjust()
<Btn1Up>:	extend-end()
<Btn3Down>:	secondary-start()
Button3<PtrMoved>:	secondary-adjust()
Ctrl<Btn3Up>:	move-to() secondary-end-and-kill()
<Btn3Up>:	copy-to() secondary-end()
<ClientMessage>:	secondary-stuff() remote-kill-selection()
<LeaveWindow>:	leave()
<FocusIn>:	focusIn()

<FocusOut>:	focusOut()
<Unmap>:	unmap()

If XmNeditMode is XmSINGLE_LINE_EDIT

<Key>Tab:	next-tab-group()
<Key>Up:	traverse-prev()
<Key>Down:	traverse-next()
<Key>Home:	traverse-home()
<Key>Return:	activate()

If XmNeditMode is XmMULTI_LINE_EDIT

<Key>Tab:	self-insert()
<Key>Up:	previous-line()
<Key>Down:	next-line()
<Key>Home:	beginning-of-file()
<Key>Return:	newline()

Public Text Widget Functions

XmTextGetString()

Retrieve the contents of the XmText widget. The application should free the string.

```
char *XmTextGetString(widget)
        Widget widget;
```

XmTextGetLastPosition()

Return the position of the end of the text buffer.

```
XmTextPosition XmTextGetLastPosition(widget)
        Widget widget;
```

XmTextSetString()

Set the contents of the text buffer to the given string.

```
void XmTextSetString(widget, value)
        XmTextWidget  widget;
        char          *value;
```

XmTextReplace()

Replace the text between two given positions with a new value.

```
void XmTextReplace(widget, frompos, topos, value)
        XmTextWidget widget;
        int          frompos, topos;
        char         *value;
```

XmTextGetEditable()

Return **TRUE** if the contents of the widget are editable.

```
unsigned int XmTextGetEditable(widget)
        Widget widget;
```

XmTextSetEditable()

Set the widget to be editable or non-editable.

```
void XmTextSetEditable(widget, editable)
        XmTextWidget widget;
        Boolean       editable;
```

XmTextGetMaxLength()

Return the maximum allowable length the to text in the buffer.

```
int XmTextGetMaxLength(widget)
        Widget widget;
```

XmTextSetMaxLength()

Set the maximum length of the text in the buffer.

```
void XmTextSetMaxLength(widget, max_length)
        XmTextWidget widget;
        int           max_length;
```

XmTextGetSelection()

Return the selected text in the XmText widget. The application is responsible for freeing the text.

```
char * XmTextGetSelection(widget)
        Widget widget;
```

XmTextSetSelection()

Set the primary selection to the area between the two given positions.

```
void XmTextSetSelection(widget, first, last, time)
        Widget widget;
        int    first, last;
        Time   time;
```

XmTextClearSelection()

Clear the XmText widget's primary selection.

```
void XmTextClearSelection(widget, time)
        Widget   widget;
        Time     time;
```

XmTextGetTopPosition()

Return the position of the top line displayed in the widget.

```
XmTextPosition XmTextGetTopPosition(widget)
        XmTextWidget widget;
```

XmTextSetTopPosition()

Set the position to be displayed at the top of the widget.

```
void XmTextSetTopPosition(widget, top_position)
        XmTextWidget   widget;
        XmTextPosition top_position;
```

XmTextGetInsertionPosition()

Return the current insertion position.

```
XmTextPosition XmTextGetInsertionPosition(widget)
        XmTextWidget widget;
```

XmTextSetInsertionPosition()

Set the current insertion position.

```
void XmTextSetInsertionPosition(widget, position)
        XmTextWidget   widget;
        XmTextPosition position;
```

XmTextGetSelectionPosition()

Retrieve the left and right positions of the selection. Return **TRUE** if successful.

```
Boolean XmTextGetSelectionPosition(widget, left, right)
        XmTextWidget   widget;
        XmTextPosition *left, *right;
```

XmTextXYToPos()

Return the text position equivalent to the (x, y) coordinate.

```
XmTextPosition XmTextXYToPos(widget, x, y)
        XmTextWidget widget;
        Position     x, y;
```

XmTextPosToXY()

Retrieve the (x, y) coordinate corresponding to the given text position.

```
Boolean XmTextPosToXY(widget, position,x, y)
        XmTextWidget    widget;
        XmTextPosition  position;
        Position        *x, *y;
```

XmTextScroll()

Scroll the buffer **n** lines. If **n** is positive, scroll the text upward, otherwise scroll text down.

```
void XmTextScroll(widget, n)
        XmTextWidget widget;
        int          n;
```

XmTextDisableRedisplay()

Turn off updating of the text displayed in XmText widget.

```
void XmTextDisableRedisplay(widget, losesbackingstore)
        XmTextWidget widget;
        Boolean      losesbackingstore;
```

XmTextEnableRedisplay()

Resume updates to the text display in the XmText widget.

```
void XmTextEnableRedisplay(widget)
        XmTextWidget widget;
```

ToggleButton

Class Pointer: `xmToggleButtonWidgetClass`
Class Name: `XmToggleButton`
Superclass: `XmLabel`
Description:

The XmToggleButton widget is a button widget with two states. The widget can be "set" or "unset". It is often used in conjunction with a RadioBox widget.

Refer To: Section 4.3.3.2, 7.5

Resources:

Name	Type	Default
XmNindicatorType	XmRIndicatorType	XmN_OF_MANY
XmNvisibleWhenOff	XmRBoolean	TRUE
XmNspacing	XmRShort	4
XmNselectPixmap	XmRPrimForegroundPixmap	XmUNSPECIFIED_PIXMAP
XmNselectInsensitivePixmap	XmRPixmap	XmUNSPECIFIED_PIXMAP
XmNset	XmRBoolean	FALSE
XmNindicatorOn	XmRBoolean	TRUE
XmNfillOnSelect	XmRBoolean	TRUE
XmNselectColor	XmRPixel	dynamic

Callbacks:

Callback List	Call Data Type	Reason
XmNvalueChangedCallback	XmToggleButtonCallbackStruct	XmCR_VALUE_CHANGED
XmNarmCallback	XmToggleButtonCallbackStruct	XmCR_ARM
XmNdisarmCallback	XmToggleButtonCallbackStruct	XmCR_DISARM

Translations:

<Btn1Down>:	Arm()
<Btn1Up>:	Select(), Disarm()
<Key>Return:	ArmAndActivate()
<Key>space:	ArmAndActivate()
<EnterWindow>:	Enter()
<LeaveWindow>:	Leave()

If used in a menu

<BtnDown>:	BtnDown()
<BtnUp>:	BtnUp()
<EnterWindow>:	Enter()
<LeaveWindow>:	Leave()
<Key>Return:	KeySelect()
<Key>Escape:	MenuShellPopdownDone()

ToggleButtonGadget

Class Pointer:	**xmToggleButtonGadgetClass**
Class Name:	**XmToggleButtonGadget**
Superclass:	**XmLabelGadget**

Description:

A gadget version of the XmToggleButton widget.

Resources:

Name	Type	Default
XmNindicatorType	XmRIndicatorType	XmN_OF_MANY

XmNvisibleWhenOff	XmRBoolean	TRUE
XmNspacing	XmRShort	4
XmNselectPixmap	XmRPixmap	XmUNSPECIFIED_PIXMAP
XmNselectInsensitivePixmap	XmRPixmap	XmUNSPECIFIED_PIXMAP
XmNset	XmRBoolean	FALSE
XmNindicatorOn	XmRBoolean	TRUE
XmNfillOnSelect	XmRBoolean	TRUE
XmNselectColor	XmRPixel	dynamic

Callbacks:

Callback List	Call Data Type	Reason
XmNvalueChangedCallback	XmToggleButtonCallbackStruct	XmCR_VALUE_CHANGED
XmNarmCallback	XmToggleButtonCallbackStruct	XmCR_ARM
XmNdisarmCallback	XmToggleButtonCallbackStruct	XmCR_DISARM

WarningDialog

Class Pointer:	**xmMessageBoxWidgetClass**
Class Name:	**XmMessage**
Superclass:	**XmBulletinBoard**
Refer To:	Section 4.4.1

WorkingDialog

Class Pointer:	**xmMessageBoxWidgetClass**
Class Name:	**XmMessage**
Superclass:	**XmBulletinBoard**
Refer To:	Section 4.4.1

FUNCTIONS FOR MANIPULATING COMPOUND STRINGS

XmStringByteCompare()

Return **TRUE** if two compound strings are byte-for-byte identical.

```
Boolean XmStringByteCompare (s1, s2)
        XmString    s1, s2;
```

XmStringCompare()

Return **TRUE** if two compound strings are identical.

```
Boolean XmStringCompare (s1, s2)
        XmString     s1, s2;
```

XmStringConcat()

Concatenate two compound strings and return the resulting new string.

```
XmString XmStringConcat (s1, s2)
        XmString    s1, s2;
```

XmStringCopy()

Return a copy of a compound string.

```
XmString XmStringCopy (string)
        XmString    string;
```

XmStringCreate()

Create a compound string to represent the given character string.

```
XmString XmStringCreate (text, charset)
        char            *text;
        XmStringCharSet   charset;
```

XmStringCreateLtoR()

Create a compound string to represent the given character string. Convert newline characters to separator components.

```
XmString XmStringCreateLtoR (text, charset)
        char            *text;
        XmStringCharSet  charset;
```

XmStringDirectionCreate()

Create a compound string with a direction component representing the given direction.

```
XmString XmStringDirectionCreate (direction)
        XmStringDirection   direction;
```

XmStringDraw()

Draw a compound string, displaying only the foreground.

```
void XmStringDraw (d, w, fontlist, string, gc, x, y,
                width, align, lay_dir, clip)
        Display    *d;
        Window     w;
        XmFontList  fontlist;
        XmString    string;
```

```
GC          gc;
Position    x, y;
Dimension   width;
UChar       align;
UChar       lay_dir;
XRectangle  *clip;
```

XmStringDrawImage()

Draw a compound string, drawing both the foreground and background.

```
void XmStringDrawImage (d, w, fontlist, string, gc, x,y,
                        width, align, lay_dir, clip)
        Display    *d;
        Window     w;
        XmFontList fontlist;
        XmString   string;
        GC         gc;
        Position   x, y;
        Dimension  width;
        UChar      align;
        UChar      lay_dir;
        XRectangle *clip;
```

XmStringDrawUnderline()

Draw an underlined compound string.

```
XmStringDrawUnderline (d, w, fontlist, string, gc,x, y,
                       width, align, lay_dir, clip, underline)
        Display    *d;
        Window     w;
        XmFontList fontlist;
        XmString   string;
        GC         gc;
        Position   x, y;
        Dimension  width;
        UChar      align;
        UChar      lay_dir;
        XRectangle *clip;
        XmString   underline;
```

XmStringEmpty()

Return **TRUE** if the compound string is **NULL** or has a length of zero.

```
Boolean XmStringEmpty (string)
        XmString     string;
```

XmStringExtent()

Return the width and height, in pixels, of a compound string.

```
void XmStringExtent (fontlist, string, width, height)
        XmFontList    fontlist;
        XmString      string;
        Dimension     *width, *height;
```

XmFontListAdd()

Return a fontlist consisting of the old fontlist plus the new **font**. The **old** fontlist is destroyed.

```
XmFontList XmFontListAdd (old, font, charset)
        XmFontList       old;
        XFontStruct      *font;
        XmStringCharSet  charset;
```

XmFontListCopy()

Return a copy of a fontlist.

```
XmFontList XmFontListCopy (fontlist)
        XmFontList   fontlist;
```

XmFontListCreate()

Create a fontlist containing the given **font**.

```
XmFontList XmFontListCreate (font, charset)
        XFontStruct      *font;
        XmStringCharSet  charset;
```

XmFontListFree()

Free the memory used by a fontlist.

```
void XmFontListFree (fontlist)
        XmFontList   fontlist;
```

XmStringFree()

Free the memory used by a compound string.

```
void XmStringFree (string)
        XmString    string;
```

XmStringFreeContext()

Free the memory used by a **XmStringContext**.

```
void XmStringFreeContext (context)
        XmStringContext  context;
```

XmStringGetLtoR()

Retrieve the first text component of the given compound string which matches the given character set.

```
Boolean XmStringGetLtoR (string, charset, text)
        XmString          string;
        XmStringCharSet   charset;
        char              **text;
```

XmStringGetNextComponent()

Retrieve the next component of a compound string.

```
XmStringComponentType
XmStringGetNextComponent(context, text, charset, direction,
                         unknown_tag, unknown_length,
                         unknown_value)
        XmStringContext         context;
        char                    **text;
        XmStringCharSet         *charset;
        XmStringDirection       *direction;
        XmStringComponentType   *unknown_tag;
        UShort                  *unknown_length;
        UChar                   **unknown_value;
```

XmStringGetNextSegment()

Retrieve the next segment of a compound string.

```
Boolean XmStringGetNextSegment (context, text, charset,
                                direction, separator)
        XmStringContext         context;
        char                    **text;
```

```
        XmStringCharSet      *charset;
        XmStringDirection    *direction;
        Boolean              *separator;
```

XmStringHeight()

Return the height, in pixels, of a compound string.

```
Dimension XmStringHeight (fontlist, string)
        XmFontList   fontlist;
        XmString     string;
```

XmStringInitContext()

Initialize an **XmStringContext**, for use with **XmStringGetNextComponent()** or **XmStringGetNextSegment()**.

```
Boolean XmStringInitContext (context, string)
        XmStringContext *context;
        XmString         string;
```

XmStringLength()

Return the size, in bytes, of a compound string.

```
int XmStringLength (string)
        XmString     string;
```

XmStringLineCount()

Return the number of lines in a compound string.

```
int XmStringLineCount (string)
        XmString string;
```

XmStringLtoRCreate()

Same as **XmStringCreateLtoR()**.

```
XmString XmStringLtoRCreate (text, charset)
        char               *text;
        XmStringCharSet   charset;
```

XmStringNCopy()

Return a copy of a compound string, up to **n** bytes long.

Syntax:

```
XmString XmStringNCopy (s1, n)
        XmString    s1;
        int         n;
```

XmStringNConcat()

Return a new compound string consisting of the first **n** bytes of s2 appended to s1.

```
XmString XmStringNConcat (s1, s2, n)
        XmString    s1, s2;
        int         n;
```

XmStringSegmentCreate()

Create a compound string segment to represent the specified text and direction. If separator is **TRUE**, append a separator component.

```
XmString XmStringSegmentCreate (text, charset,
                                direction, separator)
        char                *text;
        XmStringCharSet     charset;
        XmStringDirection   direction;
        Boolean             separator;
```

XmStringSeparatorCreate()

Return a separator component.

```
XmString XmStringSeparatorCreate ()
```

XmStringWidth()

Return the width, in pixels, of a compound string.

Syntax:

```
Dimension XmStringWidth (fontlist, string)
        XmFontList  fontlist;
        XmString    string;
```

TYPES DEFINED BY MOTIF

Motif defines a number of new resource types. This section lists the possible values that can be set programatically for each of these resource types. For example, if we refer to the resources supported by the XmArrowButton widget class, we can see that this widget's **XmNarrowDirection** resource expects a value whose type is **XmRarrowDirection**. Looking below, we can see that aceptable values for this resource type are **XmARROW_UP**, **XmARROW_DOWN**, **XmARROW_LEFT**, and **XmARROW_RIGHT**. To set these same values in a resource file, the user can simple remove the leading characters "**Xm**", and change the string to all lowercase letters. For example, the string that corresponds to the value **XmARROW_UP** is "**arrow_up**".

XmRAlignment

`XmALIGNMENT_CENTER`	`XmALIGNMENT_BEGINNING`
`XmALIGNMENT_END`	

XmRarrowDirection

`XmARROW_UP`	`XmARROW_DOWN`
`XmARROW_LEFT`	`XmARROW_RIGHT`

XmRAttachment

`XmATTACH_NONE`	`XmATTACH_FORM`
`XmATTACH_OPPOSITE_FORM`	`XmATTACH_WIDGET`
`XmATTACH_OPPOSITE_WIDGET`	`XmATTACH_POSITION`
`XmATTACH_SELF`	

XmREditMode

`XmMULTI_LINE_EDIT`	`XmSINGLE_LINE_EDIT`

XmRDefaultButtonType

`XmDIALOG_OK_BUTTON`	`XmDIALOG_CANCEL_BUTTON`
`XmDIALOG_HELP_BUTTON`	

XmRDialogStyle

`XmDIALOG_WORK_AREA`	`XmDIALOG_MODELESS`
`XmDIALOG_APPLICATION_MODAL`	`XmDIALOG_SYSTEM_MODAL`

XmRDialogType

XmDIALOG_ERROR	XmDIALOG_INFORMATION
XmDIALOG_MESSAGE	XmDIALOG_QUESTION
XmDIALOG_WARNING	XmDIALOG_WORKING
XmDIALOG_PROMPT	XmDIALOG_SELECTION
XmDIALOG_COMMAND	

XmRDisplayPolicy

XmAS_NEEDED	XmSTATIC

XmRIndicatorType

XmN_OF_MANY	XmONE_OF_MANY

XmRLabelType

XmSTRING	XmPIXMAP

XmRListSizePolicy

XmCONSTANT	XmVARIABLE	XmRESIZE_IF_POSSIBLE

XmROrientation

XmVERTICAL	XmHORIZONTAL

XmRPacking

XmPACK_NONE	XmPACK_TIGHT	XmPACK_COLUMN

XmRRowColumnType

XmWORK_AREA	XmMENU_BAR	XmMENU_POPUP
XmMENU_PULLDOWN	XmMENU_OPTION	

XmRSBPlacement

XmTOP_LEFT	XmTOP_RIGHT
XmBOTTOM_LEFT	XmBOTTOM_RIGHT

XmRProcessingDirection

XmMAX_ON_TOP	XmMAX_ON_BOTTOM
XmMAX_ON_LEFT	XmMAX_ON_RIGHT

XmRResizePolicy

`XmRESIZE_NONE`	`XmRESIZE_GROW`	`XmRESIZE_ANY`

XmRScrollPolicy

`XmAUTOMATIC`	`XmAPPLICATION_DEFINED`

XmRSelectionPolicy

`XmSINGLE_SELECT`	`XmMULTIPLE_SELECT`
`XmEXTENDED_SELECT`	`XmBROWSE_SELECT`

XmRSeparatorType

`XmNO_LINE`	`XmSINGLE_LINE`
`XmDOUBLE_LINE`	`XmSINGLE_DASHED_LINE`
`XmDOUBLE_DASHED_LINE`	`XmSHADOW_ETCHED_OUT`
`XmSHADOW_ETCHED_IN`	

XmRShadowType

`XmSHADOW_ETCHED_IN`	`XmSHADOW_ETCHED_OUT`
`XmSHADOW_IN`	`XmSHADOW_OUT`

XmRStringDirection

`XmSTRING_DIRECTION_L_TO_R`	`XmSTRING_DIRECTION_R_TO_L`

XmRUnitType

`XmPIXELS`	`Xm100TH_MILLIMETERS`	`Xm1000TH_INCHES`
`Xm100TH_POINTS`	`Xm100TH_FONT_UNITS`	

XmRVisualPolicy

`XmVARIABLE`	`XmCONSTANT`

XmRWhichButton

`Button1`	`Button2`	`Button3`
`Button4`	`Button5`	

CALLBACK DATA STRUCTURES USED BY MOTIF

XmAnyCallbackStruct

```
typedef struct {
    int       reason;
    XEvent  *event;
} XmAnyCallbackStruct;
```

XmCommandCallbackStruct

```
typedef struct {
    int       reason;
    XEvent  *event;
    XmString  value;
    int       length;
} XmCommandCallbackStruct;
```

XmDrawingAreaCallbackStruct

```
typedef struct {
    int       reason;
    XEvent  *event;
    Window   window;
} XmDrawingAreaCallbackStruct;
```

XmDrawnButtonCallbackStruct

```
typedef struct {
    int       reason;
    XEvent  *event;
    Window   window;
} XmDrawnButtonCallbackStruct;
```

XmListCallbackStruct

```
typedef struct {
    int          reason;
    XEvent     *event;
    XmString    item;
    int          item_length;
    int          item_position;
    XmString   *selected_items;
    int     selected_item_count;
    int          selection_type;
} XmListCallbackStruct;
```

XmRowColumnCallbackStruct

```
typedef struct {
    int          reason;
    XEvent     *event;
    Widget      widget;
    char       *data;
    char       *callbackstruct;
} XmRowColumnCallbackStruct;
```

XmScaleCallbackStruct

```
typedef struct {
    int       reason;
    XEvent  *event;
    int       value;
} XmScaleCallbackStruct;
```

XmScrollBarCallbackStruct

```
typedef struct {
    int       reason;
    XEvent  *event;
    int       value;
    int       pixel;
} XmScrollBarCallbackStruct;
```

XmSelectionBoxCallbackStruct

```
typedef struct {
    int         reason;
    XEvent      *event;
    XmString    value;
    int         length;
} XmSelectionBoxCallbackStruct;
```

XmToggleButtonCallbackStruct

```
typedef struct {
    int         reason;
    XEvent      *event;
    int         set;
} XmToggleButtonCallbackStruct;
```

XmFileSelectionBoxCallbackStruct

```
typedef struct{
    int         reason;
    XEvent      *event;
    XmString    value;
    int         length;
    XmString    mask;
    int         mask_length;
}
XmFileSelectionBoxCallbackStruct;
```

MOTIF PIXMAP CACHING FUNCTIONS

XmDestroyPixmap()

Destroy a cached pixmap. This function decrements a reference count for the pixmap. If the count reaches zero, the pixmap is freed.

```
Boolean XmDestroyPixmap (screen, pixmap)
        Screen * screen;
        Pixmap   pixmap;
```

XmGetPixmap()

Retrieve a pixmap matching the named pattern from the cache. This function increments a reference count associated with the pixmap.

```
Pixmap XmGetPixmap (screen, image_name, foreground, background)
        Screen  *screen;
        char    *image_name;
        Pixel   foreground;
        Pixel   background;
```

XmInstallImage()

Cache an image given in XImage format

```
Boolean XmInstallImage (image, image_name)
        XImage * image;
        char    * image_name;
```

XmInstallPixmap()

Cache an image given in Pixmap format.

```
Boolean XmInstallPixmap (pixmap, screen, image_name,
                         foreground, background)
        Pixmap    pixmap;
        Screen    *screen;
        char      *image_name;
        Pixel     foreground;
        Pixel     background;
```

XmUninstallImage()

Remove the matching XImage from the cache.

```
Boolean XmUninstallImage (image)
        XImage   *image;
```

APPENDIX C

QUICK INTRINSICS REFERENCE

This appendix lists the syntax of some commonly used Xt Intrinsics functions, and lists the form of the callbacks, event handlers and other application-defined functions used by the Intrinsics. This appendix also lists some common data structures used by the Xt Intrinsics.

SELECTED Xt INTRINSICS FUNCTIONS

XtAddActions()

Register an actions list with the Intrinsics.

Syntax:

```
void XtAddActions(actions, num_actions)
    XtActionList actions;
    Cardinal     num_actions;
```

Refer To: Section 2.4.5
See Also:

```
XtOverrideTranslations()
XtAugmentTranslations()
```

XtAddCallback()

Adds a function to one of a widget's callback lists.

Syntax:

```
void XtAddCallback(w, callback_list, callback, client_data)
      Widget          w;
      XtCallbackKind callback_list;
      XtCallbackProc callback;
      caddr_t         client_data;
```

Refer To: Section 2.4.4

See Also:

```
XtRemoveCallback()
XtRemoveCallbacks()
```

XtAddCallbacks()

Adds a list of callback procedures to a widget's callback list.

Syntax:

```
void XtAddCallbacks (widget, callback_list, callbacks)
      Widget           widget;
      String           callback_list;
      XtCallbackList   callbacks;
```

Refer To:

```
XtAddCallback()
XtRemoveCallback()
XtRemoveCallbacks()
```

XtAddConverter()

Registers a new type converter with the Intrinsics' resource manager facilities.

Syntax:

```
void XtAddConverter(from, to, converter, args, nargs)
   String           from, to;
   XtConverter      converter;
   XtConvertArgList args;
   Cardinal         nargs;
```

Refer To: Section 3.3.4

XtAddEventHandler()

Registers a function with the Intrinsics to handle an event.

Syntax:

```
void XtAddEventHandler(w, event_mask, nonmaskable, proc,
                       client_data)
        Widget          w;
        XtEventMask     event_mask;
        Boolean         nonmaskable;
        XtEventHandler  proc;
        caddr_t         client_data;
```

Refer To: Section 2.4.3
See Also:

```
XtAddRawEventHandler()
XtRemoveEventHandler()
XtRemoveRawEventHandler()
```

XtAddInput()

Adds a file descriptor as an input source and returns a unique ID. When the specified condition occurs on the source, the function **proc** is called with the ID, the **source** file descriptor, and **client_data** as arguments.

Syntax:

```
XtInputId XtAddInput(source, condition, proc, client_data)
        int                  source;
        caddr_t              condition;
        XtInputCallbackProc  proc;
        caddr_t              client_data;
```

Refer To: Section 5.8
See Also:

```
XtRemoveInput()
```

XtAddRawEventHandler()

Adds an event handler to a widget without selecting the event for the widget's window.

Syntax:

```
void XtAddRawEventHandler(widget, eventMask, nonmaskable,
                          proc, client_data)
        Widget          widget;
        EventMask       eventMask;
        Boolean         nonmaskable;
        XtEventHandler  proc;
        caddr_t         client_data ;
```

See Also:

```
XtAddEventHandler()
XtRemoveEventHandler()
XtRemoveRawEventHandler()
```

XtAddTimeOut()

Registers a callback function to be called in **interval** milliseconds. The callback is removed once it has been invoked.

Syntax:

```
XtIntervalId XtAddTimeOut(interval, proc, client_data)
        unsigned long       interval;
        XtTimerCallbackProc proc;
        caddr_t             client_data;
```

Refer To: Section 5.6
See Also:

```
XtRemoveTimeout()
```

XtAugmentTranslations()

Merges a set of translations with a widget's existing translations. Existing entries are not overriden.

Syntax:

```
void XtAugmentTranslations(widget, new)
        Widget          widget;
        XtTranslations new;
```

Refer To: Section 2.4.5
See Also:

```
XtAddActions()
XtOverrideTranslations()
```

XtCallCallbacks()

Invokes all procedures on the named callback list.

Syntax:

```
void XtCallCallbacks(w, callback_list, call_data)
        Widget      w;
        String      callback_list;
        caddr_t     call_data;
```

Refer To: Section 12.2.3.3
See Also:

```
XtAddCallbacks()
```

XtCalloc()

Calls `calloc()` and issues an error message if allocation fails.

Syntax:

```
char *XtCalloc(num, size);
      Cardinal num;
      Cardinal size;
```

See Also:

```
XtMalloc()
XtFree()
XtRealloc()
```

XtCheckSubclass()

Generates an error message if the widget is not a subclass of the named widget class.

Syntax:

```
void XtCheckSubclass(w, widget_class, message)
      Widget      w;
      WidgetClass widget_class;
      String      message;
```

See Also:

```
XtIsSubclass()
```

XtClass()

Returns a pointer to the widget's class record

Syntax:

```
WidgetClass XtClass(w)
      Widget w;
```

See Also:

```
XtSuperClass()
```

XtCreateApplicationShell()

Creates a top level shell widget.

Syntax:

```
Widget XtCreateApplicationShell (name, widget_class,
                                 args, num_args)
        String       name;
        WidgetClass  widget_class;
        ArgList      args;
        Cardinal     num_args;
```

Refer To: Section 2.5
See Also:

```
XtCreatePopupShell()
XtInitialize()
XtCreateWidget()
```

XtCreateManagedWidget()

A convenience function that creates an manages a widget with one call.

Syntax:

```
Widget XtCreateManagedWidget (name, widget_class, parent,
                              args, num_args)
        String       name;
        WidgetClass  widget_class;
        Widget       parent;
        ArgList      args;
        Cardinal     num_args;
```

Refer To: Section 2.3.3
See Also:

```
XtCreateWidget()
XtManageChild()
```

XtCreatePopupShell()

Creates a popup shell widget.

Syntax:

```
Widget XtCreatePopupShell(name, class, parent,
                          args, num_args)
        String       name;
        WidgetClass  class;
        Widget       parent;
        ArgList      args;
        Cardinal     num_args;
```

Refer To: Section 4.5
See Also:

```
XtCreateApplicationShell()
```

XtCreateWidget()

Creates and returns a new instance of the given widget class.

Syntax:

```
Widget XtCreateWidget(name, class, parent, args, num_args)
        String      name;
        WidgetClass class;
        Widget      parent;
        ArgList     args;
        Cardinal    num_args;
```

Refer To: Section 2.3.2
See Also:

```
XtCreateManagedWidget()
XtCreateApplicationShell()
```

XtDestroyWidget()

Destroys a widget and all children of the widget.

Syntax:

```
void XtDestroyWidget(w)
        Widget w;
```

See Also:

```
XtCreateWidget()
```

XtDispatchEvent()

This function looks up the widget associated with the event window in an event structure, and invokes the widget's event handlers for that event.

Syntax:

```
void XtDispatchEvent(event)
    XEvent *event;
```

See Also:

```
XtMainLoop()
XtNextEvent()
```

XtDisplay()

Returns a pointer to the **Display** structure associated with a widget.

Syntax:

```
Display *XtDisplay(w)
      Widget w;
```

Refer To: Section 2.3.2
See Also:

```
XtScreen()
```

XtError()

Calls the currently installed fatal error handler, which is expected to report the error message and then exit.

Syntax:

```
void XtError(message)
      String message;
```

See Also:

```
XtSetErrorFunction()
XtWarning()
```

XtFree()

Frees memory allocated by **XtMalloc()**, **XtCalloc()**, or **XtRealloc()**.

Syntax:

```
void XtFree(ptr);
    char *ptr;
```

See Also:

```
XtMalloc()
XtCalloc()
XtRealloc()
```

XtFreeTranslations()

Deallocates the memory used by a compiled set of translation.

Syntax:

```
void XtFreeTranslations(translations)
      XtTranslations translations;
```

See Also:

```
XtParseTranslations()
```

XtGetGC()

Returns a read-only graphics context for use with the given widget. The graphics contexts are cached for efficiency and may be shared with other widgets. **XtGetGC()** increments a reference count associated with this GC.

Syntax:

```
GC XtGetGC(w, value_mask, values)
      Widget     w;
      XtGCMask   value_mask;
      XGCValues *values;
```

Refer To: Section 8.1
See Also:

```
XtRelease()
```

XtGetValues()

Retrieves the current value of the resources specified in the **args** array.

Syntax:

```
void XtGetValues(w, args, num_args)
      Widget    w;
      ArgList   args;
      Cardinal  num_args;
```

Refer To: Section 2.3.5
See Also:

```
XtSetValues()
```

XtInitialize()

Performs initialization of the X Toolkit intrinsics. Also opens the X display and loads the user's resource data base.

Syntax:

```
Widget XtInitialize(name, class_name, options, num_options,
                    argc, argv)
      String           name;
      String           class_name;
      XrmOptionDescRec *options;
      Cardinal         num_options;
      Cardinal         *argc;
      char             *argv[];
```

> **Refer To:**   **2.3.1**

XtIsComposite()

Returns **TRUE** if the widget is a subclass of the Composite widget class.

Syntax:

```
Boolean XtIsComposite(w)
      Widget w;
```

See Also:

```
XtClass()
XtIsSubclass()
```

XtIsRealized()

Returns **TRUE** if the widget has been realized.

Syntax:

```
Boolean XtIsRealized(w)
      Widget w;
```

See Also:

```
XtRealizeWidget()
```

XtIsSubclass()

Returns **TRUE** if the widget is a subclass of the given widget class.

Syntax:

```
Boolean XtIsSubclass(w, widget_class)
      Widget      w;
      WidgetClass widget_class;
```

See Also:

```
XtClass()
```

XtMainLoop()

A convenience function that calls **XtNextEvent()** and **XtDispatchEvent()** in an infinite loop.

Syntax:

```
void XtMainLoop()
```

Refer To: Section 2.3.4
See Also:

```
XtNextEvent()
XtDispatchEvent()
```

XtMakeGeometryRequest()

Used internally by a widget to request a configuration change.   If the widget's parent suggests a compromise, the **reply** structure contains the compromise geometry.

Syntax:

```
XtGeometryResult XtMakeGeometryRequest(w, request, reply)
        Widget              w;
        XtWidgetGeometry *request;
        XtWidgetGeometry *reply;
```

Refer To: Section 13.2.3.2

See Also:

```
XtMakeResizeRequest()
```

XtMakeResizeRequest()

Provides a simpler interface to **XtMakeGeometryRequest()** when only changes to a widget's width and height are desired.

Syntax:

```
XtGeometryResult XtMakeResizeRequest(w, width, height,
                                     replyWidth, replyHeight)
        Widget      w;
        Dimension  width, height;
        Dimension *replyWidth, *replyHeight;
```

See Also:

```
XtMakeGeometryRequest
```

XtMalloc()

Calls **malloc()** and issues an error message if allocation fails.

Syntax:

```
char *XtMalloc(size)
        Cardinal size;
```

See Also:

```
XtCalloc()
XtRealloc()
XtFree()
```

XtManageChild()

Adds a single widget to its parent's managed set.

Syntax:

```
void XtManageChild(child)
        Widget child;
```

Refer To: Section 2.3.3
See Also:

```
XtUnmanageChild()
XtManageChildren()
```

XtManageChildren()

Adds a list of widgets to their parents' managed sets.

Syntax:

```
void XtManageChildren(children, num_children)
        WidgetList children;
        Cardinal   num_children;
```

Refer To: Section 2.3.3
See Also:

```
XtUnmanageChildren()
XtManageChild()
```

XtMoveWidget()

Moves a widget to the specified (x, y) position. Normally, only a widget's parent may use this function.

Syntax:

```
void XtMoveWidget(w, x, y)
        Widget   w;
        Position x;
        Position y;
```

Refer To: Section 13.2.3.2
See Also:

```
XtMakeResizeRequest()
```

XtNameToWidget()

Returns the widget structure for a named widget, within the widget tree whose root is the reference widget. The **names** argument may be a list of names separated by dots (".") to specify widgets that are not direct children of the reference widget.

Syntax:

```
Widget XtNameToWidget(reference, names)
      Widget reference;
      String names;
```

See Also:

```
XtWindowToWidget()
```

XtNextEvent()

If there is an event in the X event queue, **XtNextEvent()** removes it and returns. Otherwise, it waits until an event is available.

Syntax:

```
void XtNextEvent(event)
      XEvent *event;
```

Refer To: Section 2.3.4
See Also:

```
XtMainLoop()
```

XtNumber()

A macro that determines the number of elements in a fixed-size array.

Syntax:

```
Cardinal XtNumber(array)
      ArrayVariable array;
```

Refer To: Section 2.3.5

XtOffset()

A macro used to calculate the byte offset of a field within a structure.

Syntax:

```
Cardinal XtOffset(pointer_type, field_name)
      Type  pointer_type;
      Field field_name;
```

Refer To: Section 3.3.2

XtOverrideTranslations()

Installs a new set of translations, overriding any conflicting entries in the widget's existing translations.

Syntax:

```
void XtOverrideTranslations(widget, new)
     Widget          widget;
     XtTranslations new;
```

Refer To: Section 2.4.5

See Also:

```
XtAugmentTranslations()
XtFreeTranslations()
XtParseTranslationTable()
```

XtParseTranslationTable()

Parses a translation table (a string) and returns a compiled form.

Syntax:

```
XtTranslations XtParseTranslationTable(source)
     String source;
```

Refer To: Section 2.4.5

See Also:

```
XtAugmentTranslations()
XtFreeTranslations()
XtOverrideTranslations()
```

XtPeekEvent()

Returns the event at the head of the event queue, without removing it from the queue.

Syntax:

```
void XtPeekEvent(event)
     XEvent *event;
```

Refer To: Section 5.5

See Also:

```
XtNextEvent()
XtPending()
```

XtPending()

Returns an **XtInputMask** that indicates whether there are any events pending. The possible return values are **XtIMXEvent**, **XtIMTimer**, and **XtIMAlternateInput**. The function returns zero if there is no input pending.

Syntax:

```
XtInputMask XtPending()
```

Refer To: Section 5.5
See Also:

```
XtNextEvent()
XtPeekEvent()
```

XtPopdown()

Pops down a widget popped up with **XtPopup()**.

Syntax:

```
void XtPopdown(widget)
    Widget  widget;
```

Refer To: Section 4.5
See Also:

```
XtPopup()
XtCreatePopupShell()
```

XtPopup()

Pops up a popup shell widget.

Syntax:

```
void XtPopup(widget, grab_kind)
    Widget      widget;
    XtGrabKind  grab_kind;
```

Refer To: Section 4.5
See Also:

```
XtPopdown()
XtCreatePopupShell()
```

XtRealizeWidget()

Calls a widget's **realize** procedure, which normally creates an X window for the widget.

Syntax:

```
void XtRealizeWidget(w)
    Widget  w;
```

Refer To: 2.3.2
See Also:

```
XtIsRealized()
```

XtRealloc()

Calls **realloc()** and issues an error message if allocation fails.

Syntax:

```
char *XtRealloc(ptr, num)
    char    *ptr;
    Cardinal num;
```

See Also:

```
XtMalloc()
XtCalloc()
XtFree()
```

XtReleaseGC()

Decrements a reference count for this GC. If the reference count reaches zero, the GC is freed.

Syntax:

```
void  XtReleaseGC(widget, gc)
    Widget  widget;
    GC      gc;
```

See Also:

```
XtGetGC()
```

XtRemoveAllCallbacks()

Removes all functions from the callback list.

Syntax:

```
void XtRemoveAllCallbacks(w, callback_kind)
    Widget          w;
    XtCallbackKind  callback_kind;
```

See Also:

```
XtRemoveCallback()
XtAddCallback()
```

XtRemoveCallback()

Removes a function from a callback list.

Syntax:

```
void XtRemoveCallback(w,callback_kind,callback,client_data)
    Widget          w;
    XtCallbackKind  callback_kind;
    XtCallbackProc  callback;
    caddr_t         client_data;
```

See Also:

```
XtRemoveAllCallbacks()
XtAddCallback()
```

XtRemoveCallbacks()

Removes a list of callback functions from a widget's callback list.

Syntax:

```
void XtRemoveCallbacks (widget, callback_name, callbacks)
    Widget          widget;
    String          callback_name;
    XtCallbackList  callbacks;
```

See Also:

```
XtAddCallback()
XtRemoveAllCallbacks()
XtRemoveCallbacks()
```

XtRemoveEventHandler()

Stops the specified function, **proc**, from receiving the specified event or events. If the event handler is registered for only one event type, the function is removed from the widget's list of event handlers.

Syntax:

```
void XtRemoveEventHandler(w, event_mask, nonmaskable,
                          proc, client_data)
    Widget          w;
    XtEventMask     event_mask;
    Boolean         nonmaskable;
    XtEventHandler  proc;
    caddr_t         client_data;
```

Refer To: Section 5.4.1

See Also:

```
XtAddEventHandler()
```

XtRemoveInput()

Removes the input source associated with an **XtInputId**.

Syntax:

```
void XtRemoveInput(id)
    XtInputId id;
```

See Also:

```
XtAddInput()
```

XtRemoveRawEventHandler()

Removes an event handler added using **XtAddRawEventHandler()**.

Syntax:

```
void XtRemoveRawEventHandler(widget, eventMask, nonmaskable,
                             proc, client_data)
      Widget            widget;
      EventMask         eventMask;
      Boolean           nonmaskable;
      XtEventHandler    proc;
      caddr_t           client_data ;
```

See Also:

```
XtRemoveEventHandler()
XtAddRawEventHandler()
```

XtRemoveTimeOut()

Removes the callback associated with the timeout ID.

Syntax:

```
void XtRemoveTimeOut(id)
    XtIntervalId id;
```

Refer To: Section 5.6
See Also:

```
XtAddTimeOut()
```

XtResizeWidget()

Resizes a widget. Normally, only a widget's parent may use this function.

Syntax:

```
void XtResizeWidget(w, width, height, border_width)
    Widget    w;
    Dimension width;
    Dimension height;
    Dimension border_width;
```

See Also:

```
XtMoveWidget()
XtMakeResizeRequest()
```

XtScreen()

Returns the **Screen** structure associated with a widget.

Syntax:

```
Screen *XtScreen(w)
      Widget w;
```

Refer To: Section 2.3.2

See Also:

```
XtDisplay()
```

XtSetArg()

A macro used to set the contents of an **Arg** structure.

Syntax:

```
#define XtSetArg(arg, n, d) \
    ( (arg).name = (n), (arg).value = (XtArgVal)(d) )
```

Refer To: Section 2.3.5

See Also:

```
XtSetValues()
XtGetValues()
```

XtSetErrorHandler()

Registers an application-defined function to be called when an error occurs.

Syntax:

```
void XtSetErrorHandler(errorProc)
    void (*errorProc)();
```

See Also:

```
XtError()
```

XtSetMappedWhenManaged()

Sets a widget's **XtNmapWhenManaged** resource. If **TRUE**, the widget window will be mapped whenever the widget is managed.

Syntax:

```
void XtSetMappedWhenManaged(w, map_when_managed)
    Widget  w;
    Boolean map_when_managed;
```

See Also:

```
XtManageChild()
```

XtSetSensitive()

Sets the sensitive state of a widget. Widgets that are insensitive do not respond to events and often take on a "grayed out" appearance.

Syntax:

```
void XtSetSensitive(w, sensitive)
    Widget   w;
    Boolean  sensitive;
```

Refer To: Section 11.3.2

XtSetValues()

Modifies the current value of a resource associated with a widget.

Syntax:

```
void XtSetValues(w, args, num_args)
    Widget   w;
    ArgList  args;
    Cardinal num_args;
```

Refer To: Section 2.3.5
See Also:

```
XtGetValues()
XtSetArg()
```

XtSetWarningHandler()

Registers an application-defined function to be called when a warning is issued.

Syntax:

```
void XtSetWarningHandler(errorProc)
    void (*errorProc)();
```

See Also:

>   XtWarning()

XtSuperclass()

Returns a pointer to the class structure of a widget's superclass.

Syntax:

```
WidgetClass XtSuperclass(w)
    Widget w;
```

See Also:

>   XtClass()

XtTransformCoords()

Converts a (*x, y*) location in the coordinates of a widget to the coordinates of the root window.

Syntax:

```
void XtTransformCoords(w, x, y, rootx, rooty)
    Widget    w;
    Position  x, y;
    Position *rootx, *rooty;
```

XtUnmanageChild()

Removes a single widget from its parent's managed set.

Syntax:

```
void XtUnmanageChild(child)
    Widget child;
```

See Also:

>   XtManageChild()
>   XtUnmanageChildren()

XtUnmanageChildren()

Removes a list of widgets from their parents' managed sets.

Syntax:

```
void XtUnmanageChildren(children, num_children)
    WidgetList children;
    Cardinal   num_children;
```

Refer To: Section 13.2.4
See Also:

```
XtUnmanageChild()
XtManageChildren()
```

XtWarning()

Invokes the current non-fatal error handler with the given message.

Syntax:

```
void XtWarning(message);
    String message;
```

See Also:

```
XtSetWarningHandler()
XtError()
```

XtWindow()

Returns the X window ID used by the widget.

Syntax:

```
Window XtWindow(w)
    Widget  w;
```

Refer To: Section 2.2.2
See Also:

```
XtWindowToWidget()
```

XtWindowToWidget()

Returns the widget structure associated with a window ID.

Syntax:

```
Widget XtWindowToWidget(display, window)
    Display *display;
    Window   window;
```

See Also:

```
XtWindow()
```

CALLBACK AND EVENT HANDLER FORMATS

Action Procedures

```
void action_proc(widget,event,params, n_params)
    Widget    widget;
    XEvent    *event;
    String    *params;
    Cardinal *n_params;
```

Callbacks

```
void callback_proc (widget, client_data, call_data)
    Widget    widget;
    caddr_t   client_data;
    caddr_t   call_data;
```

Event Handlers

```
void event_handler (widget, client_data, event)
    Widget   widget;
    caddr_t client_data;
    XEvent   *event;
```

Input Callbacks

```
void input_callback (client_data, file, id)
    caddr_t    client_data;
    int        *file;
    XtInputId *id;
```

Timer Callbacks

```
void timer_callback (client_data, id)
    caddr_t        client_data;
    XtIntervalId *id;
```

Type Converters

```
void converter (args, num_arsg, from, to)
    XrmValue    *args;
    Cardinal    *num_args;
    XrmValue    *from;
    Xrmvalue    *to;
```

WorkProcs

```
Boolean work_proc (client_data)
    caddr_t client_data;
```

SELECTED DATA STRUCTURES

Arg, ArgList

Used to specify a resource value to **XtSetValues()** or **XtGetValues()**.

Syntax:

```
typedef struct {
    String     name;
    XtArgVal   value;
} Arg, *ArgList;
```

Refer To: 2.3.5
See Also:

```
XtSetArg()
XtSetValues()
XtGetValues()
```

XtConvertArgRec

Used to specify additional data to be passed to a type converter.

Syntax:

```
typedef struct {
    XtAddressMode    address_mode;
    caddr_t          address_id;
    Cardinal         size;
} XtConvertArgRec, *XtConvertArgList;
```

Refer To: 3.3.4
See Also:

    `XtAddConverter()`

XtInput Masks

These masks are used as arguments to **XtAddInput()**.

Syntax:

```
#define XtInputNoneMask        0L
#define XtInputReadMask        (1L<<0)
#define XtInputWriteMask       (1L<<1)
#define XtInputExceptMask      (1L<<2)
```

Refer To: Section 5.8
See Also:

    `XtAddInput()`

XtPopdownIDRec

A pointer to an **XtPopdownIDRec** is expected to be passed as client data to the **XtPopdownCallback()** convenience function.

Syntax:

```
typedef struct {
    Widget  shell_widget;
    Widget  enable_widget;
} XtPopdownIDRec, *XtPopdownID;
```

Refer To: Section 4.5
See Also:

    `XtPopup()`
    `XtPopdown()`

XtResource

The **XtResource** structure is used to define each entry in a widget's or application's resource list.

Syntax:

```
typedef struct _XtResource {
  String    resource_name;  /* Resource name         */
  String    resource_class; /* Resource class        */
  String    resource_type;  /* desired representation*/
  Cardinal  resource_size;  /* Size in bytes         */
```

```
    Cardinal  resource_offset;/* Offset from base      */
    String    default_type;   /* default representation*/
    caddr_t   default_addr;   /* default resource      */
} XtResource;
```

Refer To: Section 3.3.2
See Also:

```
XtGetApplicationResources()
```

XtWidgetResult

An enumerated type used by a widget's geometry manager geometry functions.

Syntax:

```
typedef enum  {
    XtGeometryYes,     /* Request accepted.        */
    XtGeometryNo,      /* Request denied.          */
    XtGeometryAlmost,/* Compromise suggested.      */
    XtGeometryDone    /* Request accepted and done.*/
} XtGeometryResult;
```

Refer To: Section 13.2.3.2
See Also:

```
XtMakeGeometryRequest()
XtMakeResizeRequest()
```

APPENDIX D

X EVENTS AND EVENT MASKS

The following table lists the event types and the union member of the **XEvent** structure corresponding to the event type. For example, the **time** member the event structure reporting ButtonPress events can be accessed as:

```
event->xbutton.time
```

The five members common to all events can be access using the **xany** member, regardless of the event type. Also the **type** member of an event structure can always be accessed directly.

Event Type	Union Member
Any Type	xany
ButtonPress	xbutton
ButtonRelease	xbutton
MotionNotify	xmotion
MapNotify	xmap
EnterNotify	xcrossing
FocusIn	xfocus
LeaveNotify	xcrossing
FocusOut	xfocus
Expose	xexpose
GraphicsExpose	xgraphicsexpose
NoExpose	xnoexpose
VisibilityNotify	xvisibility
KeyPress	xkey

DestroyNotify	xdestroywindow
UnmapNotify	xunmap
MapRequest	xmaprequest
ReparentNotify	xreparent
ResizeRequest	xresizerequest
ConfigureNotify	xconfigure
GravityNotify	xgravity
CirculateNotify	xcirculate
CirculateRequest	xcirculaterequest
PropertyNotify	xproperty
SelectionClear	xselectionclear
KeymapNotify	xkeymap
SelectionNotify	xselection
ColormapNotify	xcolormap
ClientMessage	xclient
MappingNotify	xmapping
SelectionRequest	xselectionrequest
KeyRelease	xkey
ConfigureRequest	xconfigurerequest
CreateNotify	xcreatewindow

The following table lists the event mask, its associated event type or types, and the structure name associated with the event type. Some of these structures actually are typedefs to a generic structure that is shared between two event types. Note that N.A. appears in columns for which the information is not applicable.

Event Mask	Event Type	Structure
ButtonMotionMask	MotionNotify	XPointerMovedEvent
Button1MotionMask	MotionNotify	XPointerMovedEvent
Button2MotionMask	MotionNotify	XPointerMovedEvent
Button3MotionMask	MotionNotify	XPointerMovedEvent
Button4MotionMask	MotionNotify	XPointerMovedEvent
Button5MotionMask	MotionNotify	XPointerMovedEvent
ButtonPressMask	ButtonPress	XButtonPressedEvent
ButtonReleaseMask	ButtonRelease	XButtonReleasedEvent
ColormapChangeMask	ColormapNotify	XColormapEvent
EnterWindowMask	EnterNotify	XEnterWindowEvent
LeaveWindowMask	LeaveNotify	XLeaveWindowEvent
ExposureMask	Expose	XExposeEvent
GCGraphicsExposures	GraphicsExpose	XGraphicsExposeEvent
" "	NoExpose	XNoExposeEvent
FocusChangeMask	FocusIn	XFocusInEvent
" "	FocusOut	XFocusOutEvent

KeymapStateMask	KeymapNotify	XKeymapEvent
KeyPressMask	KeyPress	XKeyPressedEvent
KeyReleaseMask	KeyRelease	XKeyReleasedEvent
OwnerGrabButtonMask	N.A.	N.A.
PointerMotionMask	MotionNotify	XPointerMovedEvent
PointerMotionHintMask	N.A.	N.A.
PropertyChangeMask	PropertyNotify	XPropertyEvent
ResizeRedirectMask	ResizeRequest	XResizeRequestEvent
StructureNotifyMask	CirculateNotify	XCirculateEvent
" "	ConfigureNotify	XConfigureEvent
" "	DestroyNotify	XDestroyWindowEvent
" "	GravityNotify	XGravityEvent
" "	MapNotify	XMapEvent
" "	ReparentNotify	XReparentEvent
" "	UnmapNotify	XUnmapEvent
SubstructureNotifyMask	CirculateNotify	XCirculateEvent
" "	ConfigureNotify	XConfigureEvent
" "	CreateNotify	XCreateWindowEvent
" "	DestroyNotify	XDestroyWindowEvent
" "	GravityNotify	XGravityEvent
" "	MapNotify	XMapEvent
" "	ReparentNotify	XReparentEvent
" "	UnmapNotify	XUnmapEvent
SubstructureRedirectMask	CirculateRequest	XCirculateRequestEvent
" "	ConfigureRequest	XConfigureRequestEvent
" "	MapRequest	XMapRequestEvent
N.A.	ClientMessage	XClientMessageEvent
N.A.	MappingNotify	XMappingEvent
N.A.	SelectionClear	XSelectionClearEvent
N.A.	SelectionNotify	XSelectionEvent
N.A.	SelectionRequest	XSelectionRequestEvent
VisibilityChangeMask	VisibilityNotify	XVisibilityEvent

APPENDIX E

TRANSLATION MANAGER SYNTAX

The translation manager syntax is specified in EBNF notation with the following conventions:

[a]   Means either nothing or "a"

{ a }   Means zero or more occurrences of "a"

All terminals are enclosed in double quotation masks (" "). Informal descriptions are enclosed in angle brackets (< >).

The syntax of the translation table file is:

translationTable	= [directive] { production }
directive	= ("#replace" | "#override" | "#augment") "\n"
production	= lhs ":" rhs "\n"
lhs	= (event | keyseq) { "," (event | keyseq) }
keyseq	= """ keychar {keychar} """
keychar	= ["^" | "$" | "\"] <ISO Latin 1 character>
event	= [modifier_list] "<"event_type">" ["(" count["+"] ")"] {detail}
modifier_list	= (["!" | ":"] {modifier}) | "None"
modifier	= ["~"] modifier_name
count	= ("1" | "2" | "3" | "4" | ...)
modifier_name	= "@" <keysym> | <see ModifierNames table below>
event_type	= <see Event Types table below>
detail	= <event specific details>
rhs	= { name "(" [params] ")" }
name	= namechar { namechar }
namechar	= { "a"-"z" | "A"-"Z" | "0"-"9" | "$" | "_" }
params	= string {"," string}.
string	= quoted_string | unquoted_string
quoted_string	= """ {<Latin 1 character>} """
unquoted_string	= {<Latin 1 character except space, tab, ",", newline, ")">}

The modifier field is used to specify normal X keyboard and button modifier mask bits. If the modifier_list has no entries and is not "None", it means "don't care" on all modifiers.

- If an exclamation point (!) is specified at the beginning of the modifier list, it means that the listed modifiers must be in the correct state and no other modifiers can be asserted.

- If any modifiers are specified and an exclamation point (!) is not specified, it means that the listed modifiers must be in the correct state and "don't care" about any other modifiers.

- If a modifier is preceded by a tilde (~), it means that the modifier must not be asserted.

- If "None" is specified, it means no modifiers can be asserted.

- If a colon (:) is specified at the beginning of the modifier list, it directs the Intrinsics to apply any standard modifiers in the event to map the event keycode into a keysym. The default standard modifiers are Shift and Lock, with the interpretation as defined in *X Window System Protocol, X Version 11*. The resulting keysym must exactly match the specified keysym, and the nonstandard modifiers in the event must match the modifier_list. For example, ":<Key>a" is distinct from ":<Key>A", and ":Shift<Key>A" is distinct from ":<Key>A".

- If a colon (:) is not specified, no standard modifiers are applied. Then, for example, "<Key>A" and "<Key>a" are equivalent.

In key sequences, a circumflex (^) is an abbreviation for the Control modifier, a dollar sign ($) is an abbreviation for Meta, and a backslash (\) can be used to quote any character, in particular a double quote ("), a circumflex (^), a dollar sign ($), and another backslash (\). Briefly:

No Modifiers:	None <event> detail
Any Modifiers:	<event> detail
Only these Modifiers:	! mod1 mod2 <event> detail
These modifiers and any others:	mod1 mod2 <event> detail

The use of "None" for a modifier_list is identical to the use of an exclamation point with no modifers. The following is a list of valid modifiers:

Ctrl	Shift	Lock	Meta	Hyper
Super	Alt	Mod1	Mod2	Mod3
Mod4	Mod5	Button1	Button2	Button3
Button4	Button5	ANY		

Supported EventTypes:

Type	Meaning	Type	Meaning
Key	KeyPress	KeyDown	KeyPress
KeyUp	KeyRelease	BtnDown	ButtonPress
BtnUp	ButtonRelease	Motion	MotionNotify
Enter	EnterWindow	Leave	LeaveWindow
FocusIn	FocusIn	FocusOut	FocusOut
Keymap	KeymapNotify	Expose	ExposeEvent
GrExp	GraphicsExpose	NoExp	NoExpose
Visible	VisibilityNotify	Create	CreateNotify
Destroy	DestroyNotify	Unmap	UnmapNotify
Map	MapNotify	MapReq	MapRequest
Reparent	ReparentNotify	Configure	ConfigureNotify
ConfigureReq	ConfigureRequest	Grav	GravityNotify
ResReq	ResizeRequest	Circ	CirculateNotify
CircReq	CirculateRequest	Prop	PropertyNotify
SelClr	SelectionClear	SelReq	SelectionRequest
Select	SelectionNotify	Clrmap	ColormapNotify
Message	ClientMessage	Mapping	MappingNotify

Supported Abreviations:

Abreviation	Meaning
Ctrl	KeyPress with control modifier
Meta	KeyPress with meta modifier
Shift	KeyPress with shift modifier
Btn1Down	ButtonPress with Btn1 detail
Btn1Up	ButtonRelease with Btn1 detail
Btn2Down	ButtonPress with Btn2 detail
Btn2Up	ButtonRelease with Btn2 detail
Btn3Down	ButtonPress with Btn3 detail
Btn3Up	ButtonRelease with Btn3 detail
Btn4Down	ButtonPress with Btn4 detail
Btn4Up	ButtonRelease with Btn4 detail
Btn5Down	ButtonPress with Btn5 detail
Btn5Up	ButtonRelease with Btn5 detail
BtnMotion	MotionNotify with any button modifier
Btn1Motion	MotionNotify with Button1 modifier
Btn2Motion	MotionNotify with Button2 modifier
Btn3Motion	MotionNotify with Button3 modifier
Btn4Motion	MotionNotify with Button4 modifier
Btn5Motion	MotionNotify with Button5 modifier

APPENDIX F

WHERE TO GET X

The complete X11 distribution is available from many sources. The complete distribution is quite large and includes X servers for many machines, various X-based toolkits, and assorted contributed software. You can get X on a 9 track, 1600bpi tape directly from MIT by contacting:

MIT Software Center Technology Licensing Office
MIT E32-300
77 Mass. Ave.
Cambridge, MA 02139
(617) 258-8330

Those with the proper network access can get the complete X distribution free via anonymous ftp from a number of sources. At publication time, the following machines were among those making the X11R3 release available.

Machine	Net Address	X directory
gatekeeper.dec.com	128.45.9.52	pub/X.V11R3/
mordred.cs.purdue.edu	192.5.48.2	pub/X11/Release3/
giza.cis.ohio-state.edu	128.146.6.150	pub/X.V11R3/
nic.mr.net	192.12.250.5	pub/X.V11R3/
uunet.uu.net	192.12.141.129	X/X.V11R3/
expo.lcs.mit.edu	18.30.0.212	pub/R3/

There is also an archive of publicly available X software known as the West Coast Xarchives. This archive can be accessed through UUCP. Users can login as "UXarchiv", with no password. Dial-in numbers are 415-967-4619 (1200/2400 baud) and 415-967-4718 (19.2K baud).

There are several electronic mailing lists and bulletin boards that pertain to X. The primary electronic mailing list is:

xpert@athena.mit.edu

X user groups can also be a good source of information. The largest group is the X User's Group (XUG). This national organization publishes a newsletter containing news and technical articles related to X. They can be reached by mail at:

XUG
c/o Integrated Computer Solutions
163 Harvard Street
Cambridge, MA 02139

or via electronic mail at xug@expo.lcs.mit .edu. Local chapters of XUG have been formed in many areas as well.

Many vendors also sell supported versions of X. The following list shows the members of the X Consortium at the time of this writing. Many of these companies have or will have X-based products.

X Consortium Members

Apollo Computer, Inc.	Apple Computer, Inc.
AT&T	Bull
CalComp	Control Data Corporation
Data General Corporation	Digital Equipment Corporation
Eastman Kodak Company	Fujitsu
Hewlett Packard	IBM
NEC Corporation	NCR Corporation
Prime Computer, Inc.	Rich, Inc
Sequent Computer Systems Inc.	Siemans AG
Silicon Graphics, Inc.	Sony Corporation
Sun Microsystems, Inc.	Tektronix, Inc.
Texas Instruments	Unisys Corporation
Wang Laboratories	Xerox Corporation

X Consortium Affiliates

Acer Copunterpoint	Adobe Systems
Ardent Computer	Carnegie Mellon University
CETIA	Evans & Sutherland
GfxBase	Integrated Solutions
Interactive Systems Corporation	Interactive Development Environments

Integrated Computer Solutions	University of Kent at Canterbury
Locus Computing	Megatek Corporation
MIPS Computer Systems	Network Computing Devices
Nova Graphics International	Open Software Foundation
O'Reilly & Associates	PCS Computer Systeme GmbH
Software Productivity Consortium	Solbourne Computer Inc.
Stellar Computer Inc.	UNICAD, Inc.
Visual Technology Inc.	Xpi, Inc

SGIP - Societe de Gestion et d'Informatique Publicis
INESC - Instituto de Engenharia de Sistemas e Computadores

The Motif widget set is not part of the X distribution. Motif can be obtained from many of the members of the Open Software Foundation, and both source and binaries are available. For more information, contact the Open Software Foundation:

Open Software Foundation
11 Cambridge Center
Cambridge, MA 02142
617-621-8700

The source code for the examples in this book are also available. Those with network access can retrieve the source at no cost via anonymous ftp from expo.lcs.mit.edu. The examples are in compressed tar format and are in the file ~ftp/contrib/young.motif.tar.Z. The code will most likely be propagated to other locations as well. To unpack a compressed tar file type the following commands in a shell window:

```
uncompress young.motif.tar.Z
tar xvf young.motif.tar
```

This will create a directory structure consisting of a directory for each chapter in this book and an additional directory for the libXs library. Follow the instructions in the README file in the top level directory to build and run the example programs.

    Prentice Hall can also provide copies of the source code, for a fee, for those without network access. For more information contact:

John Wait
Prentice Hall
Prentice Hall Building
Englewood Cliffs, NJ 07632
201-592-2149

APPENDIX G

LibXs.h

The following is the complete header file for the libXs library, a collection of routines developed in the examples in this book.

```
/*********************************************************
 * libXs.h: header file for X-sample library
 *********************************************************/
#ifndef _LIBXs_h
#define _LIBXs_h

#include <Xm/Xm.h>

#define XtRFloat "Float"
/*
 * Structure used to describe an entry in a menu. Used by
 * xs_create_menu_entries().
 */
typedef struct _menu_struct{
  char*                    name;      /* name of the button */
  void                     (*func)();/* Callback to be invoked */
  caddr_t                  data;      /* Data for the callback */
  struct _menu_struct      *sub_menu;/* data for submenu
                                        of this button */
  int                      n_sub_items; /* How many items in
                                           the sub_menu */
```

```
      char               *sub_menu_title; /* Title of submenu */
    } xs_menu_struct;

extern Widget      xs_create_quit_button ();
extern void        xs_invert_widget ();
extern XmString    xs_concat_words ();
extern void        xs_cvt_str_to_float ();
XmString           xs_str_array_to_xmstr();
extern Widget      xs_create_pixmap_button ();
extern Widget      xs_create_pixmap_browser ();
extern char        *xs_get_string_from_xmstring ();
void               xs_help_callback();
extern GC          xs_create_xor_gc ();
 /*
  * Horrible hack for BSD systems which don't have vsprintf().
  * Instead of xs_wprintf(), use the macro which matches the
  * number of args passed. Extend as needed.
  */
#define XS_WPRINTF_ONE(_widget,_format,_arg) { \
        Arg _tmp[10];   char _tmp_buf[1000]; \
        sprintf(_tmp_buf, _format, _arg); \
        XtSetArg(_tmp[0], XmNlabelString, \
                XmStringLtoRCreate(_tmp_buf, \
                                    XmSTRING_DEFAULT_CHARSET));\
        XtSetValues(_widget,_tmp, 1); \
        }

#define XS_WPRINTF_TWO(_widget,_format,_a,_b) { \
        Arg _tmp[10];   char _tmp_buf[1000]; \
        sprintf(_tmp_buf, _format, _a, _b); \
        XtSetArg(_tmp[0], XmNlabelString, \
                XmStringLtoRCreate(_tmp_buf, \
                                    XmSTRING_DEFAULT_CHARSET));\
        XtSetValues(_widget,_tmp, 1); \
        }

#endif _LIBXs_h
```

BIBLIOGRAPHY

C and UNIX Programming

[Kern84]   Kerningham, B. W. and R. Pike, *The Unix Programming Environment*, Prentice Hall, 1984.

[Kern78]   Kerningham, B. W. and D. M. Ritchie, *The C Programming Language*, Prentice Hall, 1978.

[Roch85]   Rochkind, M., *Advanced Unix Programming*, Prentice Hall, 1985.

Graphics

[Foley82]   Foley, J. D. and A. van Dam, *Fundamentals of Interactive Computer Graphics*, Addison-Wesley, 1983.

[Mand83]   Mandelbrot, B., *The Fractal Geometry of Nature*, W. H. Freeman, 1983.

Object-Oriented Programming

[Cox86]   Cox, Brad, *Object-Oriented Programming, An Evolutionary Approach*, Addison-Wesley, 1986.

[Goldb83]   Goldberg, Adele and David Robson, *Smalltalk-80: The Language and its Implementation*, Addison-Wesley, 1983.

[Meyer88]   Meyer, Bertrand, *Object-Oriented Software Construction,* Prentice Hall, 1988.

[Stroust86] Stroustrup, Bjarne, *The C++ Programming Language*, Addison-Wesley, 1986.

User Interfaces

[Schneid87] Shneiderman, Ben , *Designing the User Interface*, Addison-Wesley, 1987.

[Smith89]   Smith, Wanda, *Using Computer Color Effectively*, Prentice-Hall, 1989.

Window Systems

[Hopgood86]   Hopgood, F. R. A., *Methodology of Window Management*, Springer-Verlag, New York, 1986.

[Myers88]   Myers, Brad A., "Window Interfaces: A Taxonomy of Window Manager User Interfaces," *IEEE Computer Graphics & Applications*, vol. 8, no. 5, pp. 65-84, September, 1988.

[Pike88]   Pike, Rob, "Window Systems Should Be Transparent," *USENIX Computing Systems*, vol. 1, no. 3, pp. 279-296, Summer, 1988.

The X Window System

[Asente88]   Asente, Paul, "Simplicity and Productivity," *UNIX Review*, vol. 6, no. 9, pp. 57-63.

[Gettys88]   Gettys, Jim, "Flexibility Is Key To Meet Requirements For X Window System Design," *Computer Technology Review*, pp. 87-89, Summer, 1988.

[Gettys86]   Gettys, Jim, "Problems Implementing Window Systems in UNIX," in *Proceedings of the Winter, 1986 USENIX Conference*, pp. 89-97.

[Johnson89]   Johnson, Eric F. and Kevin Reichard, *X Window Applications Programming*, MIS Press, 1989

[Jones89]   Jones, Oliver, *Introduction to the X Window System*, Prentice-Hall, 1989.

[Lemke89]   Lemke, David and S. H. Rosenthall, "Visualizing X11 Clients", in *Proceedings of the Winter, 1989 USENIX Conference*, pp. 125-138.

[Linton89]   Linton, Mark A., John M. Vlissides, and Paul R. Calder, "Composing User Interfaces with InterViews", *IEEE Computer*, vol. 22, no. 2, pp. 65-84, February, 1989.

[McCorm88]   McCormack, Joel and Paul Asente, "Using the X Toolkit or How to Write a Widget," in *Proceedings of the Summer, 1988 USENIX Conference*, pp. 1-13.

[McCorm88]   McCormack, Joel and Paul Asente, "An Overview of the X Toolkit," in *Proceedings of the ACM SIGGRAPH Symposium on User Interface Software*, pp. 46-55, October, 1988.

[Nadeau88]   Nadeau, David R., "High-Performance 3-D Graphics In A Window Environment," *Computer Technology Review*, pp. 89-93, Fall,1988.

[Nye88]   Nye, Adrian, *The Xlib Programming Manul*, O'Reilly and Associates, 1988.

[Nye88]   Nye, Adrian, *The Xlib Reference Manul*, O'Reilly and Associates, 1988.

[O'Reilly89]   O'Reilly, Tim, "The Toolkits (and Politics) of X Windows," *UNIX World*, vol. 6, no. 2, pp. 66-73, February, 1989.

[Rao87]   Rao, R. and S. Wallace, "The X Toolkit," in *Proceedings of the Summer, 1987 USENIX Conference.*

[Roch89]   Rochkind, Marc. "XVTL: A Virtual Toolkit for Portability Between Window Systems," in *Proceedings of the Winter, 1989 USENIX Conference*, pp. 151-163.

[Rosen88]   Rosenthal, David S., "A Simple X.11 Client Program, or, How Hard Can It Really Be to Write 'Hello, World'?," in *Proceedings of the Winter, 1988 USENIX Conference*, pp. 229-235.

[Rost88]   Rost, Randi J., "Adding a Dimension to X," *UNIX Review*, vol. 6, no. 10, pp. 51-59.

[Schaufler88] Schaufler, Robin, "X11/NeWS Design Overview," in *Proceedings of the Summer, 1988 USENIX Conference*, pp. 23-35.

[Scheifler88] Scheifler, Robert W., James Gettys, and Ron Newman, *X Window System*, DEC Press, 1988.

[Scheifler86] Scheifler, Robert W. and Jim Gettys, "The X Window System," *ACM Transactions on Graphics*, vol. 5, no. 2, pp. 79-109, April, 1986.

[Swick88]   Swick, Ralph R. and Mark S. Ackerman, "The X Toolkit: More Bricks for Building User Interfaces," in *Proceedings of the Winter, 1988 USENIX Conference*, pp. 221-233.

Motif

Five books on Motif are expected from the Open Software Foundation, available through Prentice Hall. The planned titles are:

OSF/Motif Style Guide

OSF/Motif Application Environment Specification (AES) User Environment Volume

OSF/Motif Programmer's Guide

OSF/Motif Programmer's Reference

OSF/Motif User's Guide

EXAMPLE INDEX

INDEX

When there are multiple entries for an item, the pages listed in **bold** type indicate the principle reference, if any, for that item.

E

Q

R